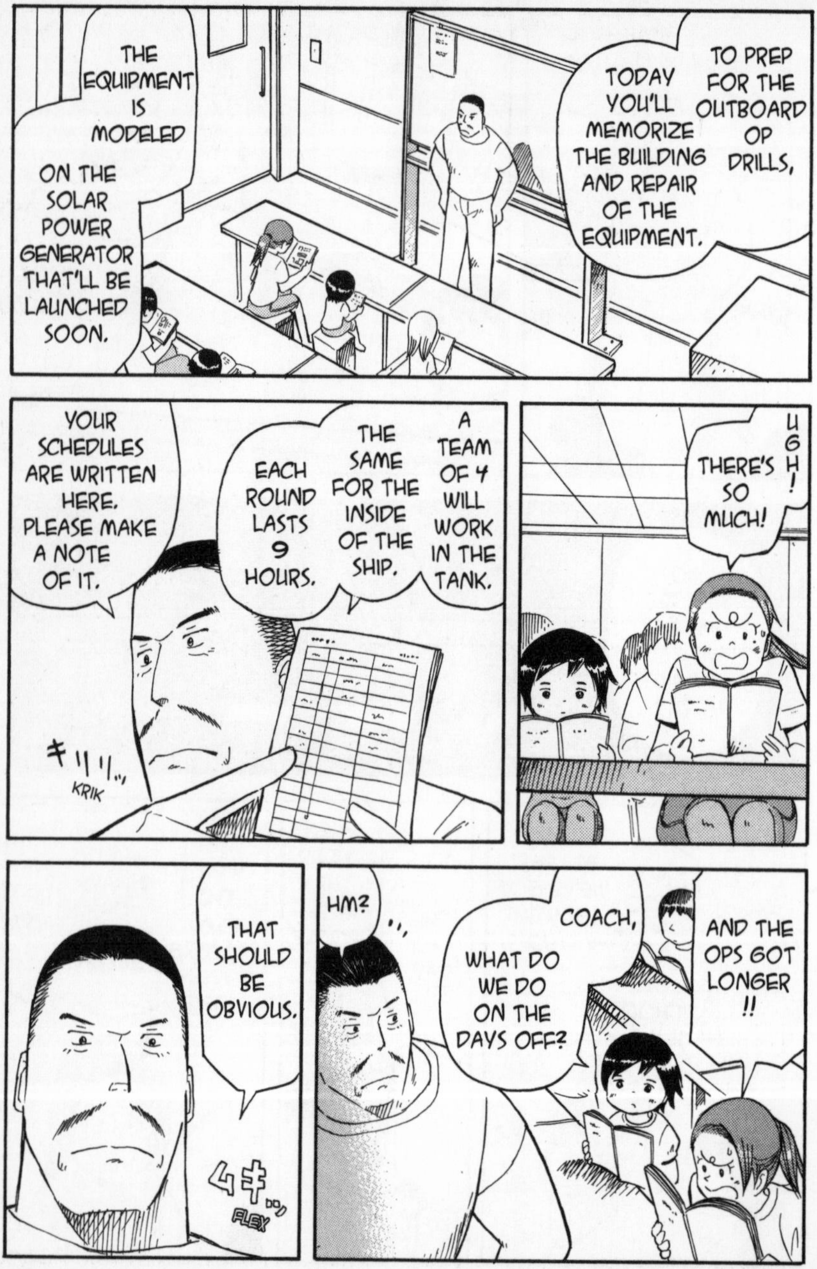
TO PREP FOR THE OUTBOARD OP DRILLS,
TODAY YOU'LL MEMORIZE THE BUILDING AND REPAIR OF THE EQUIPMENT.
THE EQUIPMENT IS MODELED
ON THE SOLAR POWER GENERATOR THAT'LL BE LAUNCHED SOON.
UGH!
THERE'S SO MUCH!
A TEAM OF 4 WILL WORK IN THE TANK.
THE SAME FOR THE INSIDE OF THE SHIP.
EACH ROUND LASTS 9 HOURS.
YOUR SCHEDULES ARE WRITTEN HERE. PLEASE MAKE A NOTE OF IT.
KRIK
AND THE OPS GOT LONGER !!
COACH,
WHAT DO WE DO ON THE DAYS OFF?
HM?
THAT SHOULD BE OBVIOUS.
FLEX

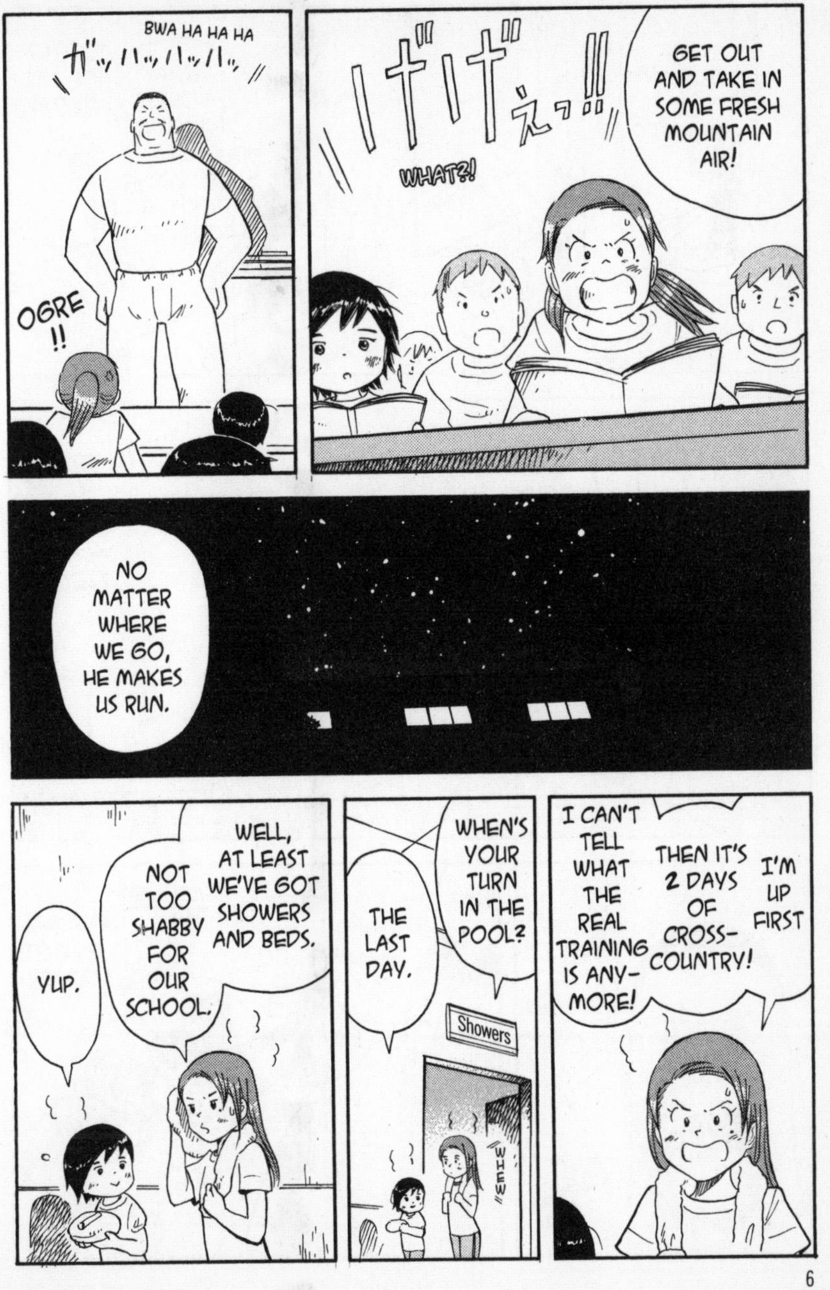
GET OUT AND TAKE IN SOME FRESH MOUNTAIN AIR!
げげえっ!!
WHAT?!
BWA HA HA HA
ガッハッハッハッ
OGRE !!
NO MATTER WHERE WE GO, HE MAKES US RUN.
I'M UP FIRST
THEN IT'S 2 DAYS OF CROSS-COUNTRY!
I CAN'T TELL WHAT THE REAL TRAINING IS ANYMORE!
WHEN'S YOUR TURN IN THE POOL?
THE LAST DAY.
Showers
WHEW
WELL, AT LEAST WE'VE GOT SHOWERS AND BEDS.
NOT TOO SHABBY FOR OUR SCHOOL.
YUP.

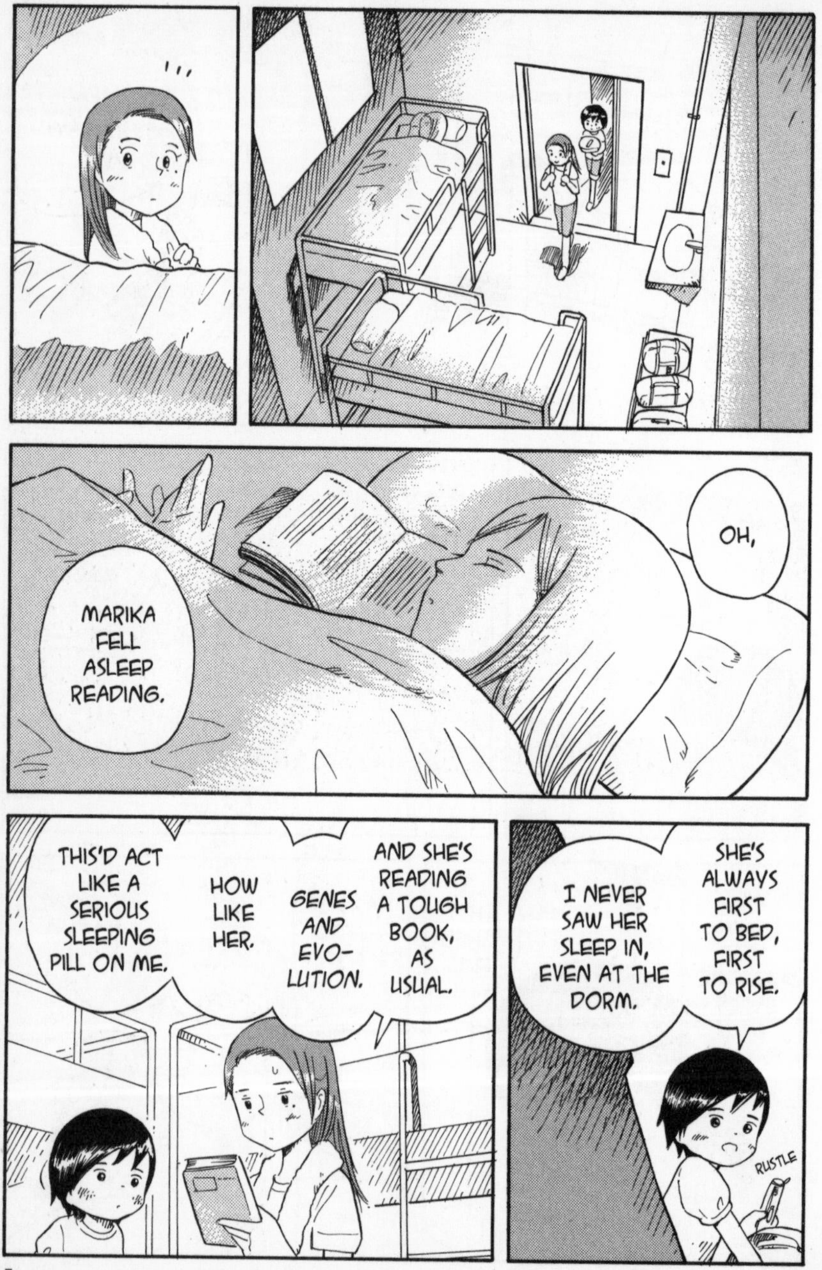
OH,
MARIKA FELL ASLEEP READING.
SHE'S ALWAYS FIRST TO BED, FIRST TO RISE.
I NEVER SAW HER SLEEP IN, EVEN AT THE DORM.
RUSTLE
AND SHE'S READING A TOUGH BOOK, AS USUAL.
GENES AND EVO-LUTION.
HOW LIKE HER.
THIS'D ACT LIKE A SERIOUS SLEEPING PILL ON ME.

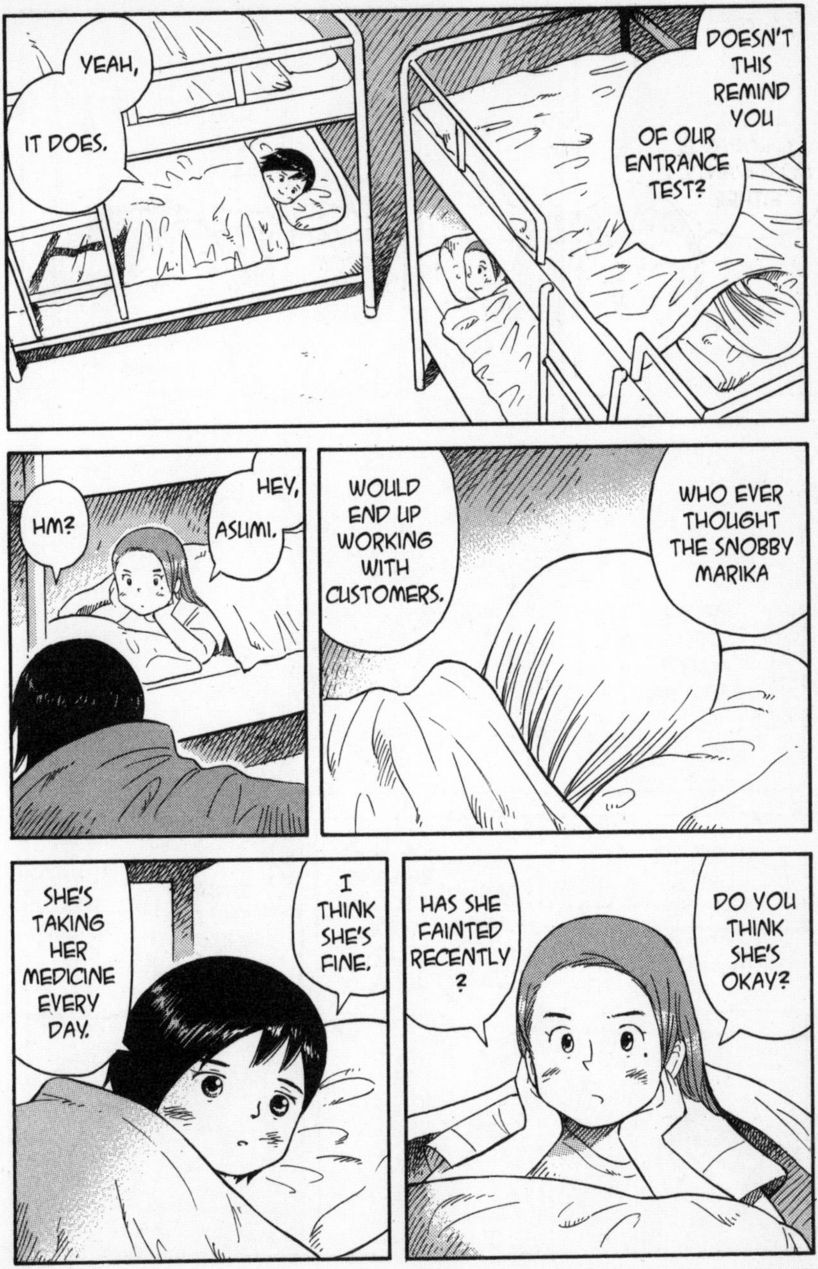
DOESN'T THIS REMIND YOU
OF OUR ENTRANCE TEST?
YEAH,
IT DOES.
WHO EVER THOUGHT THE SNOBBY MARIKA
WOULD END UP WORKING WITH CUSTOMERS.
HEY, ASUMI.
HM?
DO YOU THINK SHE'S OKAY?
HAS SHE FAINTED RECENTLY?
I THINK SHE'S FINE.
SHE'S TAKING HER MEDICINE EVERY DAY.

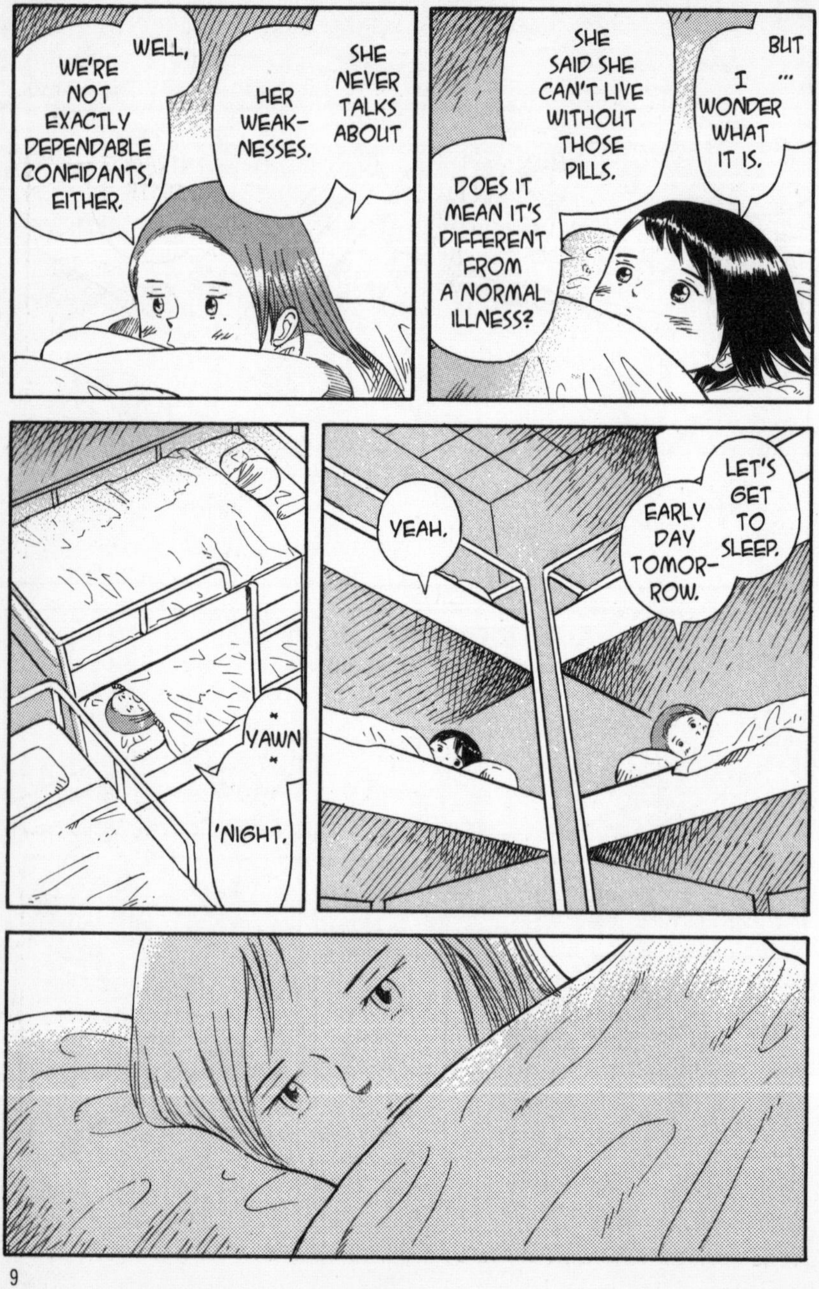
BUT ... I WONDER WHAT IT IS.
SHE SAID SHE CAN'T LIVE WITHOUT THOSE PILLS.
DOES IT MEAN IT'S DIFFERENT FROM A NORMAL ILLNESS?
SHE NEVER TALKS ABOUT HER WEAK-NESSES.
WELL, WE'RE NOT EXACTLY DEPENDABLE CONFIDANTS, EITHER.
LET'S GET TO SLEEP.
EARLY DAY TOMOR-ROW.
YEAH.
YAWN
'NIGHT.

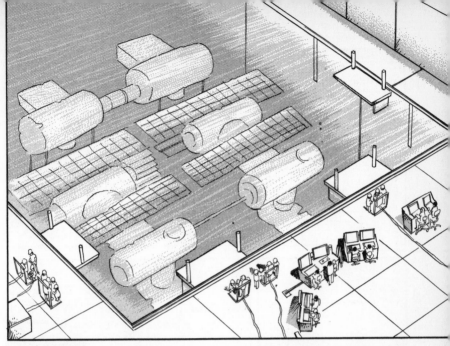

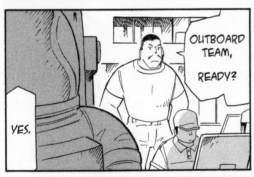

OUTBOARD TEAM, READY?

YES.

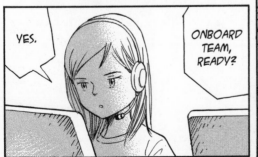

YES.

ONBOARD TEAM, READY?

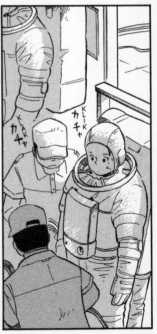

カチャ カチャ

K-I-K カチャ

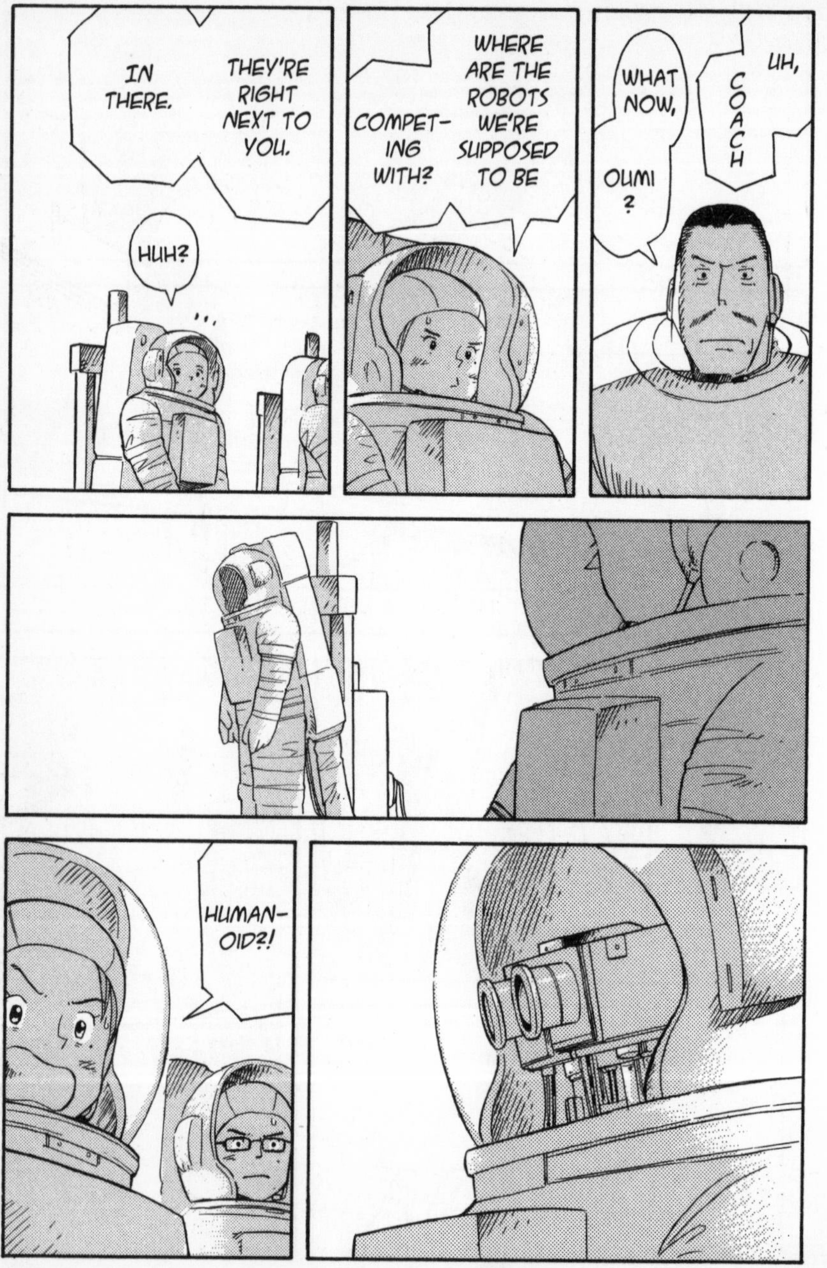
UH, COACH
WHAT NOW, OUMI?
WHERE ARE THE ROBOTS WE'RE SUPPOSED TO BE COMPETING WITH?
THEY'RE RIGHT NEXT TO YOU.
IN THERE.
HUH?
...
HUMAN-OID?!

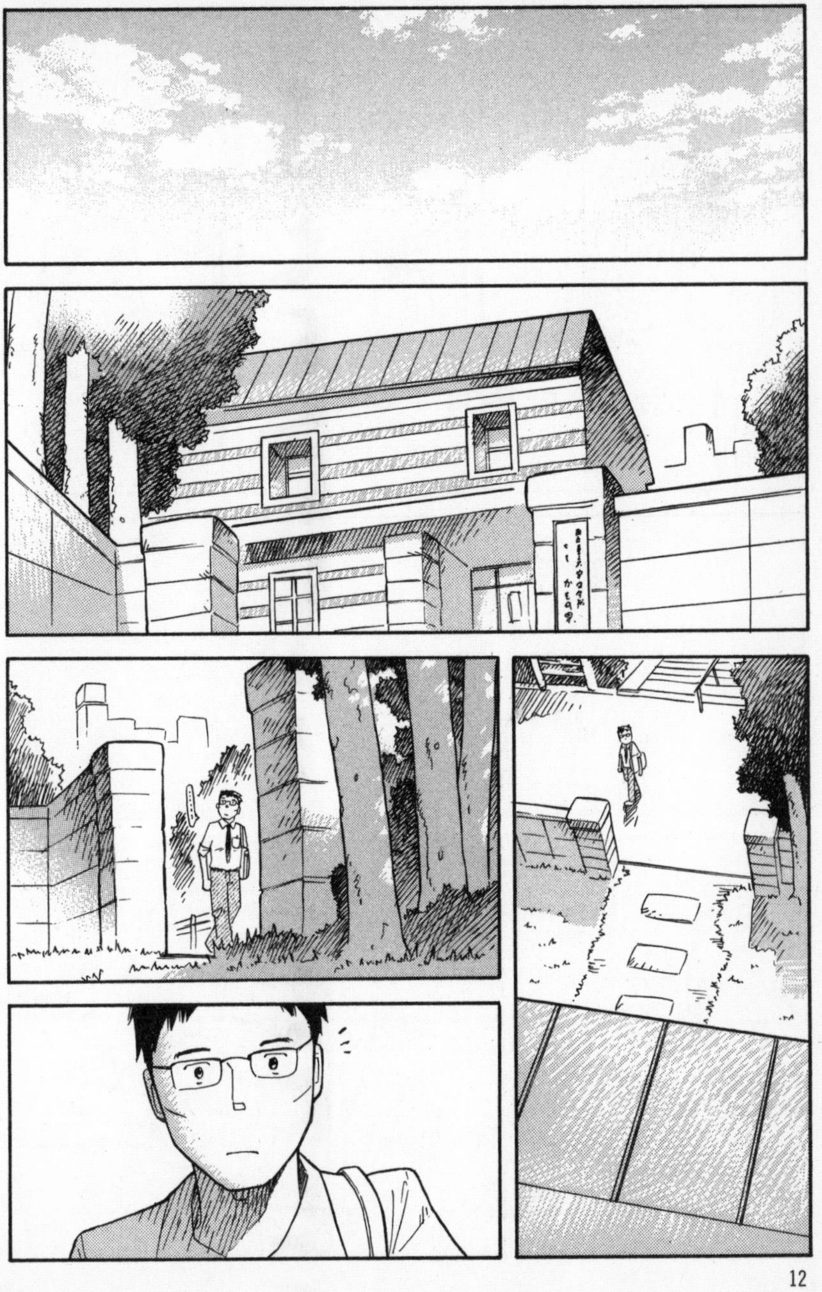
……

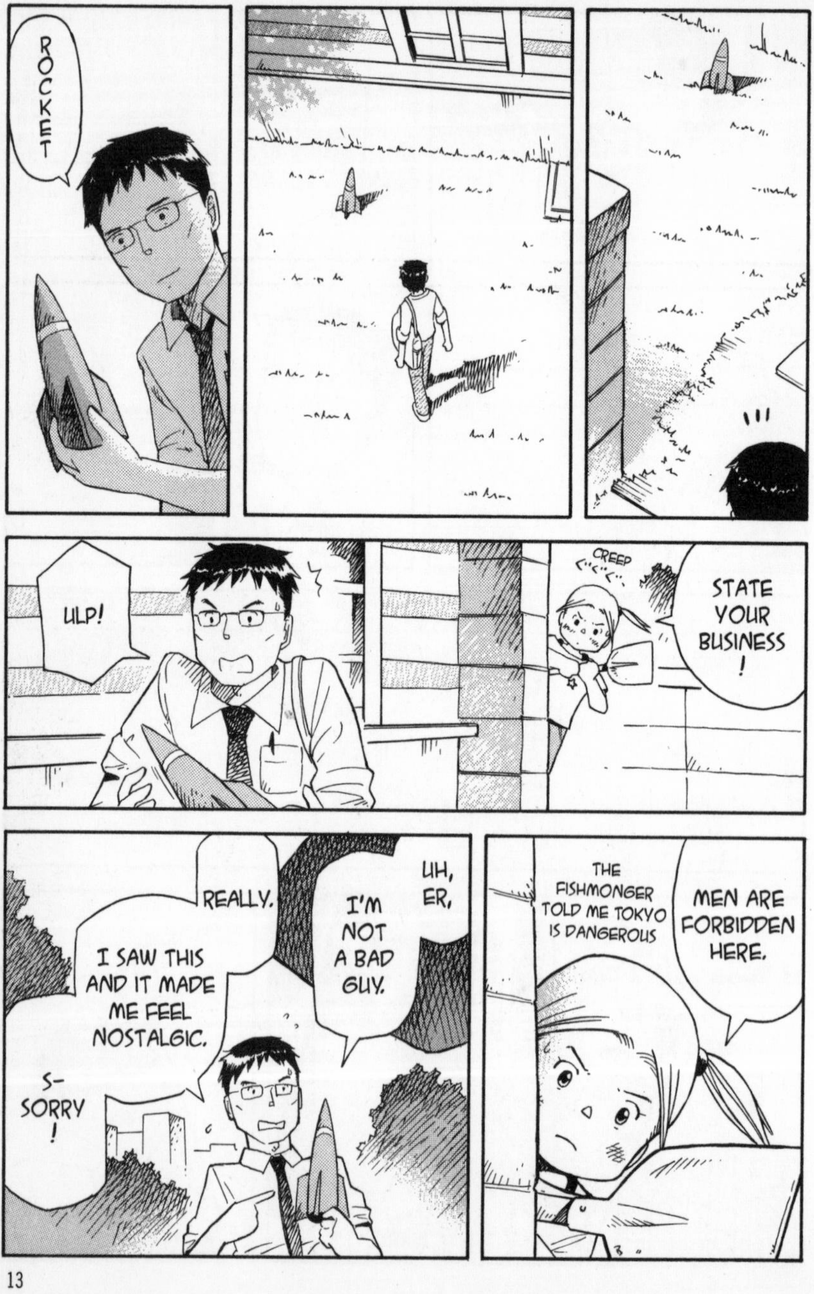
!!!
ROCKET
STATE YOUR BUSINESS !
CREEP
ULP!
MEN ARE FORBIDDEN HERE.
THE FISHMONGER TOLD ME TOKYO IS DANGEROUS
UH, ER,
I'M NOT A BAD GUY.
REALLY.
I SAW THIS AND IT MADE ME FEEL NOSTALGIC.
S- SORRY !

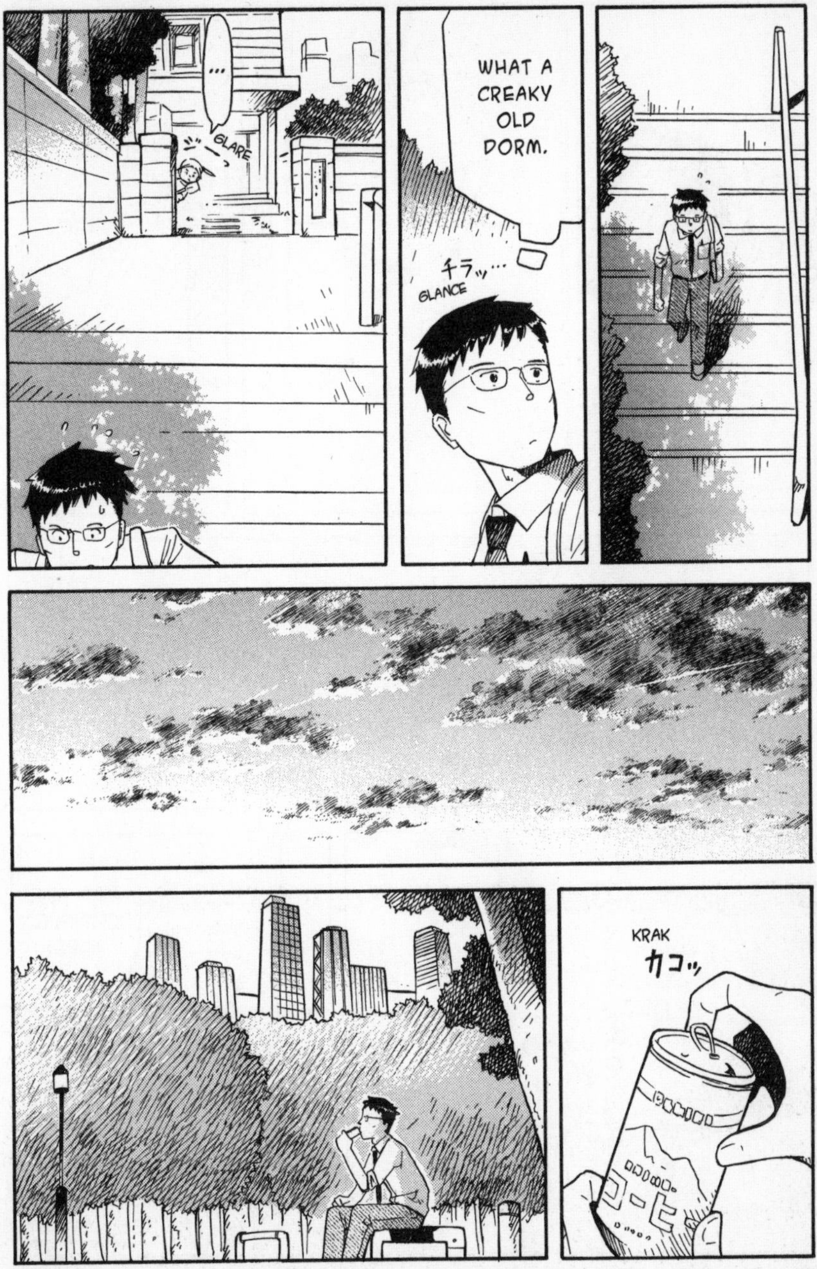
WHAT A CREAKY OLD DORM.
チラッ…
GLANCE
…
ジー
GLARE
KRAK
カコッ

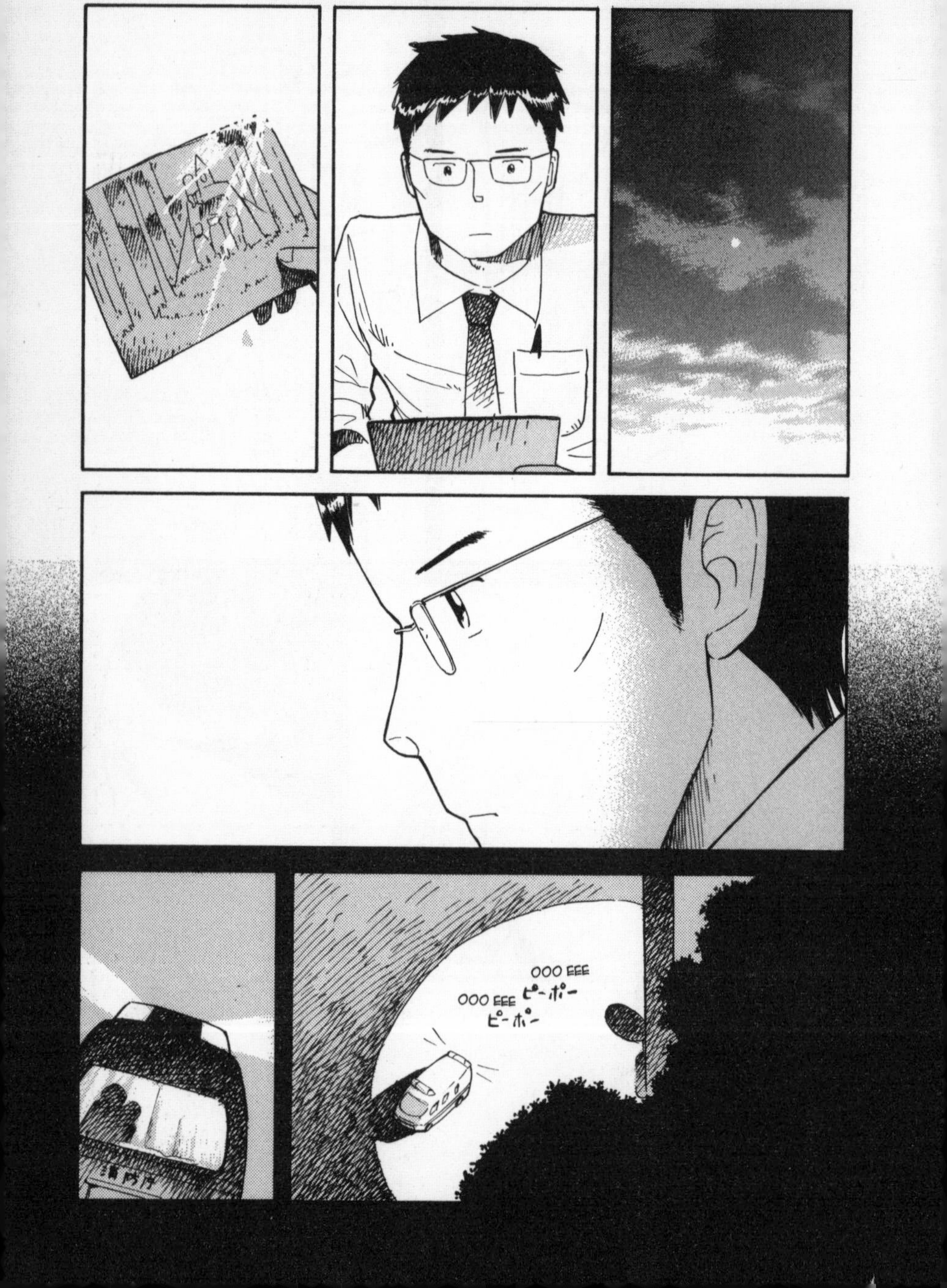
OOO EEE
ピーポー
OOO EEE
ピーポー

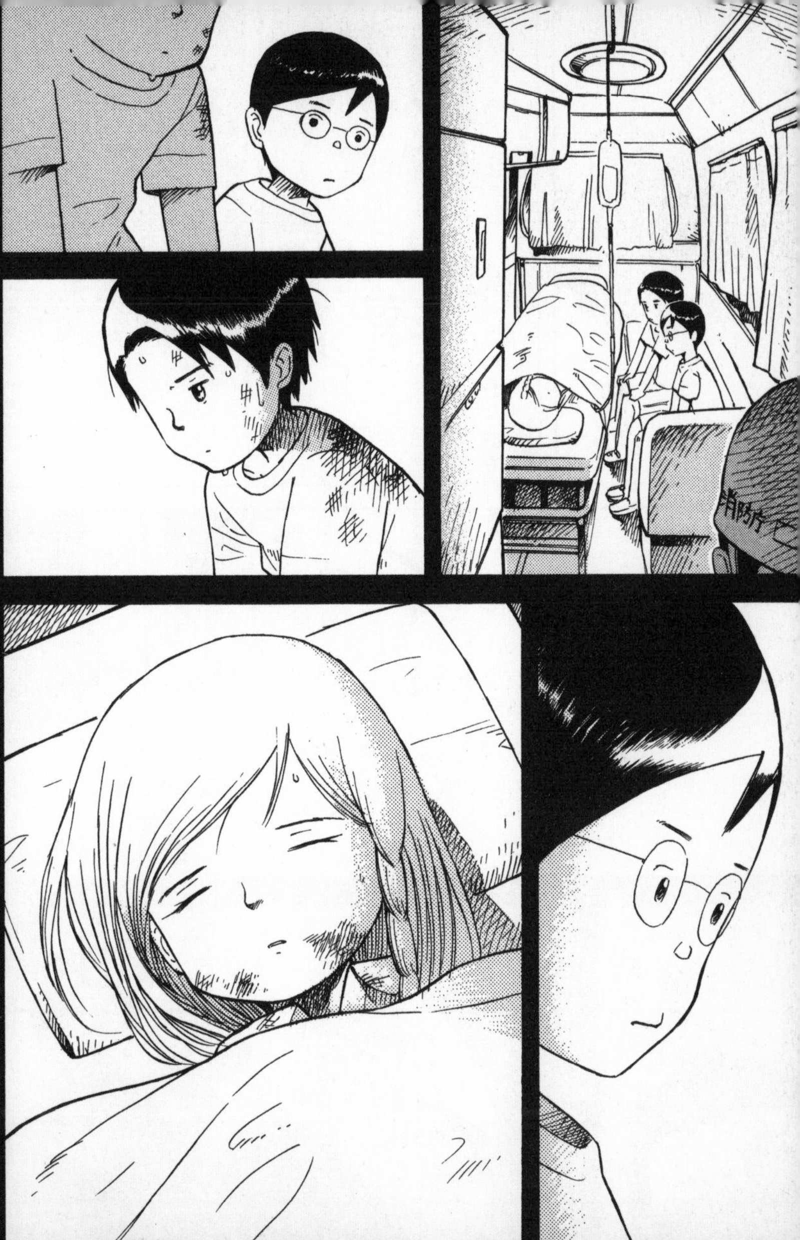
消防庁

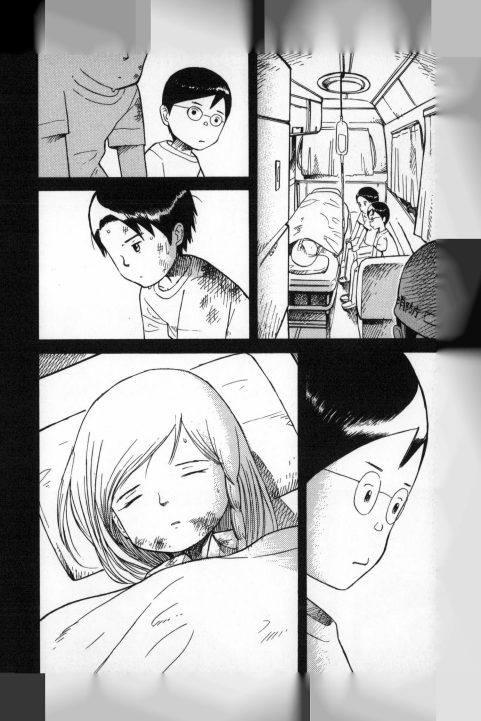

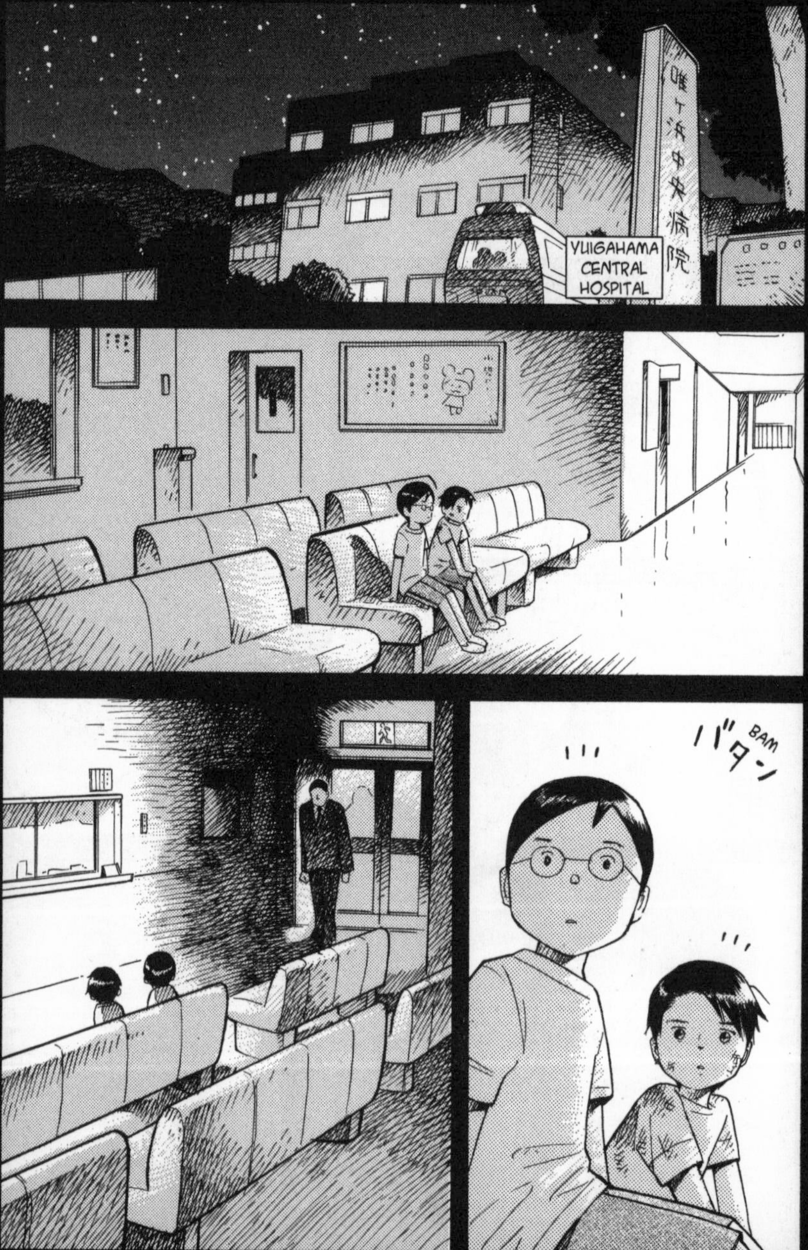
唯ケ浜中央病院
YUIGAHAMA CENTRAL HOSPITAL
バタン
BAM

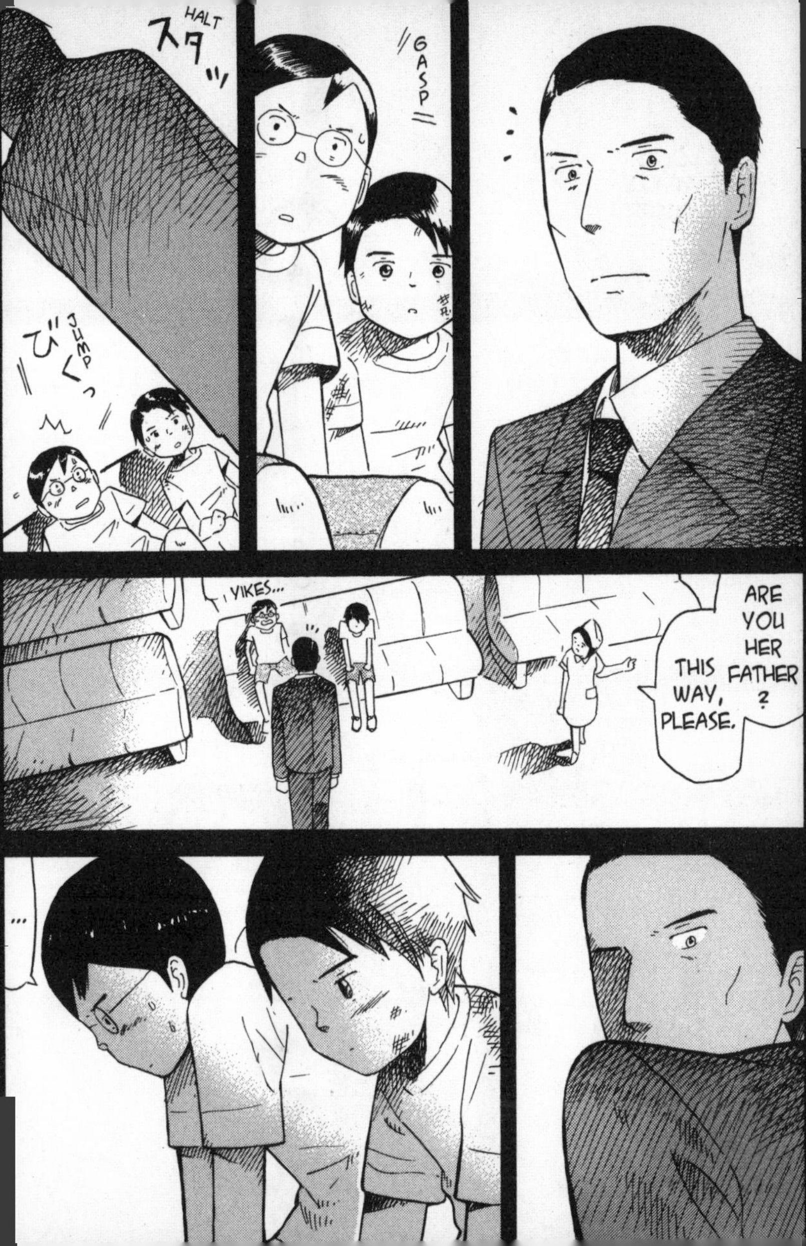
GASP
HALT
スタッ
JUMP
びくっ
ARE YOU HER FATHER?
THIS WAY, PLEASE.
YIKES...
...

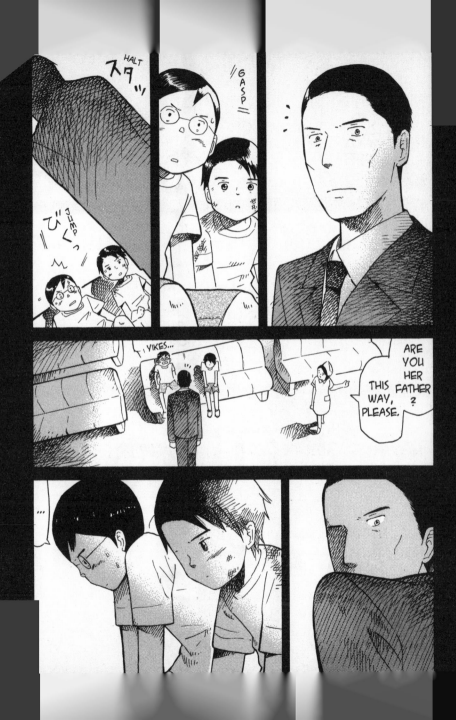

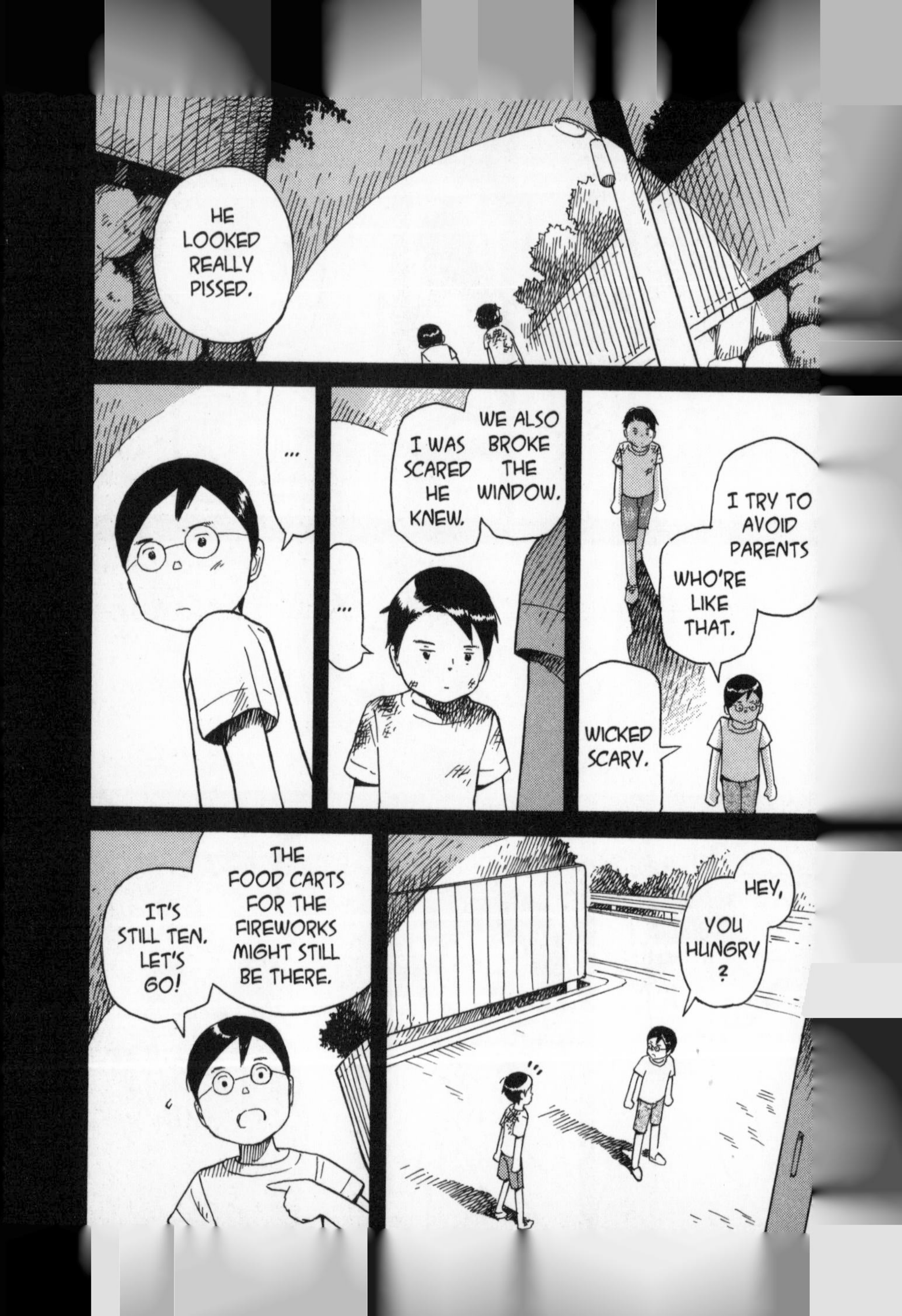
HE LOOKED REALLY PISSED.
I TRY TO AVOID PARENTS
WHO'RE LIKE THAT.
WICKED SCARY.
WE ALSO BROKE THE WINDOW.
I WAS SCARED HE KNEW.
...
...
HEY, YOU HUNGRY?
THE FOOD CARTS FOR THE FIREWORKS MIGHT STILL BE THERE.
IT'S STILL TEN. LET'S GO!

YAKISOBA
わたがし
やきそば 400円
TAKOYAKI
たこ焼き
たこ焼き 300円
HERE,
TAKE HALF.
パクッ
MUNCH
ICK, THEY'RE COLD.
MUNCH
パクッ

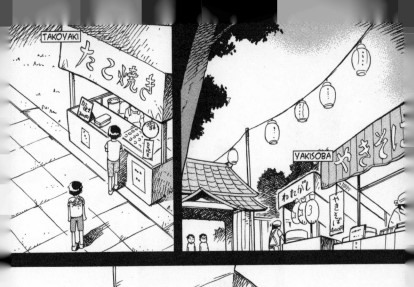

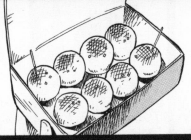

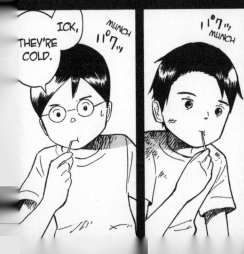

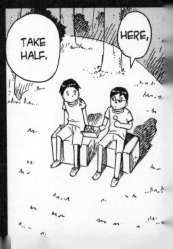

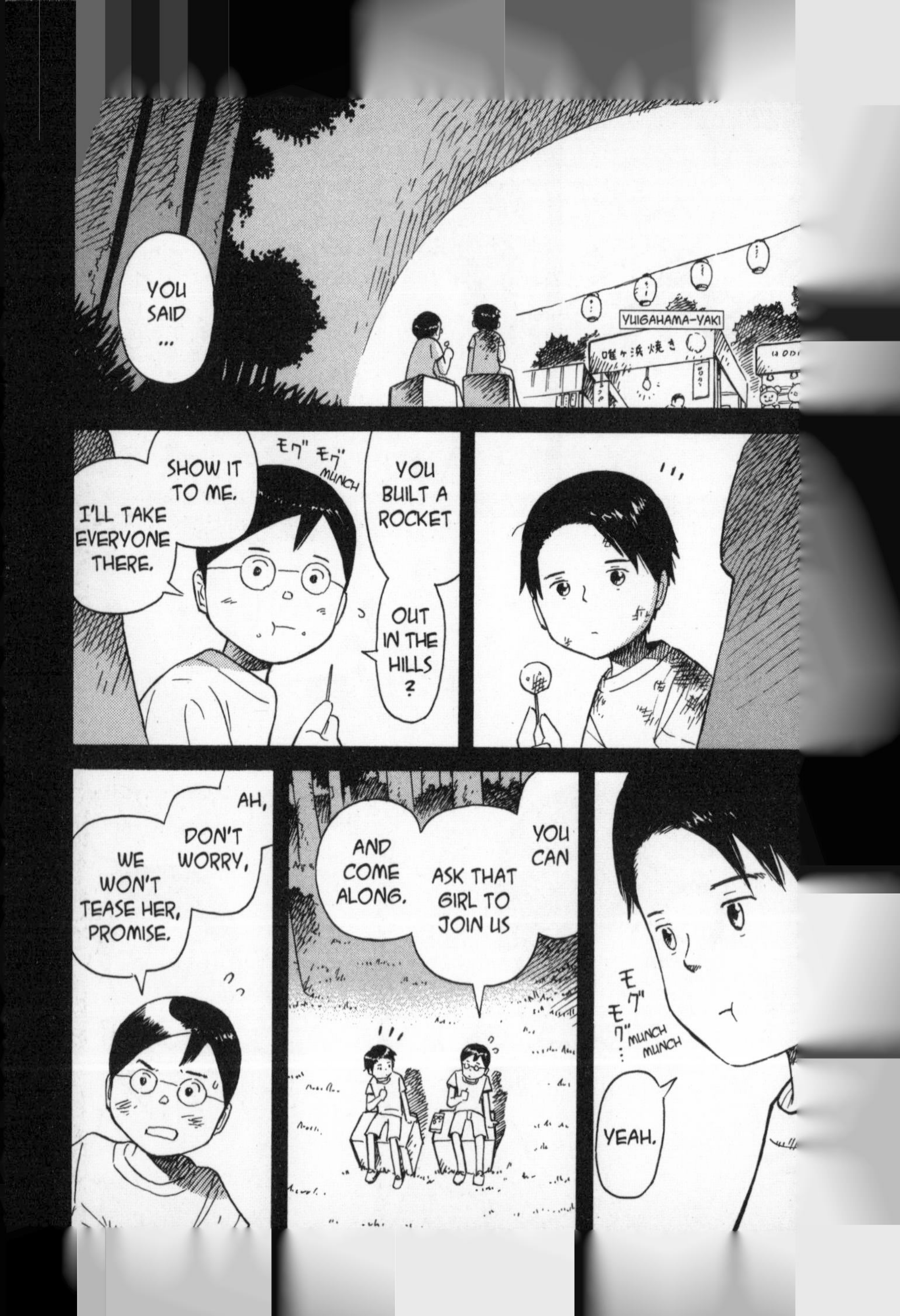
YOU SAID ...
YUIGAHAMA-YAKI
唯ヶ浜焼き
YOU BUILT A ROCKET
OUT IN THE HILLS?
モグモグ MUNCH
SHOW IT TO ME.
I'LL TAKE EVERYONE THERE.
モグモグ… MUNCH MUNCH
YEAH.
YOU CAN
ASK THAT GIRL TO JOIN US
AND COME ALONG.
AH,
DON'T WORRY,
WE WON'T TEASE HER, PROMISE.

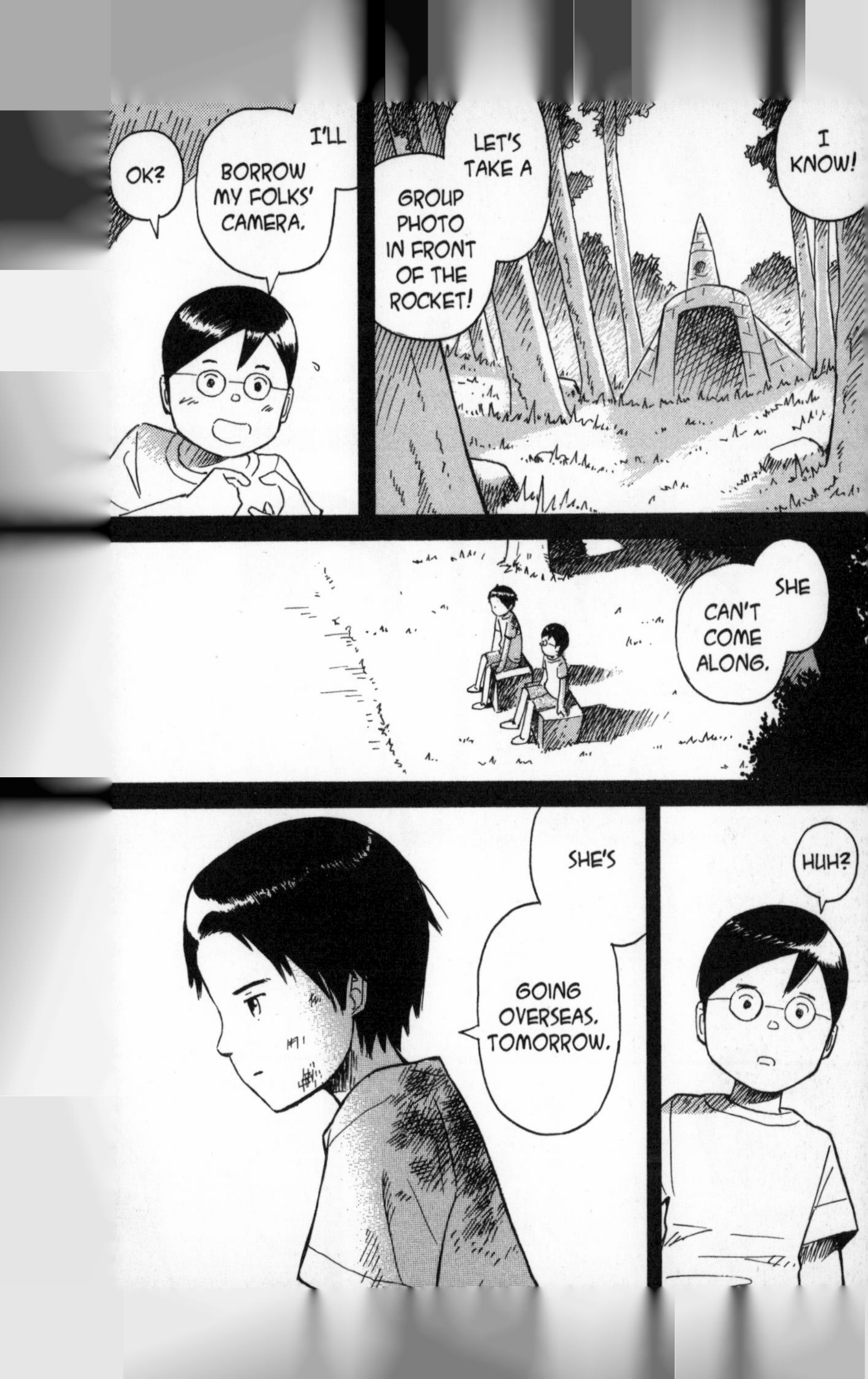
I KNOW!
LET'S TAKE A GROUP PHOTO IN FRONT OF THE ROCKET!
I'LL BORROW MY FOLKS' CAMERA.
OK?
SHE CAN'T COME ALONG.
HUH?
SHE'S GOING OVERSEAS. TOMORROW.

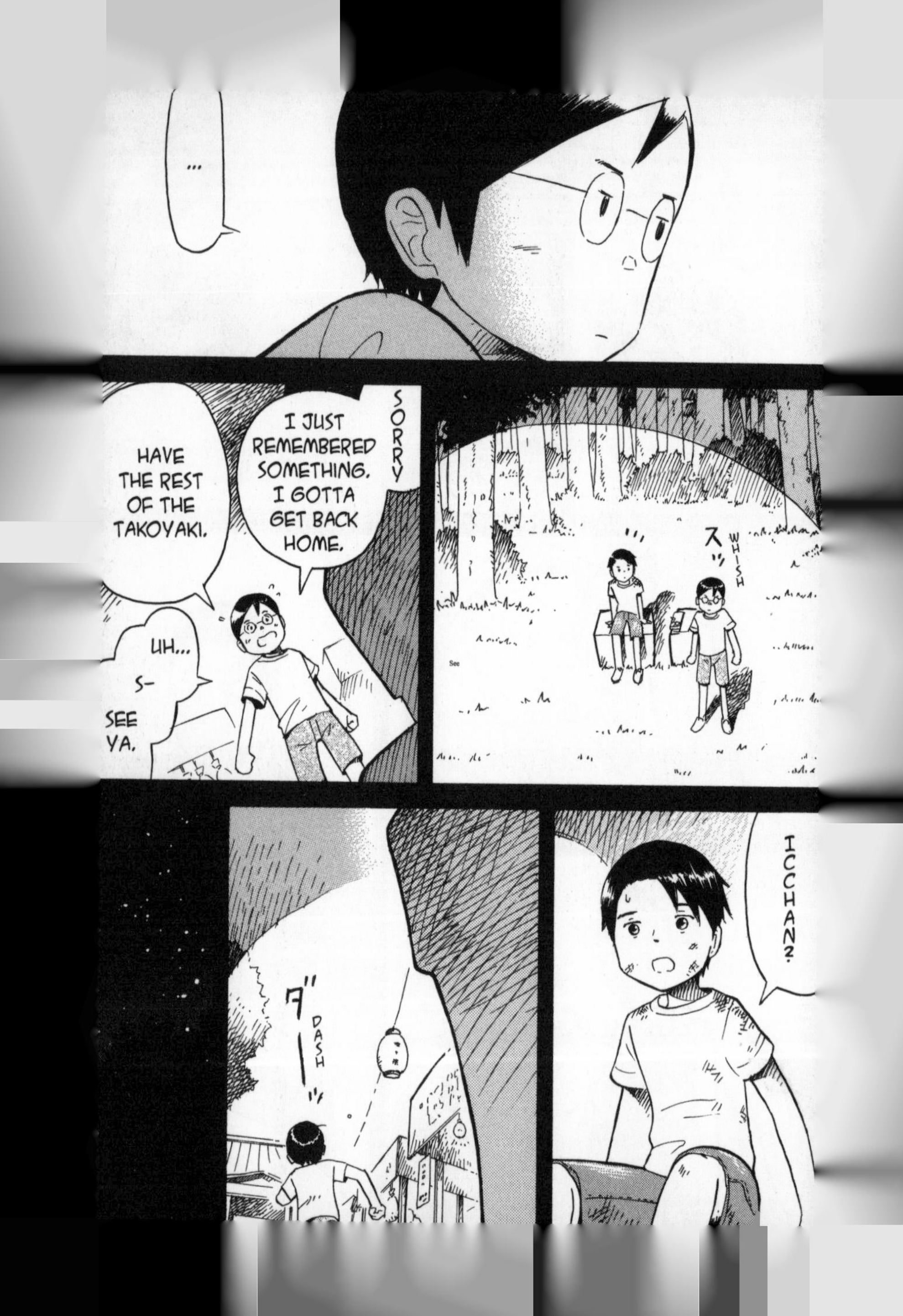
...
スッ
WHISH
SORRY
I JUST REMEMBERED SOMETHING. I GOTTA GET BACK HOME.
HAVE THE REST OF THE TAKOYAKI.
UH...
S- SEE YA.
ICCHAN?
ダー
DASH

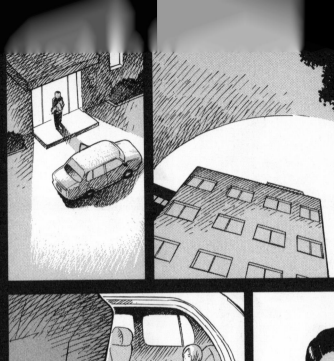

YUIGAHAMA
CENTRAL
HOSPITAL

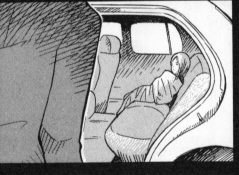

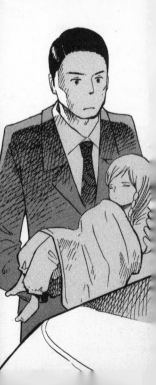

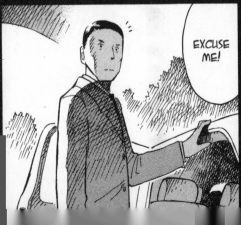

EXCUSE
ME!

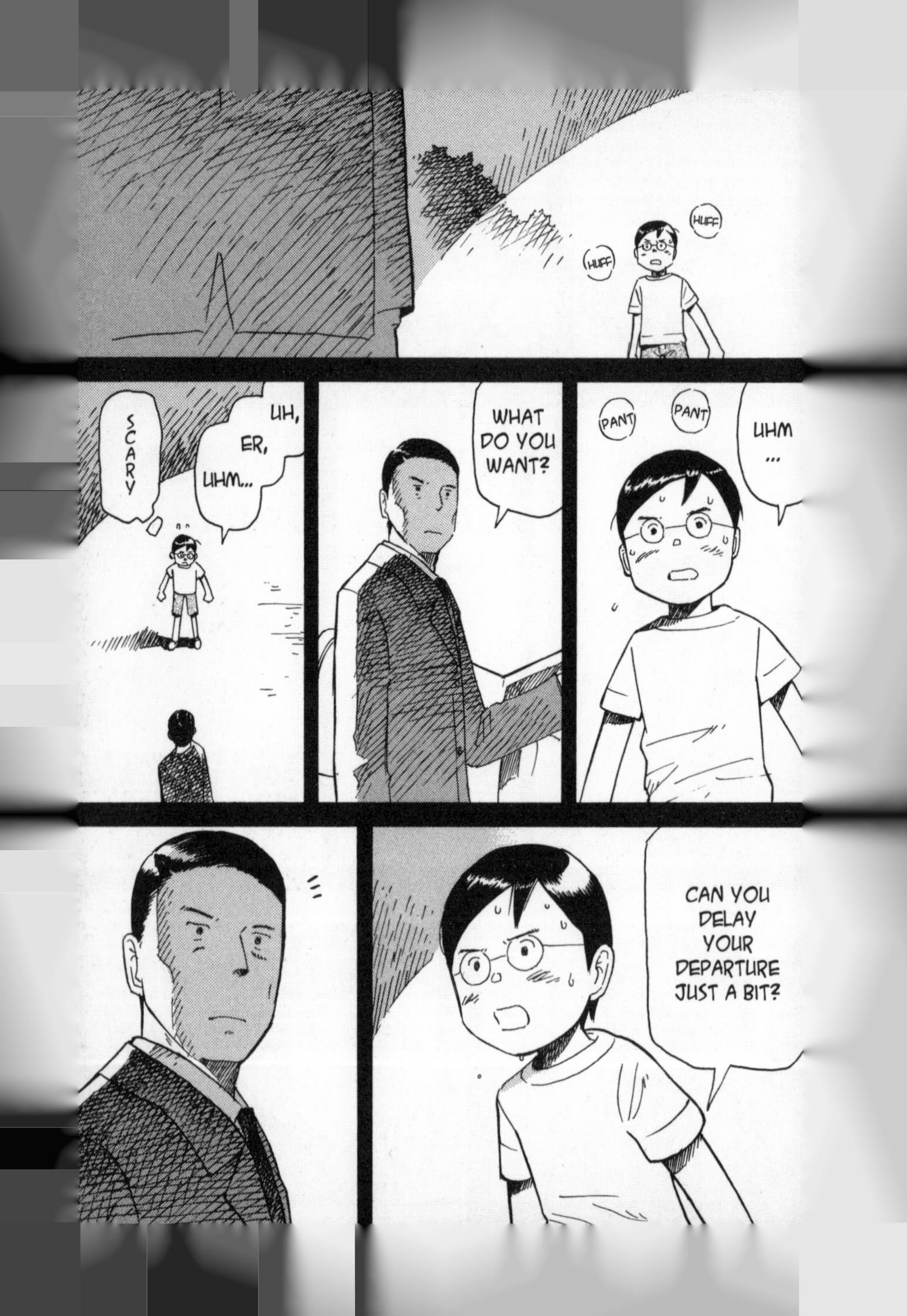
HUFF
HUFF
UHM ...
PANT
PANT
WHAT DO YOU WANT?
UH, ER, UHM...
SCARY
CAN YOU DELAY YOUR DEPARTURE JUST A BIT?

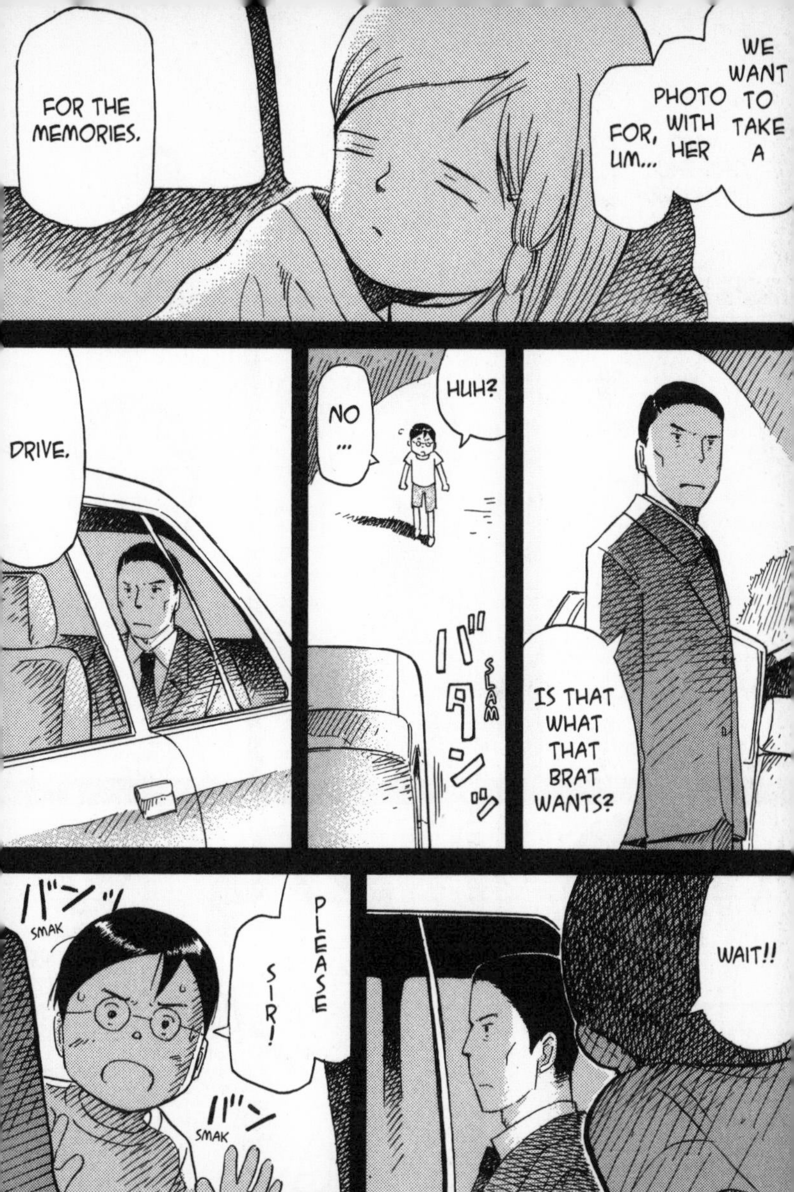
WE WANT TO TAKE A PHOTO WITH HER FOR, UM...
FOR THE MEMORIES.
IS THAT WHAT THAT BRAT WANTS?
HUH?
NO ...
バタンッ
SLAM
DRIVE.
WAIT!!
PLEASE SIR!
バンッ
SMAK
バン
SMAK

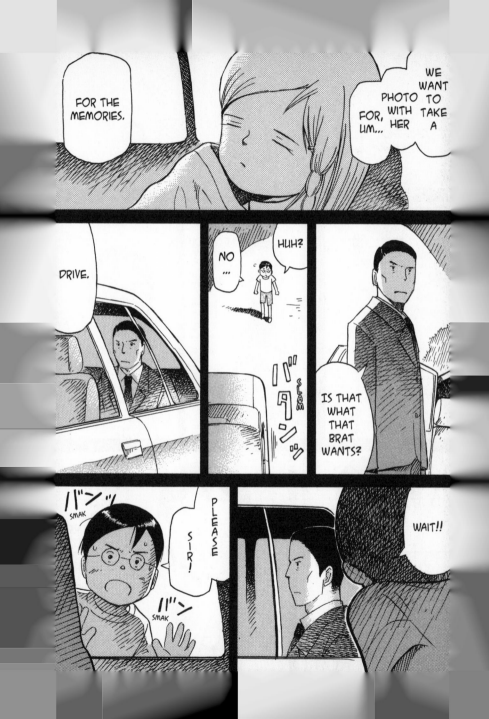

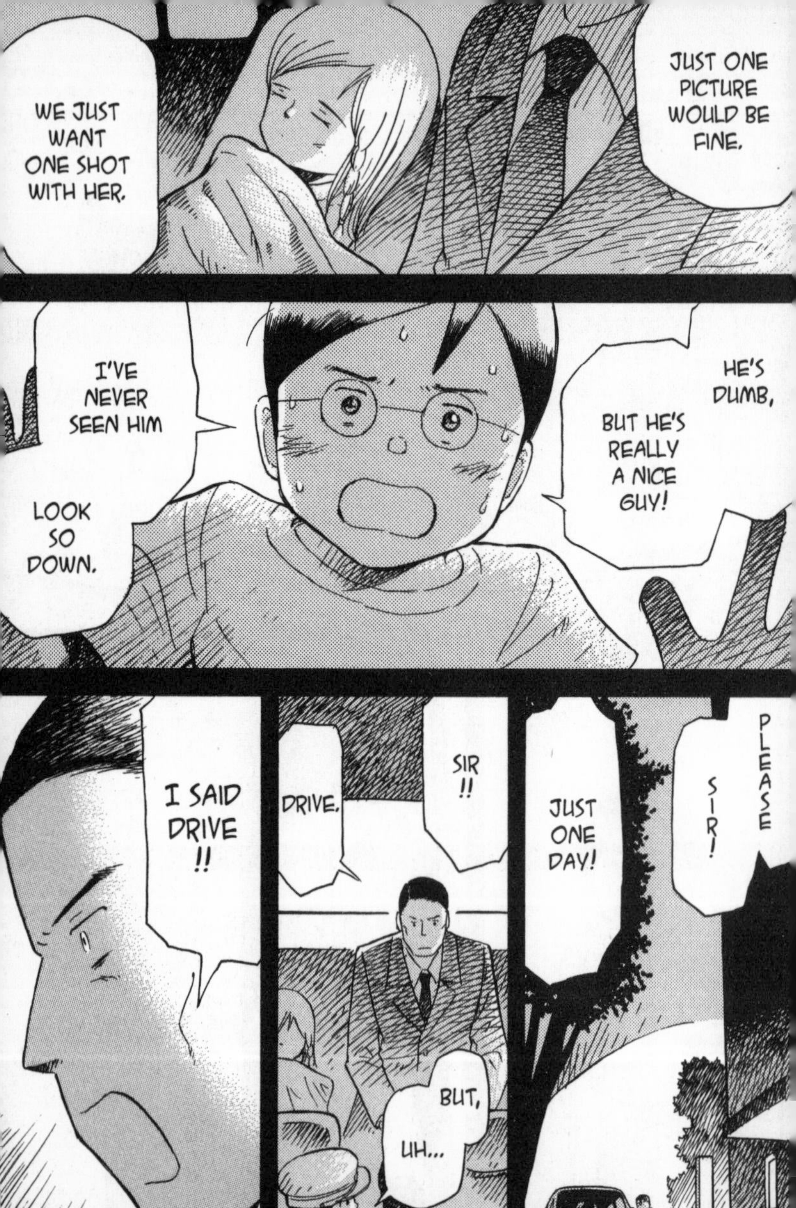
JUST ONE PICTURE WOULD BE FINE.
WE JUST WANT ONE SHOT WITH HER.
HE'S DUMB,
BUT HE'S REALLY A NICE GUY!
I'VE NEVER SEEN HIM
LOOK SO DOWN.
PLEASE
SIR!
JUST ONE DAY!
SIR!!
DRIVE.
BUT,
UH...
I SAID DRIVE!!

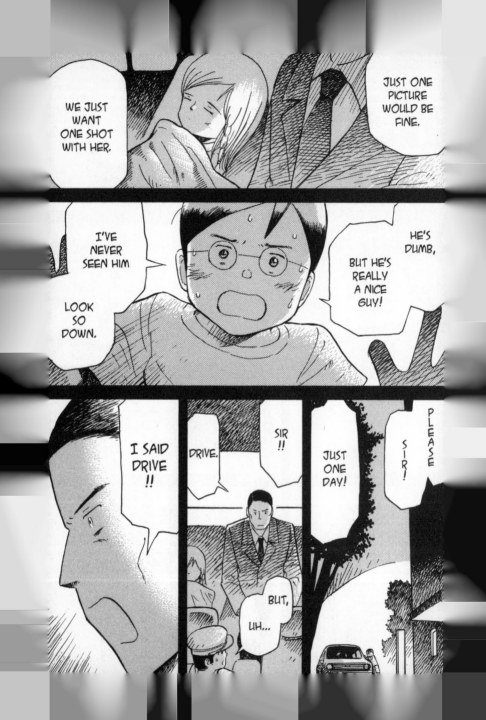

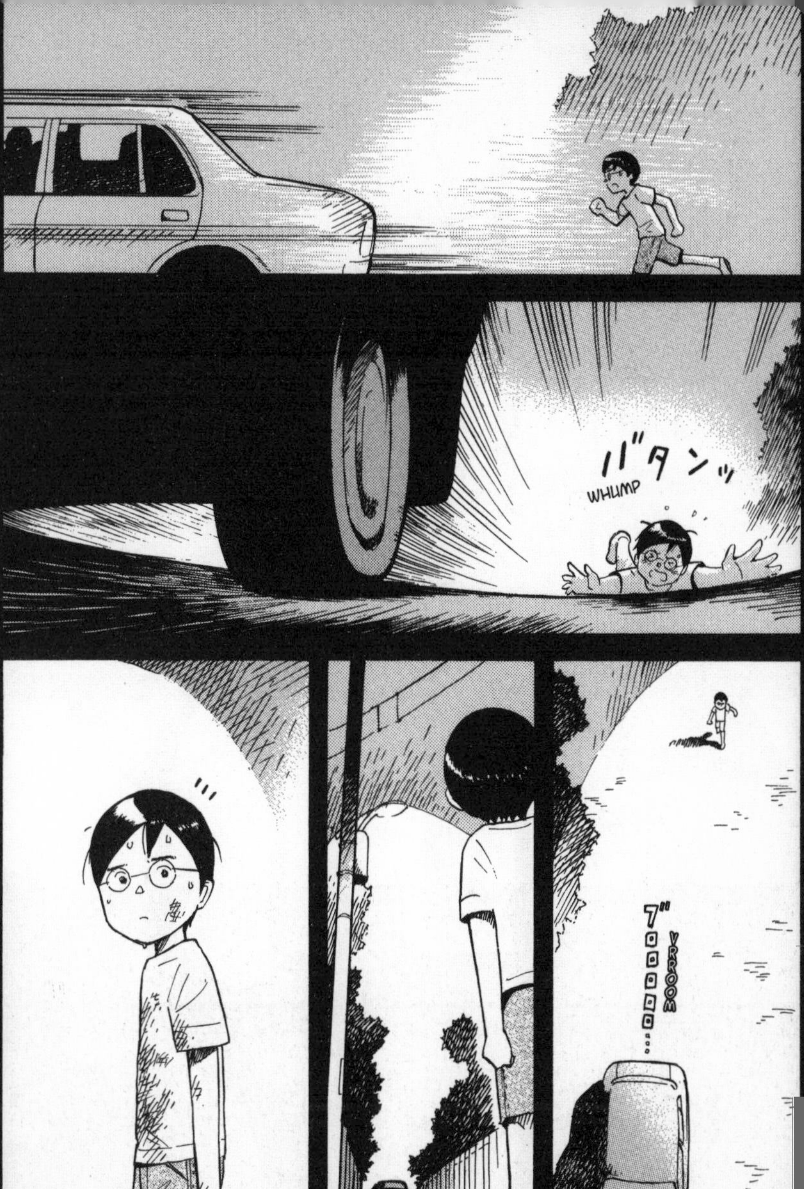
バタンッ
WHUMP
ブロロロロロ…
VRROOM

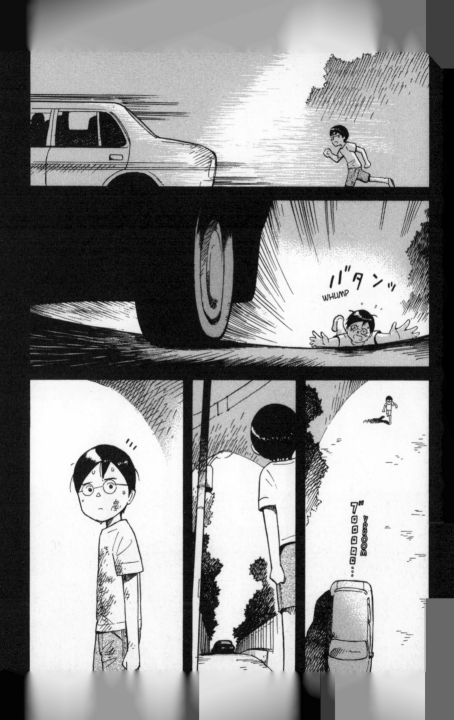

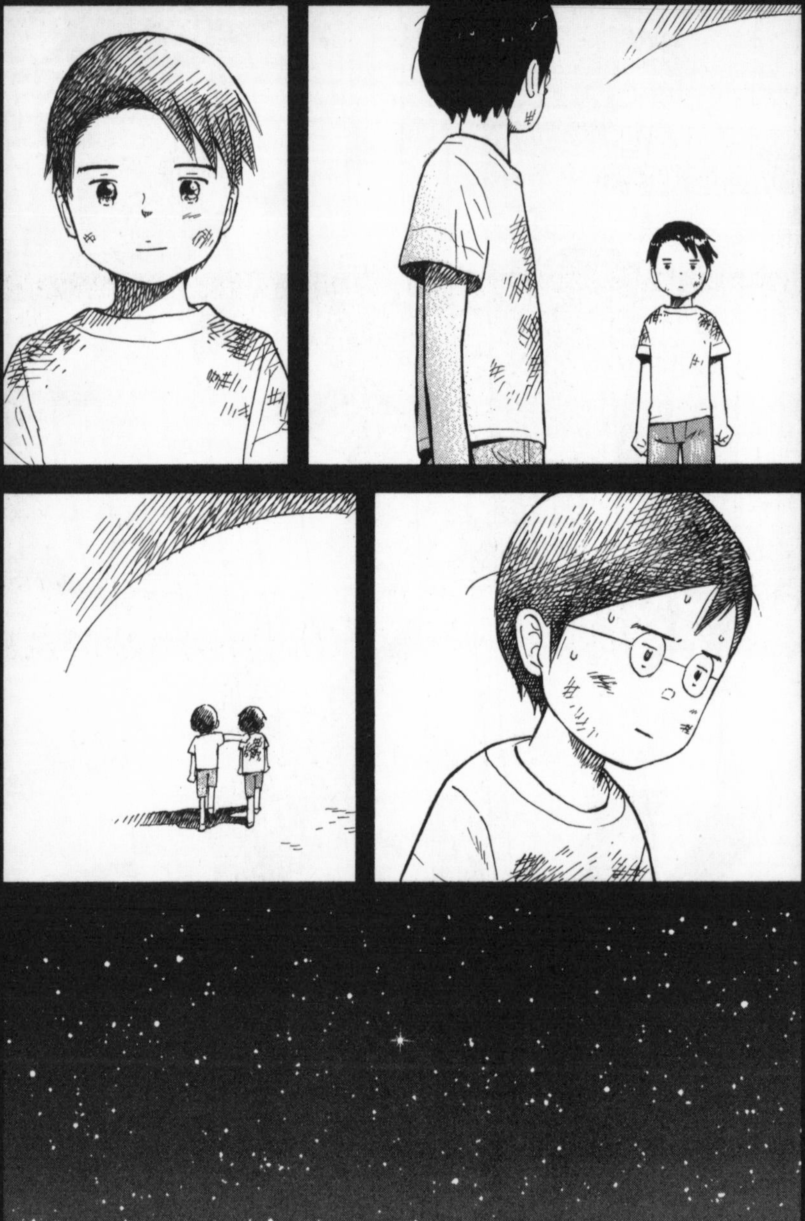

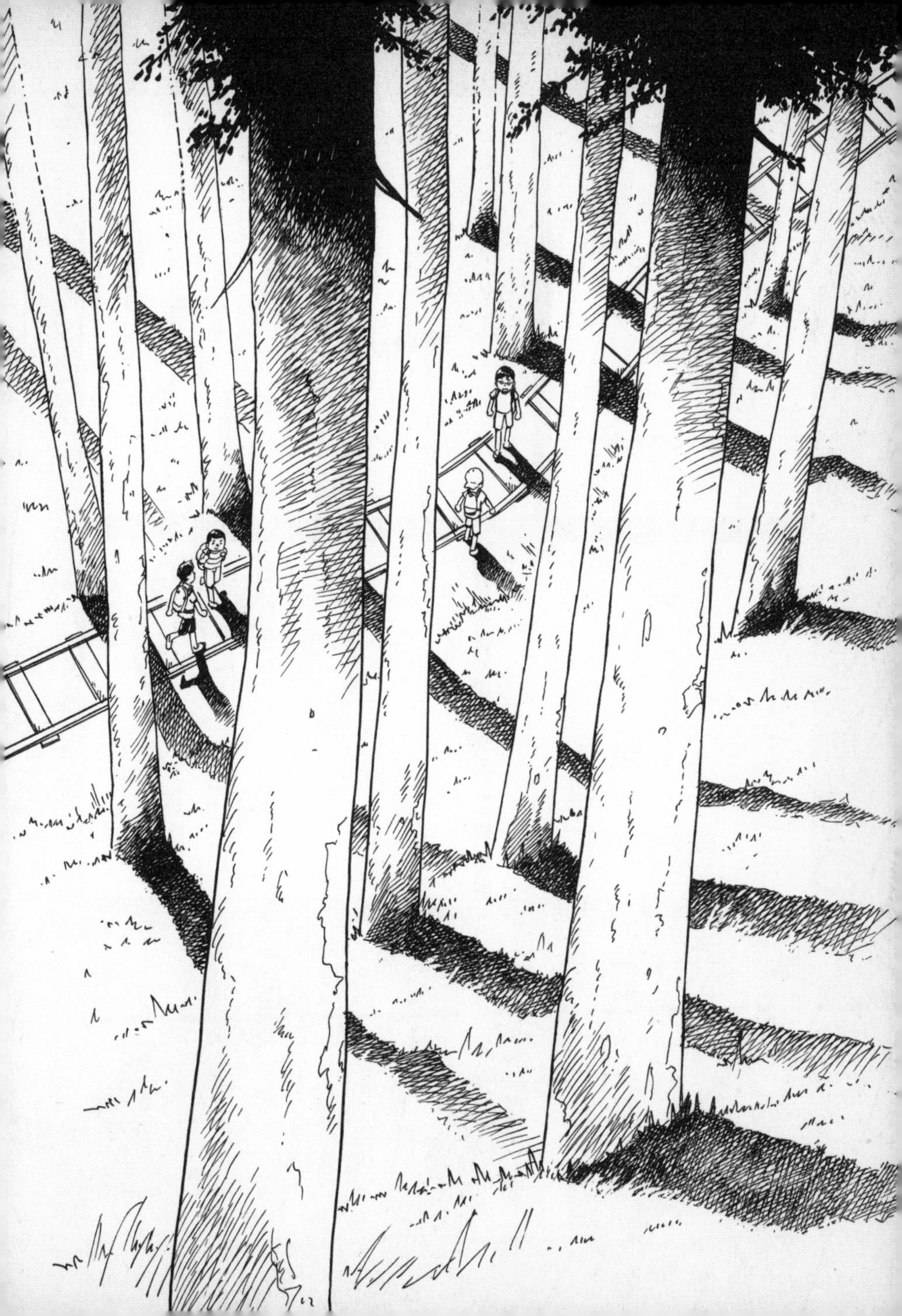

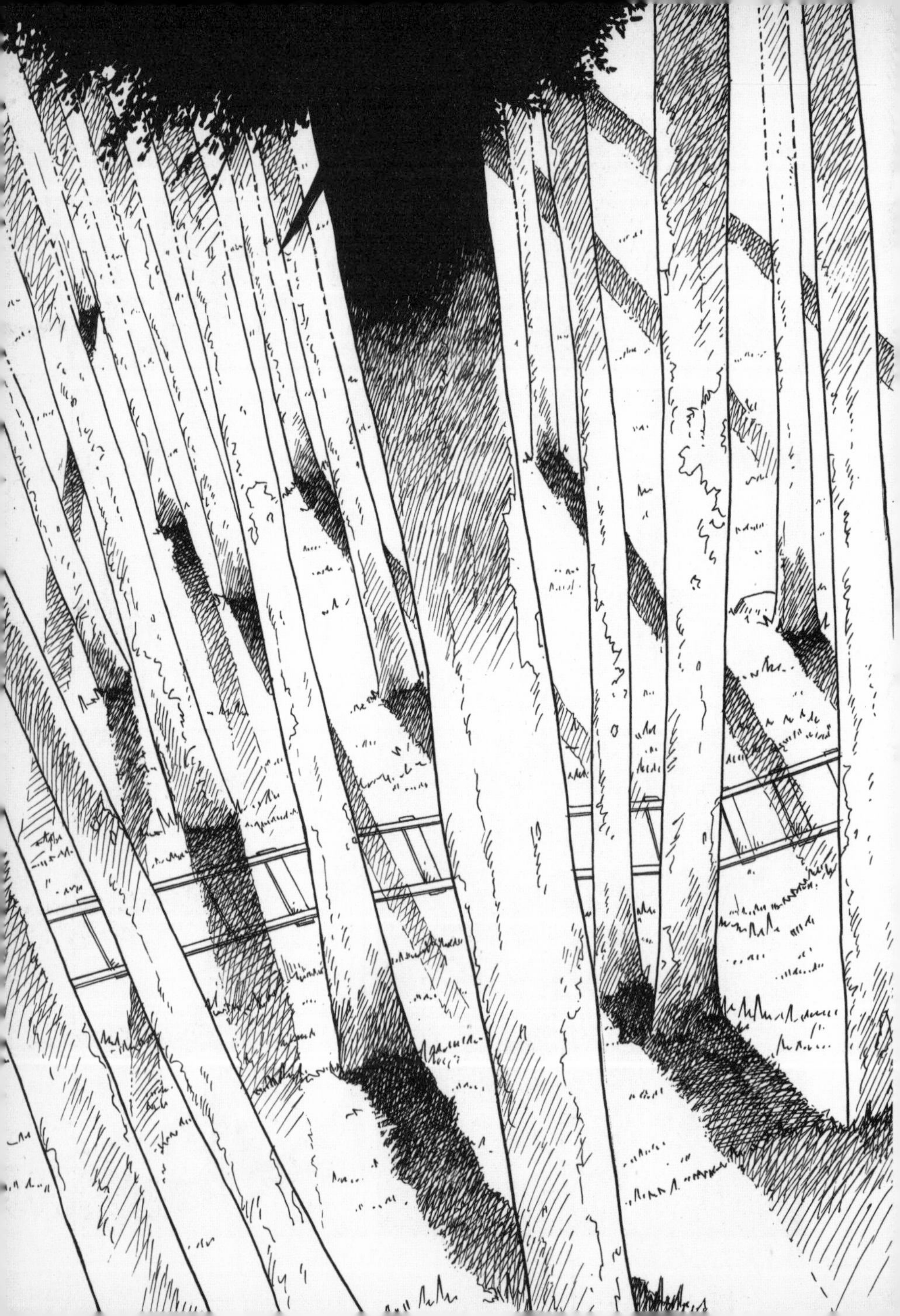

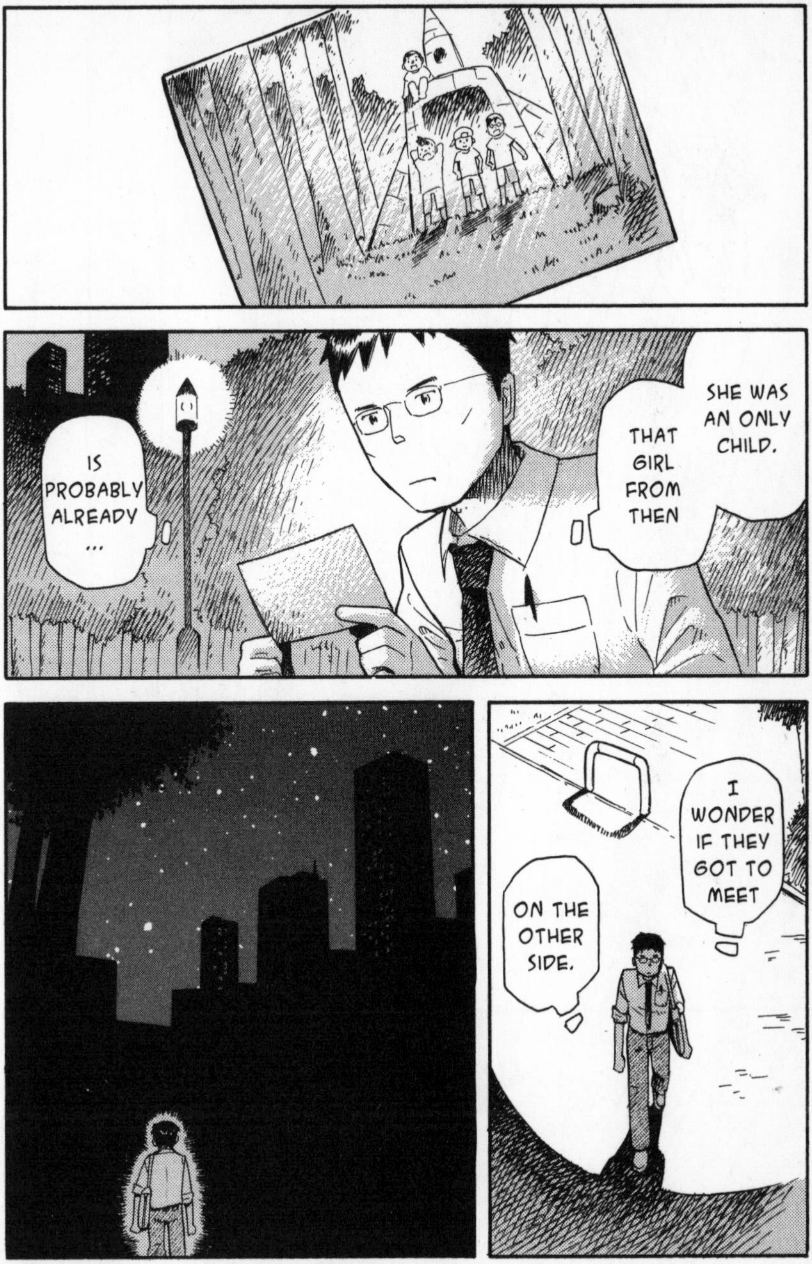
SHE WAS AN ONLY CHILD.
THAT GIRL FROM THEN
IS PROBABLY ALREADY ...
I WONDER IF THEY GOT TO MEET
ON THE OTHER SIDE.

MISSION:57

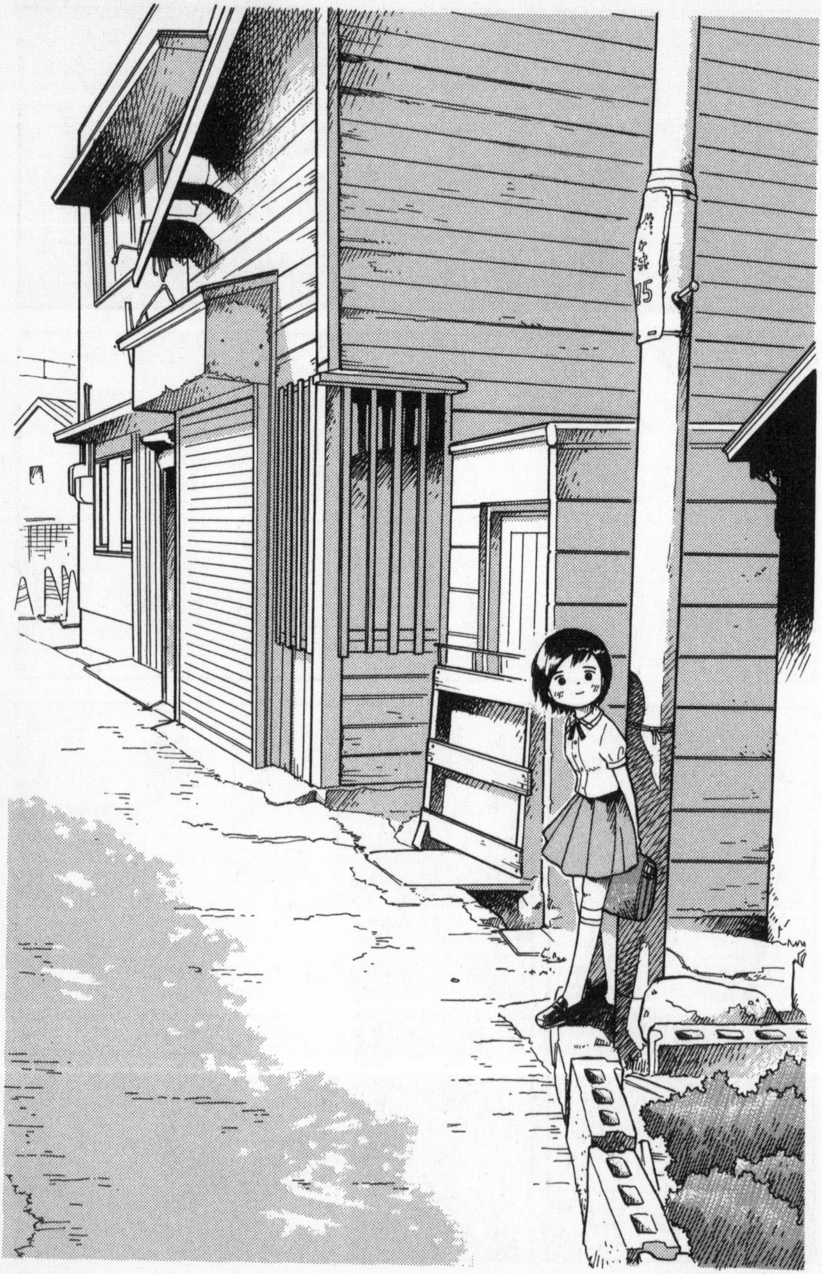

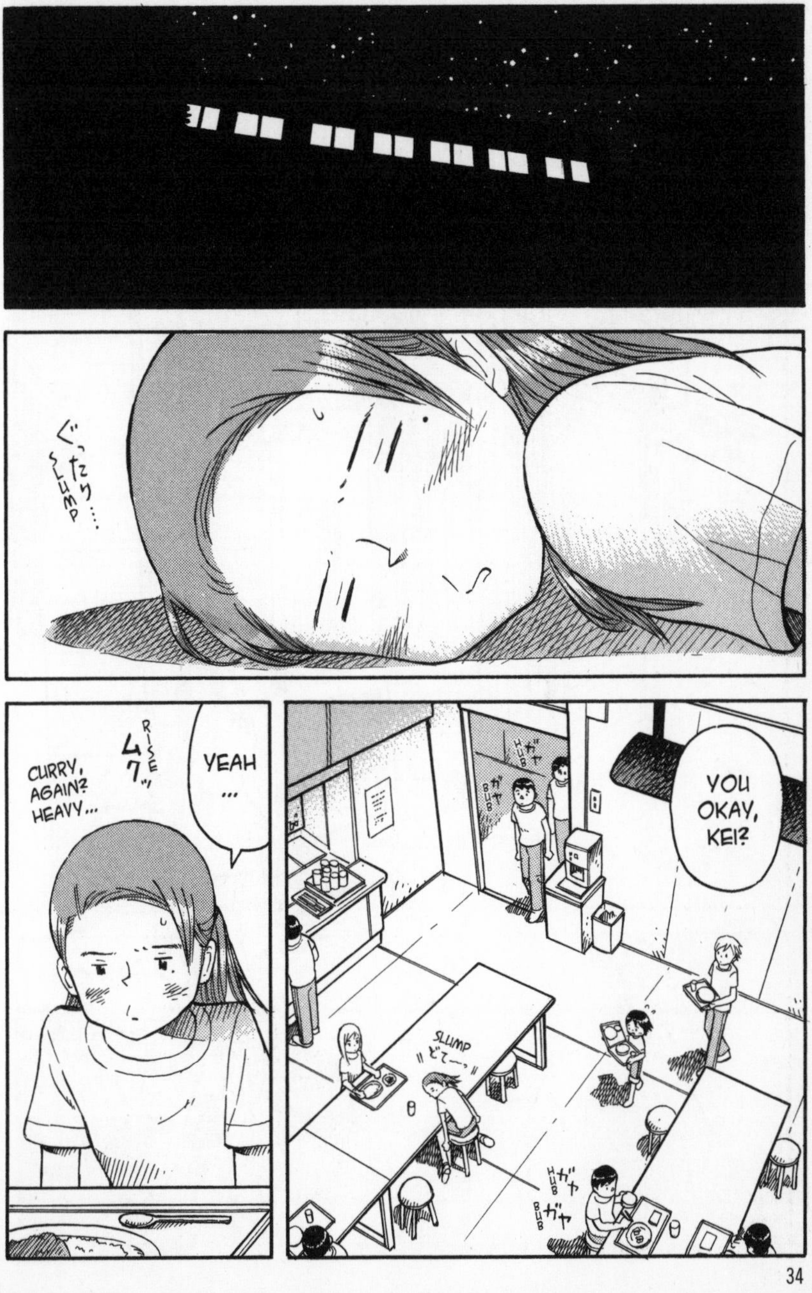
ぐったり....
SLUMP
YOU OKAY, KEI?
ガヤ HUB
ガヤ BUB
SLUMP
どてーっ
ガヤ HUB
ガヤ BUB
YEAH ...
ムクッ
RISE
CURRY, AGAIN? HEAVY...

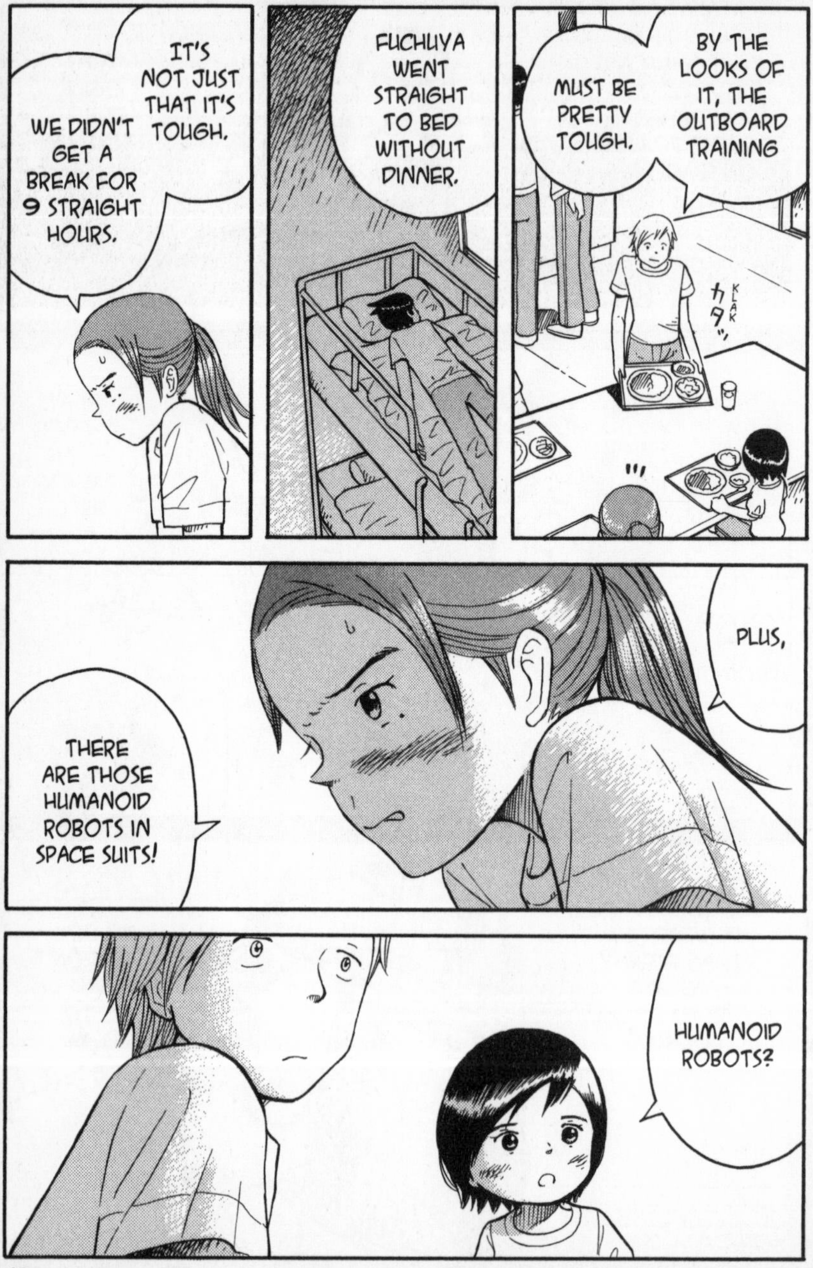
BY THE LOOKS OF IT, THE OUTBOARD TRAINING
MUST BE PRETTY TOUGH.
カタッ KLAK
FUCHUYA WENT STRAIGHT TO BED WITHOUT DINNER.
IT'S NOT JUST THAT IT'S TOUGH.
WE DIDN'T GET A BREAK FOR 9 STRAIGHT HOURS.
PLUS,
THERE ARE THOSE HUMANOID ROBOTS IN SPACE SUITS!
HUMANOID ROBOTS?

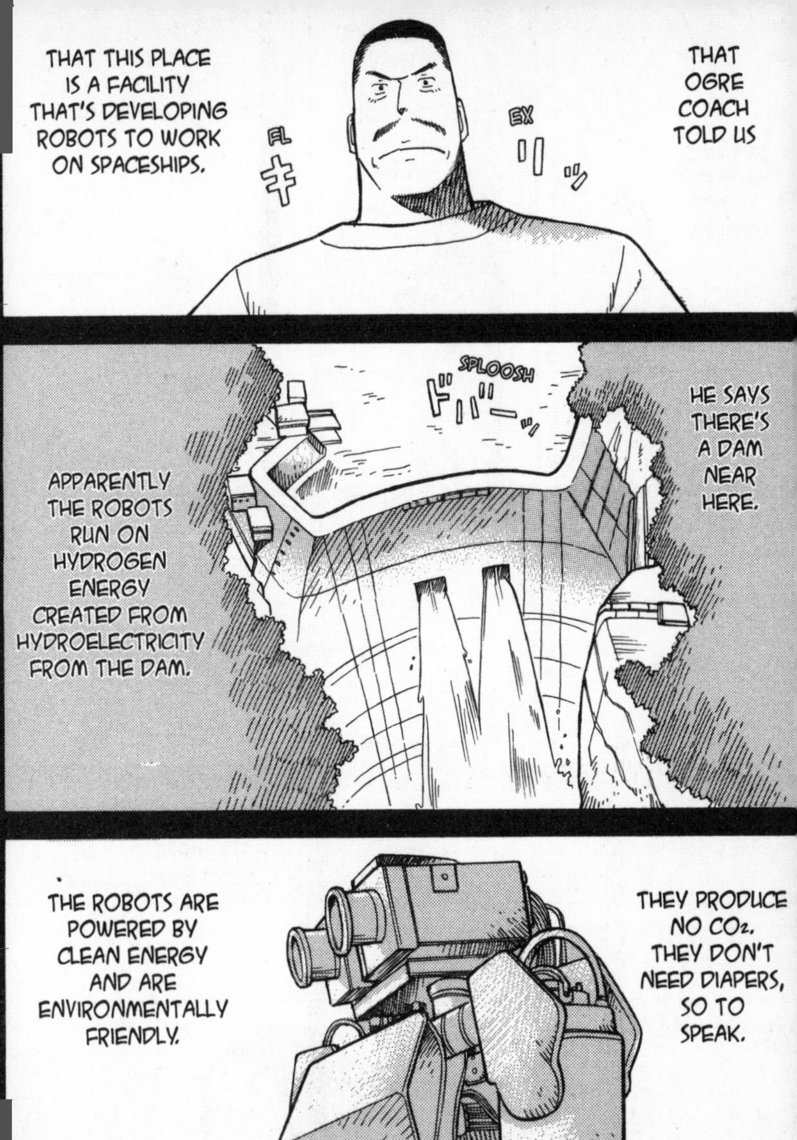
THAT OGRE COACH TOLD US
EX
FL
THAT THIS PLACE IS A FACILITY THAT'S DEVELOPING ROBOTS TO WORK ON SPACESHIPS.
HE SAYS THERE'S A DAM NEAR HERE.
SPLOOSH
APPARENTLY THE ROBOTS RUN ON HYDROGEN ENERGY CREATED FROM HYDROELECTRICITY FROM THE DAM.
THEY PRODUCE NO CO2. THEY DON'T NEED DIAPERS, SO TO SPEAK.
THE ROBOTS ARE POWERED BY CLEAN ENERGY AND ARE ENVIRONMENTALLY FRIENDLY.

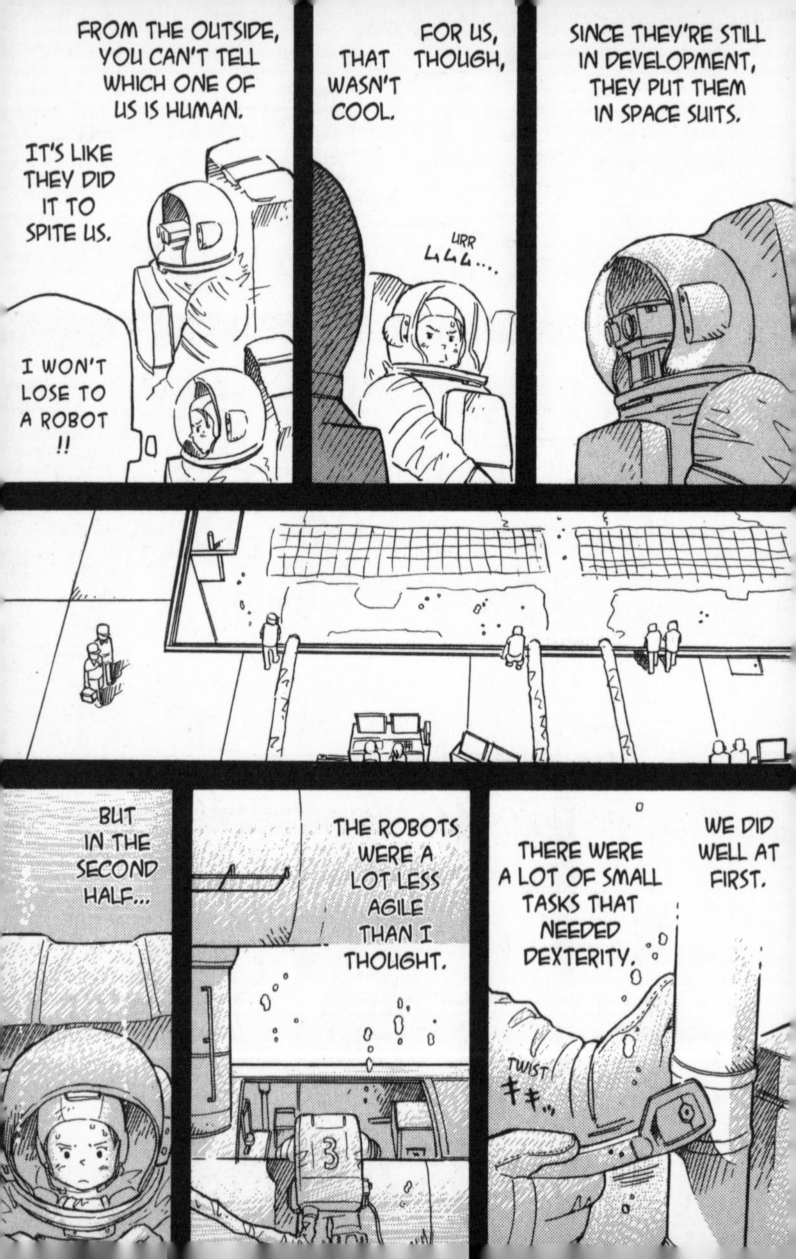
SINCE THEY'RE STILL IN DEVELOPMENT, THEY PUT THEM IN SPACE SUITS.
FOR US, THOUGH,
THAT WASN'T COOL.
URR
ムムム…
FROM THE OUTSIDE, YOU CAN'T TELL WHICH ONE OF US IS HUMAN.
IT'S LIKE THEY DID IT TO SPITE US.
I WON'T LOSE TO A ROBOT !!
WE DID WELL AT FIRST.
THERE WERE A LOT OF SMALL TASKS THAT NEEDED DEXTERITY.
TWIST
キキッ
THE ROBOTS WERE A LOT LESS AGILE THAN I THOUGHT.
3
BUT IN THE SECOND HALF...

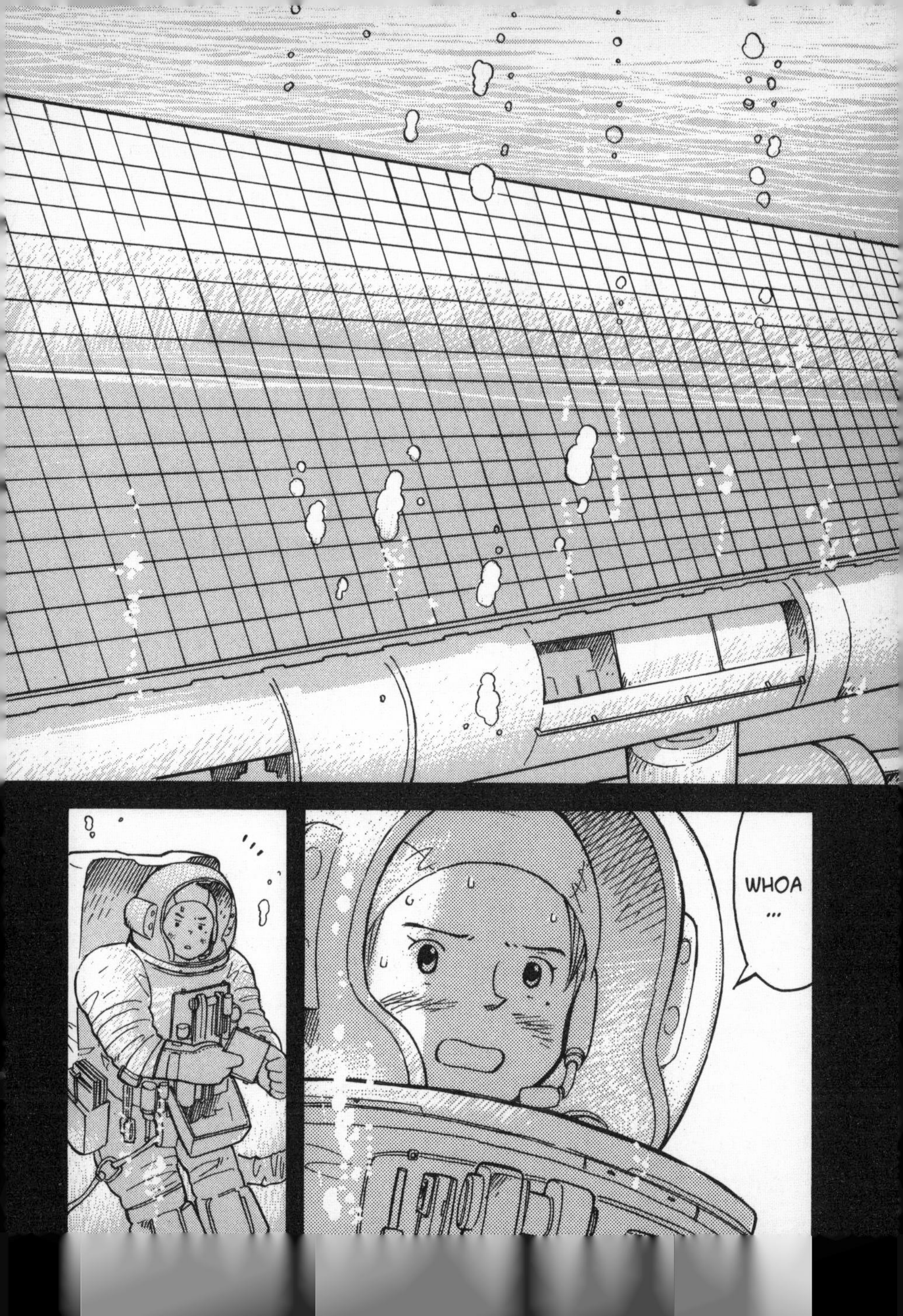
WHOA ...

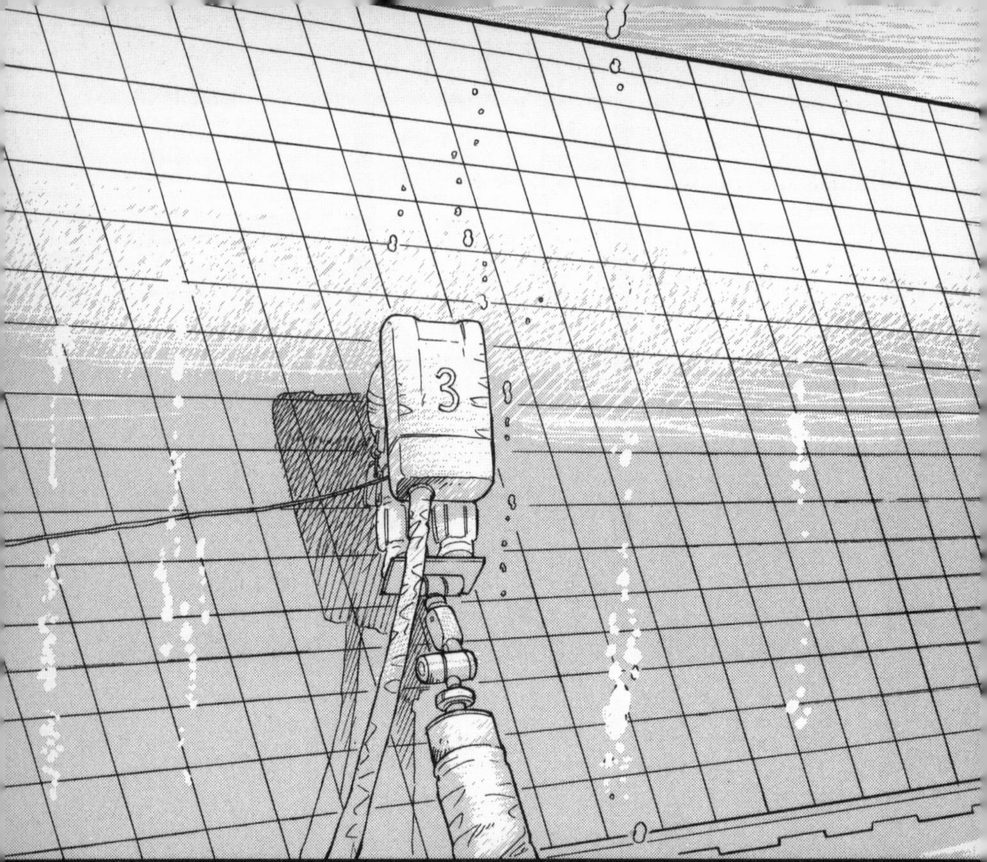

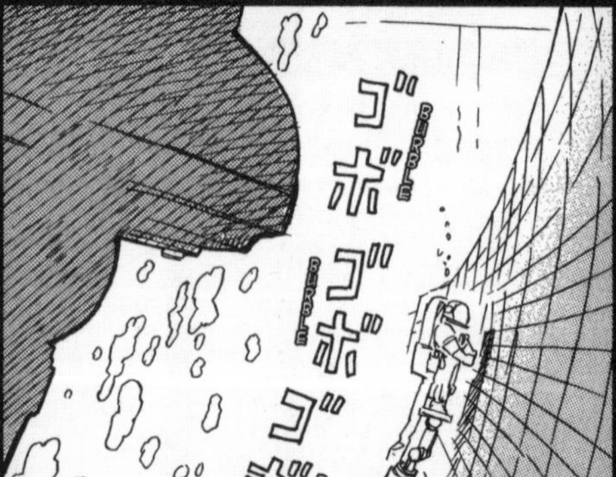
ゴボゴボゴボゴボ
BUBBLE
BUBBLE
BUBBLE

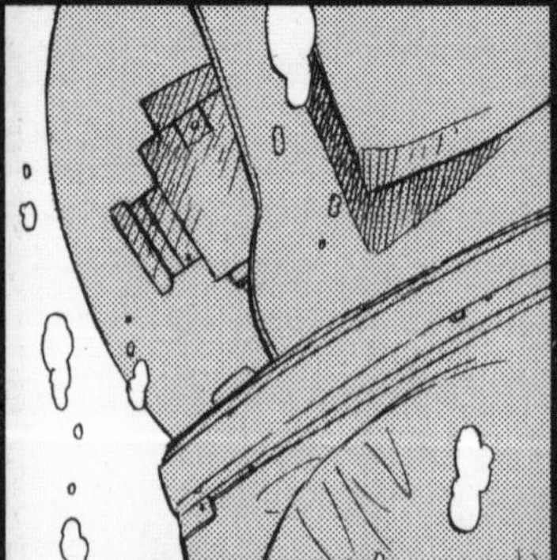

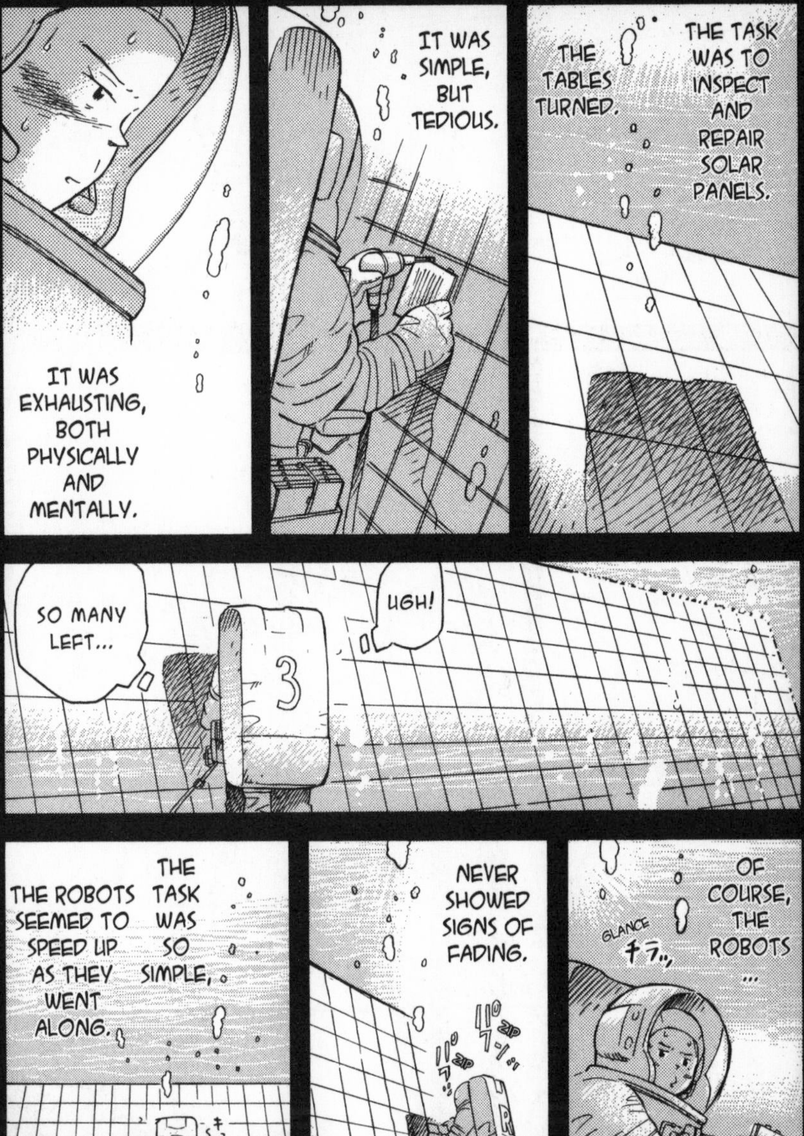
THE TASK WAS TO INSPECT AND REPAIR SOLAR PANELS.
THE TABLES TURNED.
IT WAS SIMPLE, BUT TEDIOUS.
IT WAS EXHAUSTING, BOTH PHYSICALLY AND MENTALLY.
UGH!
SO MANY LEFT...
OF COURSE, THE ROBOTS ...
GLANCE
チラッ
NEVER SHOWED SIGNS OF FADING.
ZIP
ZIP
THE TASK WAS SO SIMPLE,
THE ROBOTS SEEMED TO SPEED UP AS THEY WENT ALONG.
SQEEEEE

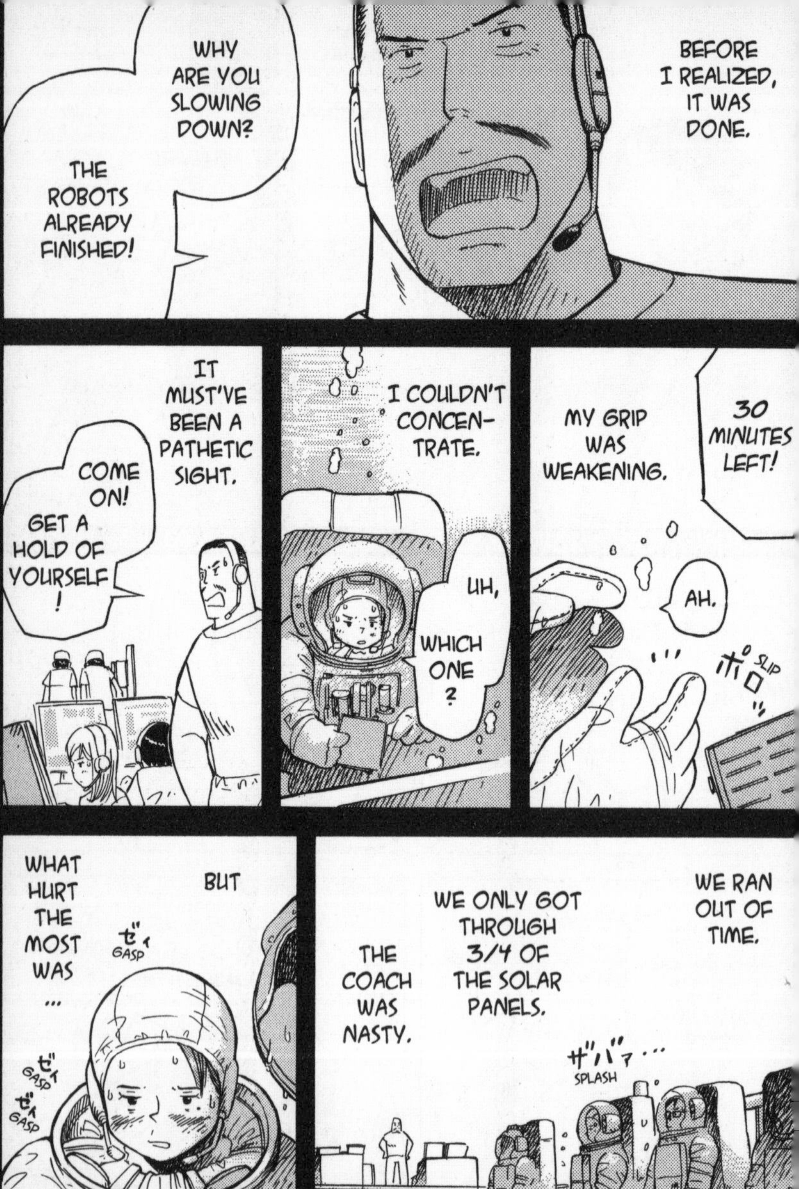
BEFORE I REALIZED, IT WAS DONE.
WHY ARE YOU SLOWING DOWN?
THE ROBOTS ALREADY FINISHED!
30 MINUTES LEFT!
MY GRIP WAS WEAKENING.
AH.
ポロ SLIP
I COULDN'T CONCEN-TRATE.
UH,
WHICH ONE?
IT MUST'VE BEEN A PATHETIC SIGHT.
COME ON!
GET A HOLD OF YOURSELF!
WE RAN OUT OF TIME.
WE ONLY GOT THROUGH 3/4 OF THE SOLAR PANELS.
THE COACH WAS NASTY.
ザバァ… SPLASH
BUT
WHAT HURT THE MOST WAS...
ゼィ GASP
ゼィ GASP
ゼィ GASP

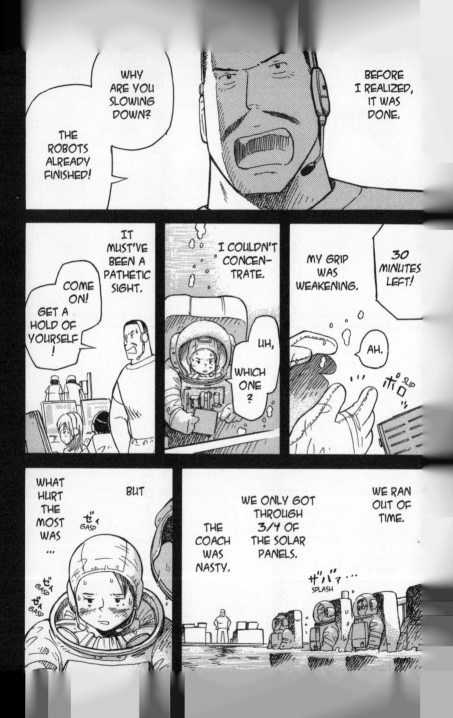

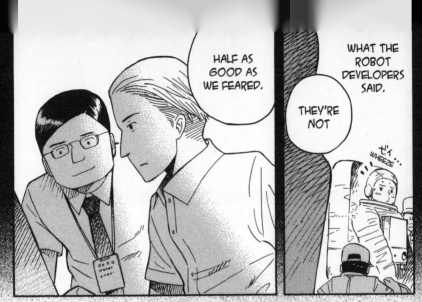

WHAT THE ROBOT DEVELOPERS SAID.
THEY'RE NOT
ゼィ…
WHEEZE
HALF AS GOOD AS WE FEARED.
GRRR!
JUST THINKING ABOUT IT
MAKES ME ANGRY!!
THEY SNEERED AT US AND
THREW DOWN THE GAUNTLET!
KEI, CALM DOWN.
KLATTER
SLAM
IT PISSES ME OFF!
HOW DARE THEY JUDGE US AFTER JUST ONE TEST?
IT WAS HUMILIATING!

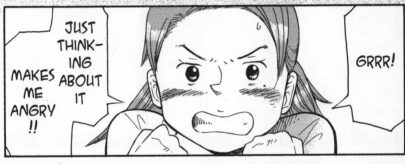

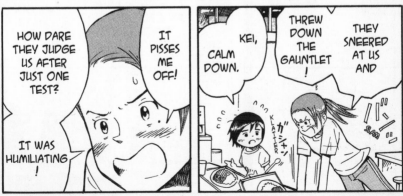

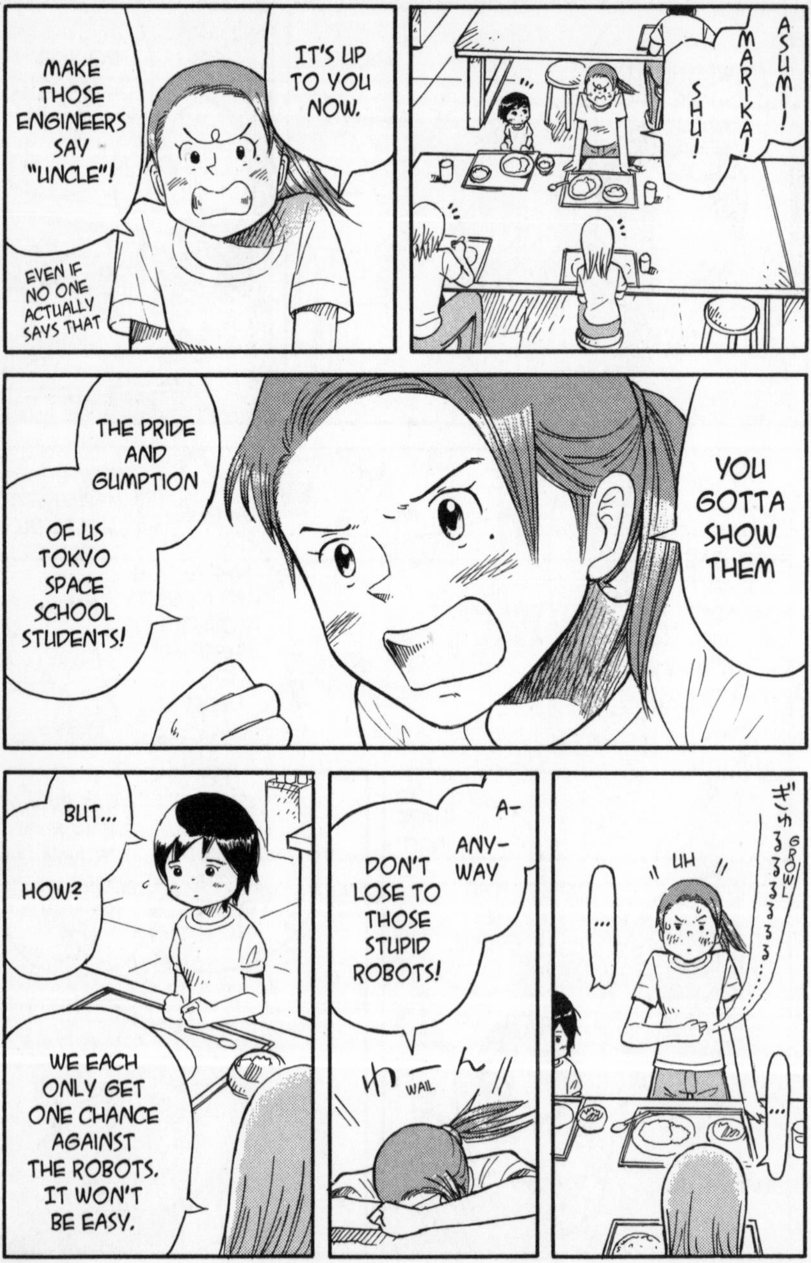
ASUMI!
MARIKA!
SHU!
IT'S UP TO YOU NOW.
MAKE THOSE ENGINEERS SAY "UNCLE"!
EVEN IF NO ONE ACTUALLY SAYS THAT
YOU GOTTA SHOW THEM
THE PRIDE AND GUMPTION
OF US TOKYO SPACE SCHOOL STUDENTS!
ぎゅるるるる… GROWL
UH
…
…
A- ANYWAY
DON'T LOSE TO THOSE STUPID ROBOTS!
わーん WAIL
BUT...
HOW?
WE EACH ONLY GET ONE CHANCE AGAINST THE ROBOTS. IT WON'T BE EASY.

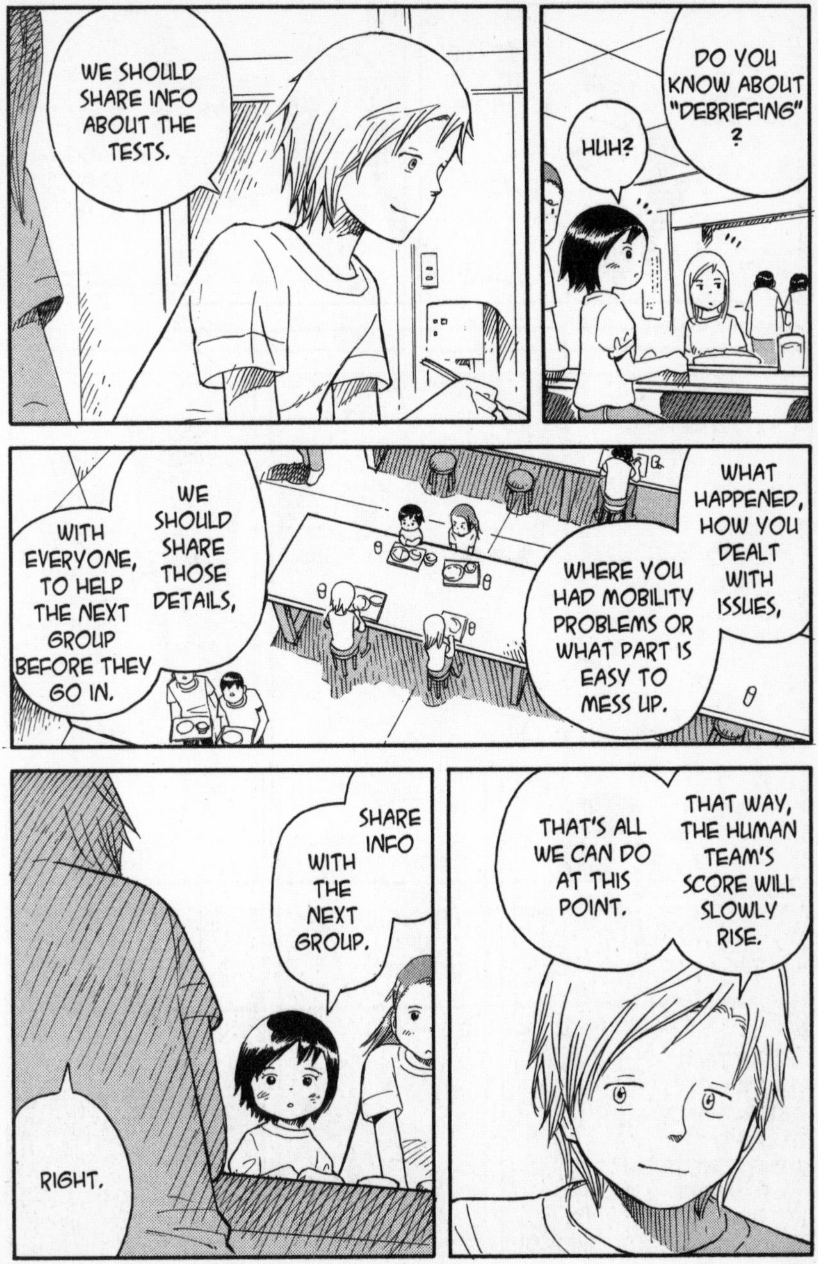
DO YOU KNOW ABOUT "DEBRIEFING"?
HUH?
WE SHOULD SHARE INFO ABOUT THE TESTS.
WHAT HAPPENED, HOW YOU DEALT WITH ISSUES,
WHERE YOU HAD MOBILITY PROBLEMS OR WHAT PART IS EASY TO MESS UP.
WE SHOULD SHARE THOSE DETAILS,
WITH EVERYONE, TO HELP THE NEXT GROUP BEFORE THEY GO IN.
THAT WAY, THE HUMAN TEAM'S SCORE WILL SLOWLY RISE.
THAT'S ALL WE CAN DO AT THIS POINT.
SHARE INFO
WITH THE NEXT GROUP.
RIGHT.

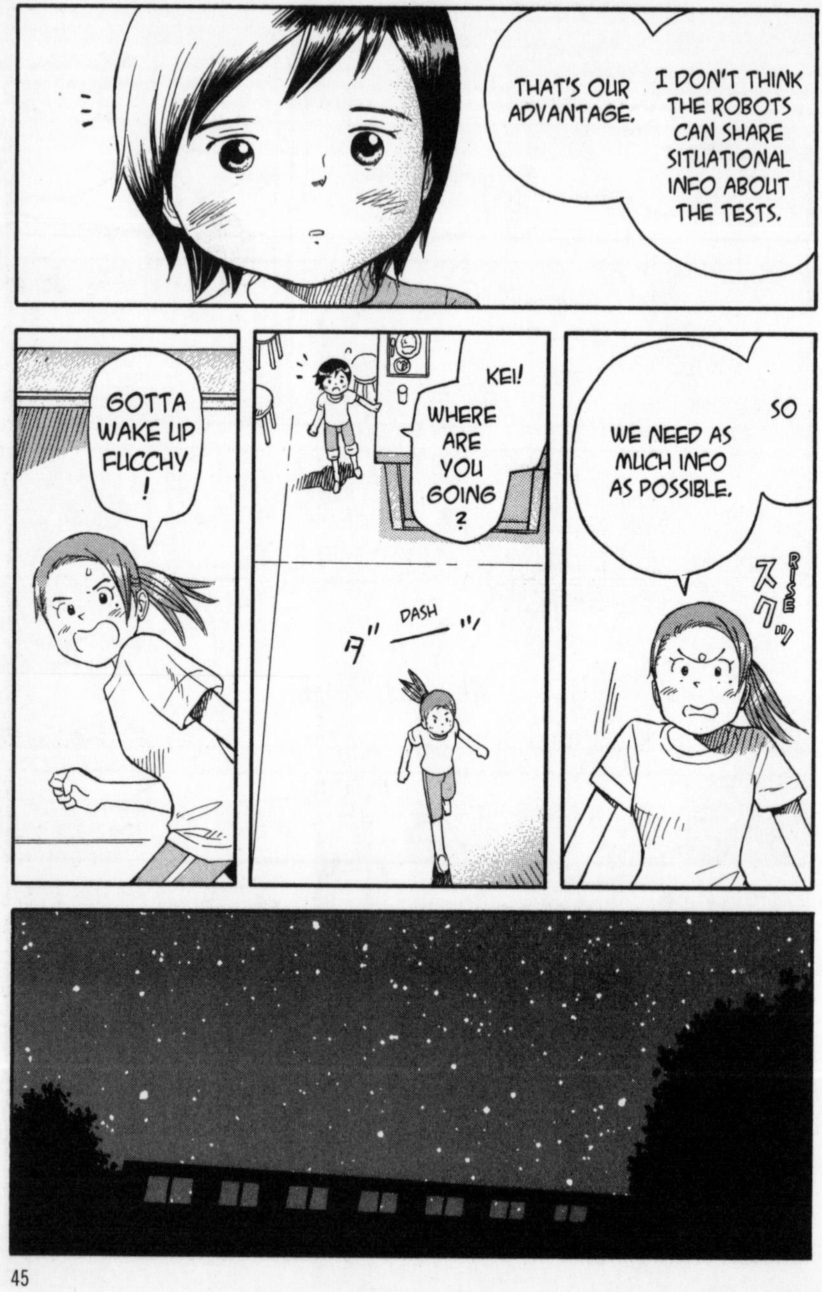
I DON'T THINK THE ROBOTS CAN SHARE SITUATIONAL INFO ABOUT THE TESTS.
THAT'S OUR ADVANTAGE.
SO
WE NEED AS MUCH INFO AS POSSIBLE.
スクッ
RISE
KEI!
WHERE ARE YOU GOING?
ダーッ
DASH
GOTTA WAKE UP FUCCHY!

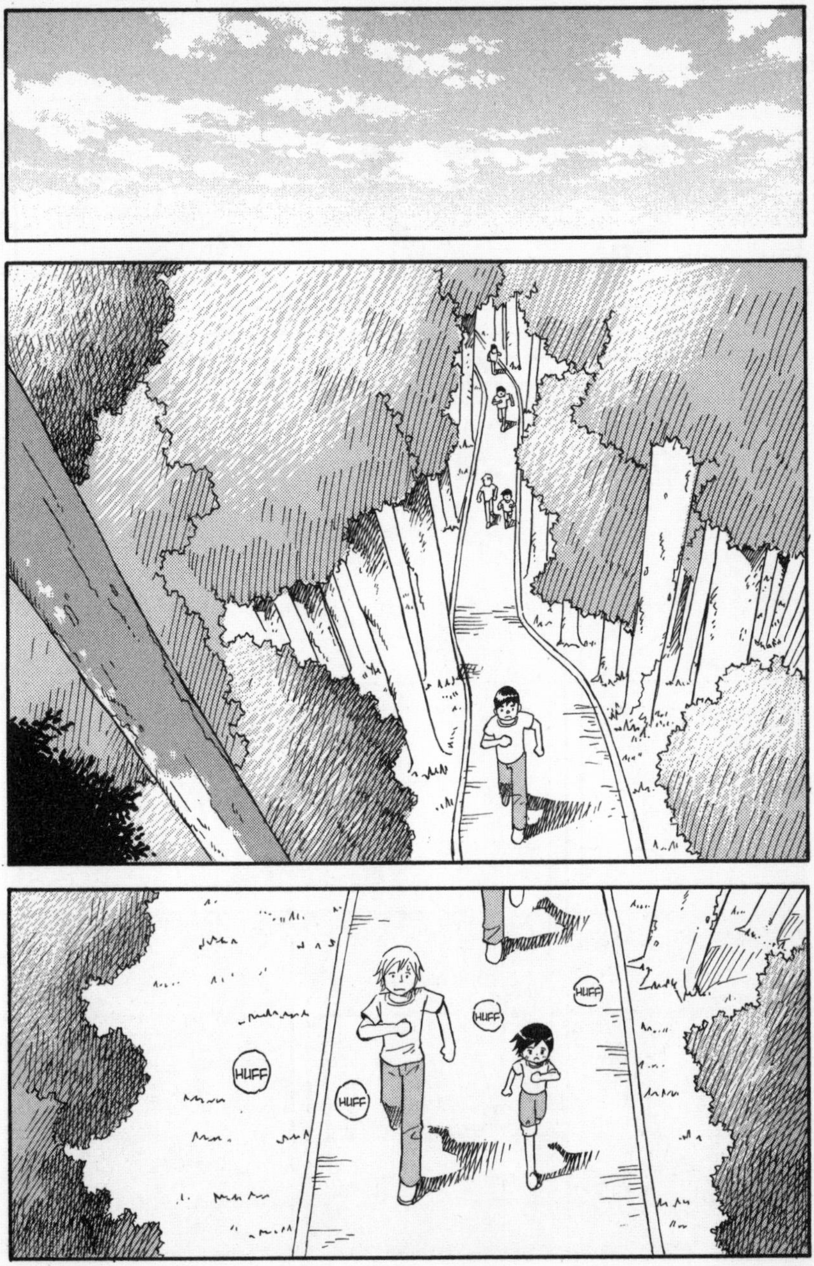
HUFF
HUFF
HUFF
HUFF

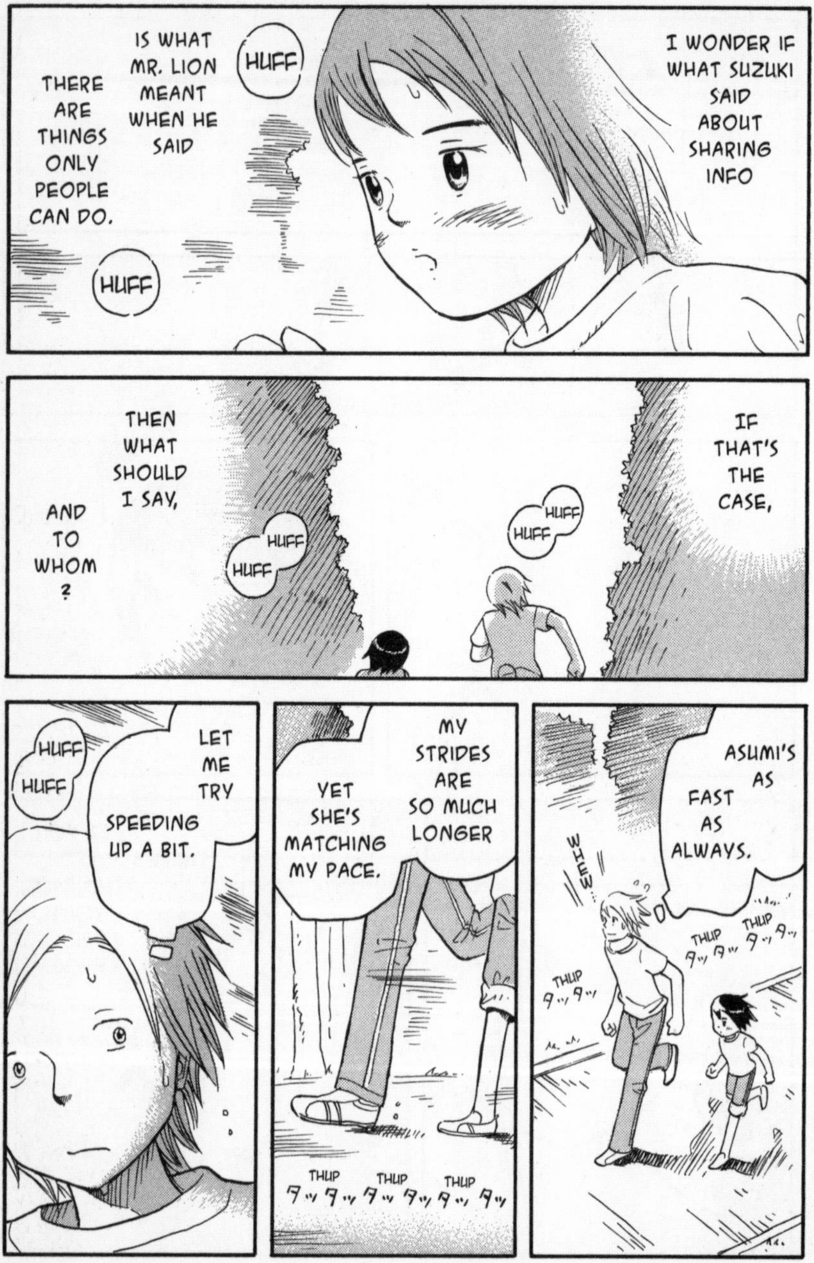
I WONDER IF WHAT SUZUKI SAID ABOUT SHARING INFO
HUFF
IS WHAT MR. LION MEANT WHEN HE SAID
THERE ARE THINGS ONLY PEOPLE CAN DO.
HUFF
IF THAT'S THE CASE,
HUFF HUFF
THEN WHAT SHOULD I SAY,
HUFF HUFF
AND TO WHOM ?
ASUMI'S AS FAST AS ALWAYS.
THUP THUP
WHEW...
THUP
MY STRIDES ARE SO MUCH LONGER
YET SHE'S MATCHING MY PACE.
THUP THUP THUP
LET ME TRY SPEEDING UP A BIT.
HUFF HUFF

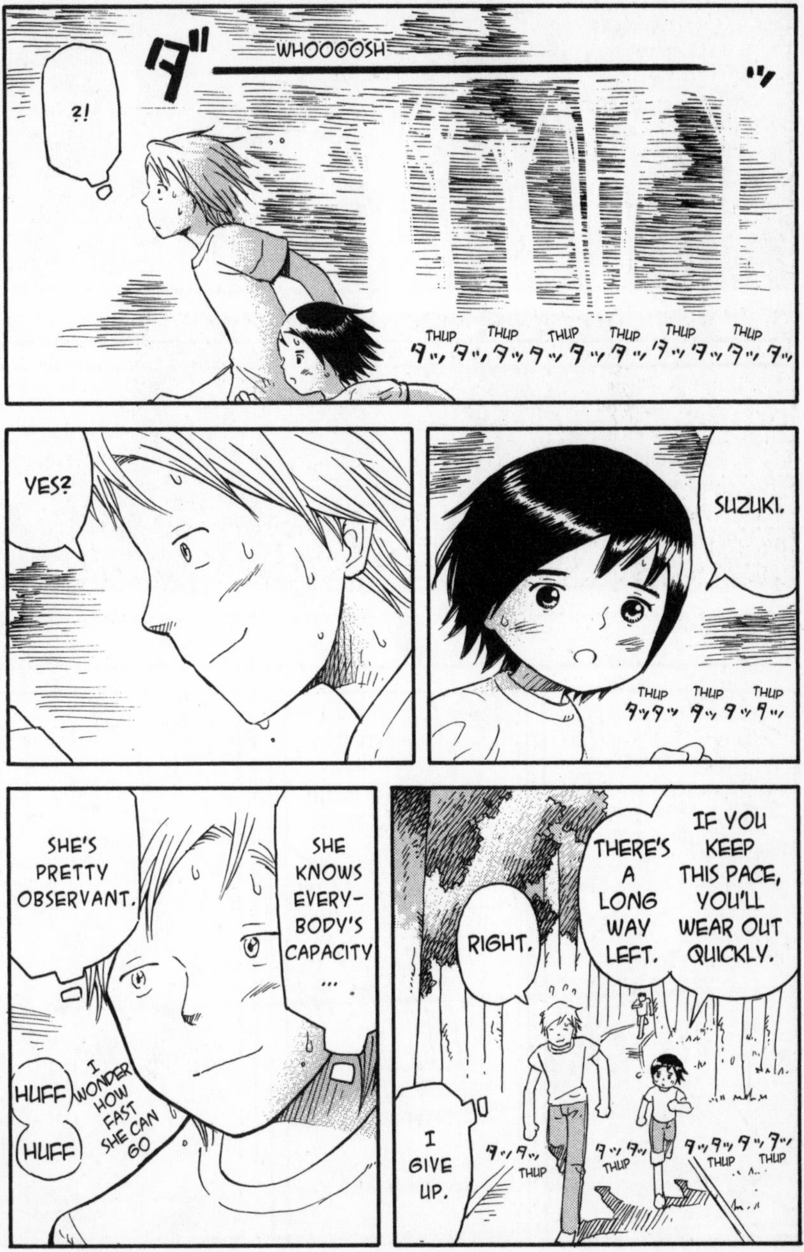
ダ
WHOOOOSH
ッ
?!
THUP THUP THUP THUP THUP THUP
SUZUKI.
THUP THUP THUP
YES?
IF YOU KEEP THIS PACE, YOU'LL WEAR OUT QUICKLY.
THERE'S A LONG WAY LEFT.
RIGHT.
I GIVE UP.
THUP THUP THUP THUP
SHE KNOWS EVERY-BODY'S CAPACITY ...
SHE'S PRETTY OBSERVANT.
I WONDER HOW FAST SHE CAN GO
HUFF
HUFF

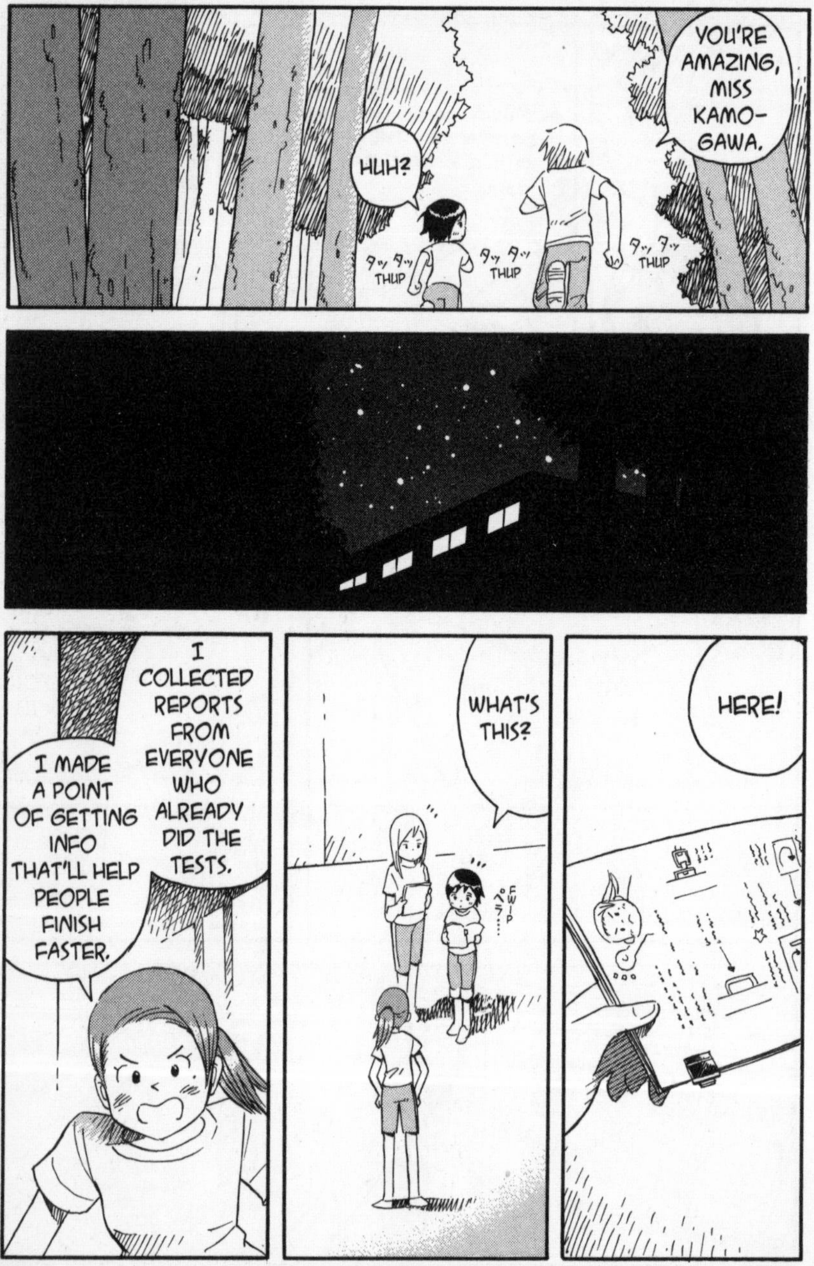
YOU'RE AMAZING, MISS KAMO-GAWA.
HUH?
タッ タッ THUP
タッ タッ THUP
タッ タッ THUP
HERE!
WHAT'S THIS?
ペラ… FWIP
I COLLECTED REPORTS FROM EVERYONE WHO ALREADY DID THE TESTS.
I MADE A POINT OF GETTING INFO THAT'LL HELP PEOPLE FINISH FASTER.

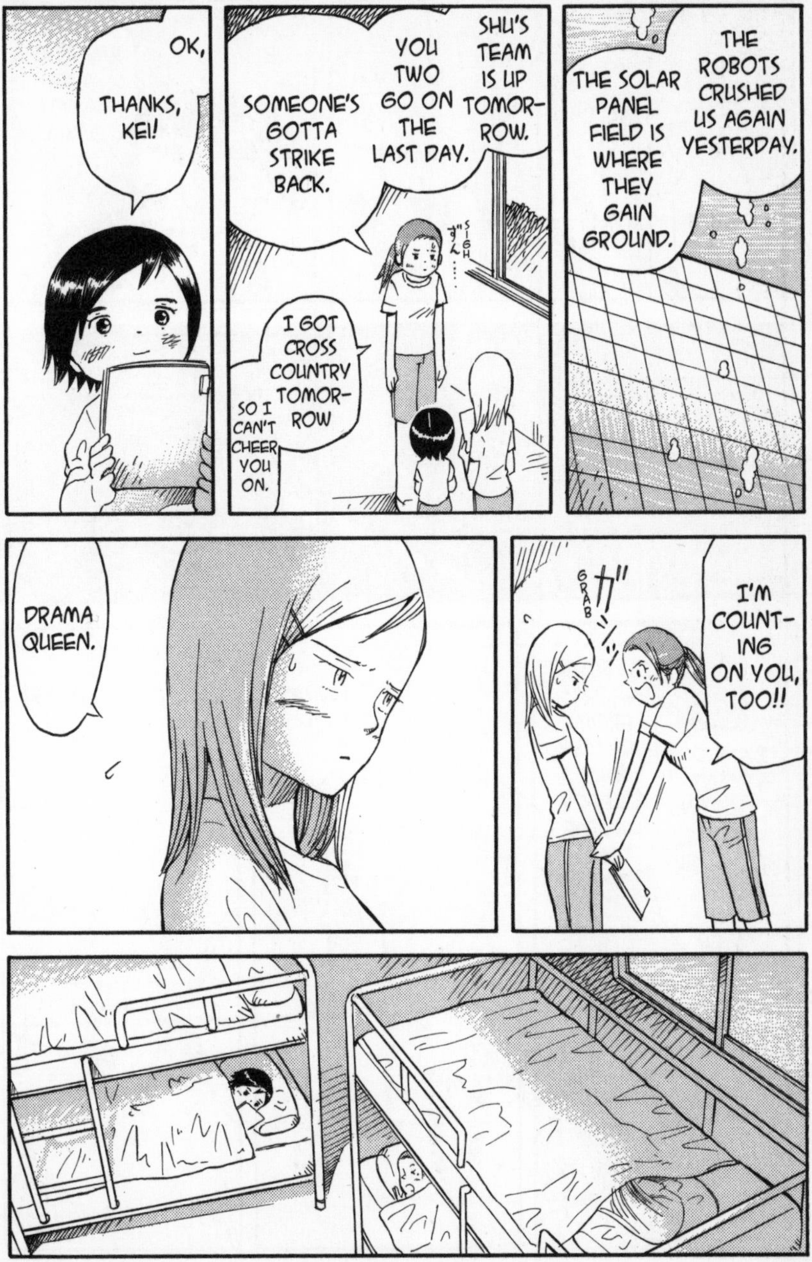
THE ROBOTS CRUSHED US AGAIN YESTERDAY.
THE SOLAR PANEL FIELD IS WHERE THEY GAIN GROUND.
SHU'S TEAM IS UP TOMORROW.
YOU TWO GO ON THE LAST DAY.
SOMEONE'S GOTTA STRIKE BACK.
SIGH.....
I GOT CROSS COUNTRY TOMORROW
SO I CAN'T CHEER YOU ON.
OK,
THANKS, KEI!
GRAB
I'M COUNTING ON YOU, TOO!!
DRAMA QUEEN.

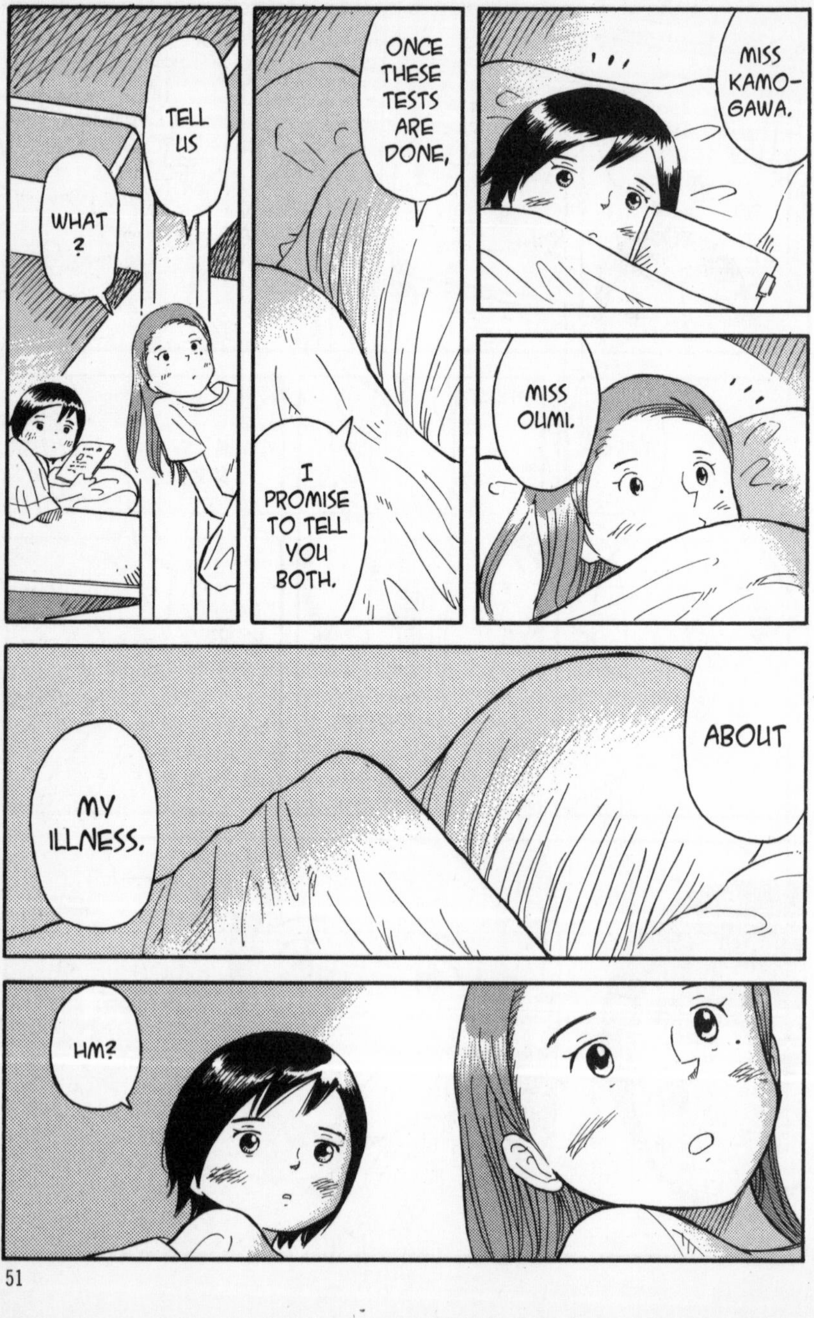
MISS KAMOGAWA.
MISS OUMI.
ONCE THESE TESTS ARE DONE,
I PROMISE TO TELL YOU BOTH.
TELL US
WHAT?
ABOUT
MY ILLNESS.
HM?

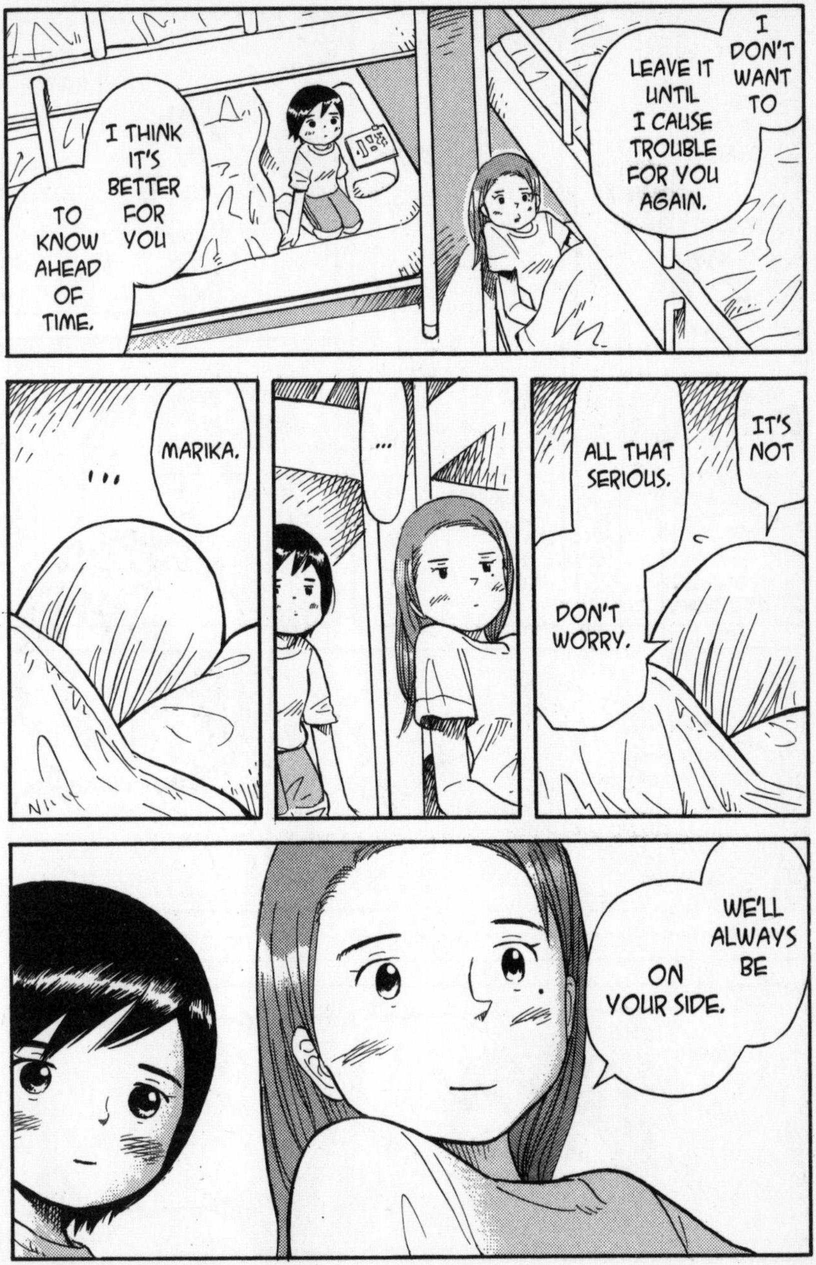
I DON'T WANT TO LEAVE IT UNTIL I CAUSE TROUBLE FOR YOU AGAIN.
I THINK IT'S BETTER FOR YOU TO KNOW AHEAD OF TIME.
IT'S NOT ALL THAT SERIOUS.
DON'T WORRY.
...
MARIKA.
...
WE'LL ALWAYS BE ON YOUR SIDE.

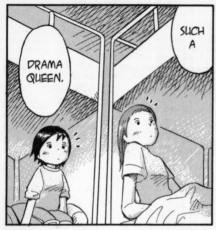

SUCH A

DRAMA QUEEN.

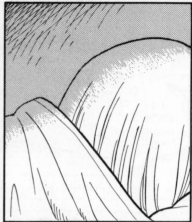

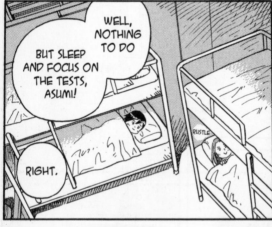

WELL, NOTHING TO DO

BUT SLEEP AND FOCUS ON THE TESTS, ASUMI!

RIGHT.

RUSTLE

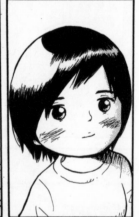

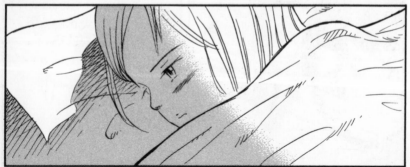

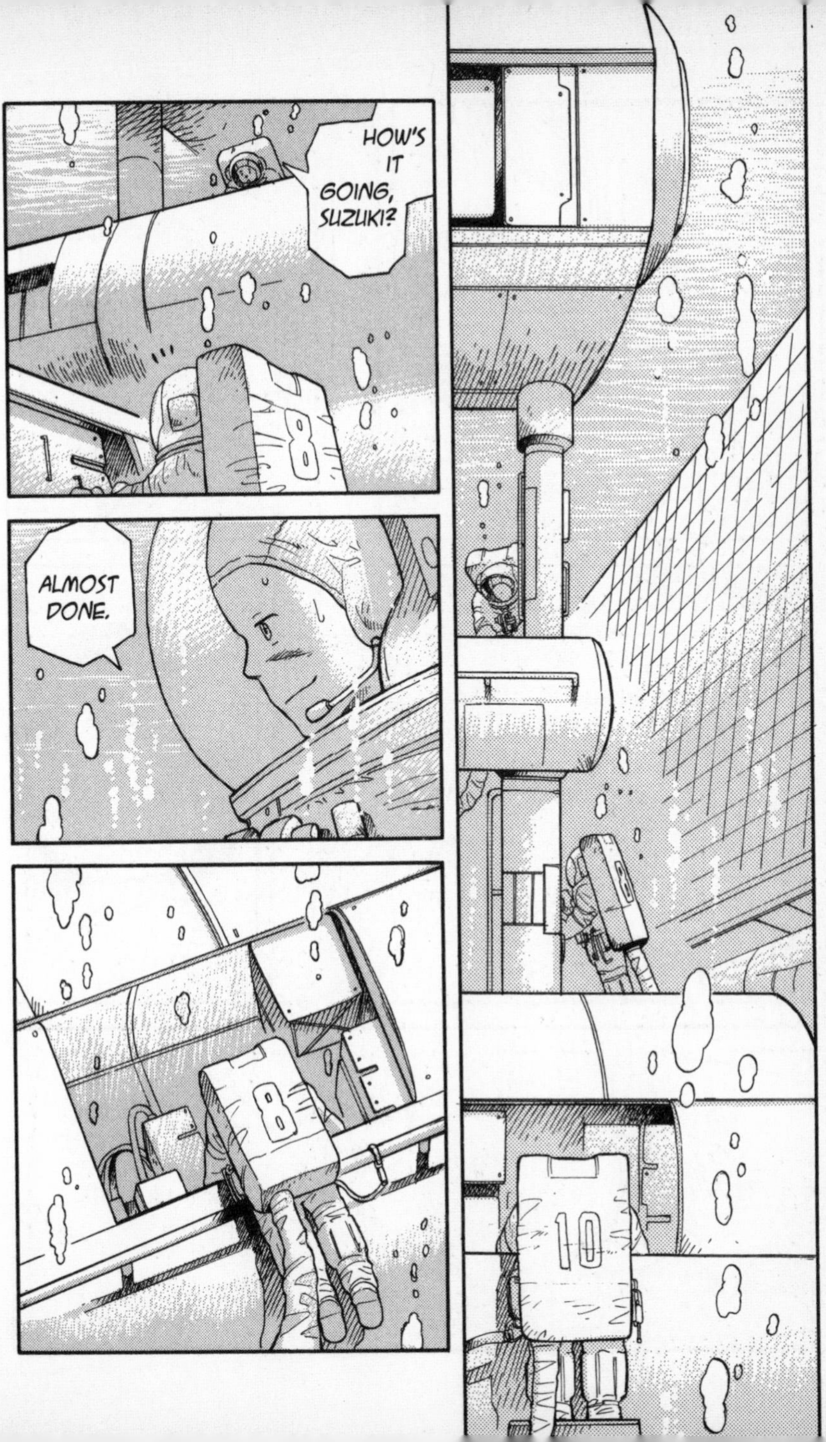
HOW'S IT GOING, SUZUKI!?
ALMOST DONE.

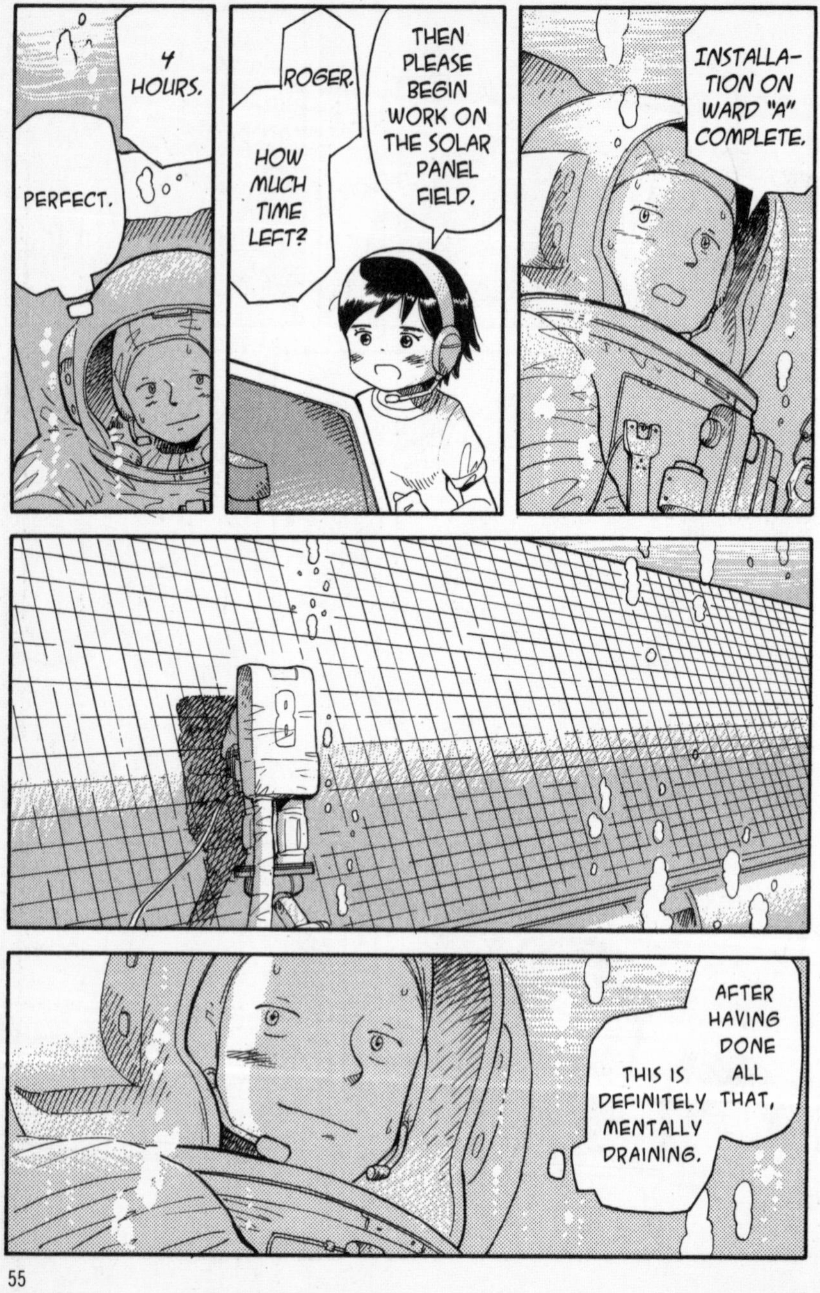
INSTALLATION ON WARD "A" COMPLETE.
THEN PLEASE BEGIN WORK ON THE SOLAR PANEL FIELD.
ROGER.
HOW MUCH TIME LEFT?
4 HOURS.
PERFECT.
AFTER HAVING DONE ALL THAT,
THIS IS DEFINITELY MENTALLY DRAINING.

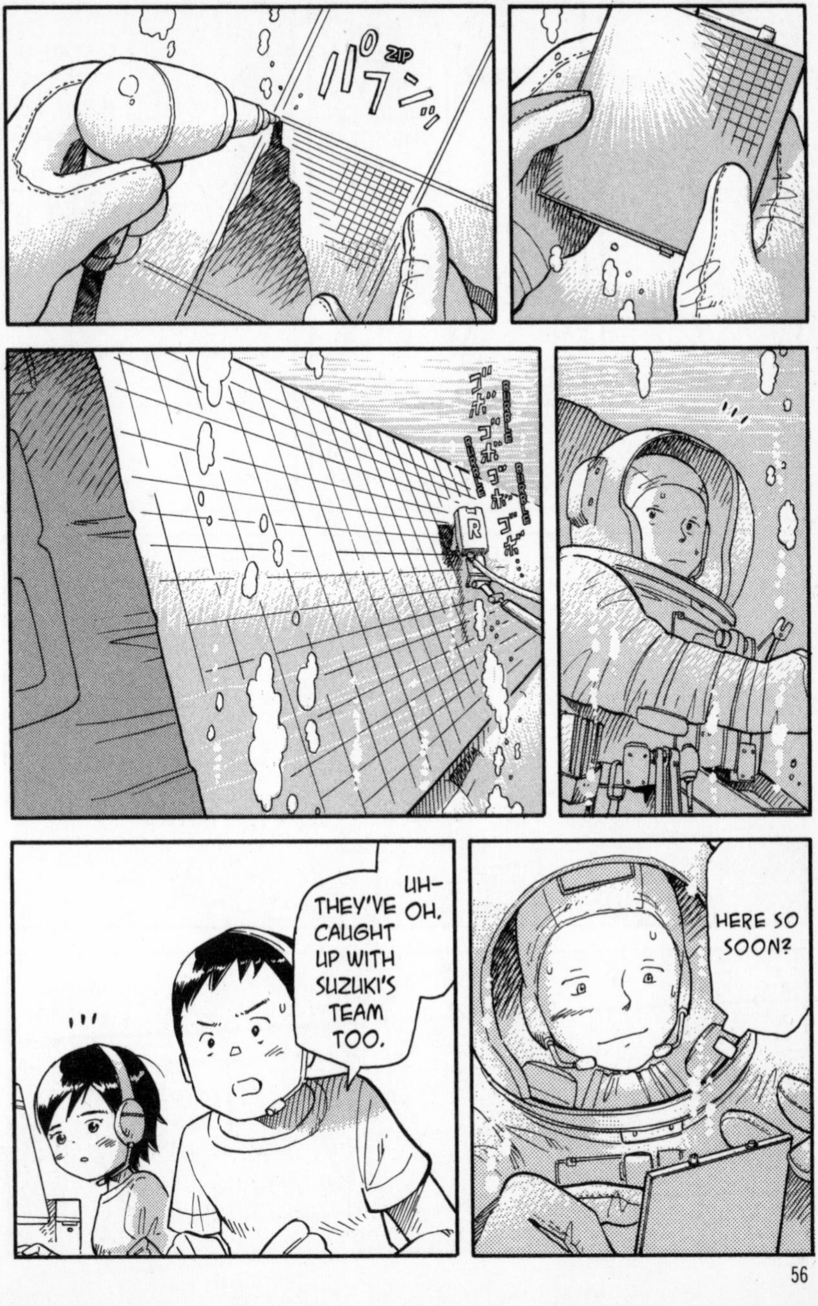
ZIP
パフンッ
ゴボゴボゴボゴボ…
BURBLE
BURBLE
BURBLE
R
HERE SO SOON?
UH-OH.
THEY'VE CAUGHT UP WITH SUZUKI'S TEAM TOO.

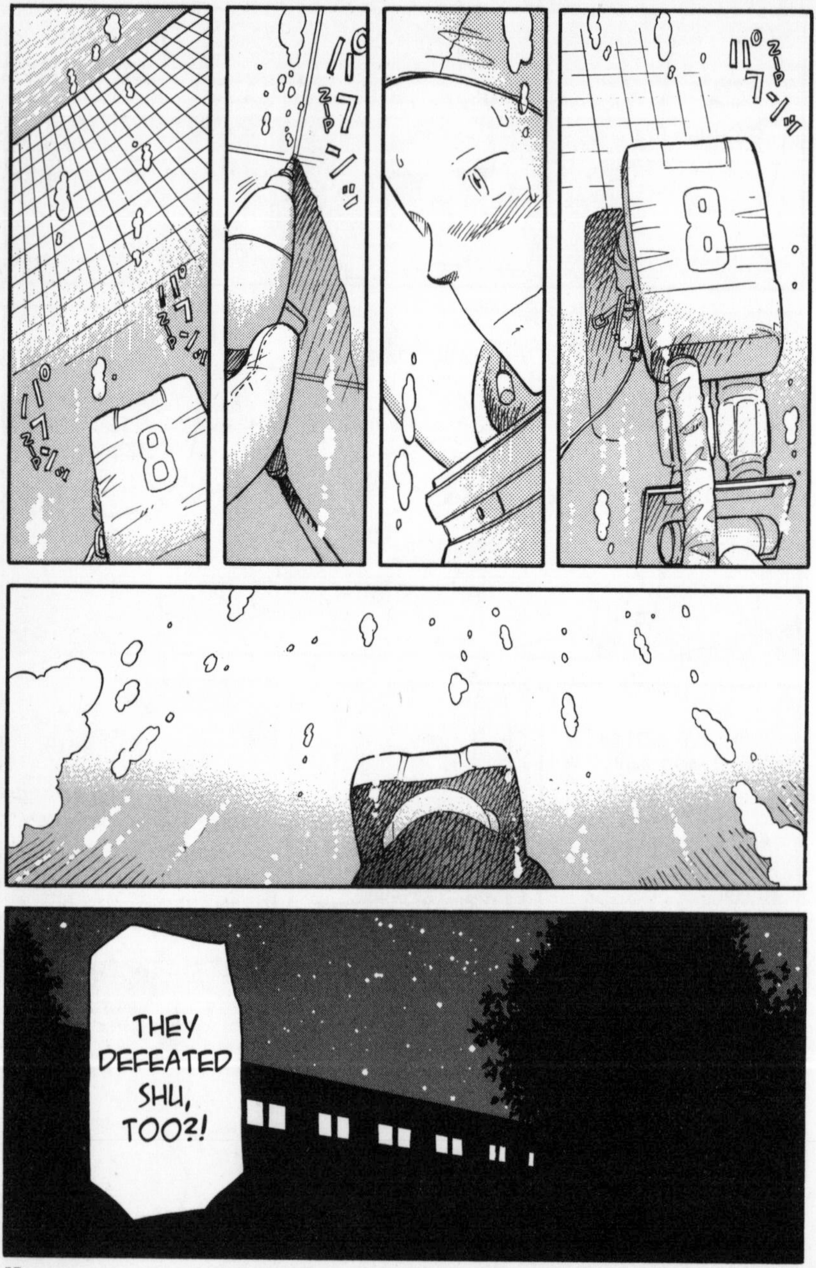
ZIP
ZIP
ZIP
ZIP
THEY DEFEATED SHU, TOO?!

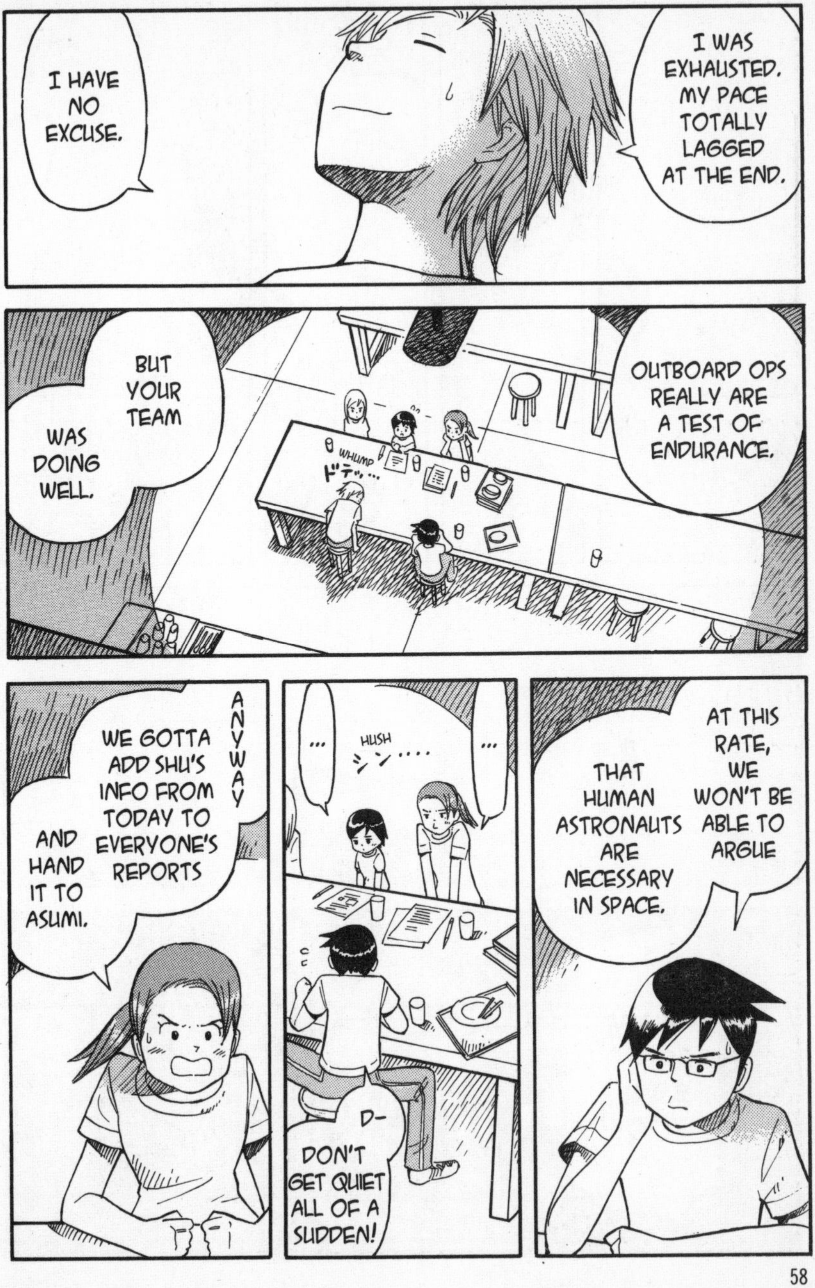
I WAS EXHAUSTED. MY PACE TOTALLY LAGGED AT THE END.
I HAVE NO EXCUSE.
OUTBOARD OPS REALLY ARE A TEST OF ENDURANCE.
BUT YOUR TEAM WAS DOING WELL.
WHUMP
ドテッ…
AT THIS RATE, WE WON'T BE ABLE TO ARGUE
THAT HUMAN ASTRONAUTS ARE NECESSARY IN SPACE.
…
…
HUSH
シン….
D- DON'T GET QUIET ALL OF A SUDDEN!
ANYWAY
WE GOTTA ADD SHU'S INFO FROM TODAY TO EVERYONE'S REPORTS
AND HAND IT TO ASUMI.

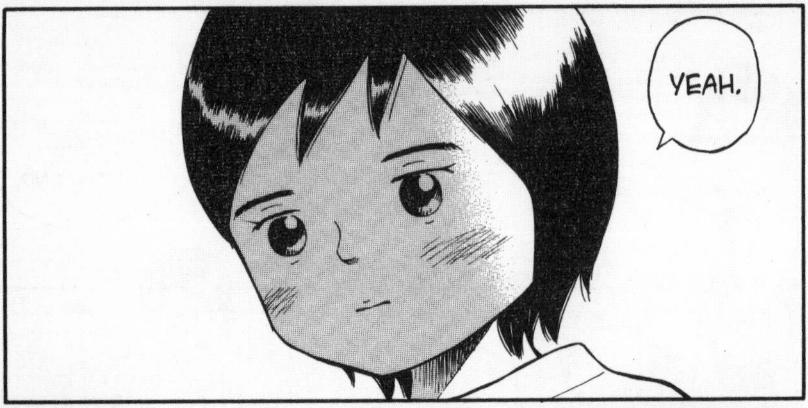
YEAH.

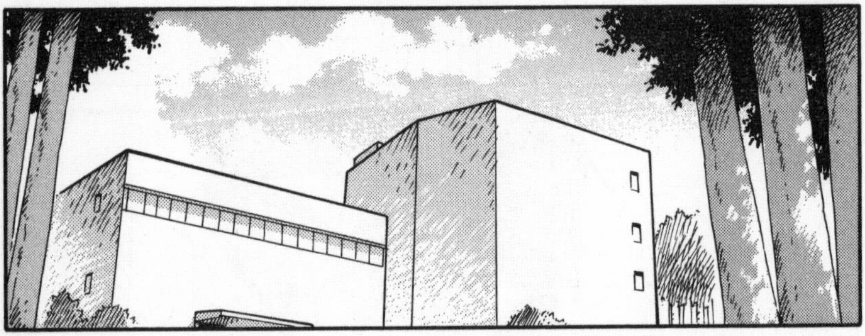

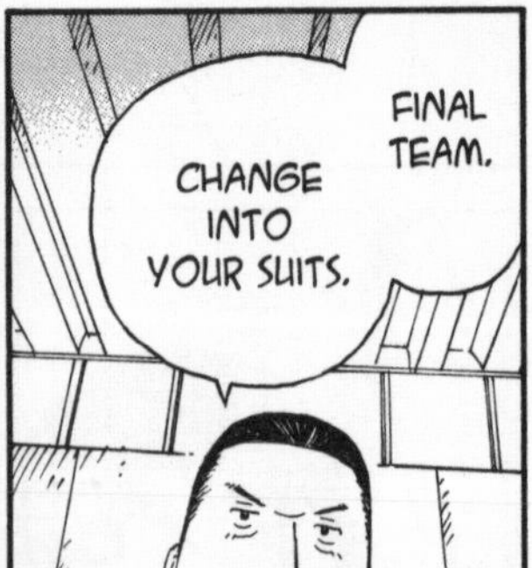
FINAL TEAM.
CHANGE INTO YOUR SUITS.
ムキ
FLEX

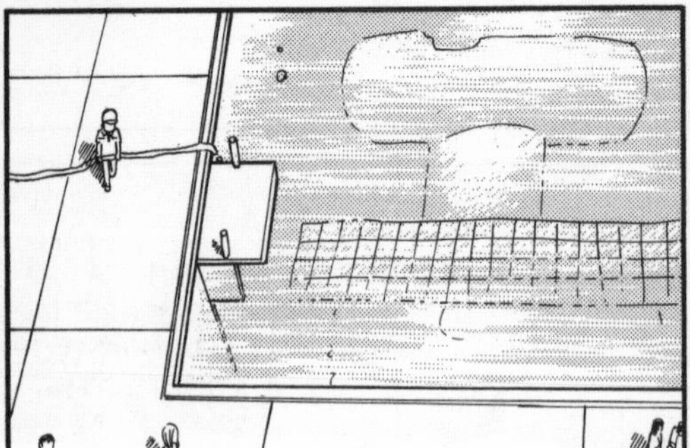

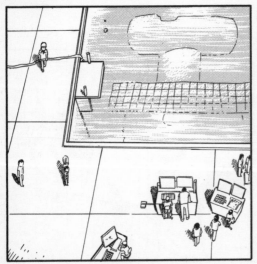

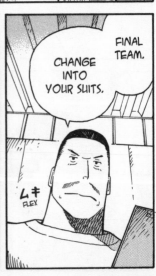

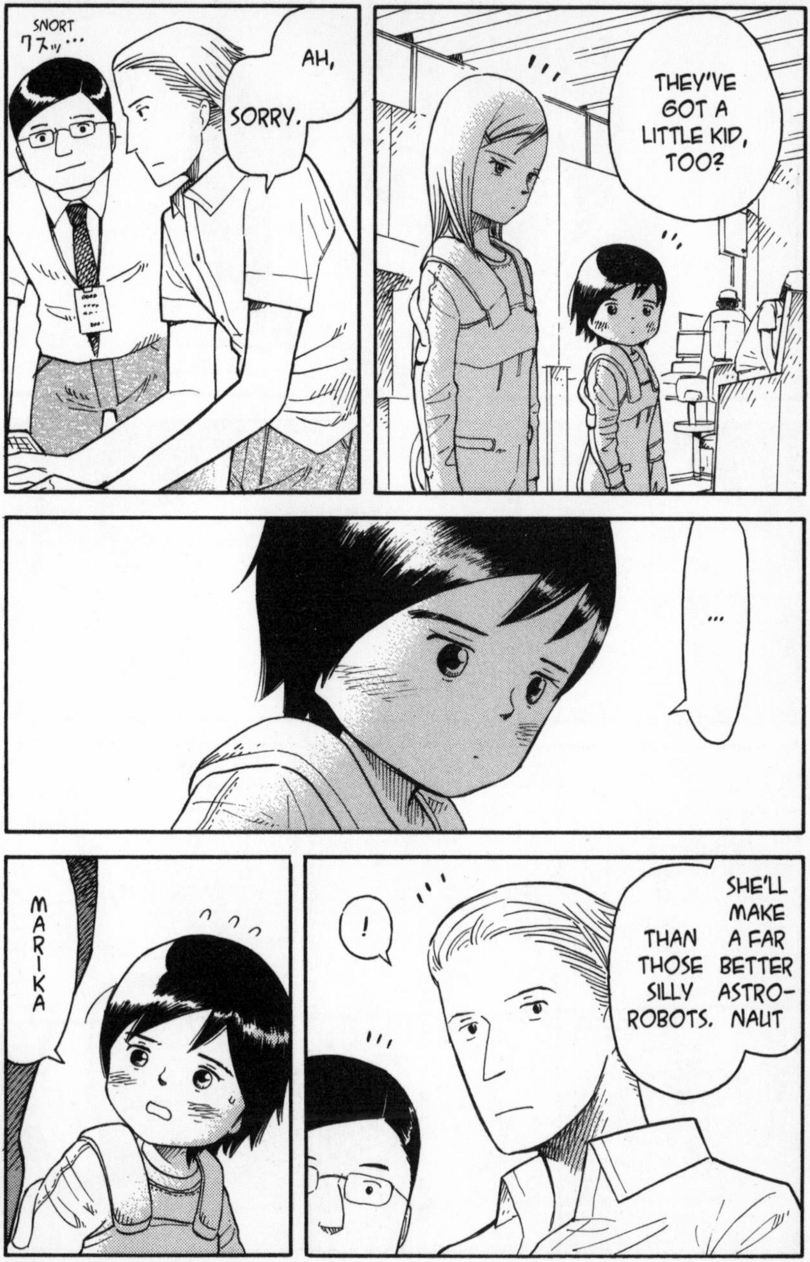
THEY'VE GOT A LITTLE KID, TOO?
SNORT
クスッ…
AH,
SORRY.
...
SHE'LL MAKE A FAR BETTER ASTRONAUT THAN THOSE SILLY ROBOTS.
!
MARIKA

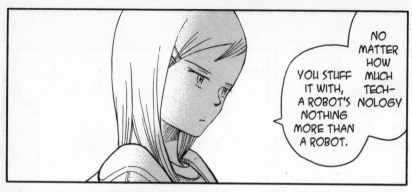

NO MATTER HOW MUCH TECH-NOLOGY YOU STUFF IT WITH, A ROBOT'S NOTHING MORE THAN A ROBOT.
YOU'VE GOT QUITE A TONGUE, YOUNG LADY.
BEATS ME...
ARE YOU SAY-ING YOU CAN COMPLETE THE TESTS FASTER THAN OUR ROBOTS?
LET'S GO, MARIKA
OF COURSE.
MARIKA.
?!
OH?
WELL, THEN ...
WHAT'LL YOU DO WHEN THEY END UP FLOORING YOU?

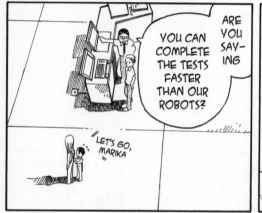

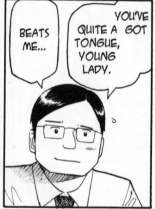

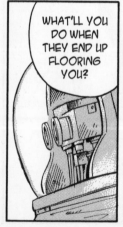

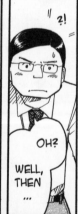

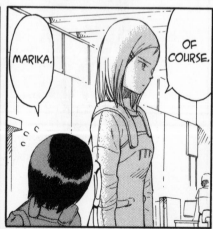

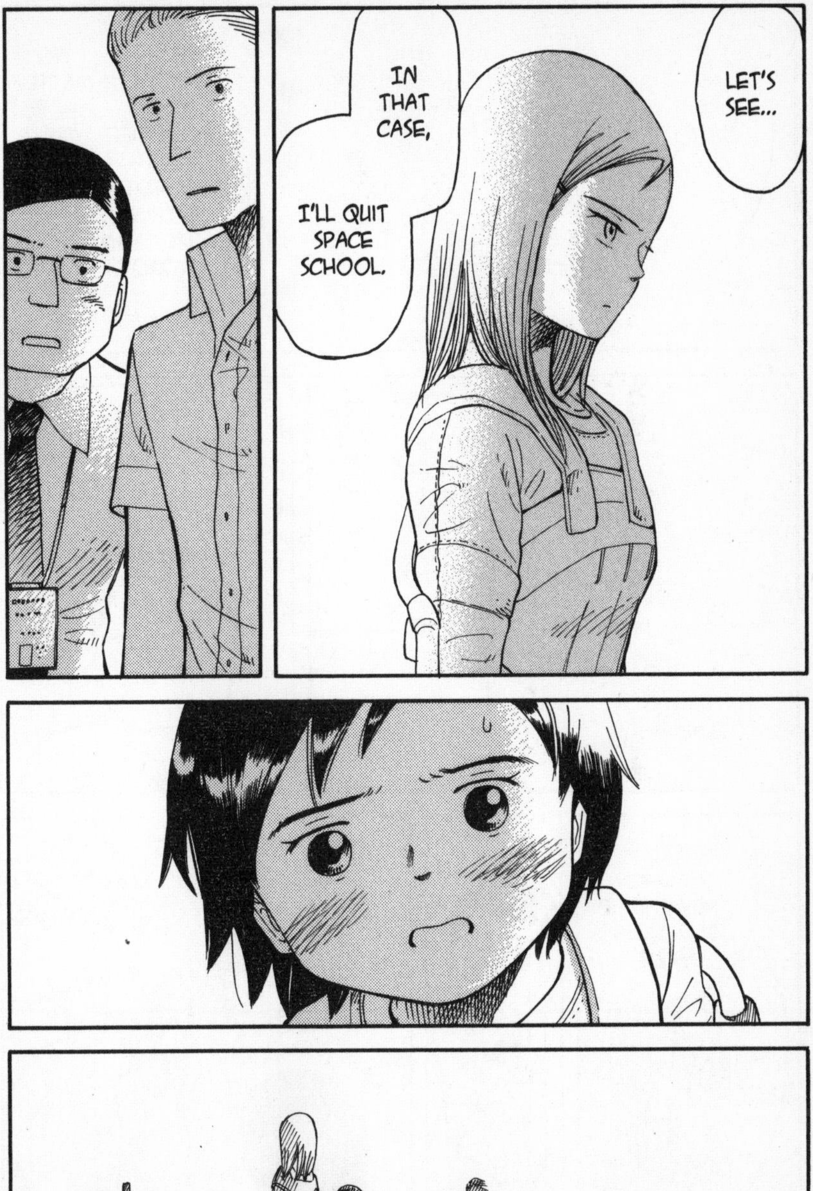
LET'S SEE...
IN THAT CASE,
I'LL QUIT SPACE SCHOOL.

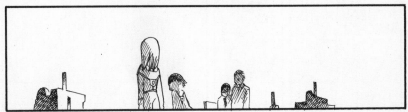

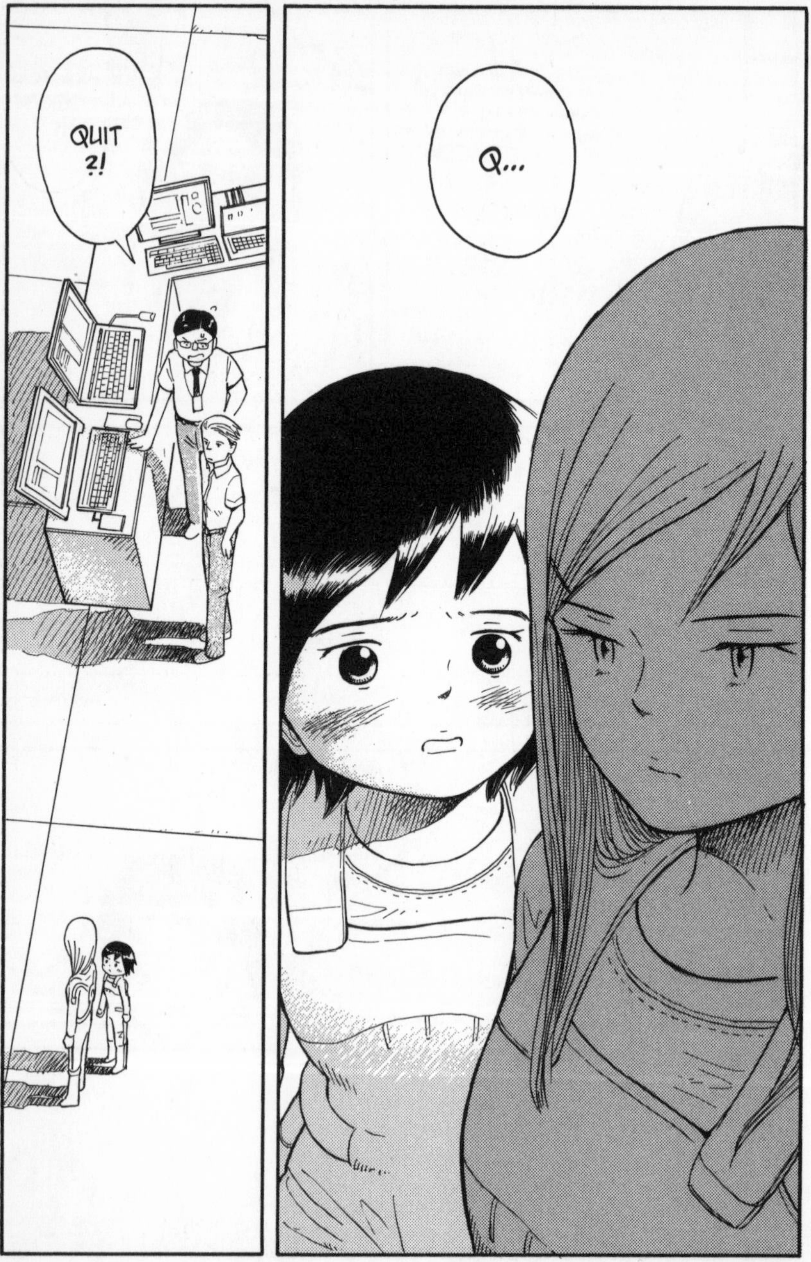
Q...
QUIT ?!

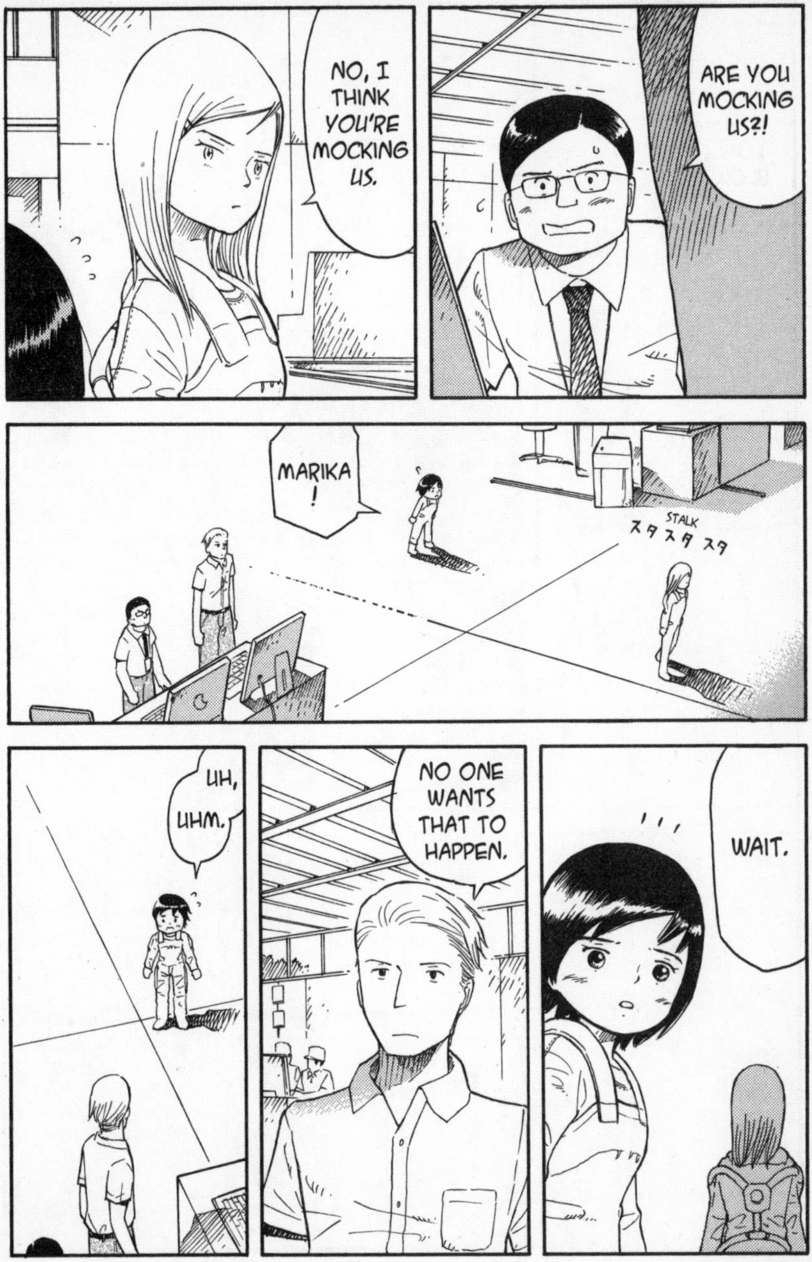
ARE YOU MOCKING US?!
NO, I THINK YOU'RE MOCKING US.
MARIKA!
STALK
スタスタスタ
WAIT.
NO ONE WANTS THAT TO HAPPEN.
UH, UHM.

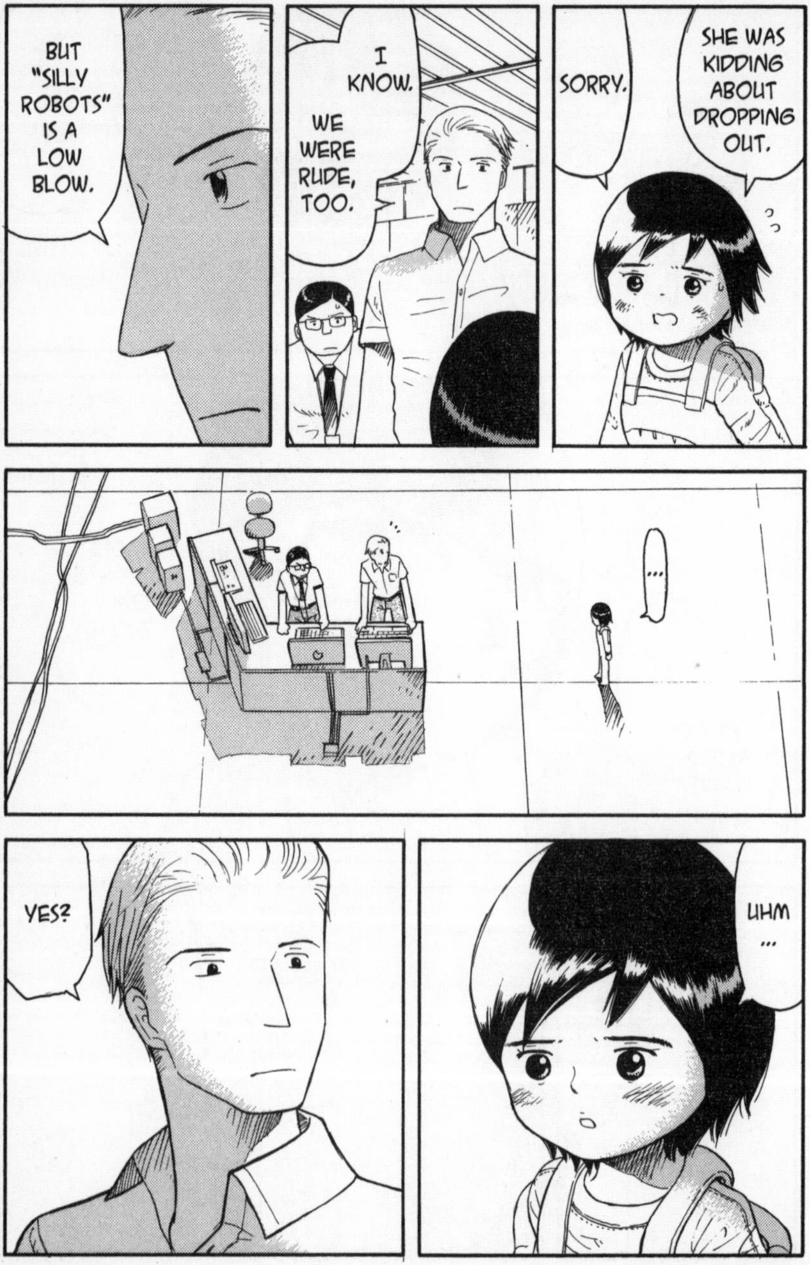
SHE WAS KIDDING ABOUT DROPPING OUT.
SORRY.
I KNOW.
WE WERE RUDE, TOO.
BUT "SILLY ROBOTS" IS A LOW BLOW.
...
UHM ...
YES?

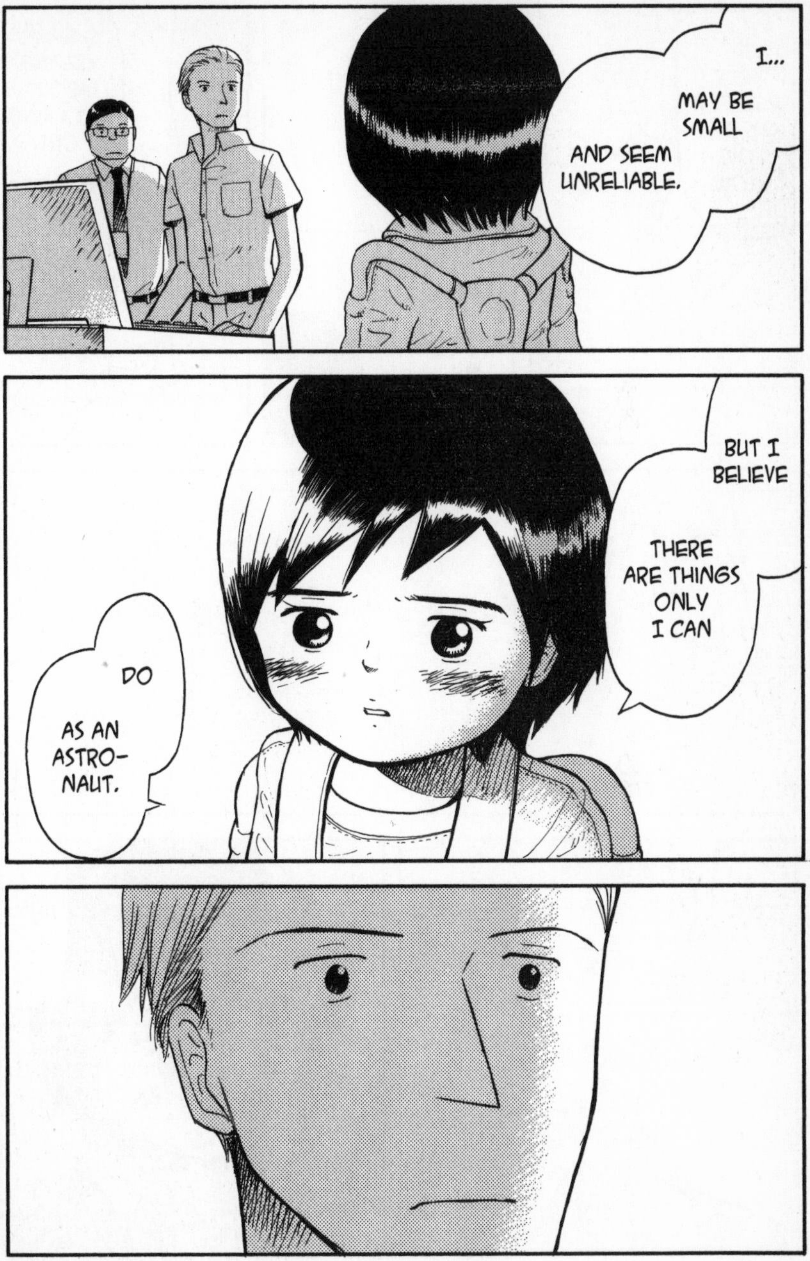
I...
MAY BE SMALL
AND SEEM UNRELIABLE.
BUT I BELIEVE
THERE ARE THINGS ONLY I CAN
DO
AS AN ASTRO-NAUT.

MISSION:58

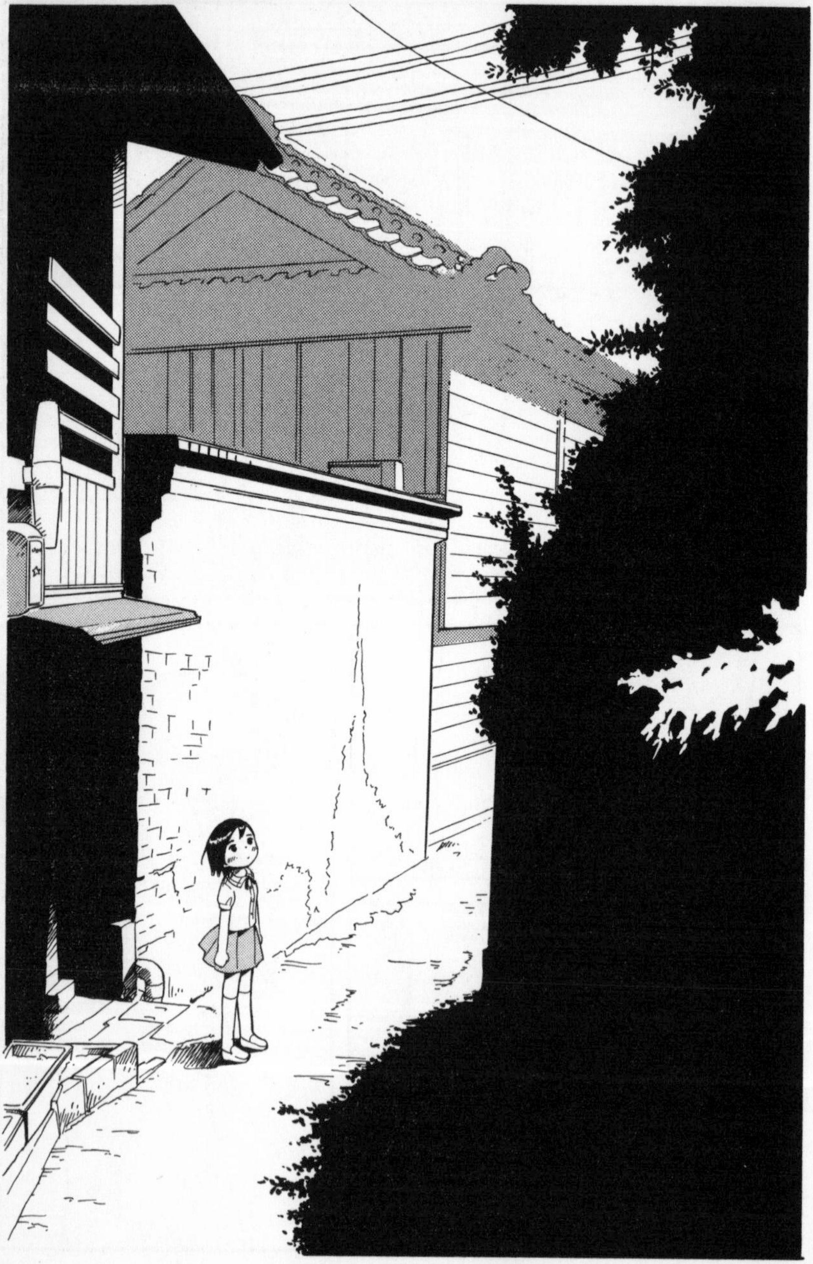

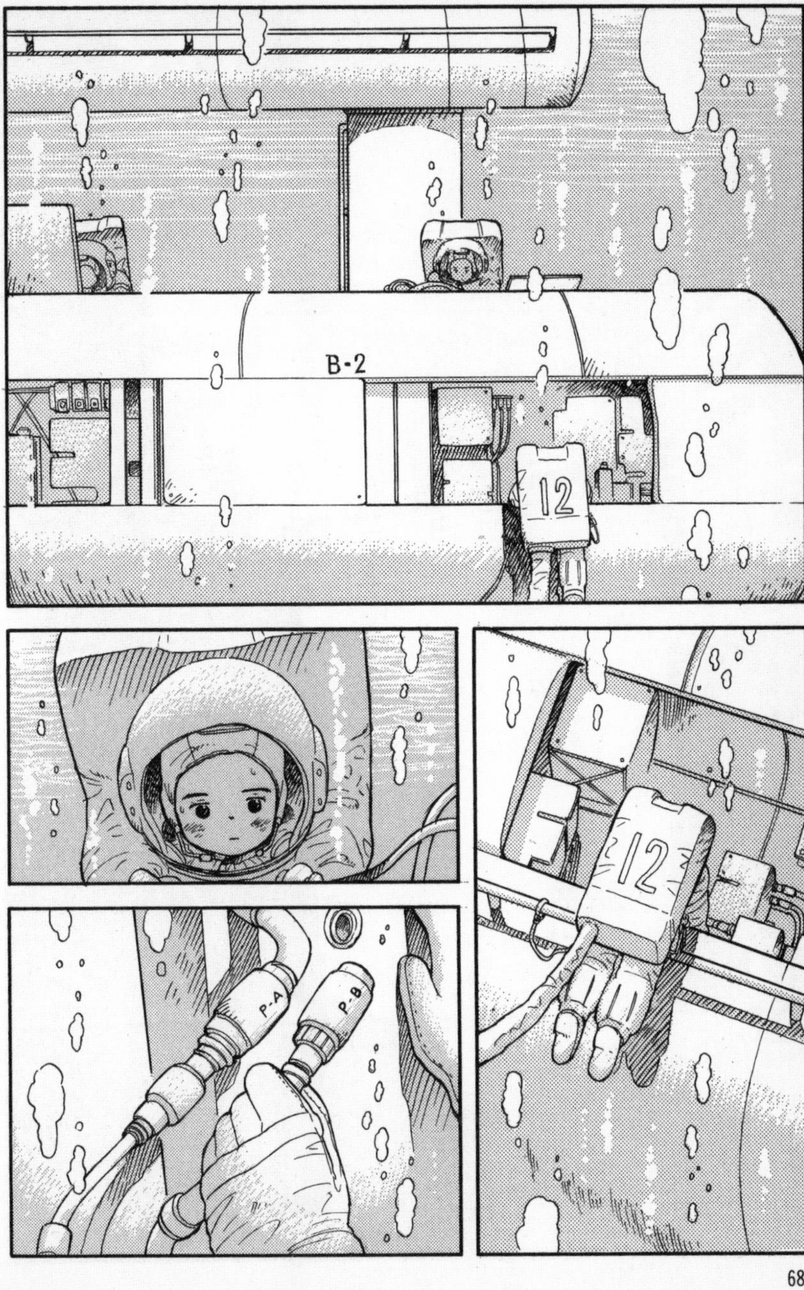
B-2
12
12
P-A
P-B

P-C
HM?
ポコッ
KLMP
THE C PLUG GOES IN SMOOTHLY IF YOU TUG IT JUST SLIGHTLY TOWARDS YOU AS YOU TWIST IT.
AH ...
カチッ
KLIK
P-C
IT'S JUST LIKE KEI SAID.

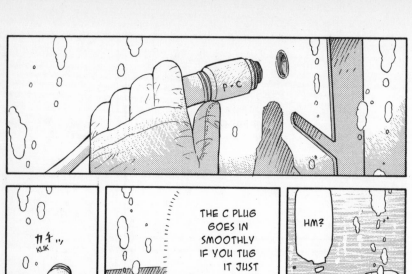

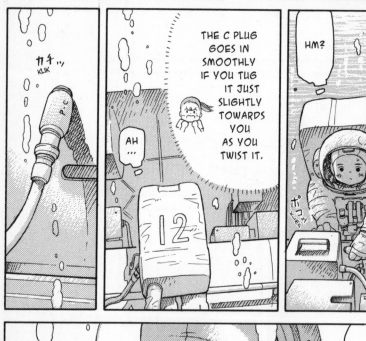

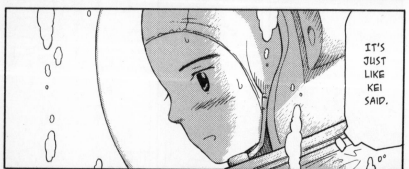

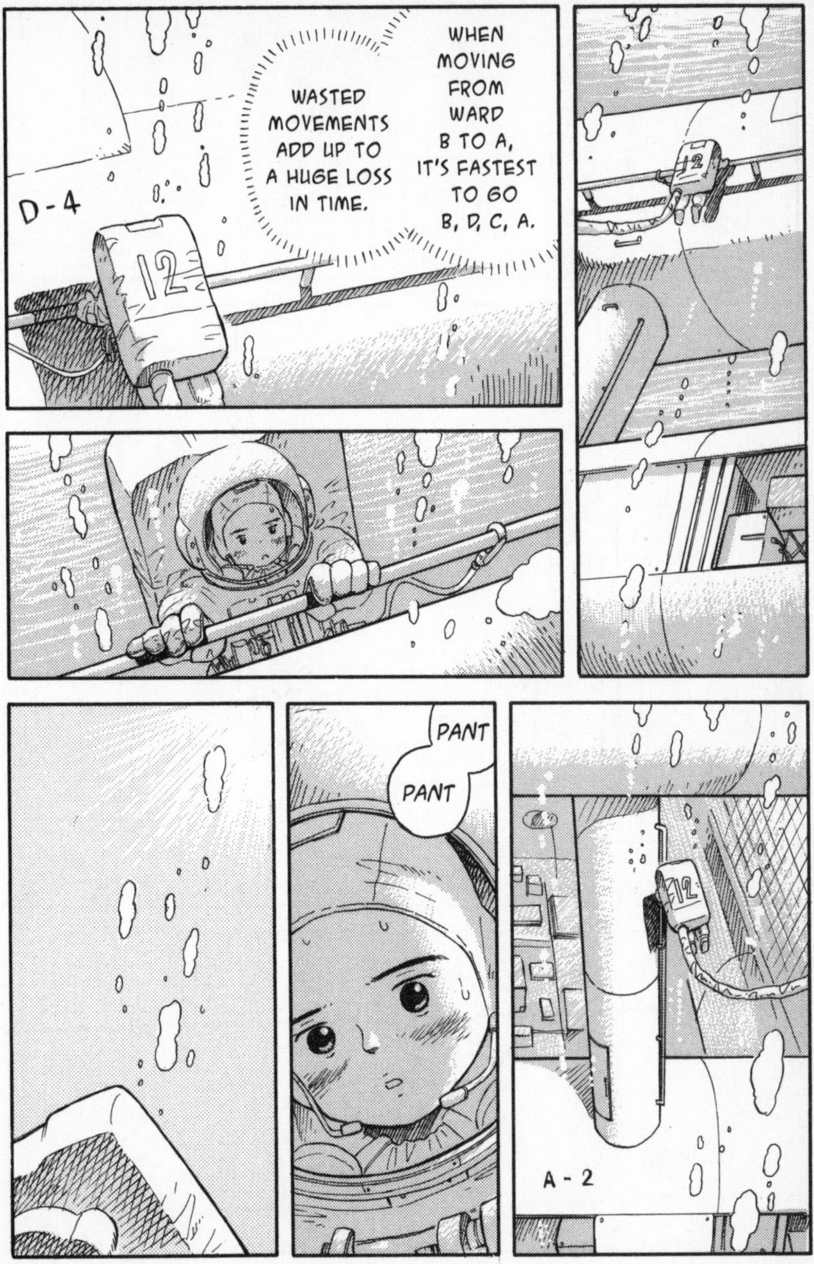
WHEN MOVING FROM WARD B TO A, IT'S FASTEST TO GO B, D, C, A.
WASTED MOVEMENTS ADD UP TO A HUGE LOSS IN TIME.
D-4
A-2
PANT
PANT

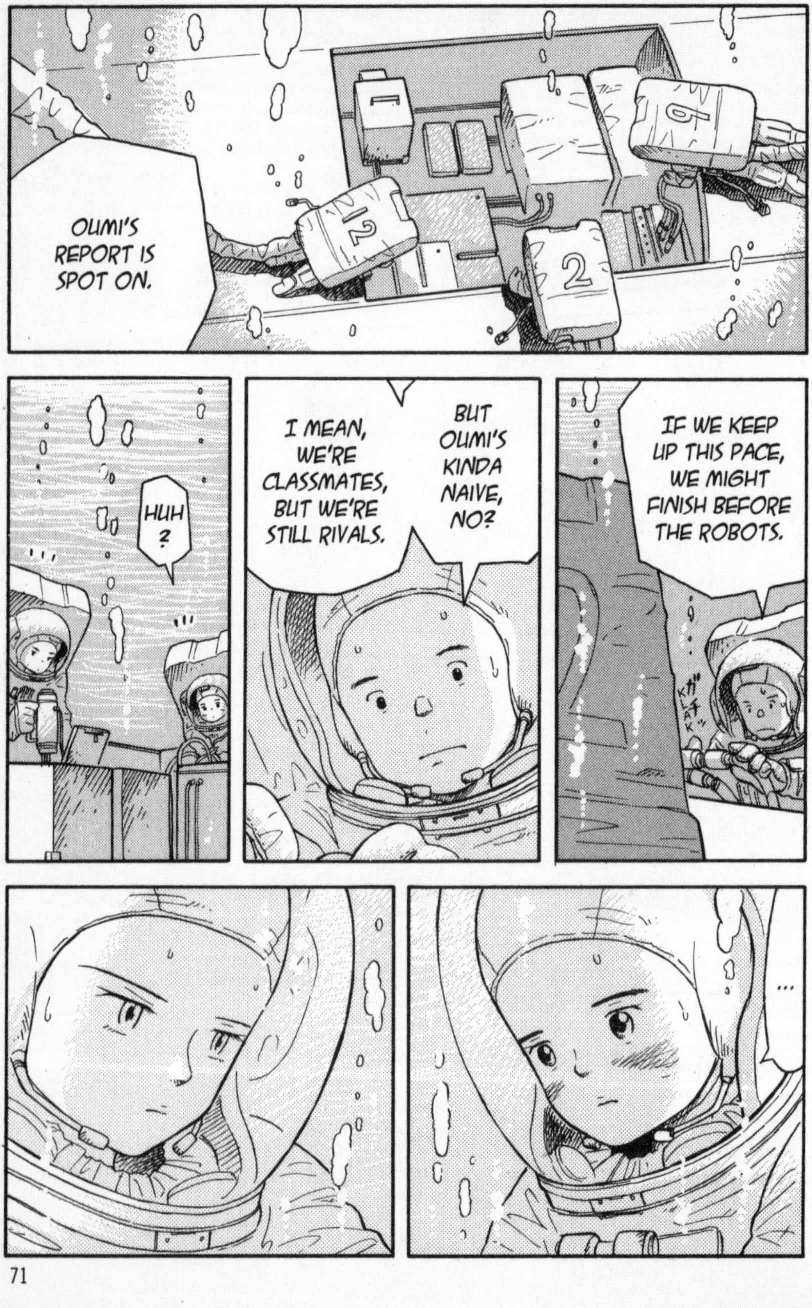
OUMI'S REPORT IS SPOT ON.
IF WE KEEP UP THIS PACE, WE MIGHT FINISH BEFORE THE ROBOTS.
BUT OUMI'S KINDA NAIVE, NO?
I MEAN, WE'RE CLASSMATES, BUT WE'RE STILL RIVALS.
HUH?
...

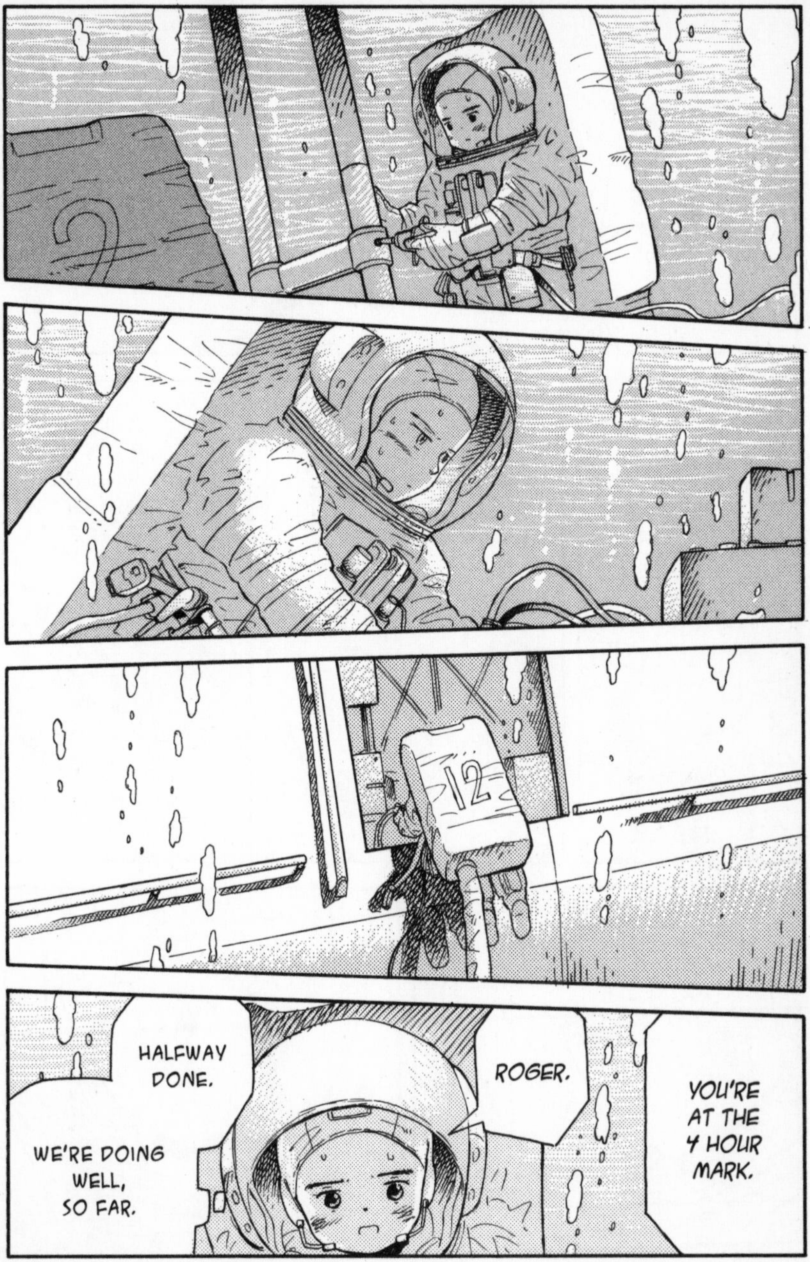
YOU'RE AT THE 4 HOUR MARK.
ROGER.
HALFWAY DONE.
WE'RE DOING WELL, SO FAR.

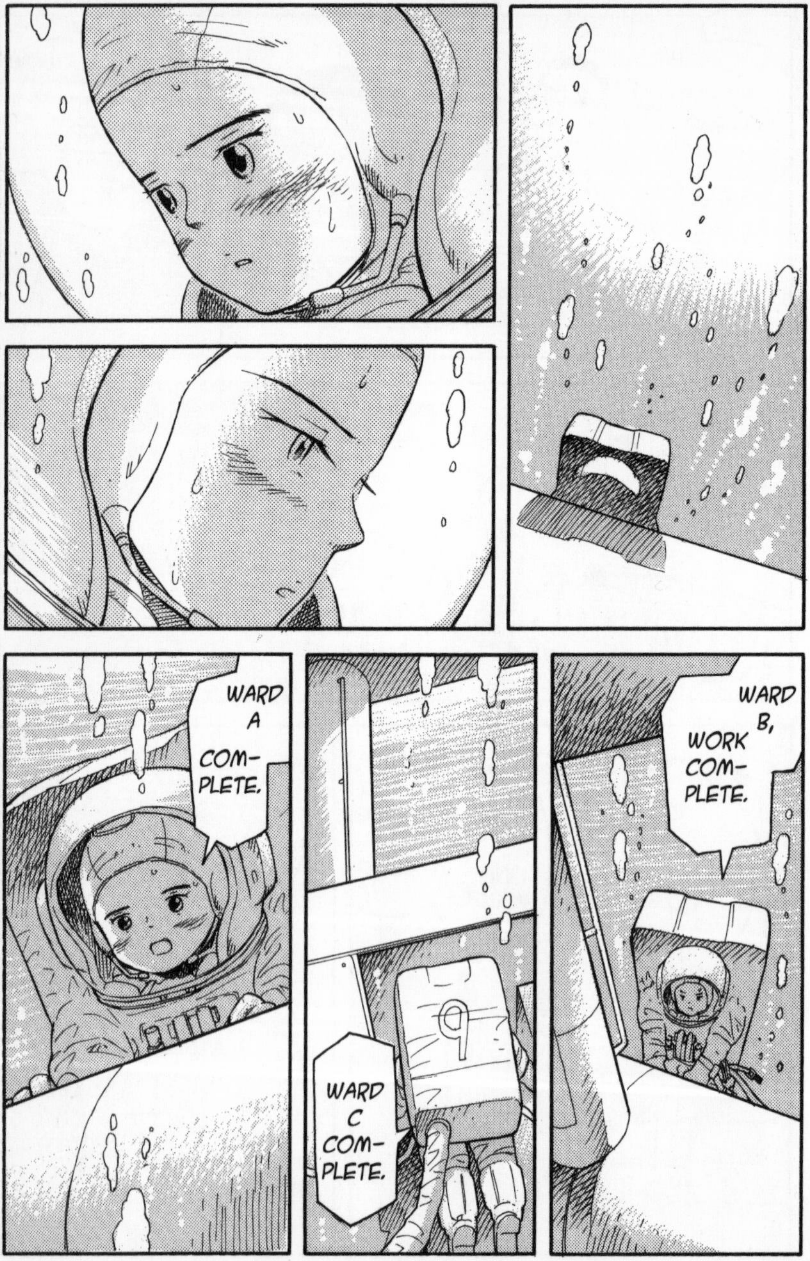
WARD B, WORK COMPLETE.
WARD C COMPLETE.
WARD A COMPLETE.

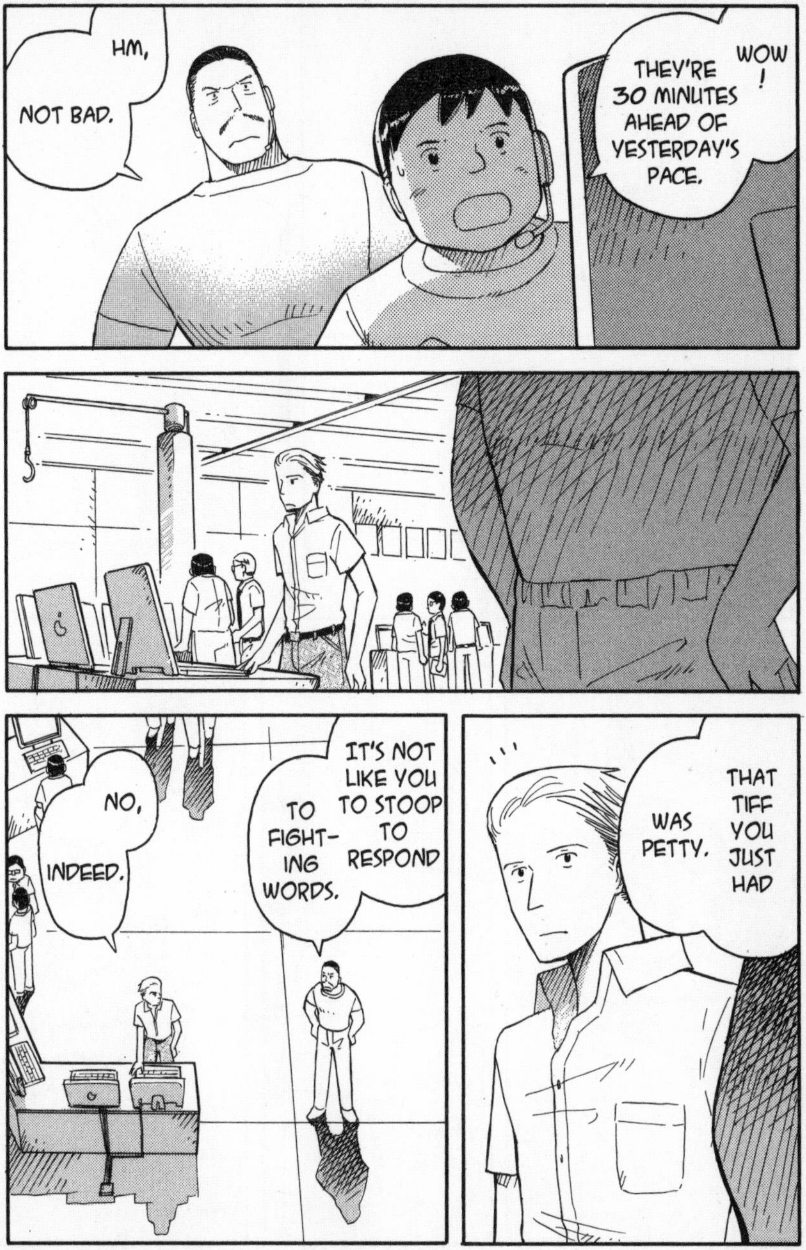
WOW! THEY'RE 30 MINUTES AHEAD OF YESTERDAY'S PACE.
HM, NOT BAD.
THAT TIFF YOU JUST HAD WAS PETTY.
IT'S NOT LIKE YOU TO STOOP TO RESPOND TO FIGHTING-ING WORDS.
NO, INDEED.

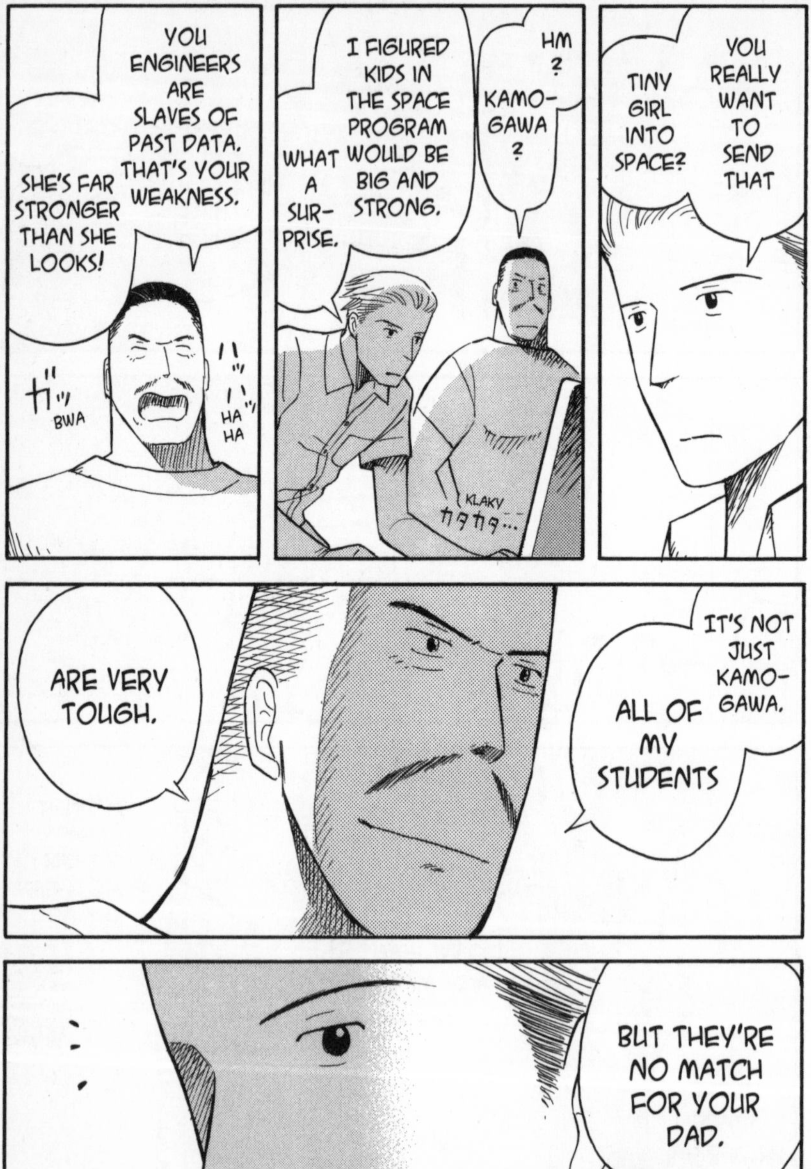

YOU REALLY WANT TO SEND THAT TINY GIRL INTO SPACE?
HM? KAMOGAWA?
I FIGURED KIDS IN THE SPACE PROGRAM WOULD BE BIG AND STRONG.
WHAT A SURPRISE.
KLAKY
カタカタ…
YOU ENGINEERS ARE SLAVES OF PAST DATA. THAT'S YOUR WEAKNESS.
SHE'S FAR STRONGER THAN SHE LOOKS!
ハッハッ
HA HA
ガッ
BWA
IT'S NOT JUST KAMOGAWA.
ALL OF MY STUDENTS
ARE VERY TOUGH.
BUT THEY'RE NO MATCH FOR YOUR DAD.
…

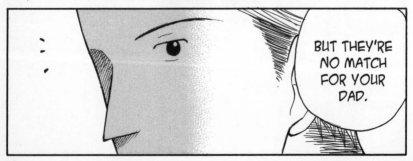

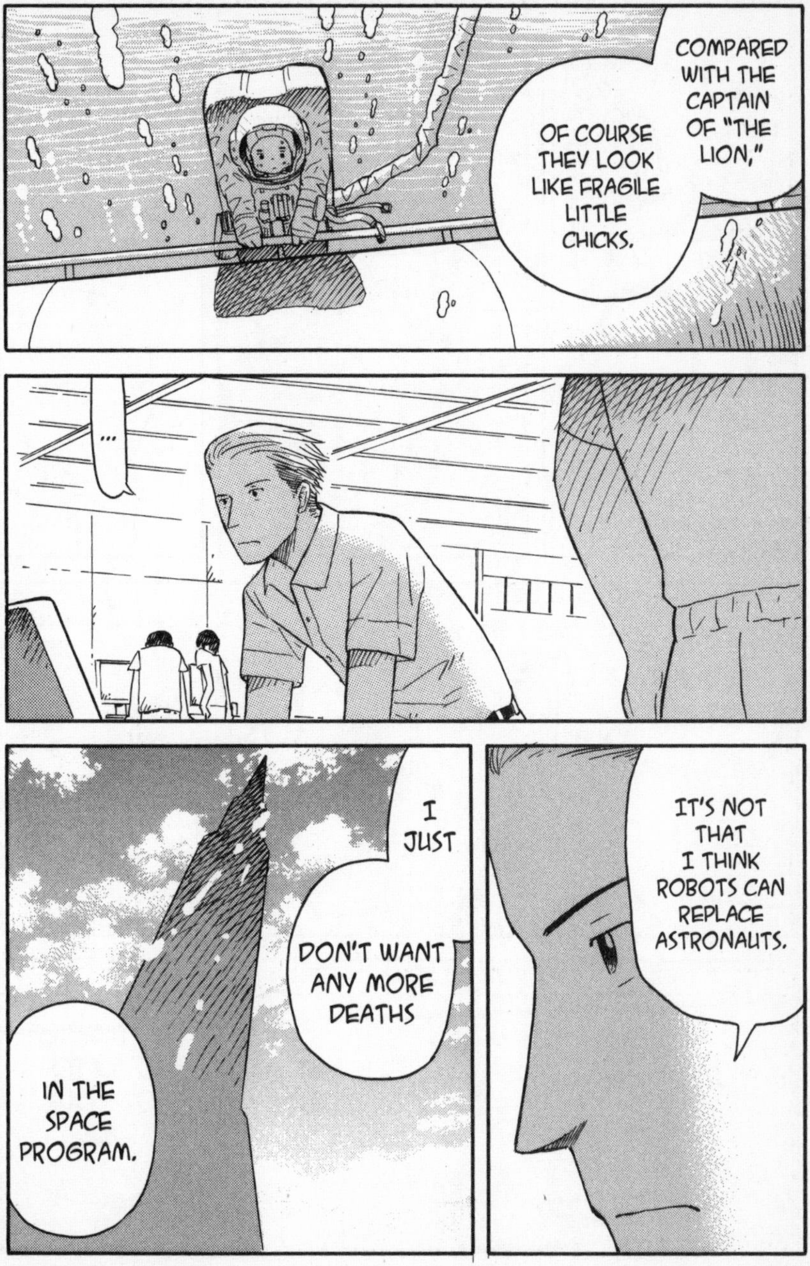
COMPARED WITH THE CAPTAIN OF "THE LION,"
OF COURSE THEY LOOK LIKE FRAGILE LITTLE CHICKS.
...
IT'S NOT THAT I THINK ROBOTS CAN REPLACE ASTRONAUTS.
I JUST
DON'T WANT ANY MORE DEATHS
IN THE SPACE PROGRAM.

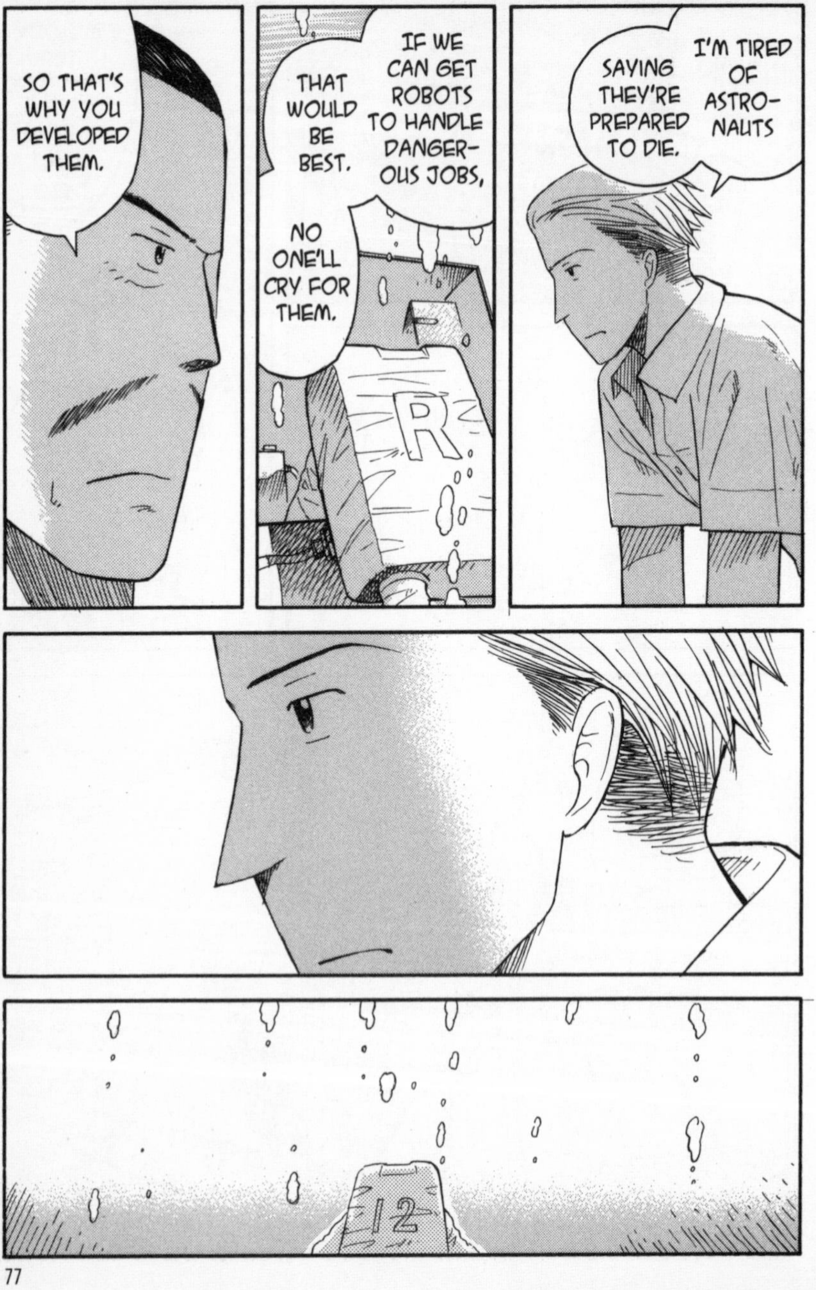
I'M TIRED OF ASTRONAUTS
SAYING THEY'RE PREPARED TO DIE.
IF WE CAN GET ROBOTS TO HANDLE DANGEROUS JOBS,
THAT WOULD BE BEST.
NO ONE'LL CRY FOR THEM.
SO THAT'S WHY YOU DEVELOPED THEM.
R
12

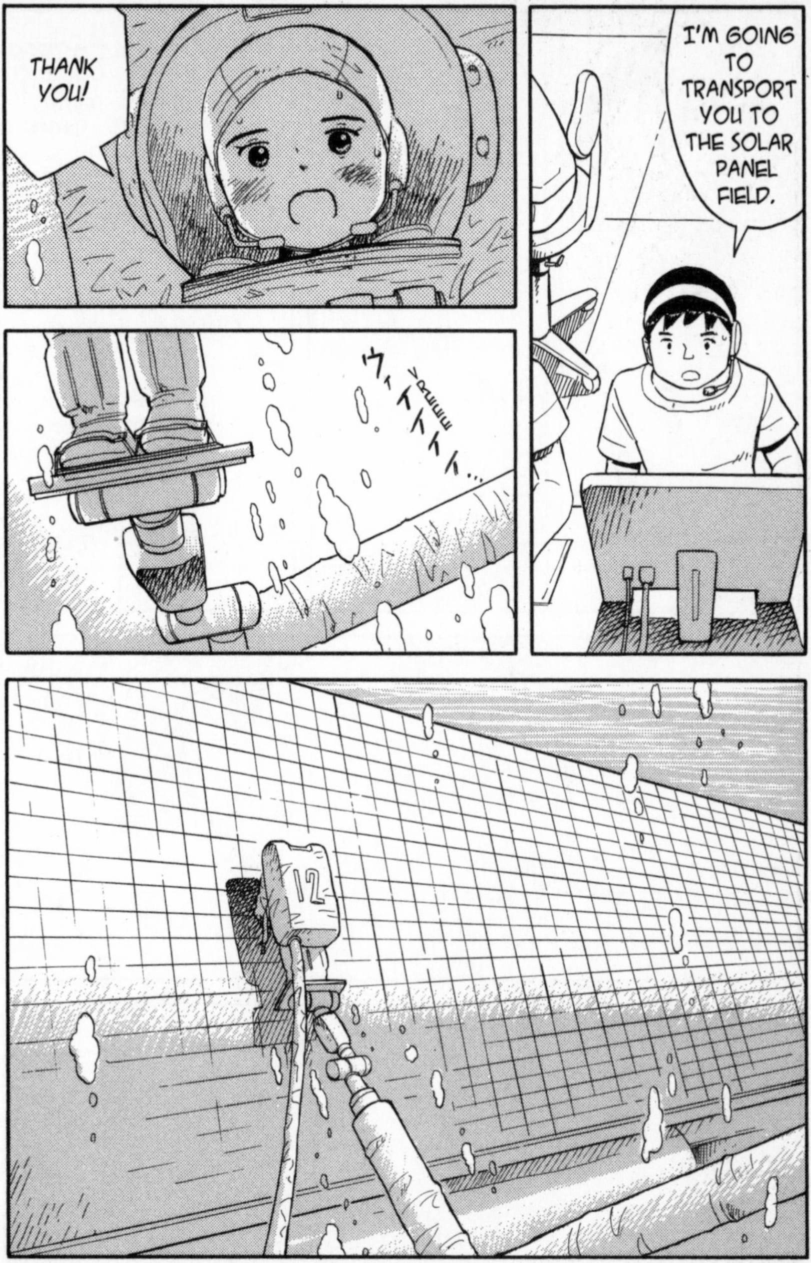
I'M GOING TO TRANSPORT YOU TO THE SOLAR PANEL FIELD.
THANK YOU!
ウィイイイイ…
VREEEE

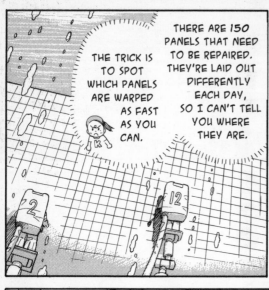

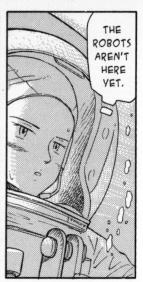

THE ROBOTS AREN'T HERE YET.
THERE ARE 150 PANELS THAT NEED TO BE REPAIRED. THEY'RE LAID OUT DIFFERENTLY EACH DAY, SO I CAN'T TELL YOU WHERE THEY ARE.
THE TRICK IS TO SPOT WHICH PANELS ARE WARPED AS FAST AS YOU CAN.
THE FASTEST WAY IS TO LOOK UP FROM THE BOTTOM
AND SEE WHERE THE LIGHT REFRACTS.
GLIMMER
キラッ

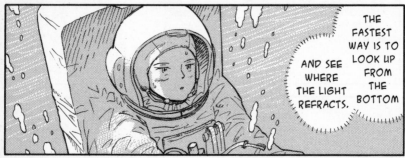

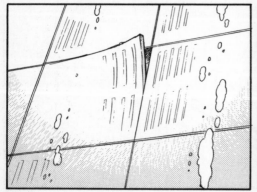

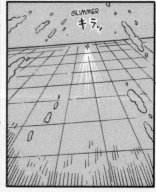

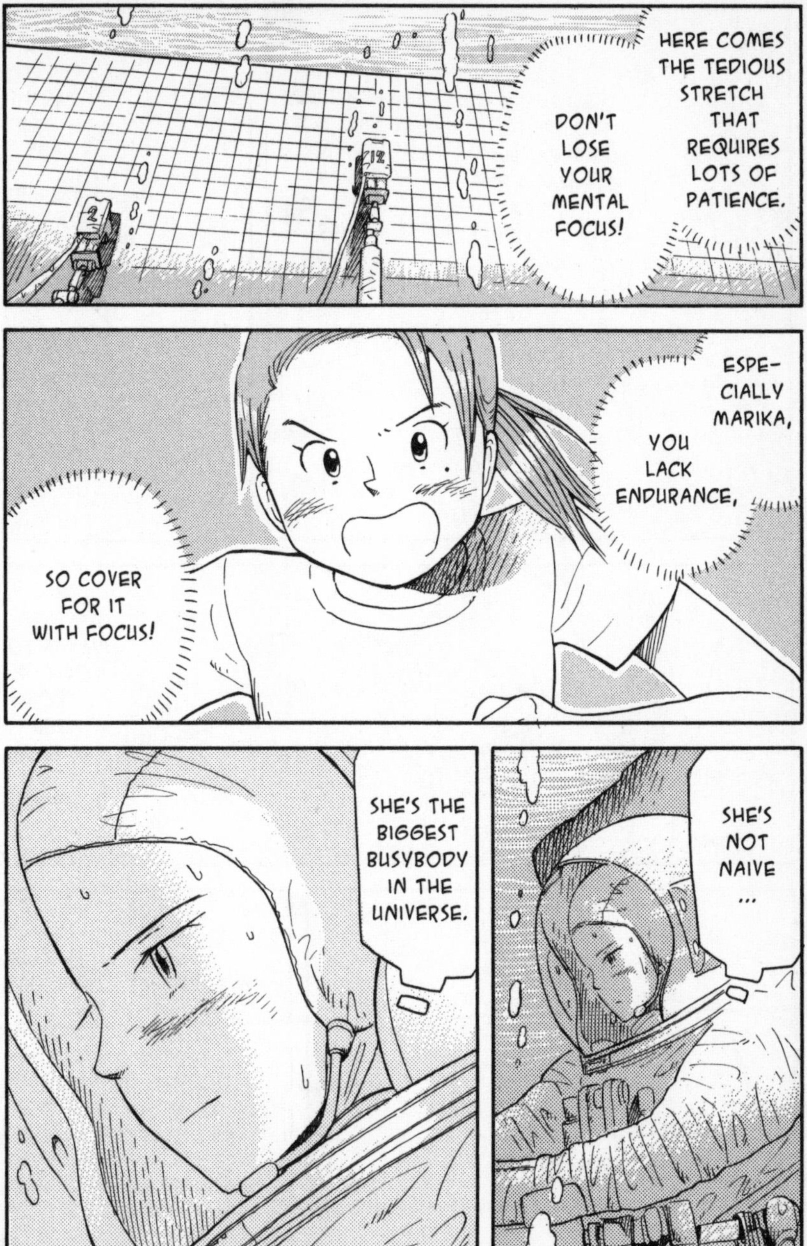
HERE COMES THE TEDIOUS STRETCH THAT REQUIRES LOTS OF PATIENCE.
DON'T LOSE YOUR MENTAL FOCUS!
ESPECIALLY MARIKA, YOU LACK ENDURANCE,
SO COVER FOR IT WITH FOCUS!
SHE'S NOT NAIVE ...
SHE'S THE BIGGEST BUSYBODY IN THE UNIVERSE.

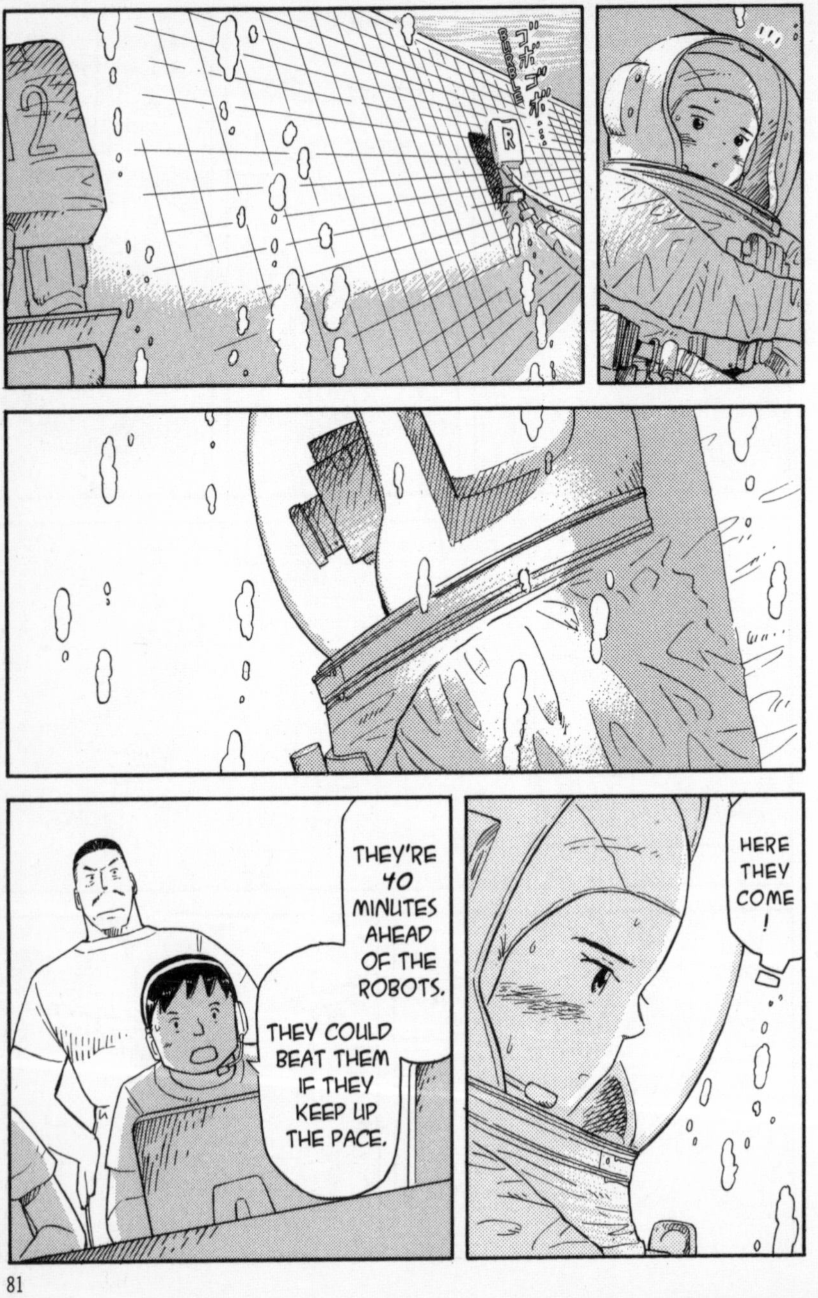
BURBLE
HERE THEY COME!
THEY'RE 40 MINUTES AHEAD OF THE ROBOTS.
THEY COULD BEAT THEM IF THEY KEEP UP THE PACE.

MY GRIP IS GETTING WEAK...
I CAN'T ...
LIFT MY ARM AS HIGH.
HUFF
HUFF
MARIKA
DON'T LET UP!
YOU DON'T NEED TO TELL ME.

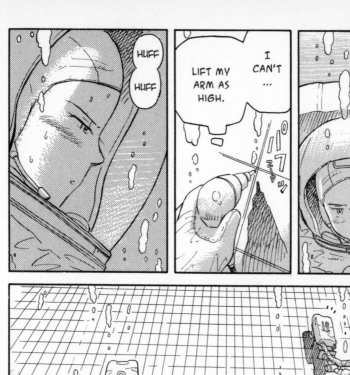

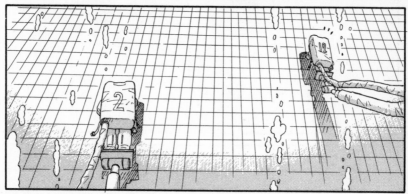

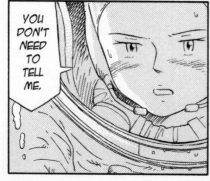

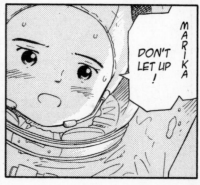

KAMOGAWA AND UKITA HAVE SPED UP!
THEY CAN MAKE IT!
1 HOUR LEFT.

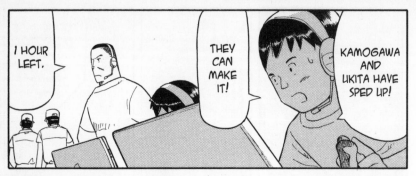

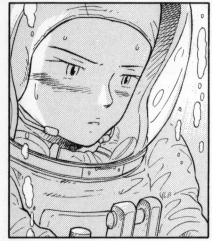

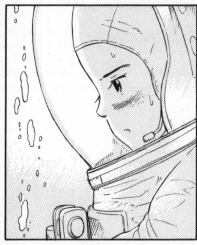

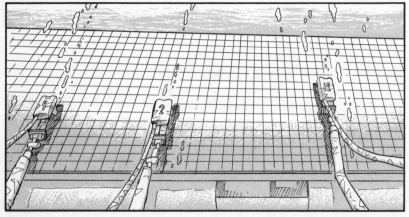

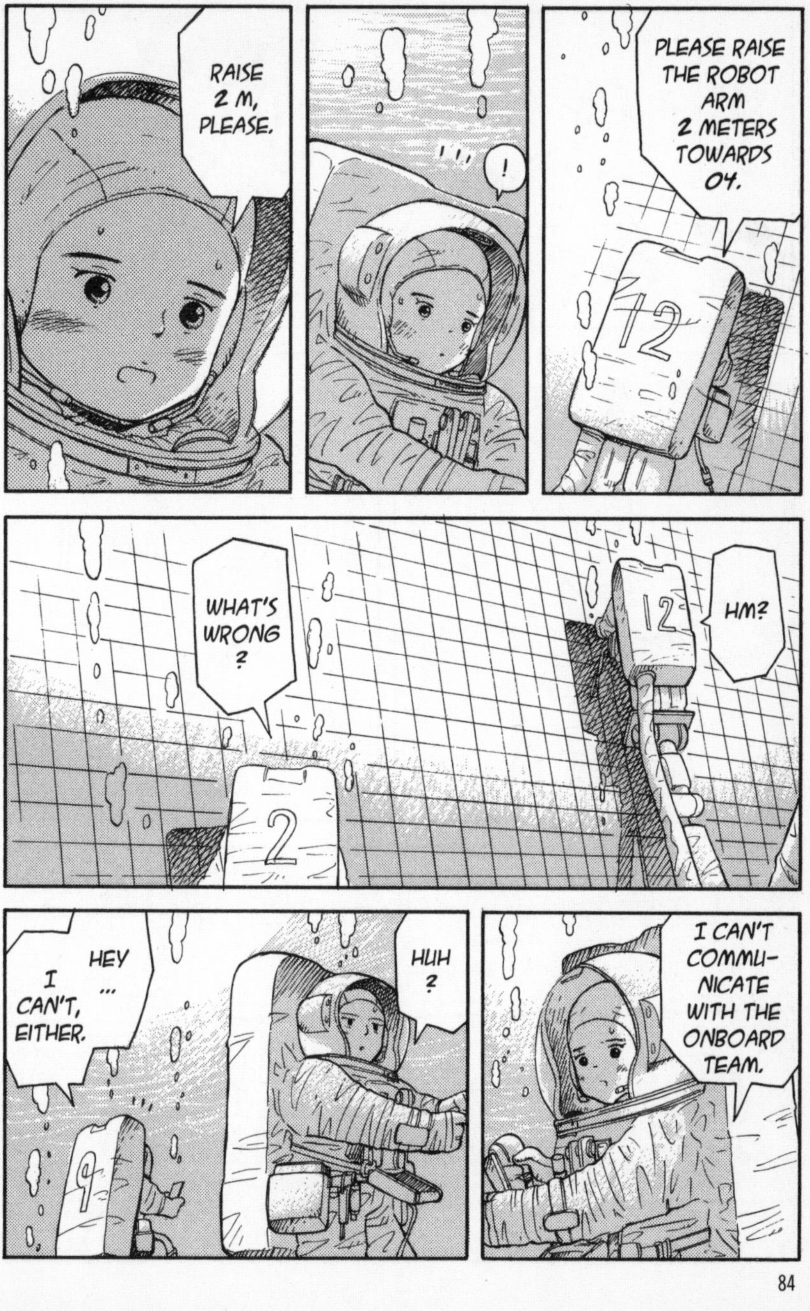
PLEASE RAISE THE ROBOT ARM 2 METERS TOWARDS 04.
!
RAISE 2 M, PLEASE.
HM?
WHAT'S WRONG ?
I CAN'T COMMU-NICATE WITH THE ONBOARD TEAM.
HUH ?
HEY ... I CAN'T, EITHER.

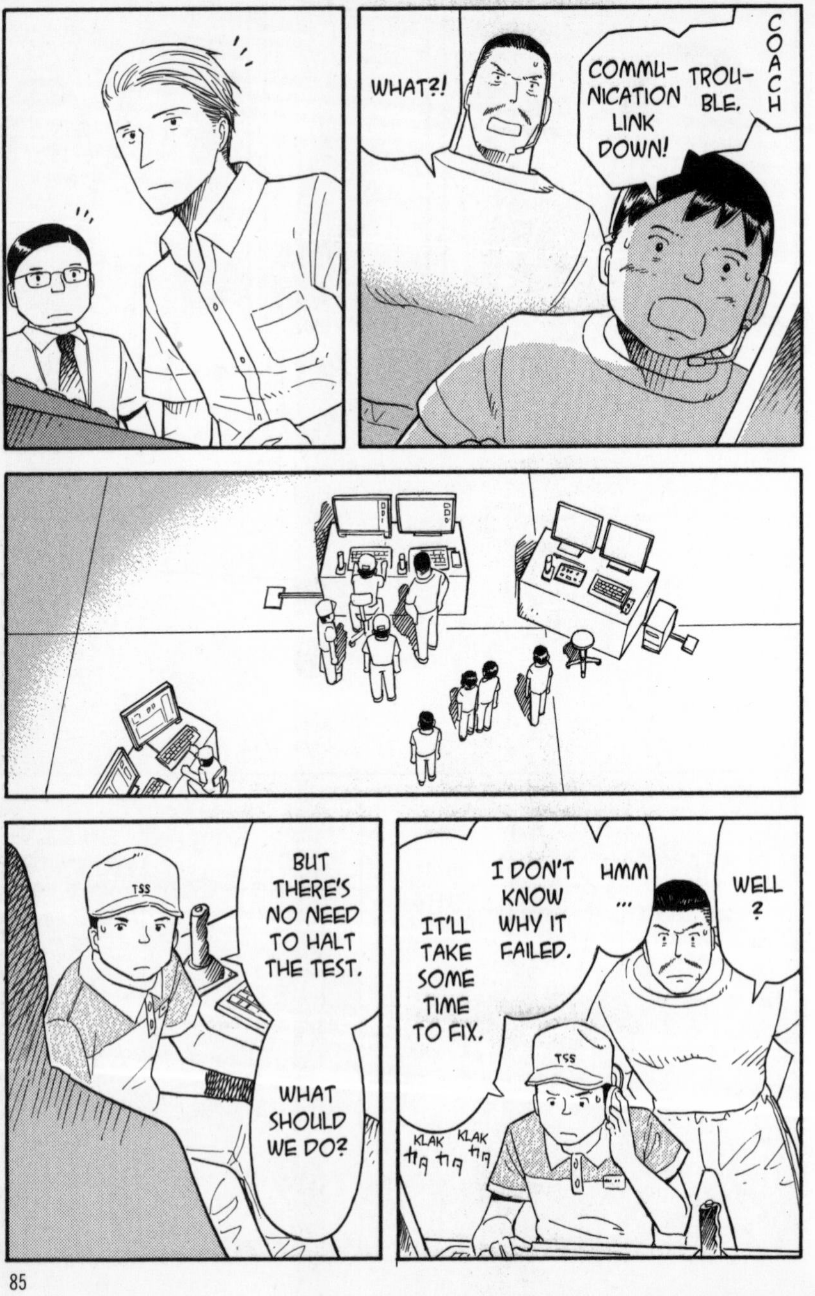
COACH
TROUBLE.
COMMUNICATION LINK DOWN!
WHAT?!
WELL?
HMM...
I DON'T KNOW WHY IT FAILED.
IT'LL TAKE SOME TIME TO FIX.
KLAK KLAK
BUT THERE'S NO NEED TO HALT THE TEST.
WHAT SHOULD WE DO?

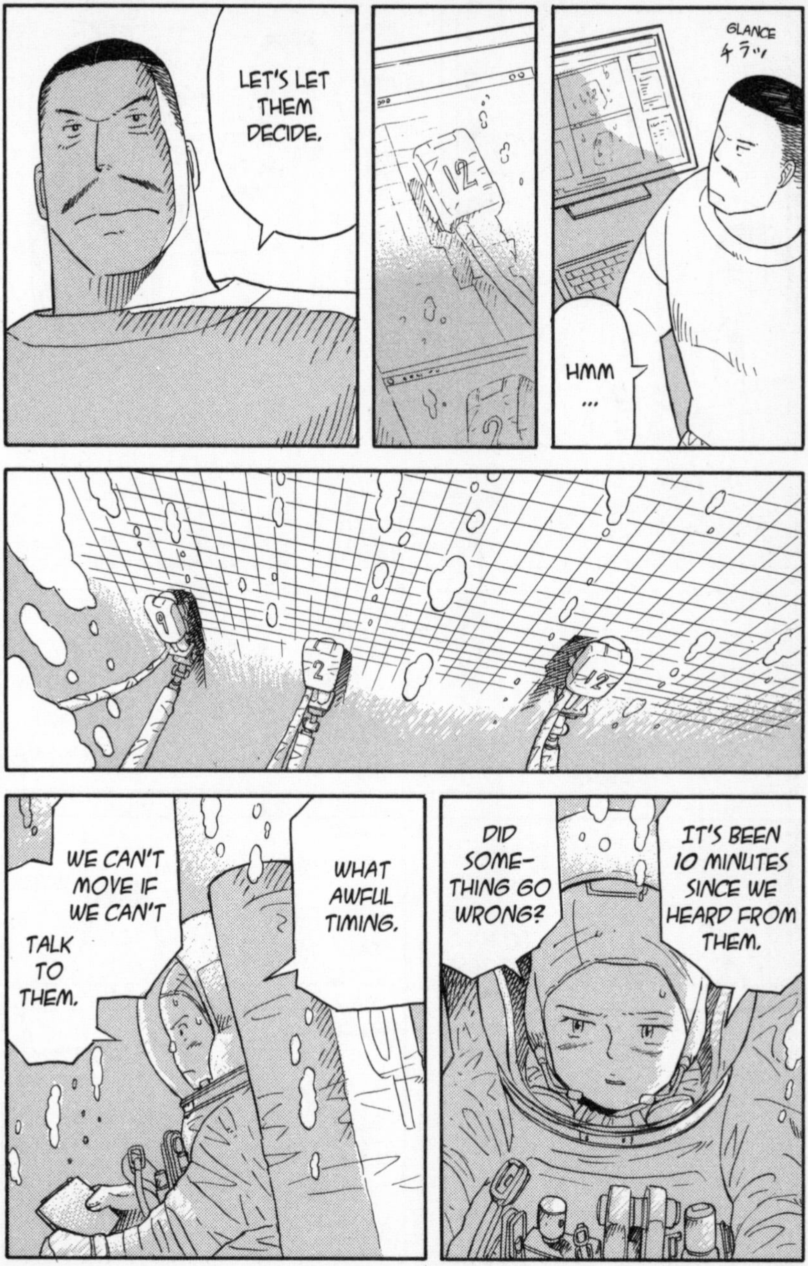
GLANCE
チラッ
HMM ...
LET'S LET THEM DECIDE.
IT'S BEEN 10 MINUTES SINCE WE HEARD FROM THEM.
DID SOME-THING GO WRONG?
WHAT AWFUL TIMING.
WE CAN'T MOVE IF WE CAN'T TALK TO THEM.

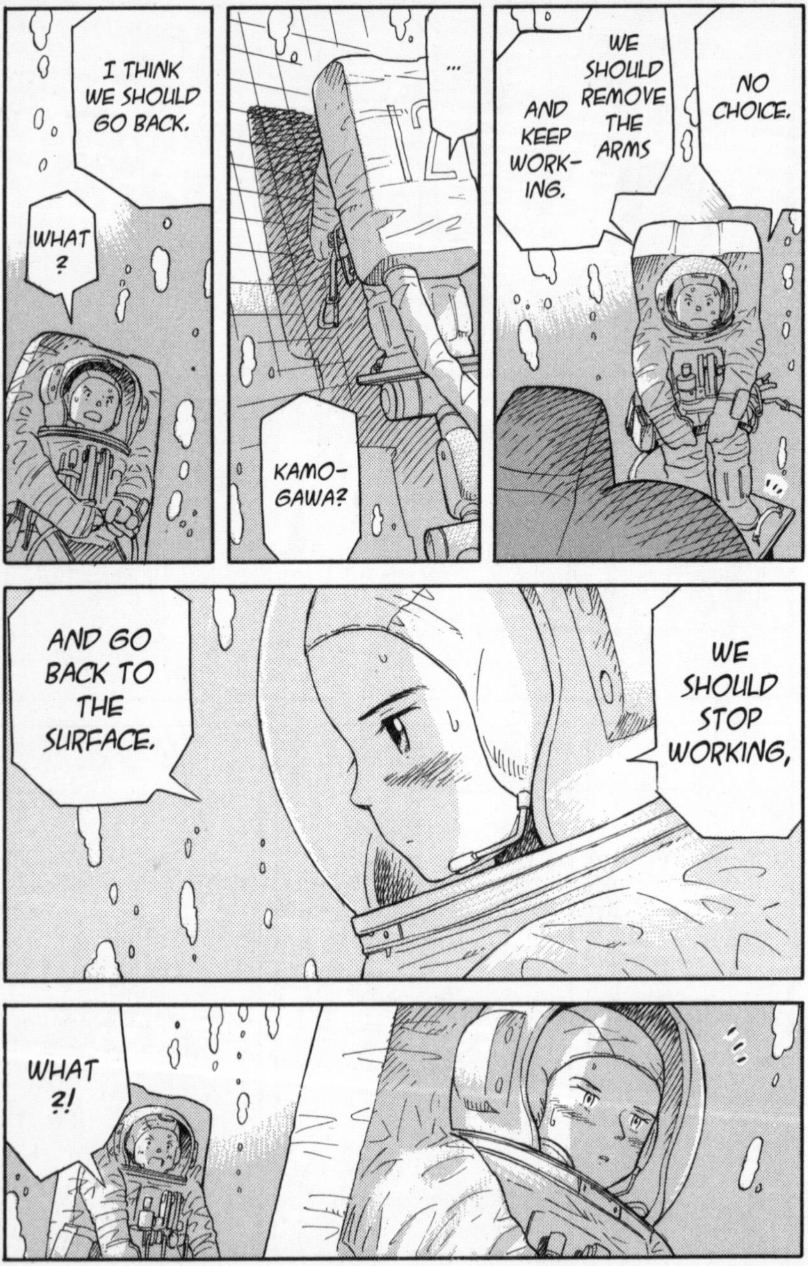
NO CHOICE.
WE SHOULD REMOVE THE ARMS
AND KEEP WORK-ING.
...
KAMO-GAWA?
I THINK WE SHOULD GO BACK.
WHAT?
WE SHOULD STOP WORKING,
AND GO BACK TO THE SURFACE.
WHAT?!

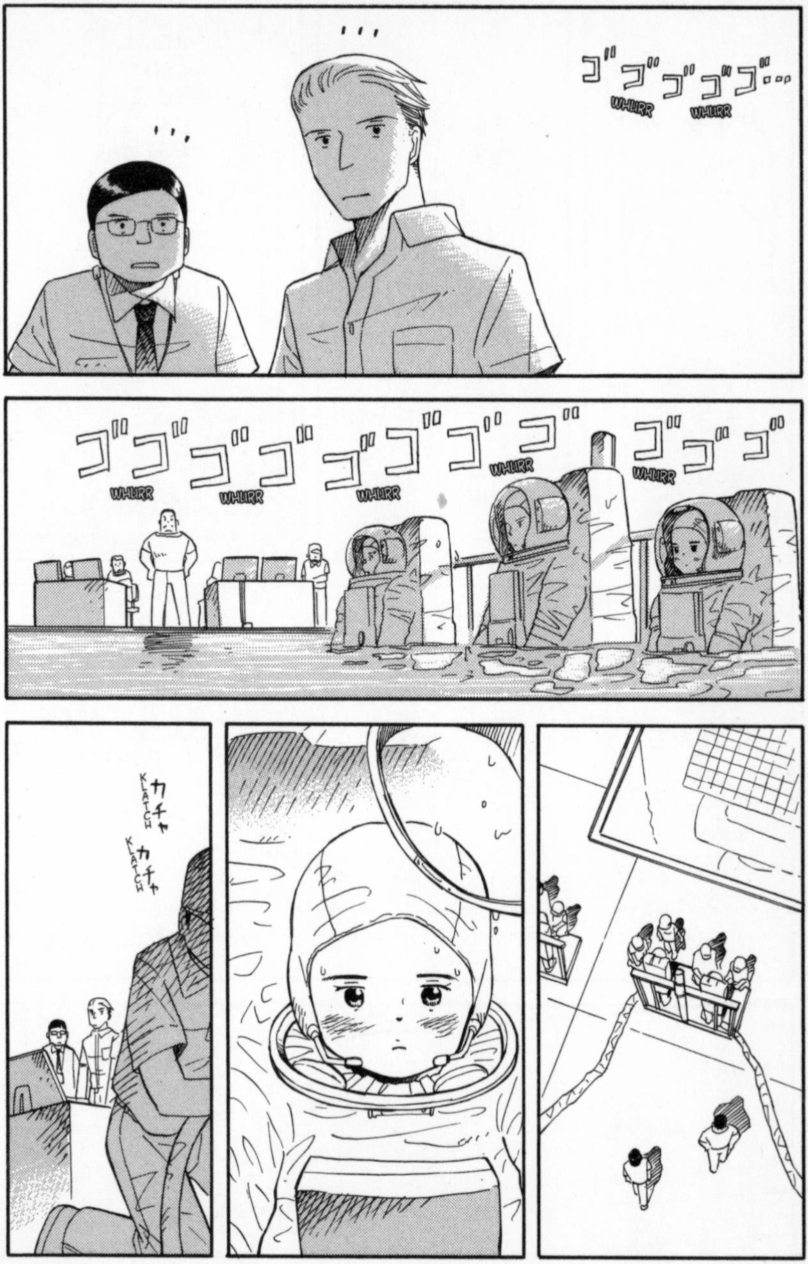
ゴゴゴゴゴ...
WHURR
WHURR
ゴゴゴゴゴゴゴゴ
WHURR
WHURR
WHURR
ゴゴゴ
WHURR
WHURR
カチャ
KLATCH
カチャ
KLATCH

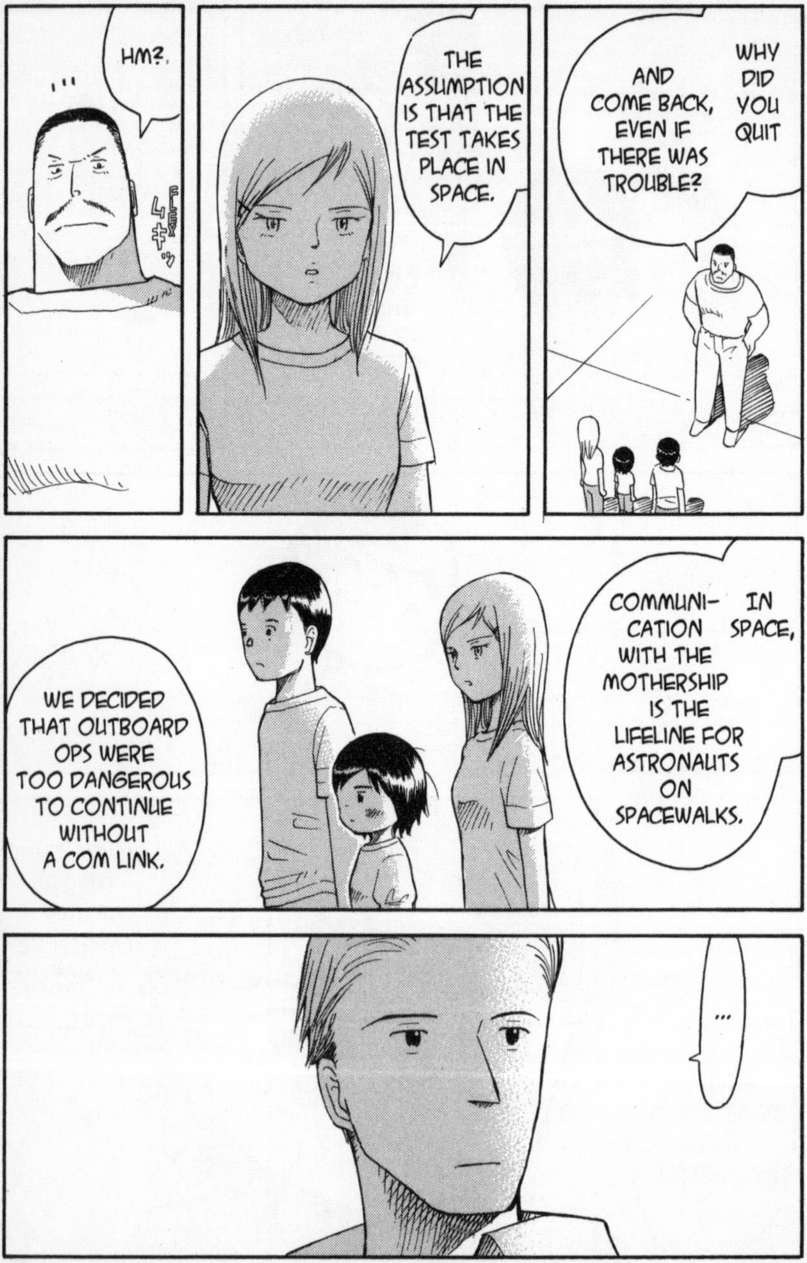
WHY DID YOU QUIT AND COME BACK, EVEN IF THERE WAS TROUBLE?
THE ASSUMPTION IS THAT THE TEST TAKES PLACE IN SPACE.
HM?
...
FLEX ムキッ
IN SPACE, COMMUNICATION WITH THE MOTHERSHIP IS THE LIFELINE FOR ASTRONAUTS ON SPACEWALKS.
WE DECIDED THAT OUTBOARD OPS WERE TOO DANGEROUS TO CONTINUE WITHOUT A COM LINK.
...

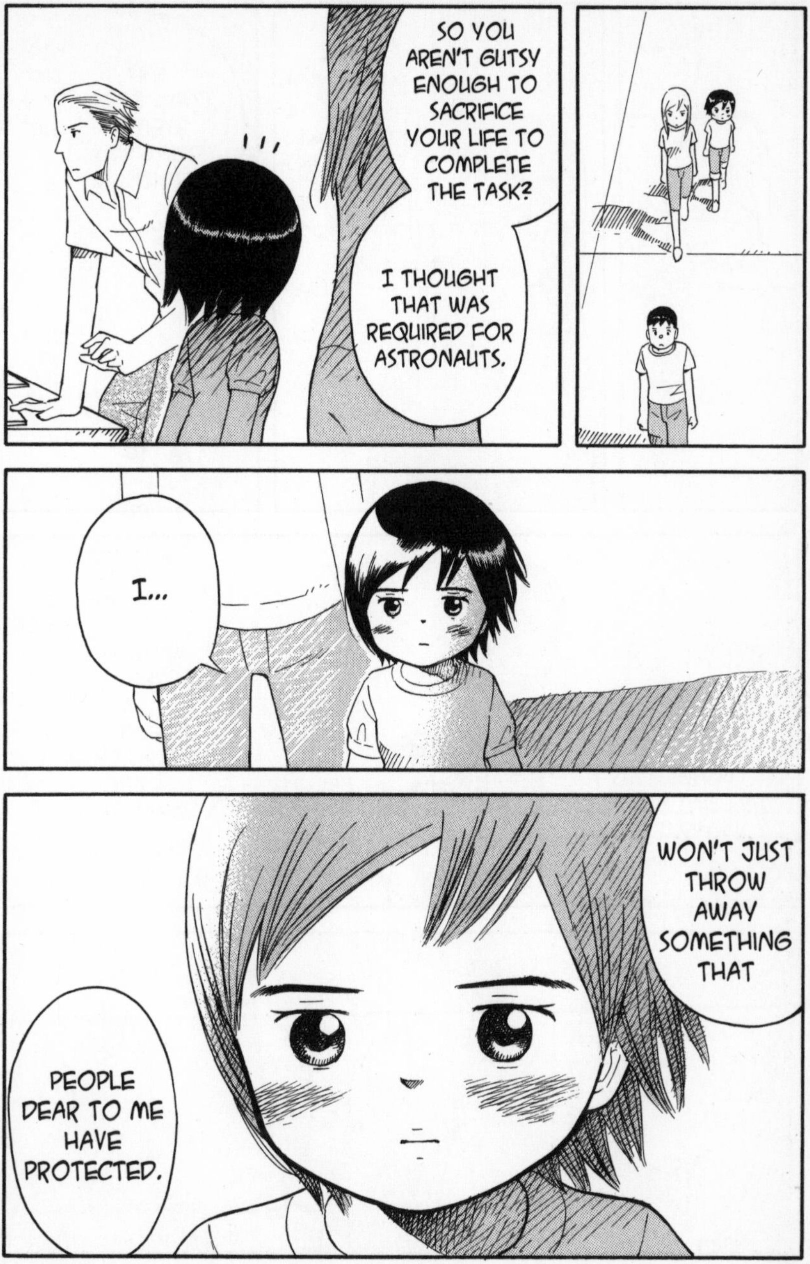
SO YOU AREN'T GUTSY ENOUGH TO SACRIFICE YOUR LIFE TO COMPLETE THE TASK?
I THOUGHT THAT WAS REQUIRED FOR ASTRONAUTS.
I...
WON'T JUST THROW AWAY SOMETHING THAT
PEOPLE DEAR TO ME HAVE PROTECTED.

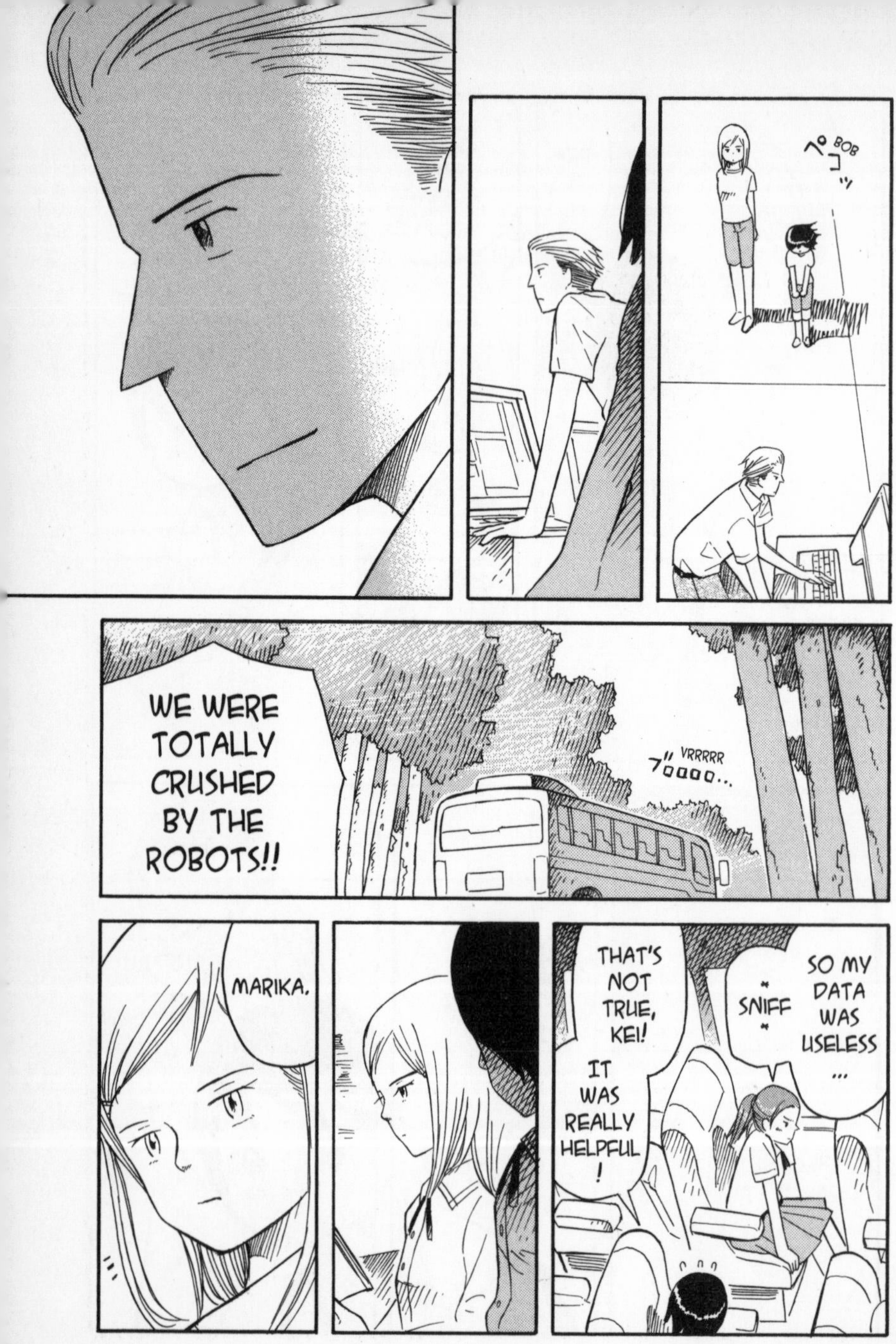
ペコッ BOB
ブロロロ... VRRRRR
WE WERE TOTALLY CRUSHED BY THE ROBOTS!!
SO MY DATA WAS USELESS ...
SNIFF
THAT'S NOT TRUE, KEI!
IT WAS REALLY HELPFUL!
MARIKA.

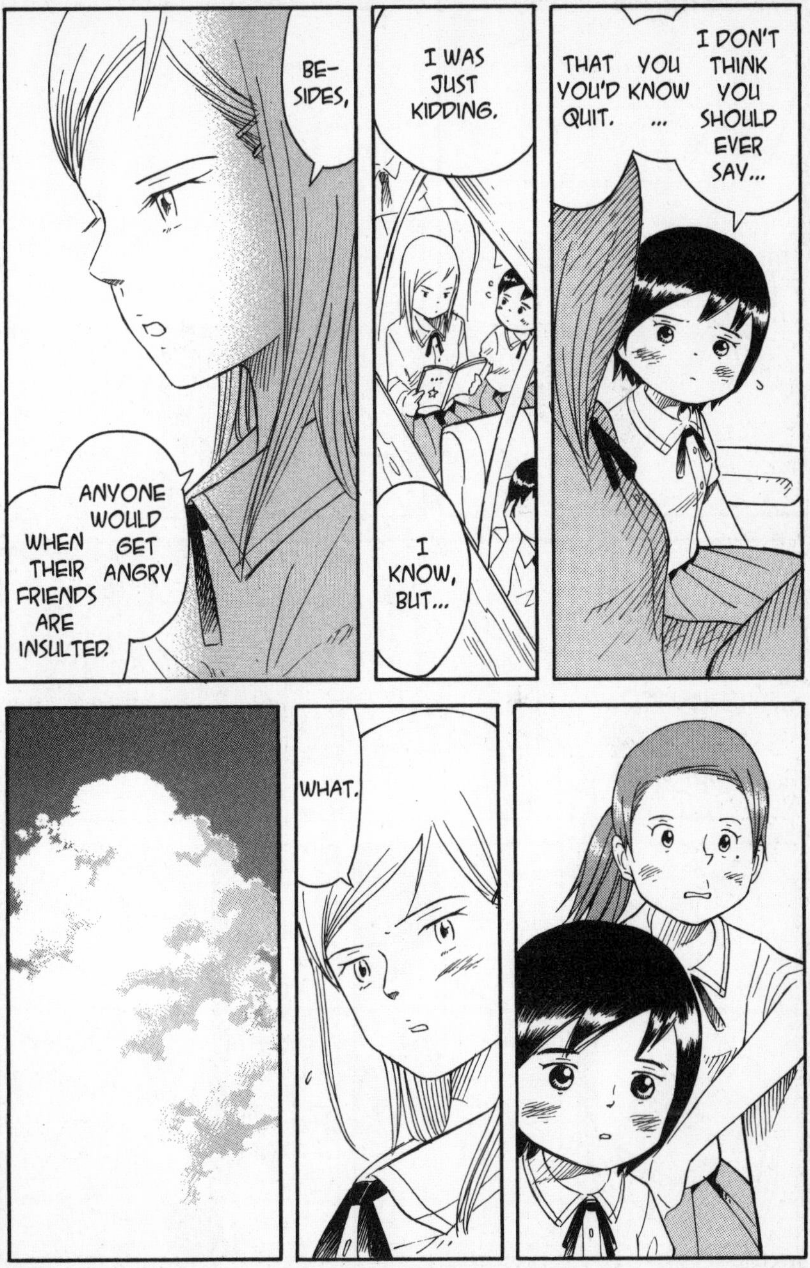
I DON'T THINK YOU SHOULD EVER SAY... YOU KNOW ... THAT YOU'D QUIT.
I WAS JUST KIDDING.
I KNOW, BUT...
BE-SIDES,
ANYONE WOULD GET ANGRY WHEN THEIR FRIENDS ARE INSULTED.
WHAT.

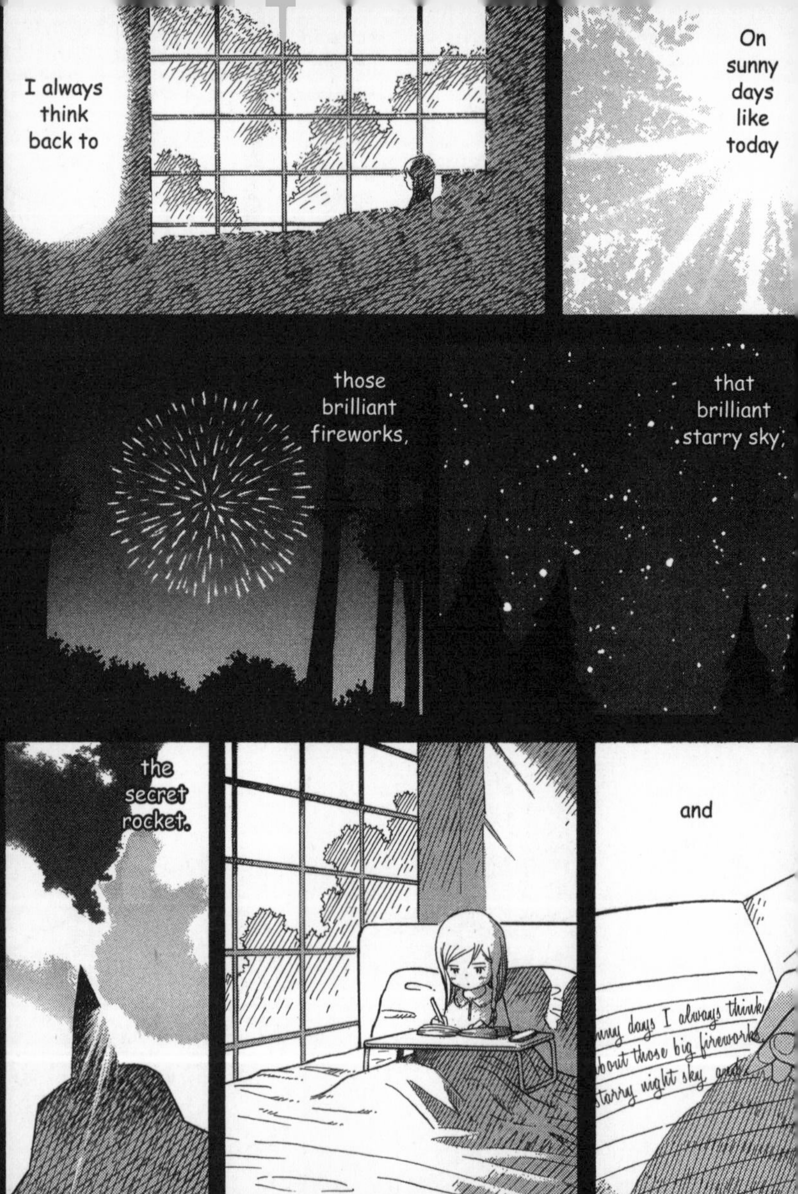

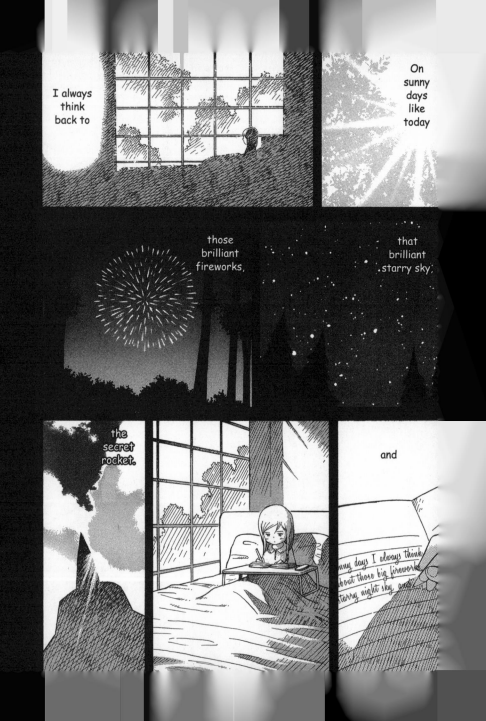

On sunny days like today
I always think back to
that brilliant starry sky,
those brilliant fireworks,
and
nny days I always think
about those big fireworks
starry night sky, and
the secret rocket.

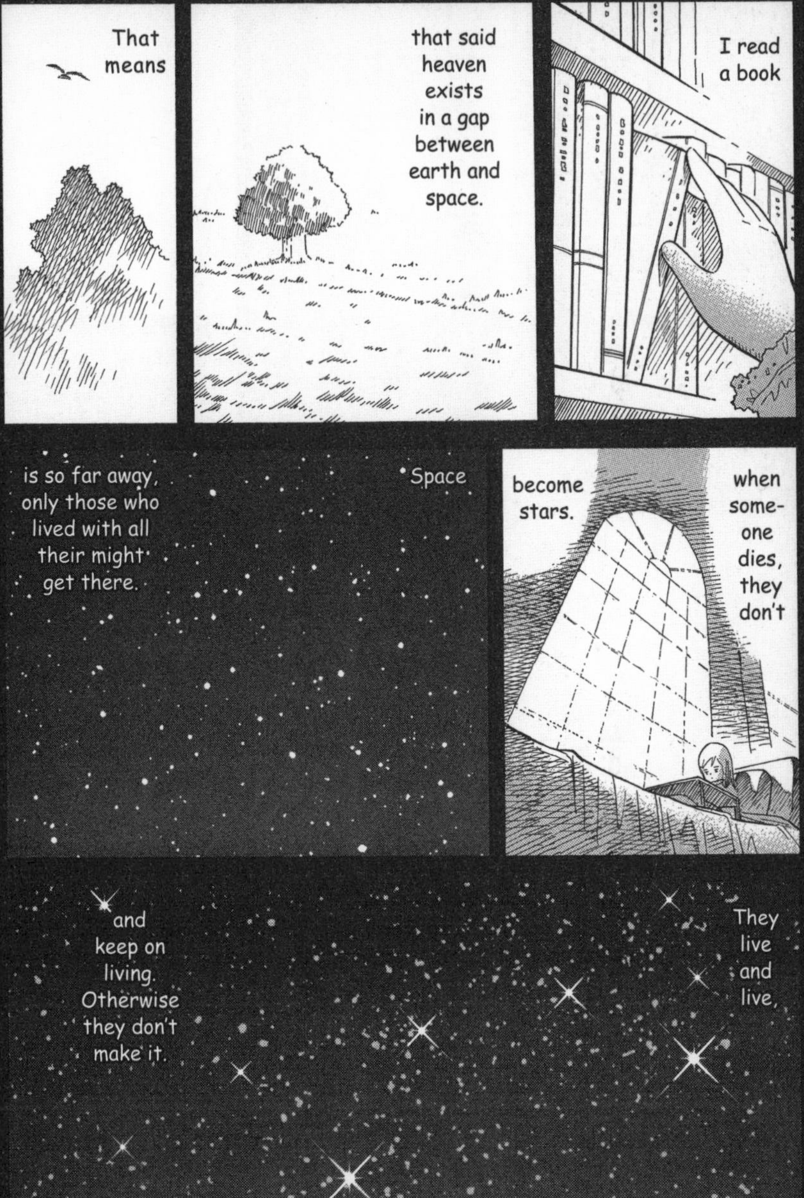
I read a book
that said heaven exists in a gap between earth and space.
That means
when some-one dies, they don't
become stars.
Space
is so far away, only those who lived with all their might get there.
They live and live,
and keep on living. Otherwise they don't make it.

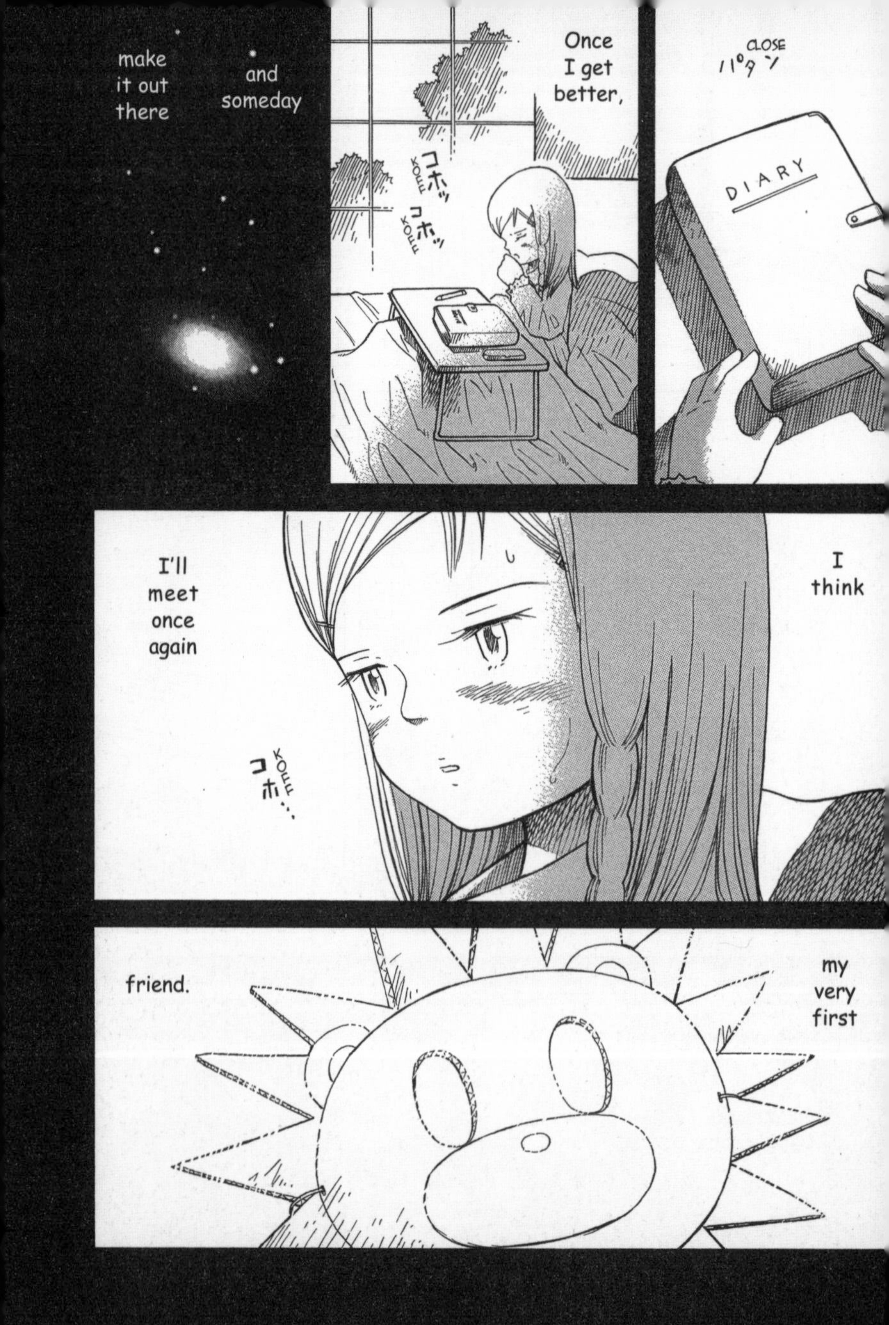
CLOSE
パタン
Once I get better,
コホッ
KOFF
コホッ
KOFF
and someday
make it out there
I think
I'll meet once again
コホ…
KOFF
my very first
friend.

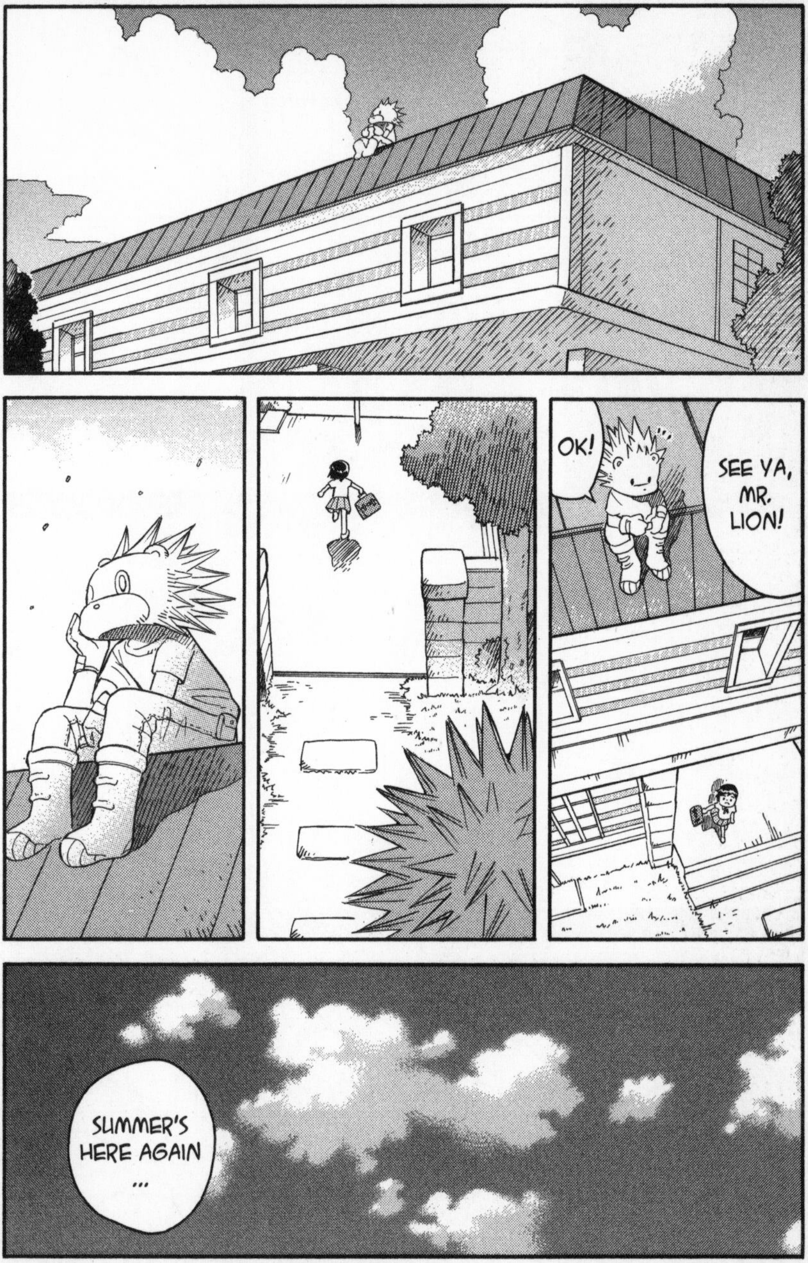
SEE YA, MR. LION!
OK!
SUMMER'S HERE AGAIN ...

MISSION:59

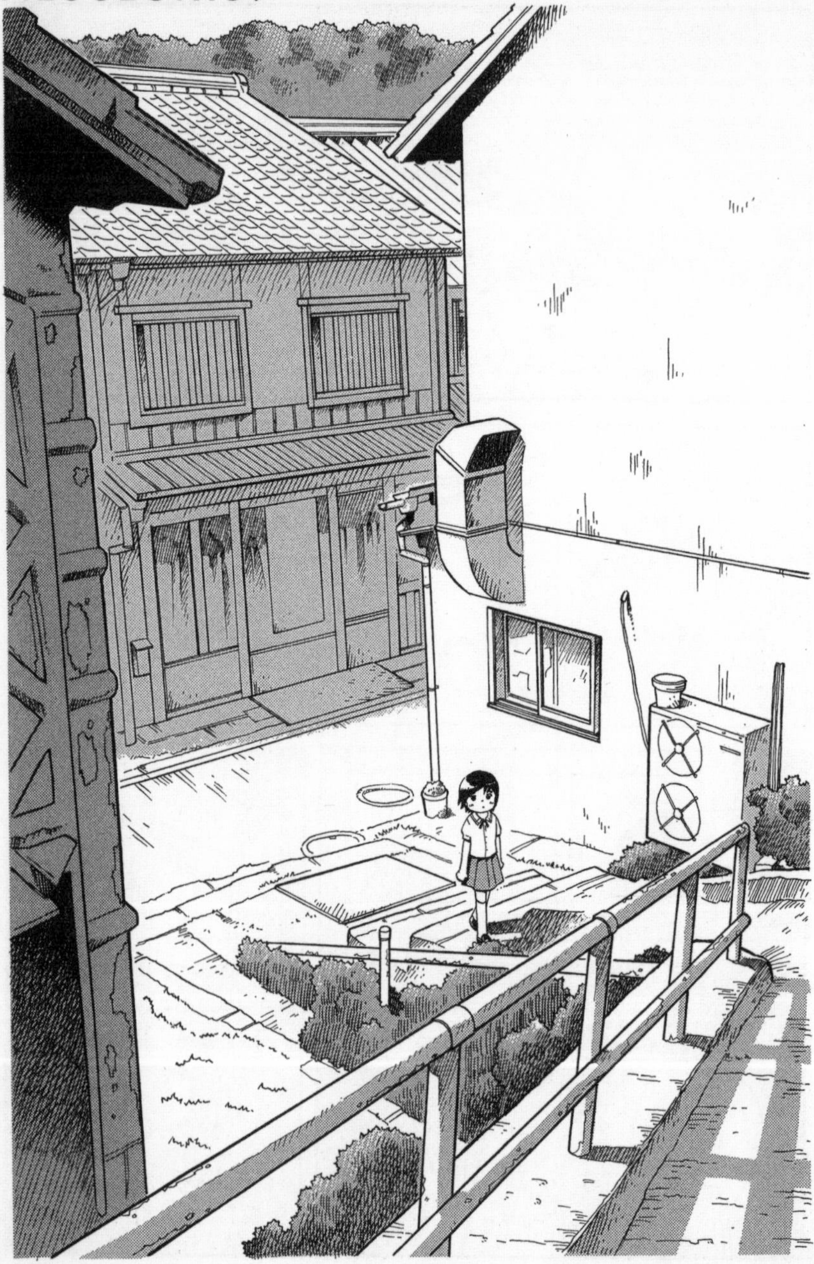

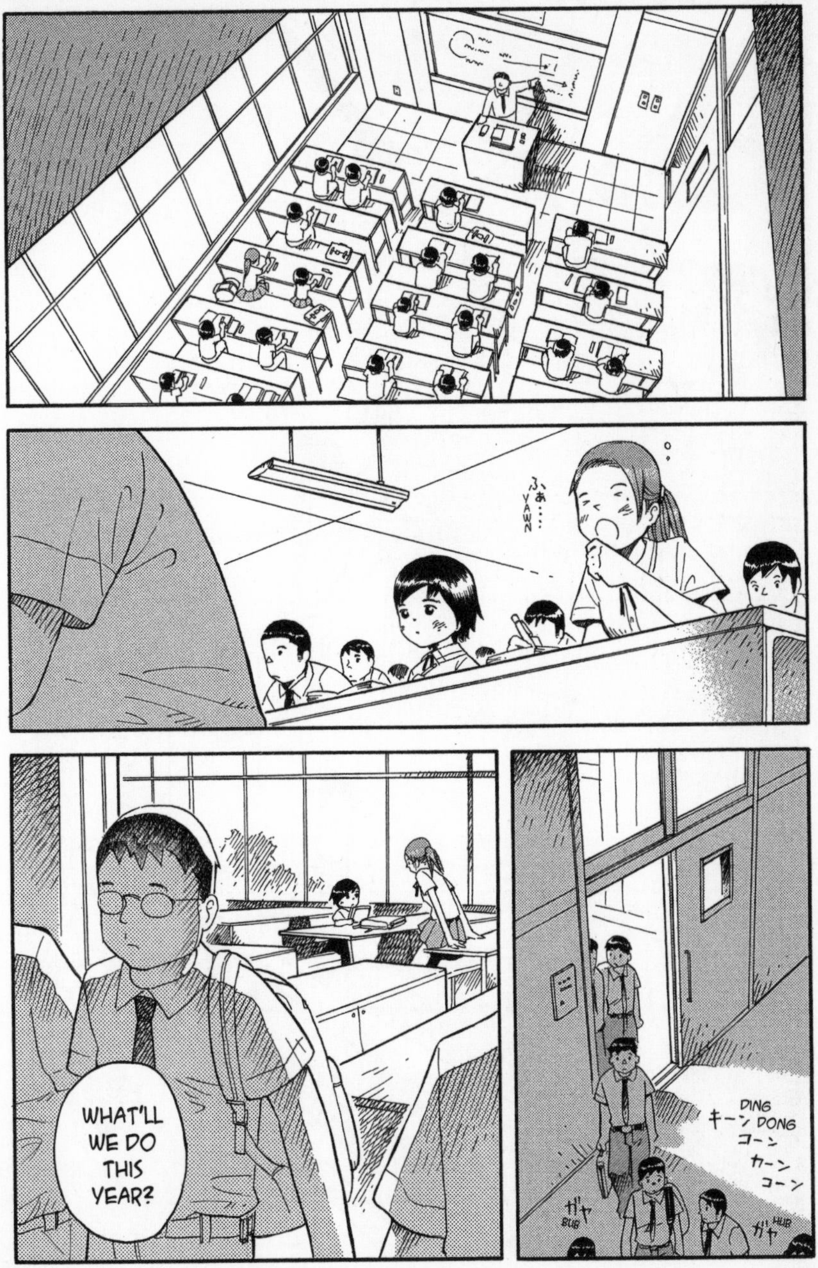
ふあ…
YAWN
キーン
DING
コーン
DONG
カーン
コーン
ガヤ
BUB
ガヤ
HUB
WHAT'LL WE DO THIS YEAR?

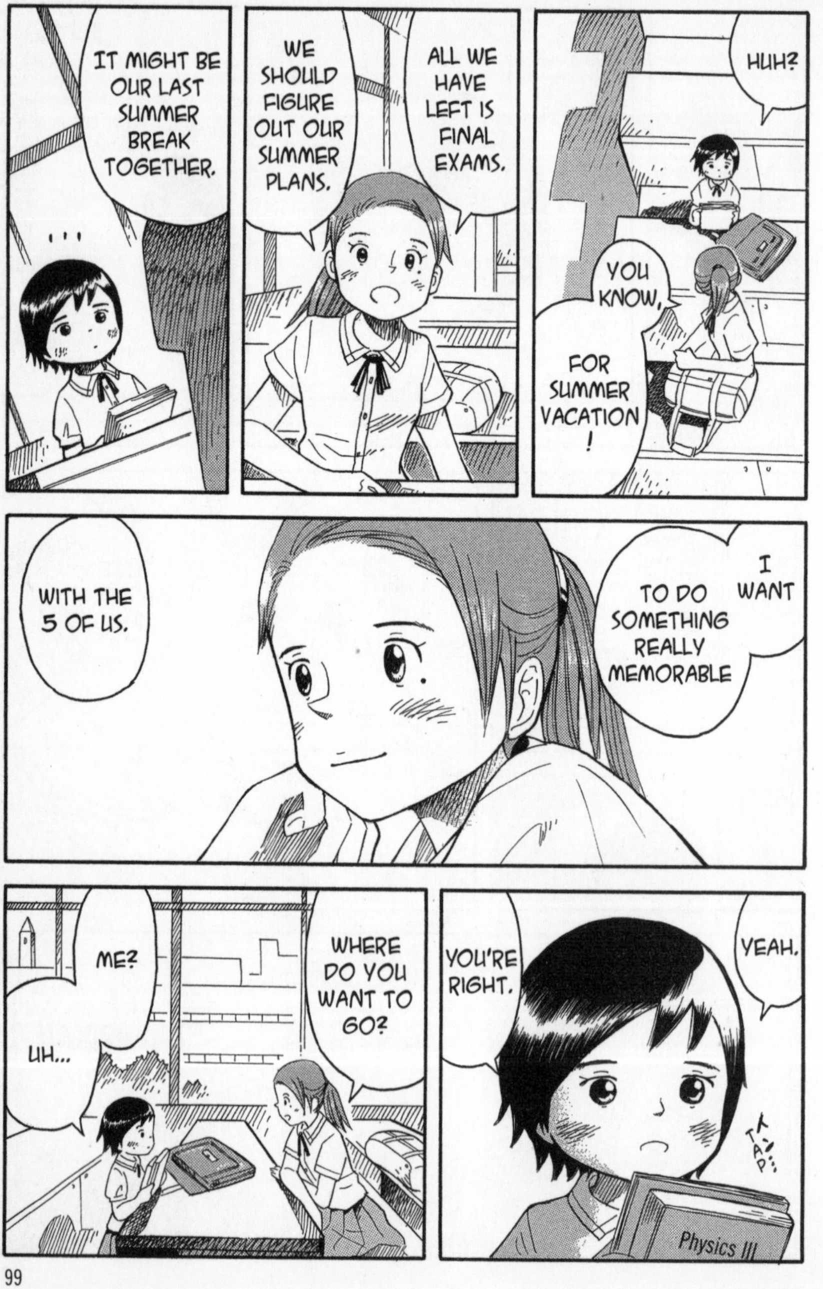
HUH?
YOU KNOW,
FOR SUMMER VACATION!
ALL WE HAVE LEFT IS FINAL EXAMS.
WE SHOULD FIGURE OUT OUR SUMMER PLANS.
IT MIGHT BE OUR LAST SUMMER BREAK TOGETHER.
...
I WANT TO DO SOMETHING REALLY MEMORABLE
WITH THE 5 OF US.
YEAH.
YOU'RE RIGHT.
TAP...
Physics III
WHERE DO YOU WANT TO GO?
ME?
UH...

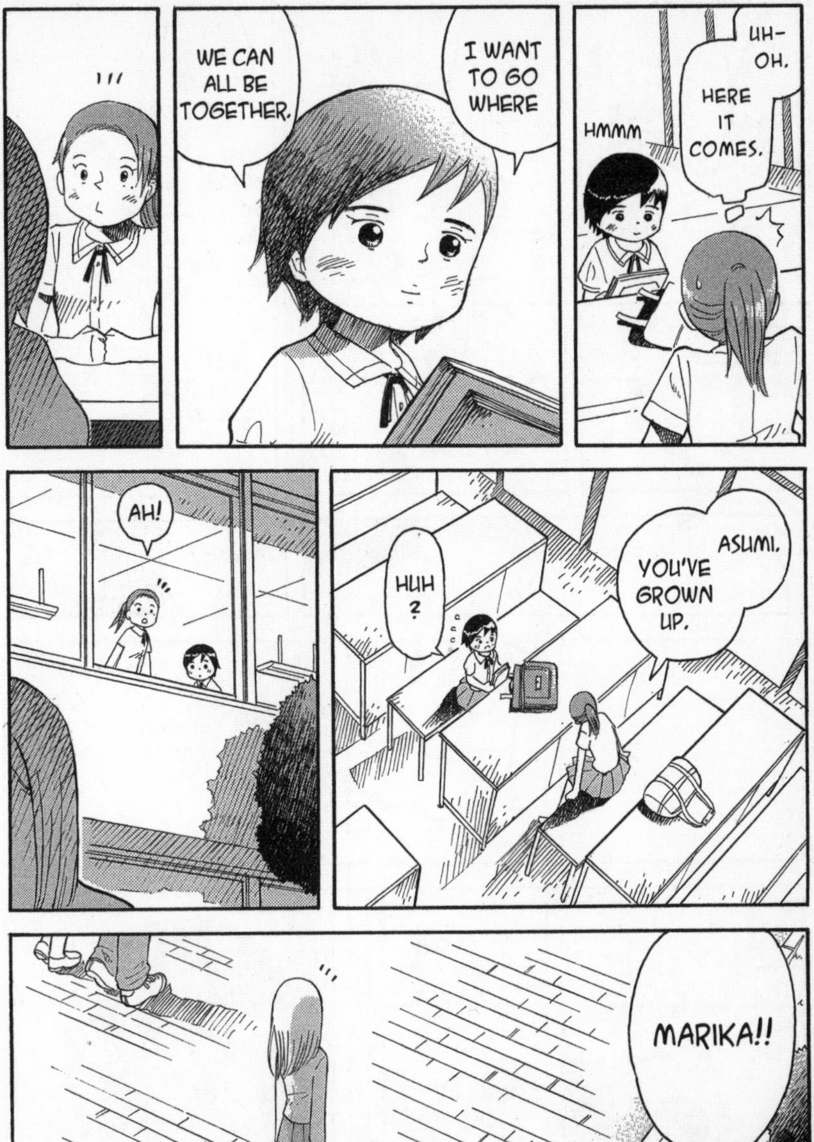
UH-OH.
HERE IT COMES.
HMMM
I WANT TO GO WHERE
WE CAN ALL BE TOGETHER.
ASUMI. YOU'VE GROWN UP.
HUH?
AH!
MARIKA!!

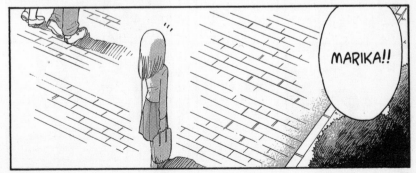

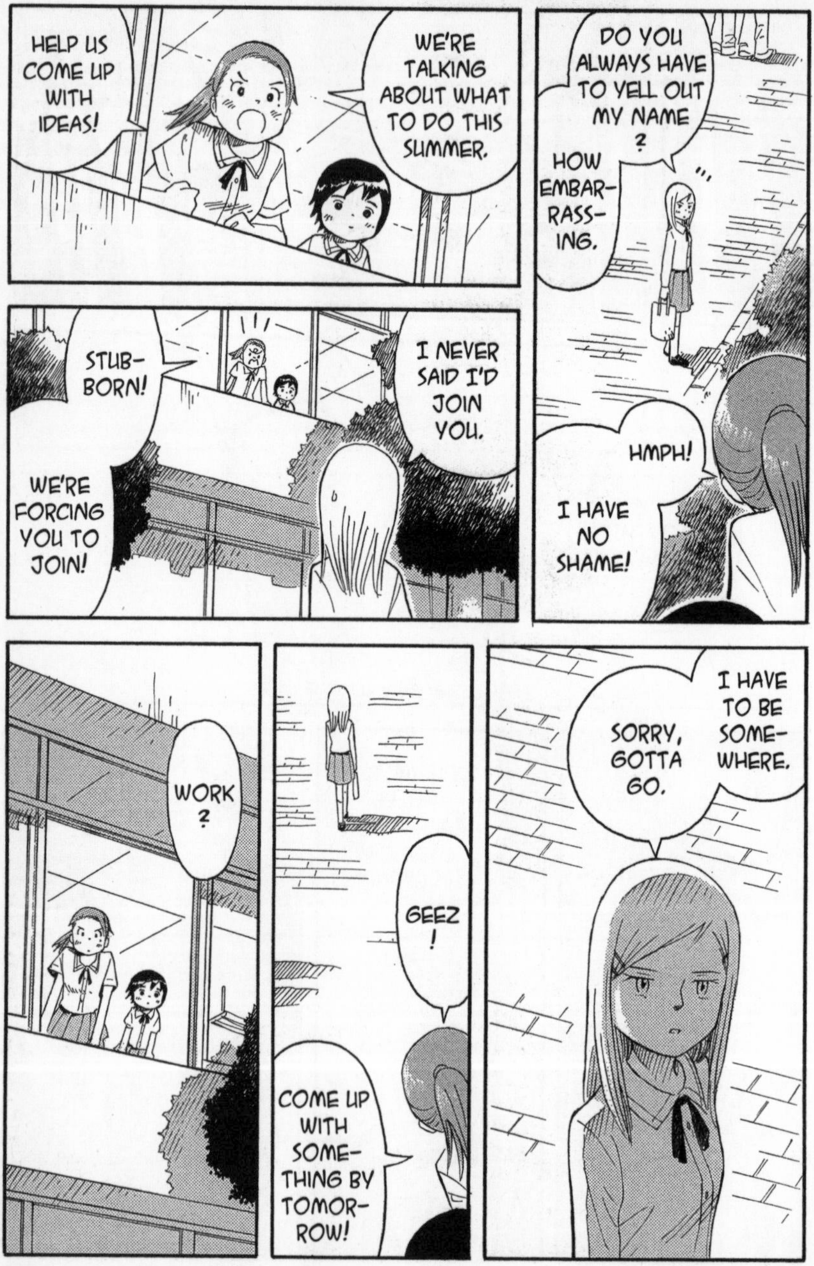
DO YOU ALWAYS HAVE TO YELL OUT MY NAME?
HOW EMBAR-RASS-ING.
HMPH!
I HAVE NO SHAME!
WE'RE TALKING ABOUT WHAT TO DO THIS SUMMER.
HELP US COME UP WITH IDEAS!
I NEVER SAID I'D JOIN YOU.
STUB-BORN!
WE'RE FORCING YOU TO JOIN!
I HAVE TO BE SOME-WHERE.
SORRY, GOTTA GO.
GEEZ!
COME UP WITH SOME-THING BY TOMOR-ROW!
WORK?

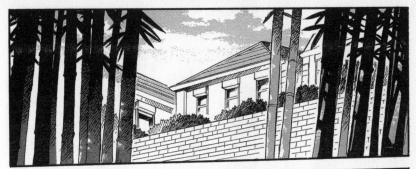

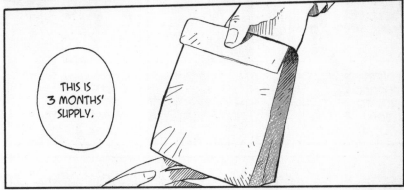

THIS IS
3 MONTHS'
SUPPLY.

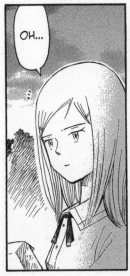

OH...

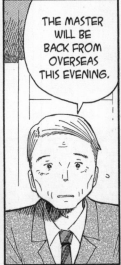

THE MASTER
WILL BE
BACK FROM
OVERSEAS
THIS EVENING.

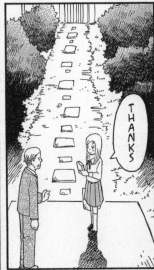

THANKS

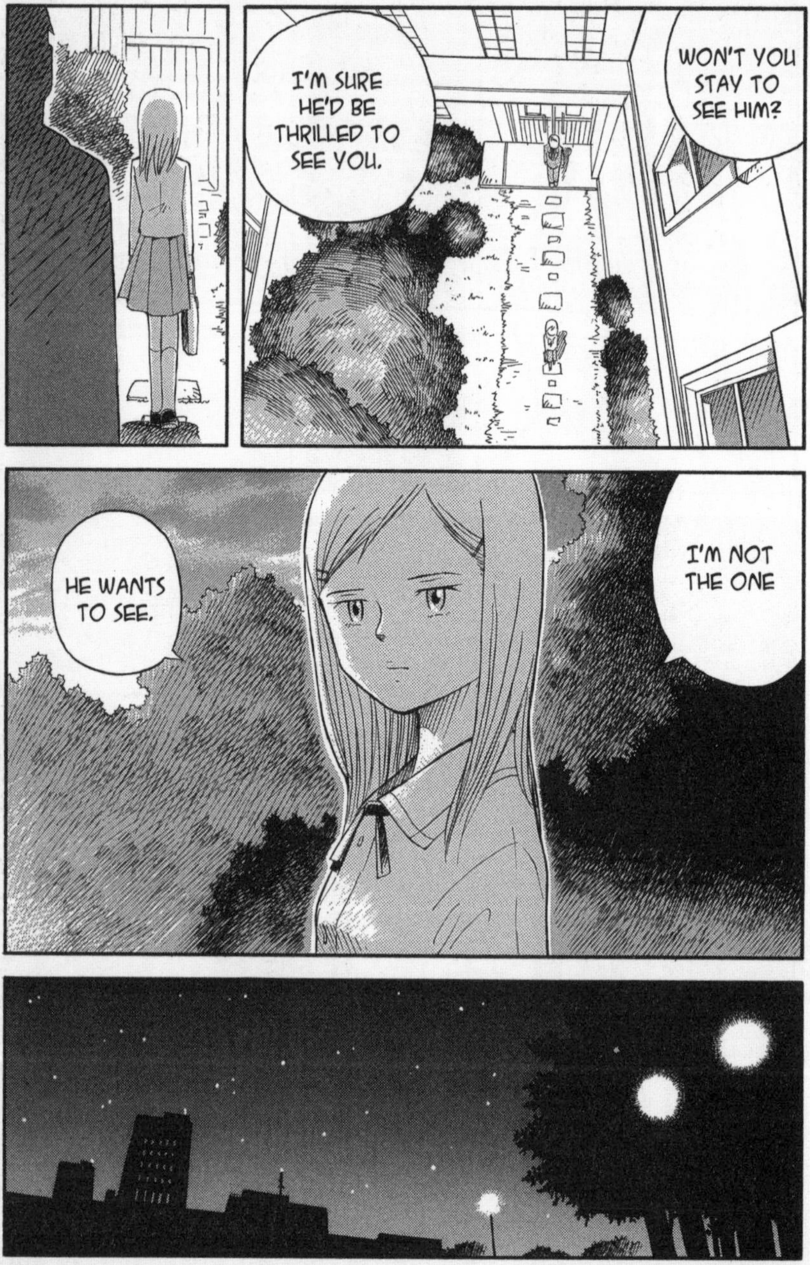
WON'T YOU STAY TO SEE HIM?
I'M SURE HE'D BE THRILLED TO SEE YOU.
I'M NOT THE ONE
HE WANTS TO SEE.

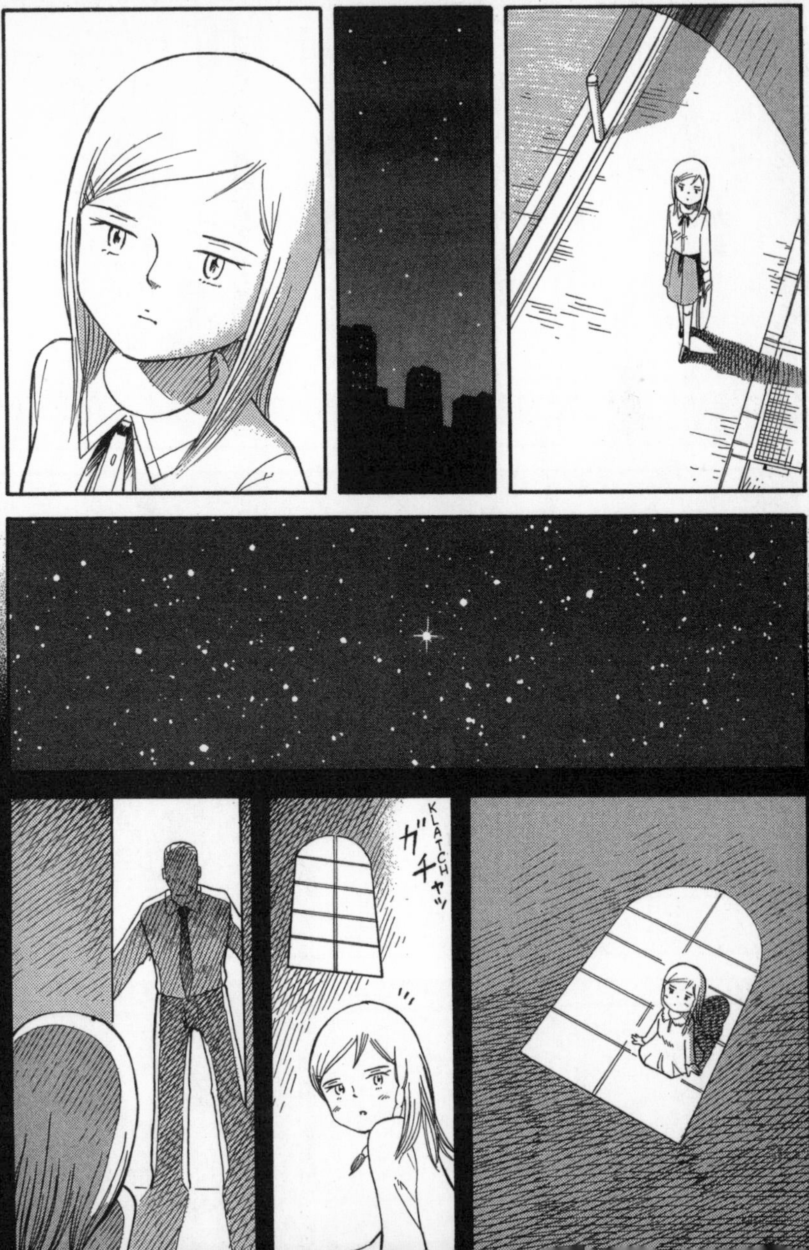
ガチャッ
KLATCH

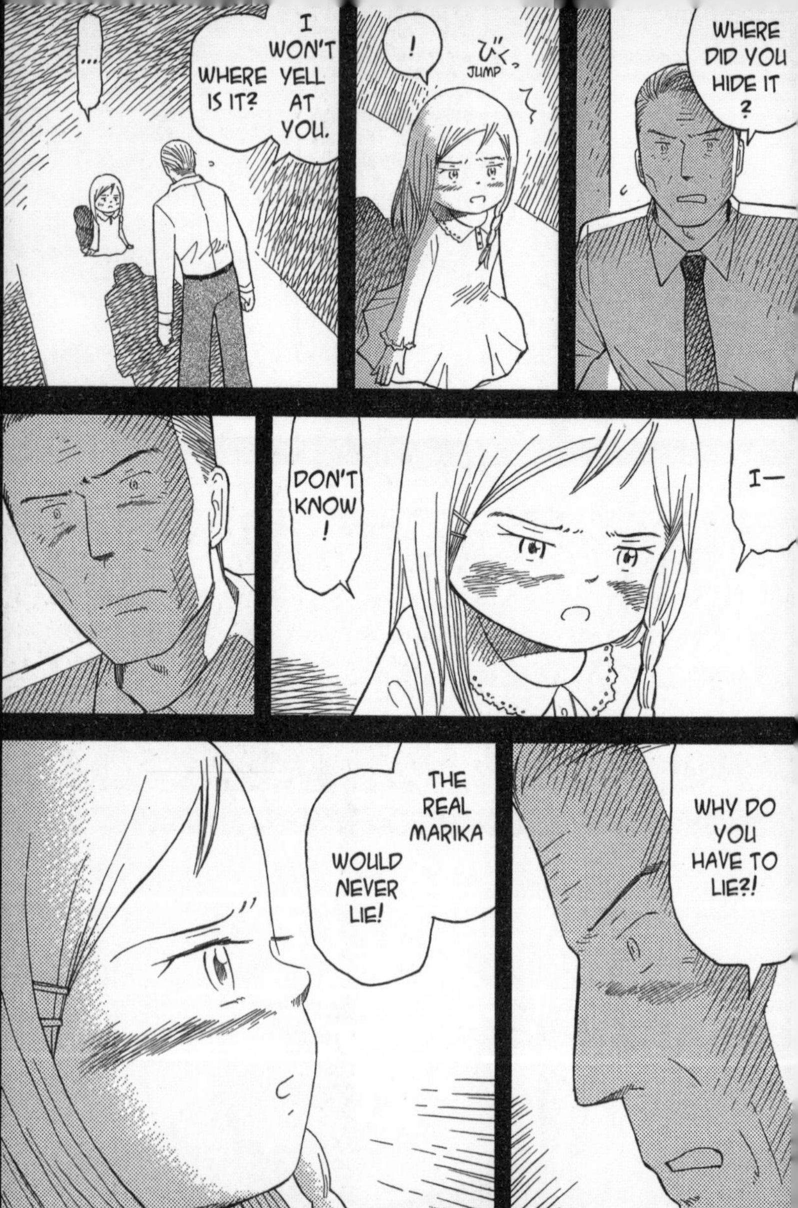
WHERE DID YOU HIDE IT?
!
びくっ
JUMP
I WON'T YELL AT YOU.
WHERE IS IT?
…
I—
DON'T KNOW!
WHY DO YOU HAVE TO LIE?!
THE REAL MARIKA
WOULD NEVER LIE!

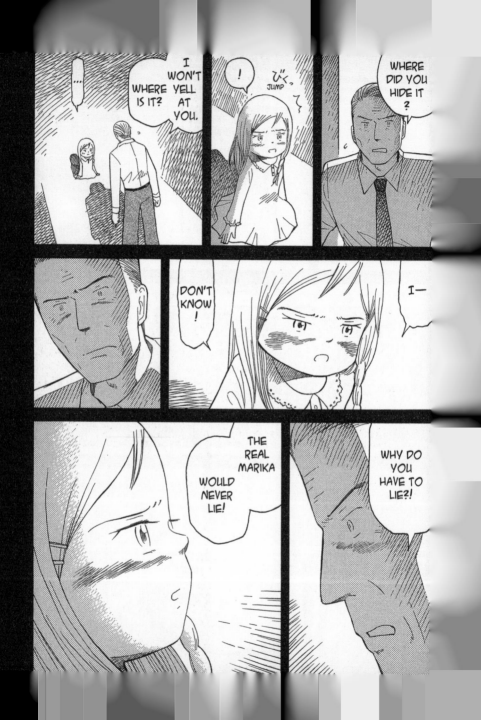

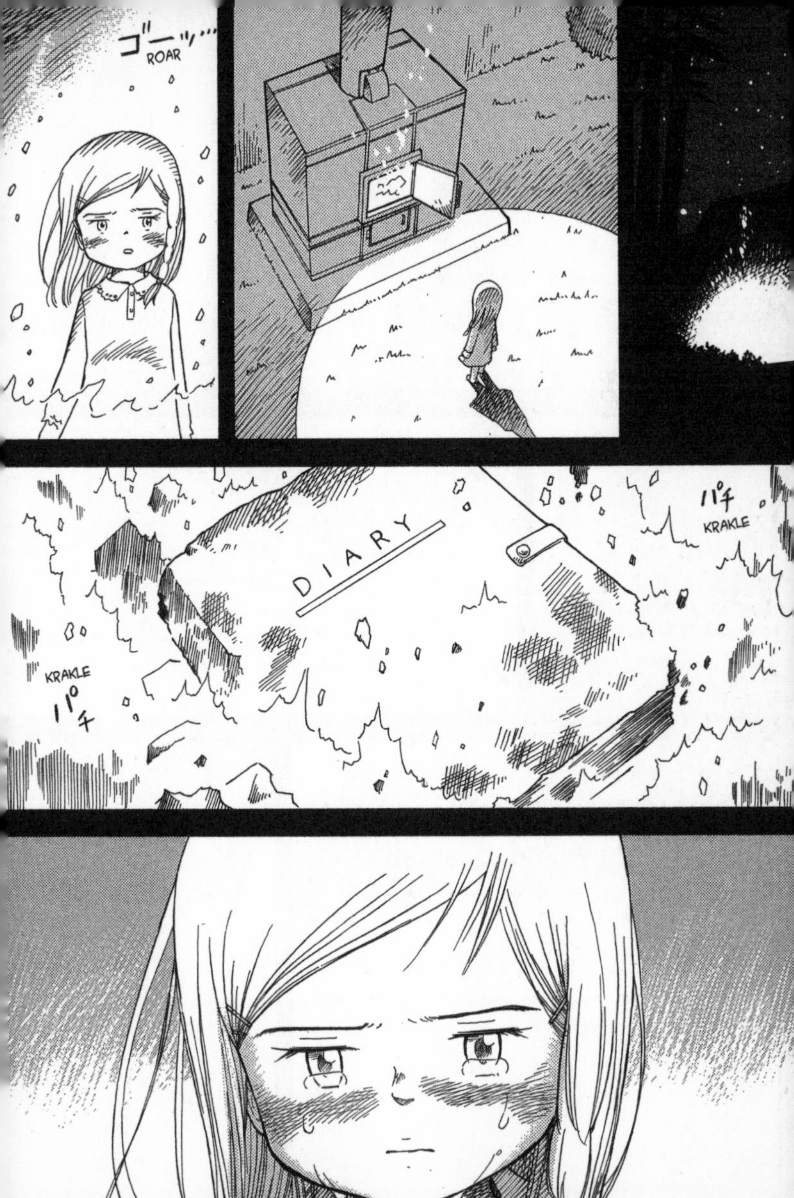
ゴーッ…
ROAR
パチ
KRAKLE
KRAKLE
パチ
DIARY

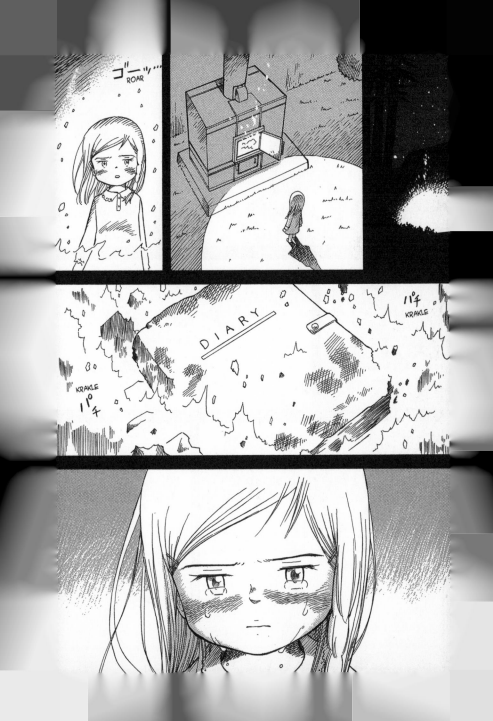

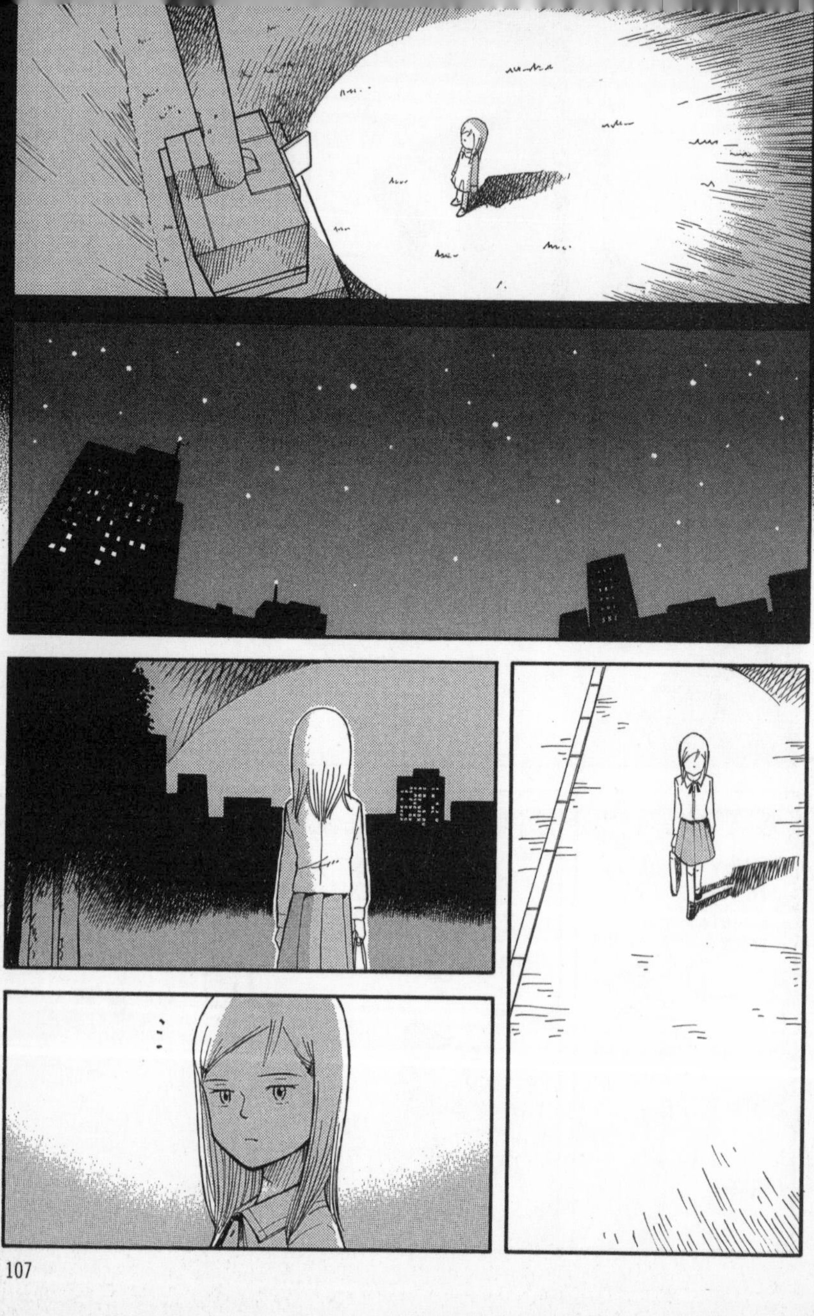

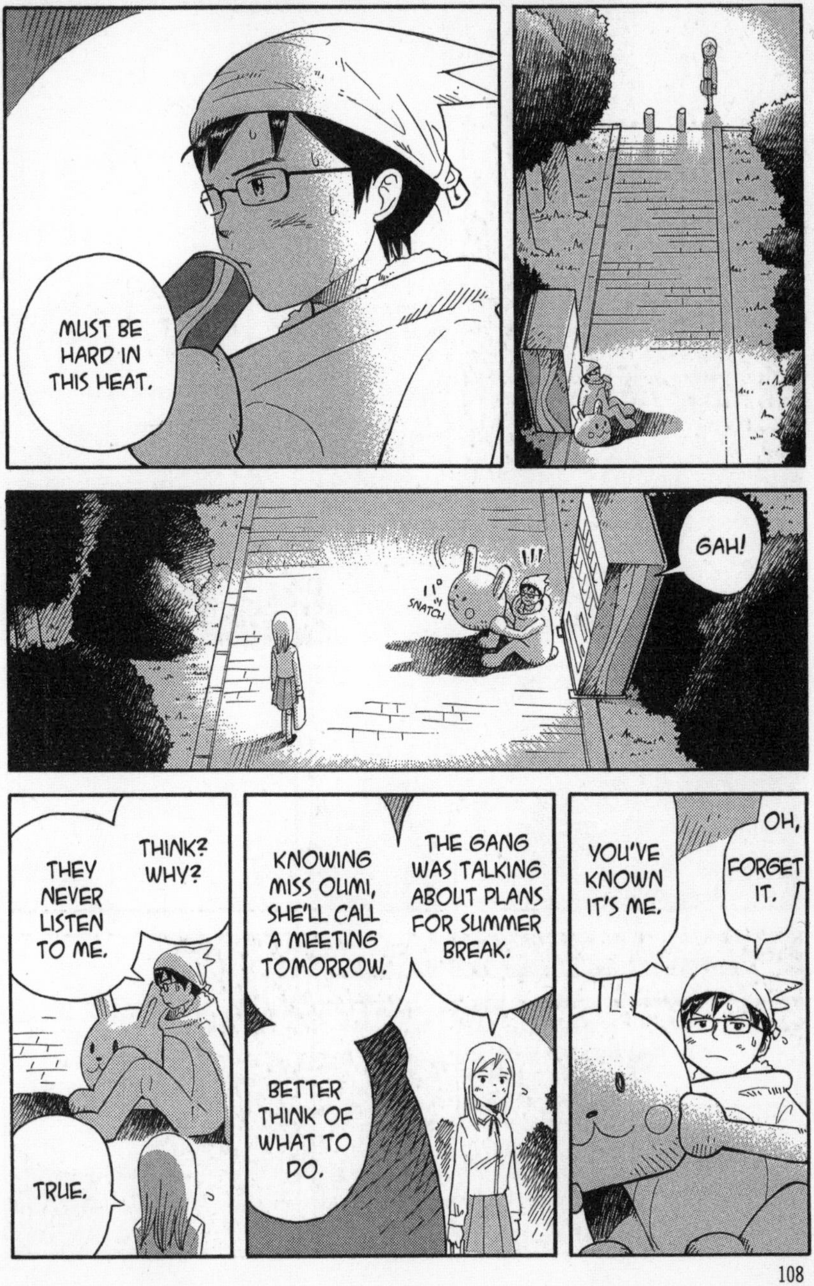
MUST BE HARD IN THIS HEAT.
GAH!
!!!
SNATCH
OH, FORGET IT.
YOU'VE KNOWN IT'S ME.
THE GANG WAS TALKING ABOUT PLANS FOR SUMMER BREAK.
KNOWING MISS OUMI, SHE'LL CALL A MEETING TOMORROW.
BETTER THINK OF WHAT TO DO.
THINK? WHY?
THEY NEVER LISTEN TO ME.
TRUE.

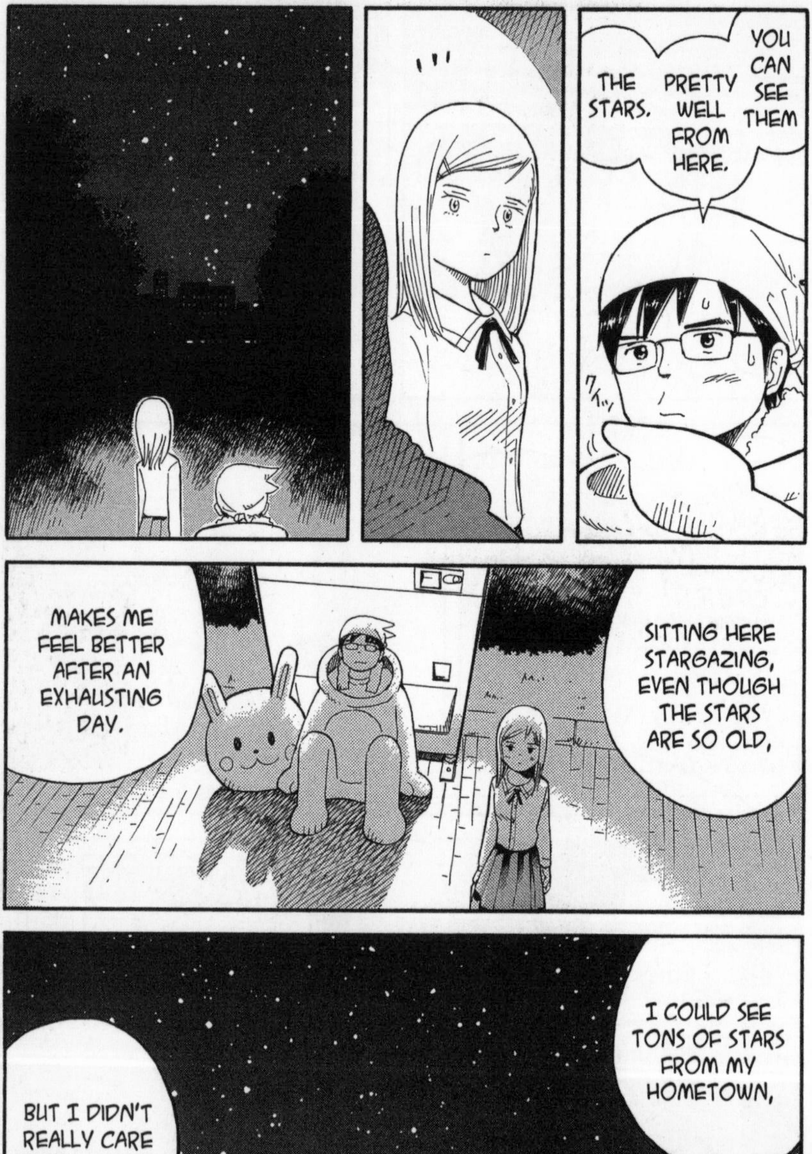
YOU CAN SEE THEM PRETTY WELL FROM HERE.
THE STARS.
SITTING HERE STARGAZING, EVEN THOUGH THE STARS ARE SO OLD,
MAKES ME FEEL BETTER AFTER AN EXHAUSTING DAY.
I COULD SEE TONS OF STARS FROM MY HOMETOWN,
BUT I DIDN'T REALLY CARE ABOUT THEM BACK THEN.

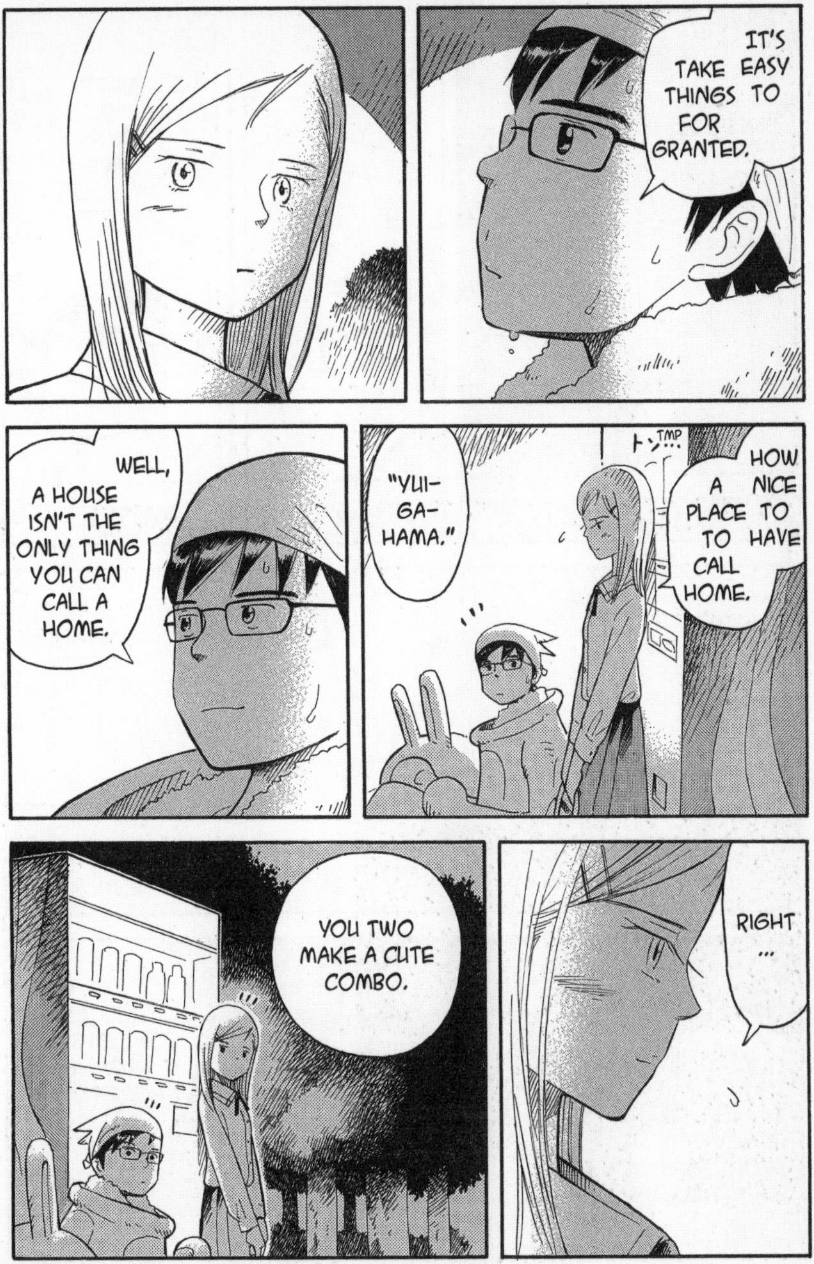
IT'S TAKE EASY THINGS TO FOR GRANTED.
トン TMP...
HOW A NICE PLACE TO TO HAVE CALL HOME.
"YUI-GA-HAMA."
WELL, A HOUSE ISN'T THE ONLY THING YOU CAN CALL A HOME.
RIGHT ...
YOU TWO MAKE A CUTE COMBO.

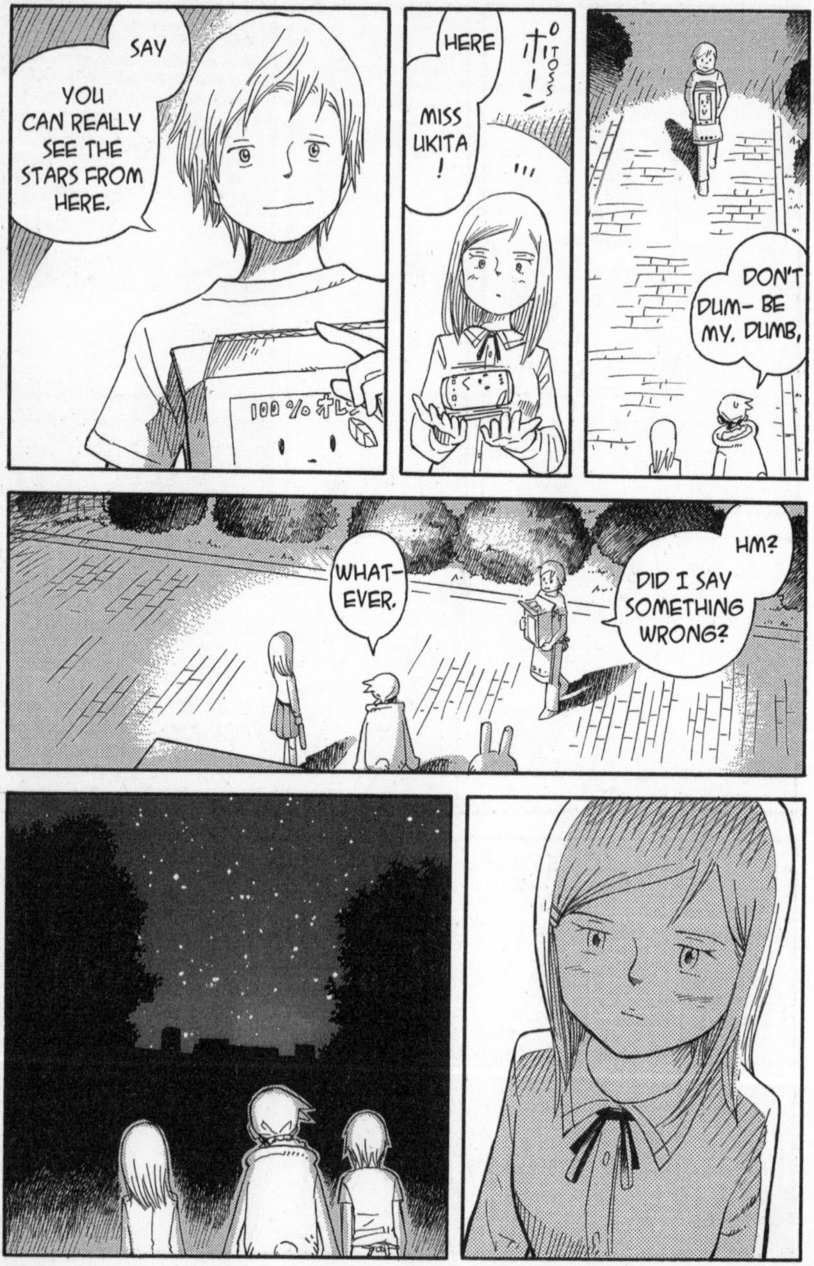
DON'T DUM- BE MY. DUMB,
HERE
MISS UKITA!
TOSS
...
SAY
YOU CAN REALLY SEE THE STARS FROM HERE.
HM?
DID I SAY SOMETHING WRONG?
WHAT-EVER.

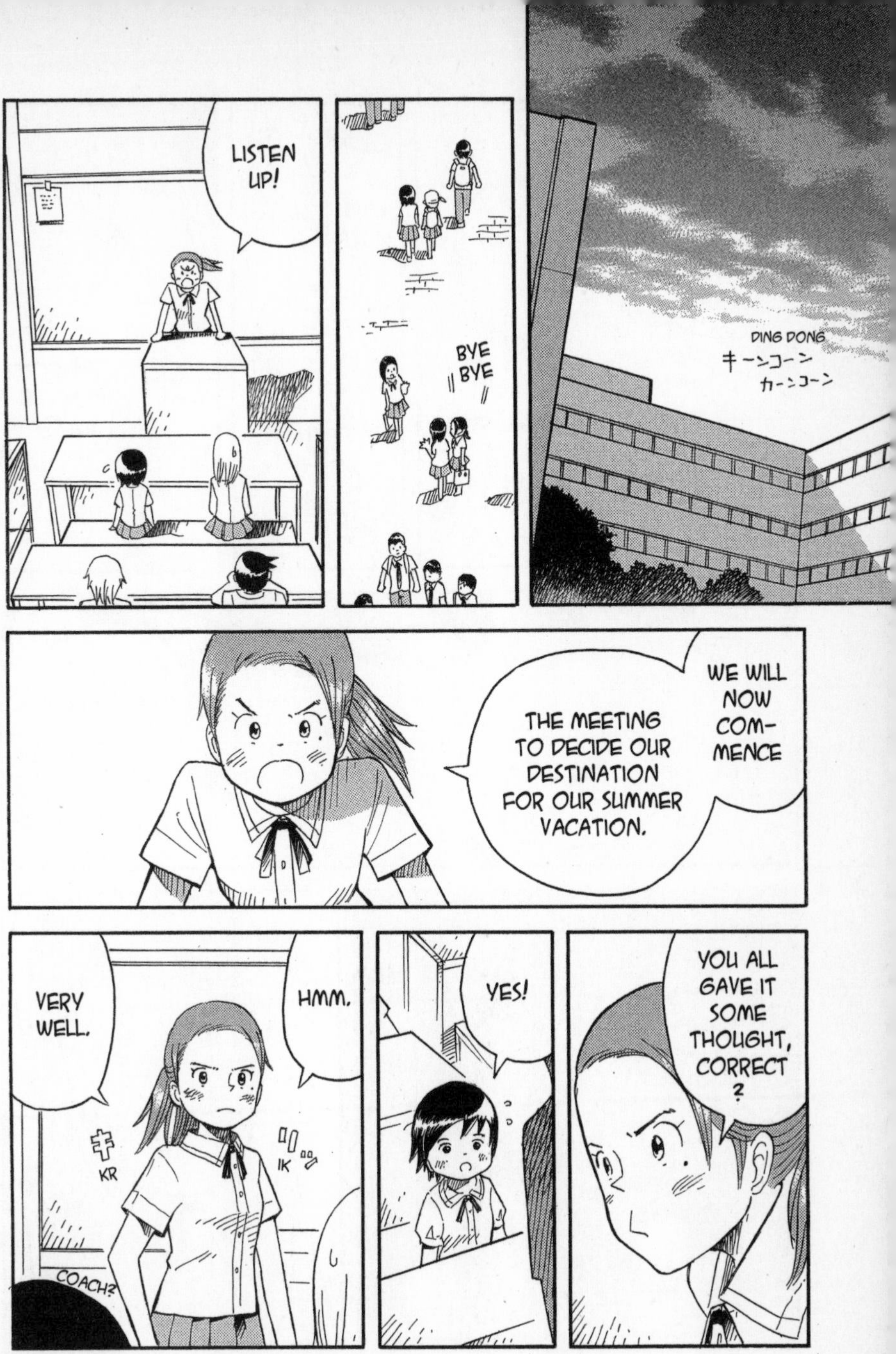
DING DONG
キーンコーン
カーンコーン
BYE BYE
LISTEN UP!
WE WILL NOW COMMENCE
THE MEETING TO DECIDE OUR DESTINATION FOR OUR SUMMER VACATION.
YOU ALL GAVE IT SOME THOUGHT, CORRECT?
YES!
HMM.
VERY WELL.
キ
KR
IK
COACH?

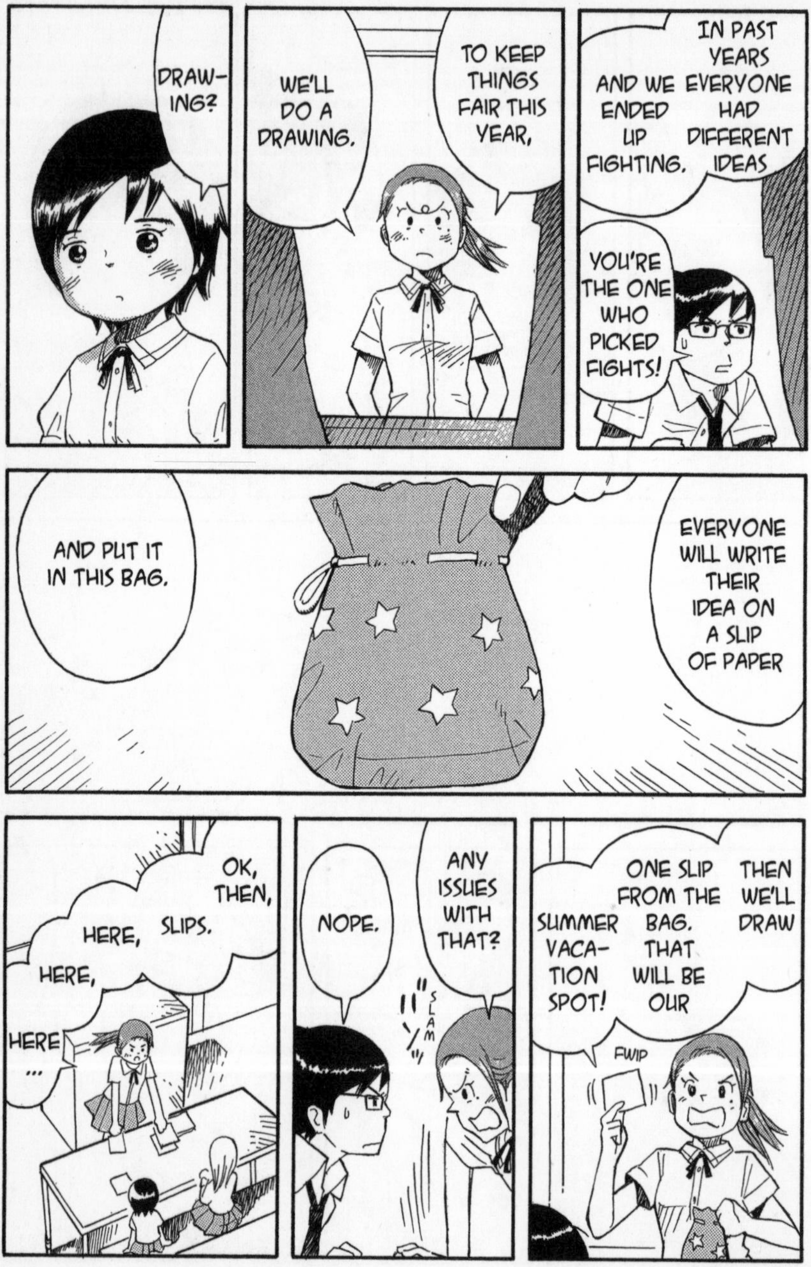
IN PAST YEARS EVERYONE HAD DIFFERENT IDEAS
AND WE ENDED UP FIGHTING.
YOU'RE THE ONE WHO PICKED FIGHTS!
TO KEEP THINGS FAIR THIS YEAR,
WE'LL DO A DRAWING.
DRAWING?
EVERYONE WILL WRITE THEIR IDEA ON A SLIP OF PAPER
AND PUT IT IN THIS BAG.
THEN WE'LL DRAW ONE SLIP FROM THE BAG. THAT WILL BE OUR SUMMER VACATION SPOT!
FWIP
ANY ISSUES WITH THAT?
SLAM
NOPE.
OK, THEN, SLIPS.
HERE,
HERE,
HERE ...

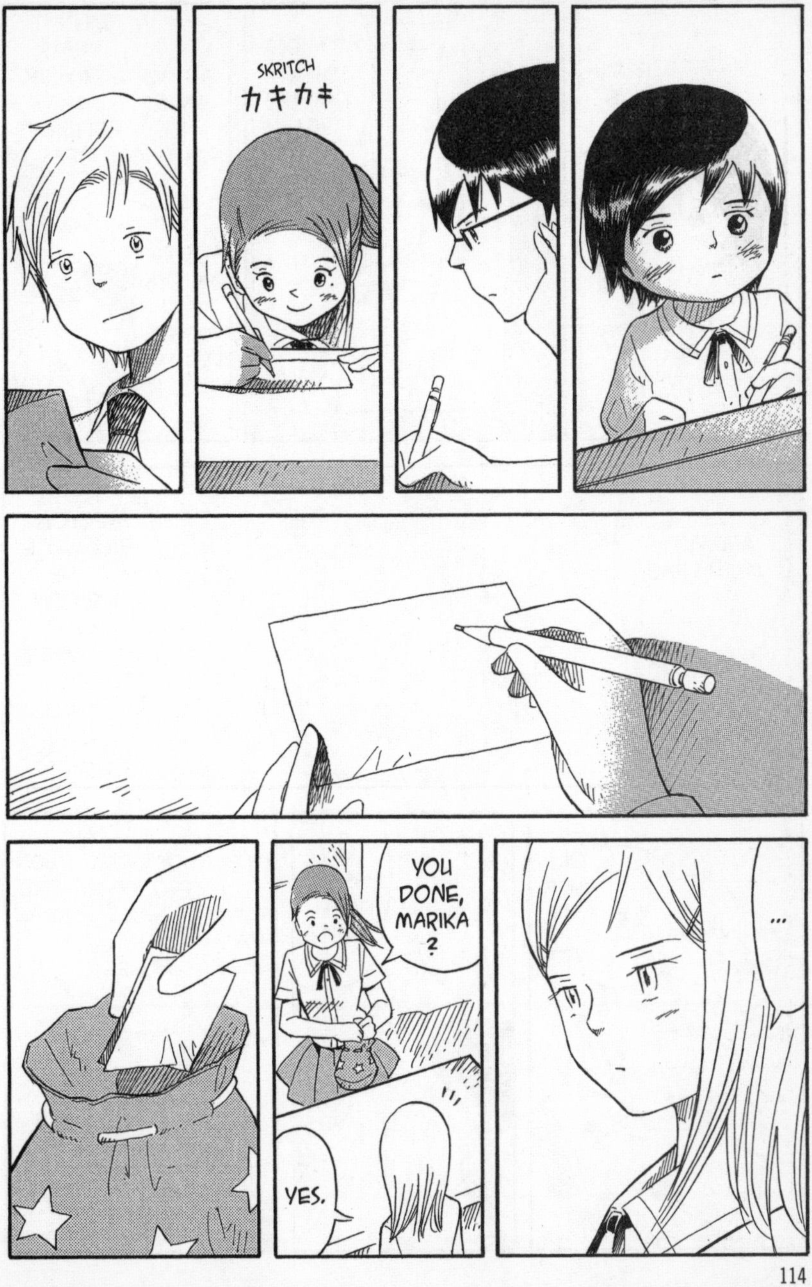
SKRITCH
カキカキ
...
YOU DONE, MARIKA?
YES.

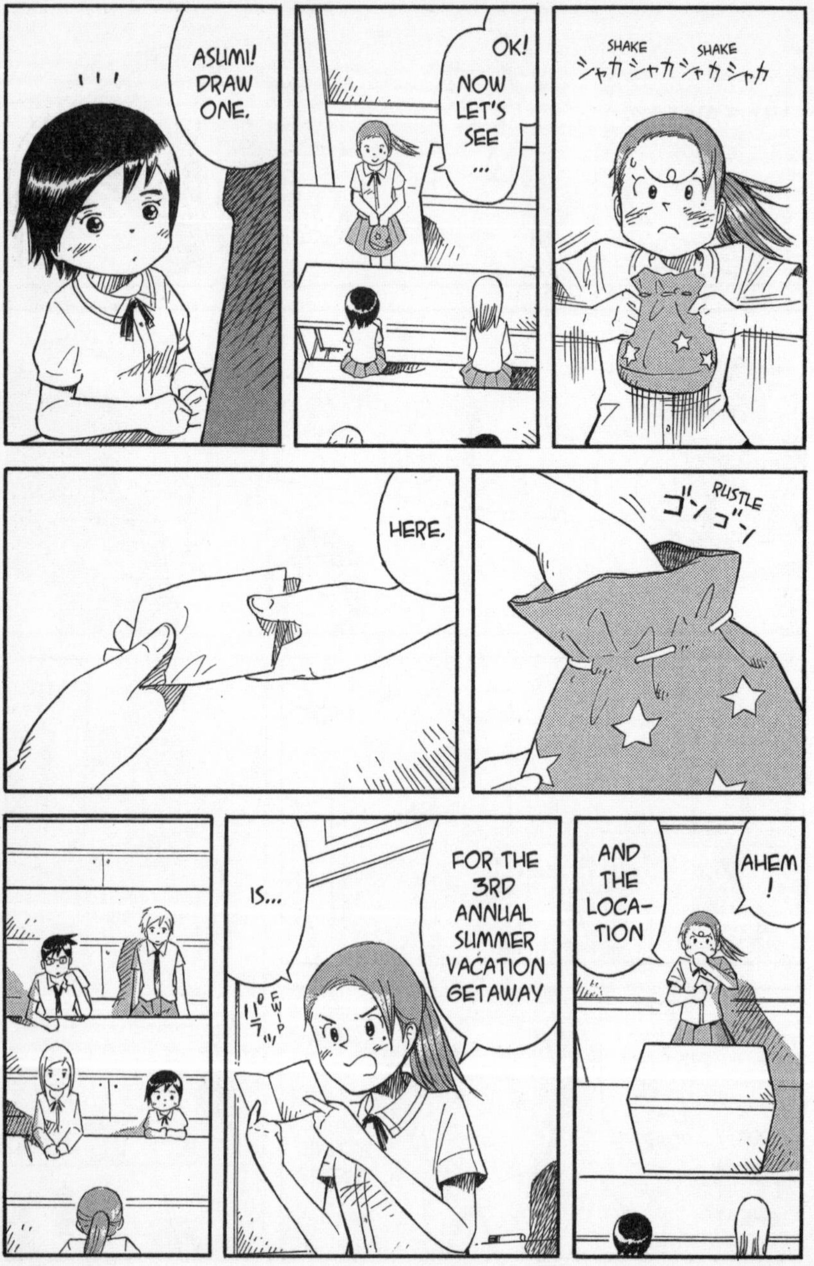
SHAKE SHAKE
シャカシャカシャカシャカ
OK! NOW LET'S SEE ...
ASUMI! DRAW ONE.
RUSTLE
ゴソゴソ
HERE.
AHEM !
AND THE LOCA-TION
FOR THE 3RD ANNUAL SUMMER VACATION GETAWAY
IS...
FWIP
パラッ

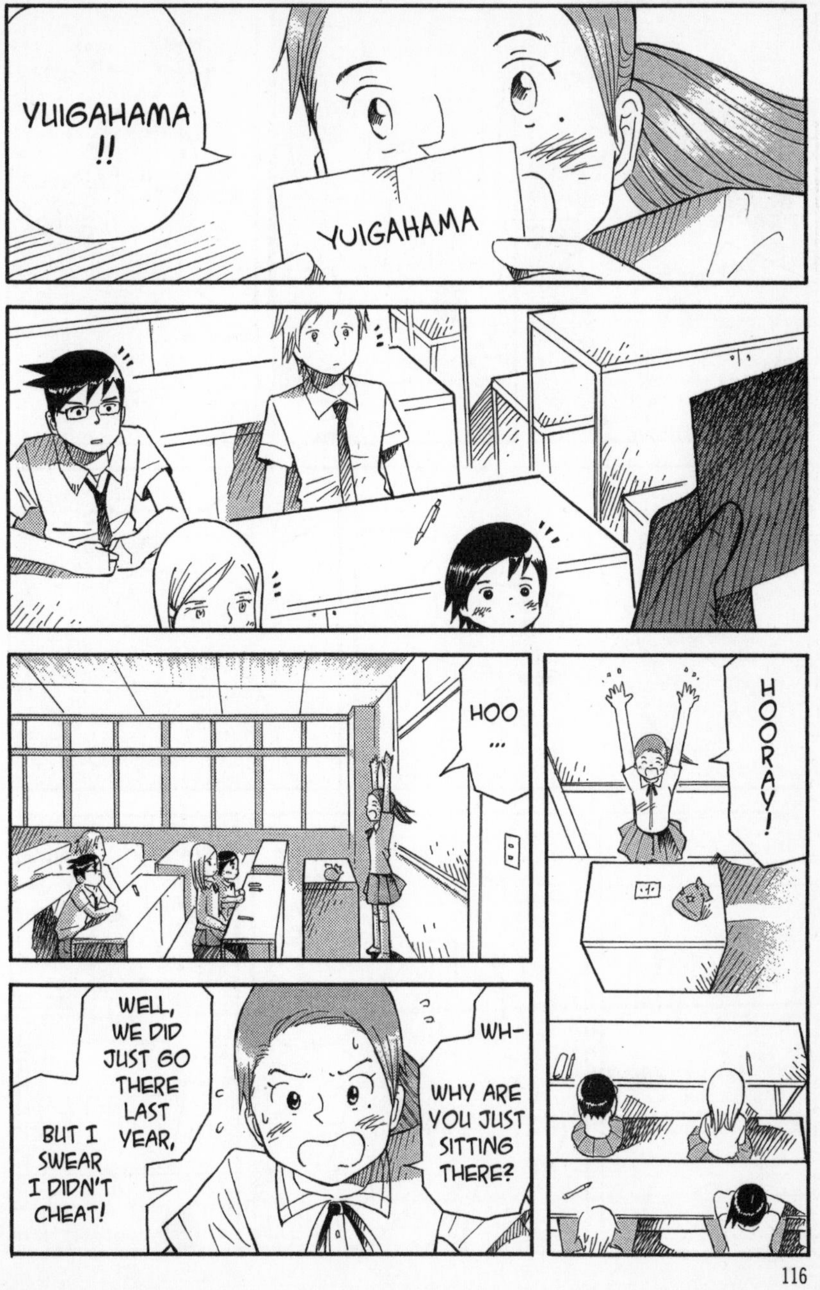
YUIGAHAMA
YUIGAHAMA !!
HOORAY!
HOO ...
WH- WHY ARE YOU JUST SITTING THERE?
WELL, WE DID JUST GO THERE LAST YEAR,
BUT I SWEAR I DIDN'T CHEAT!

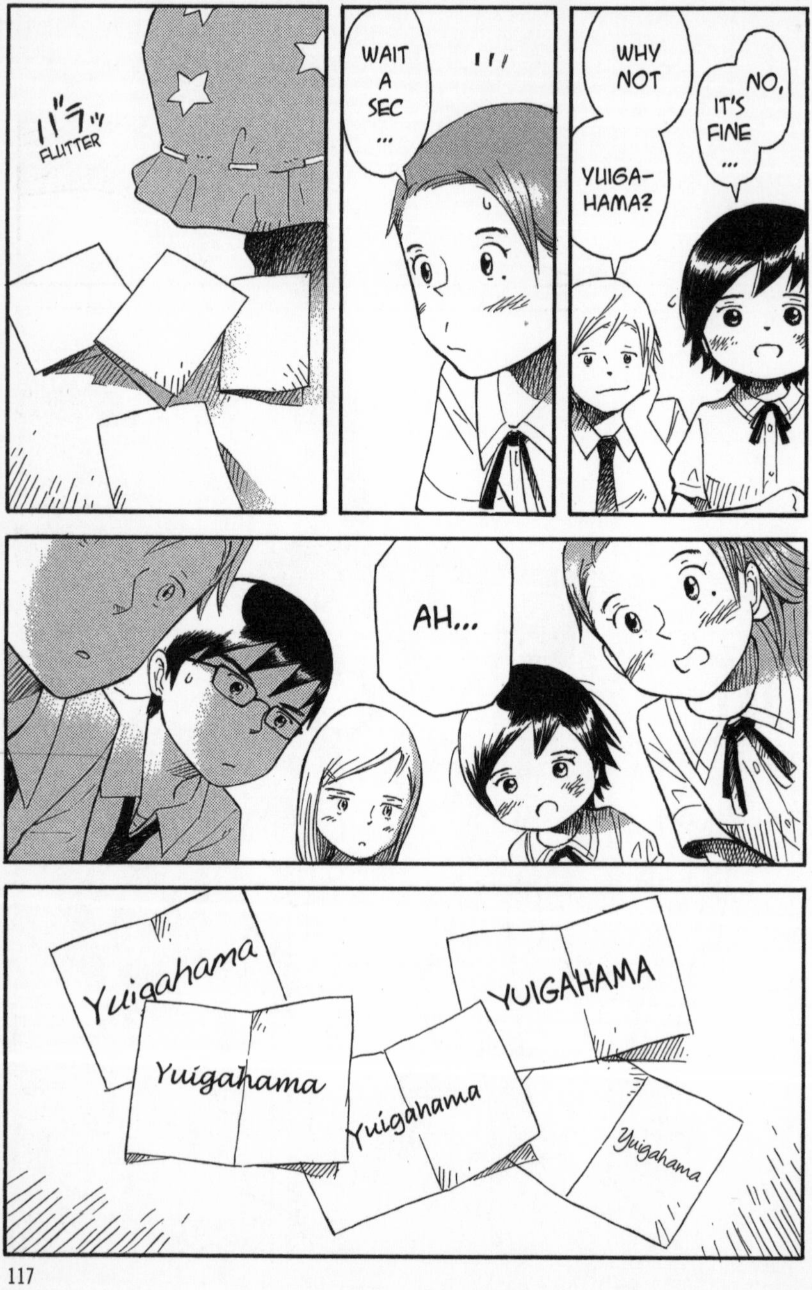
NO, IT'S FINE ...
WHY NOT YUIGA-HAMA?
WAIT A SEC ...
バラッ
FLUTTER
AH...
YUIGAHAMA
Yuigahama
Yuigahama
Yuigahama
Yuigahama
Yuigahama

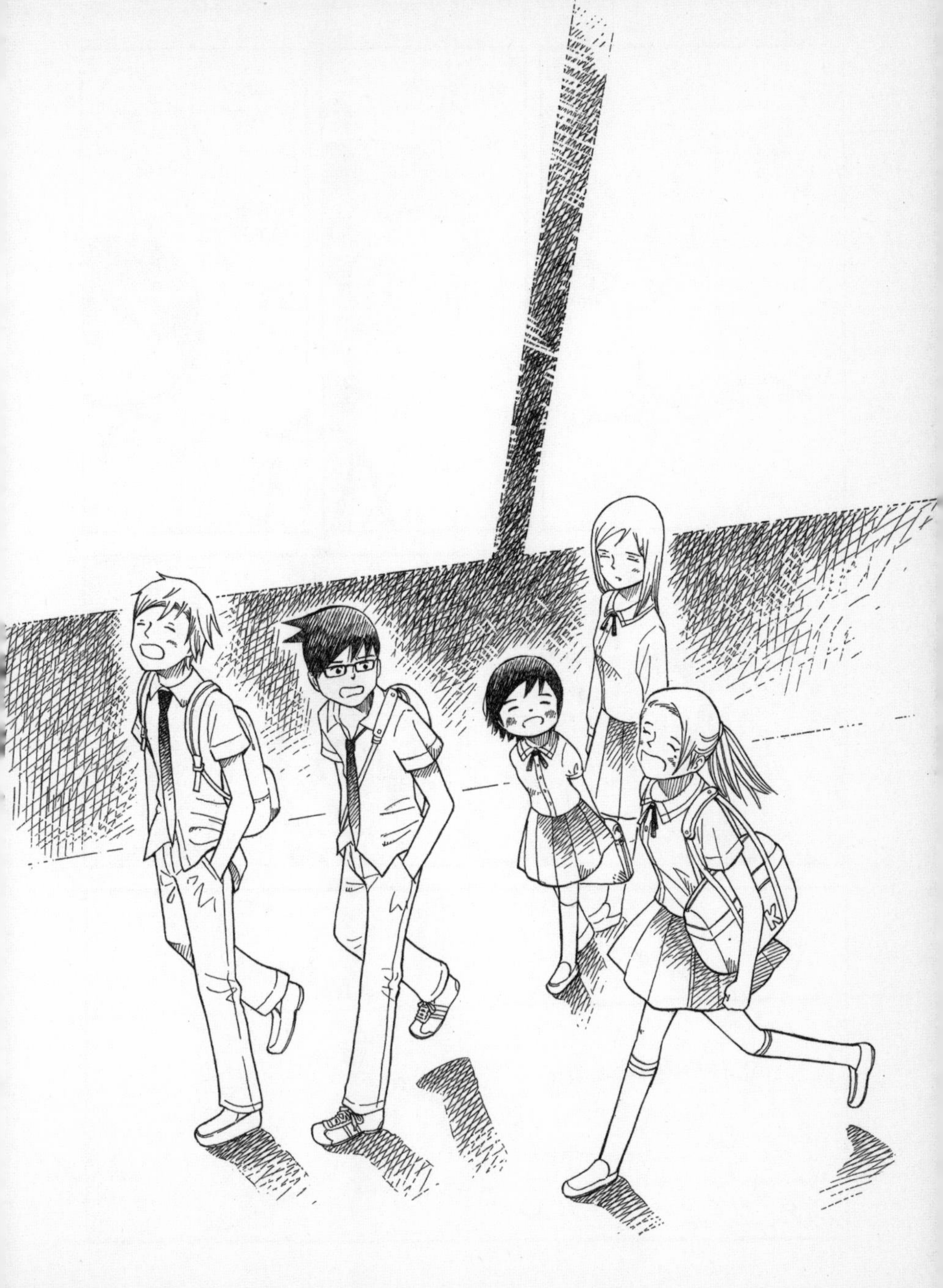

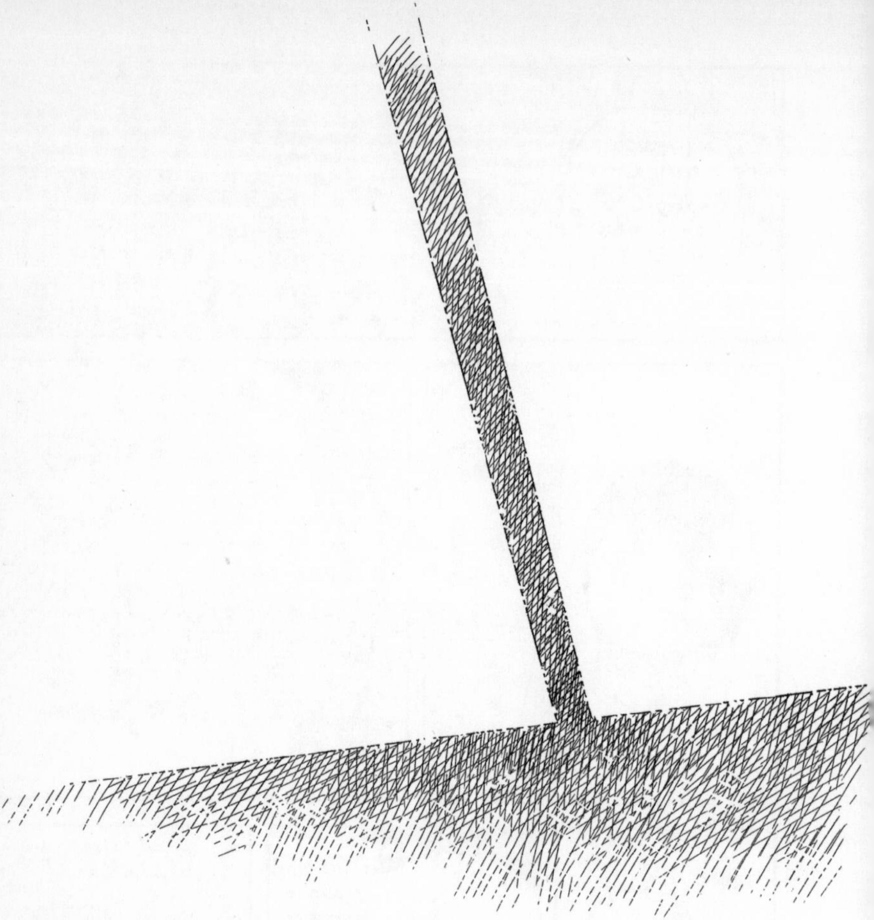

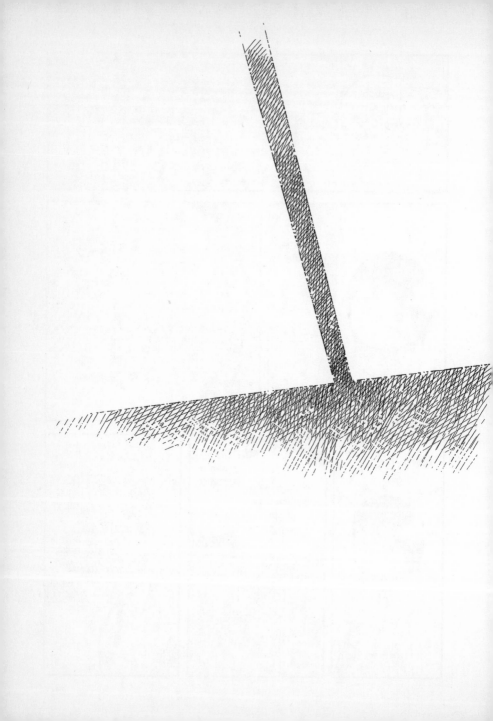

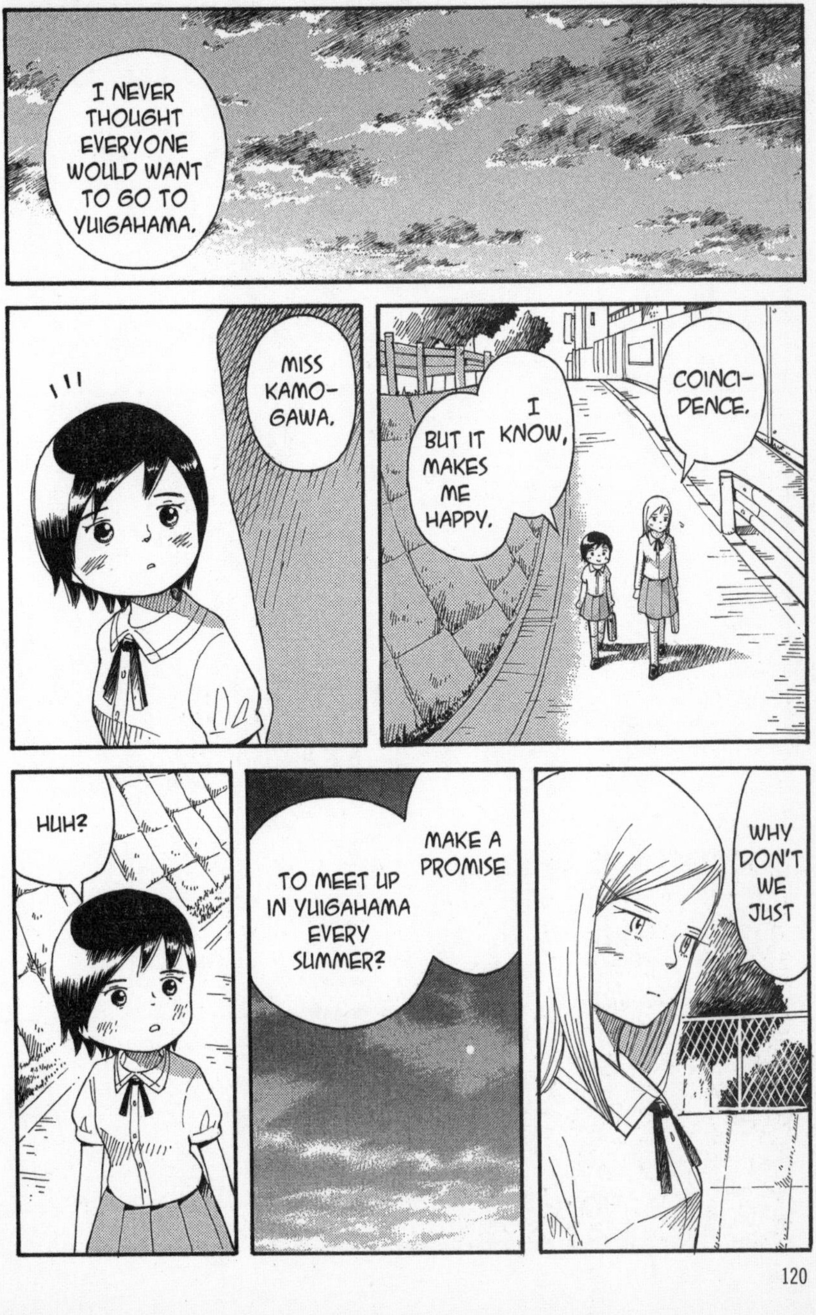
I NEVER THOUGHT EVERYONE WOULD WANT TO GO TO YUIGAHAMA.
COINCI-DENCE.
I KNOW, BUT IT MAKES ME HAPPY.
MISS KAMO-GAWA.
WHY DON'T WE JUST
MAKE A PROMISE
TO MEET UP IN YUIGAHAMA EVERY SUMMER?
HUH?

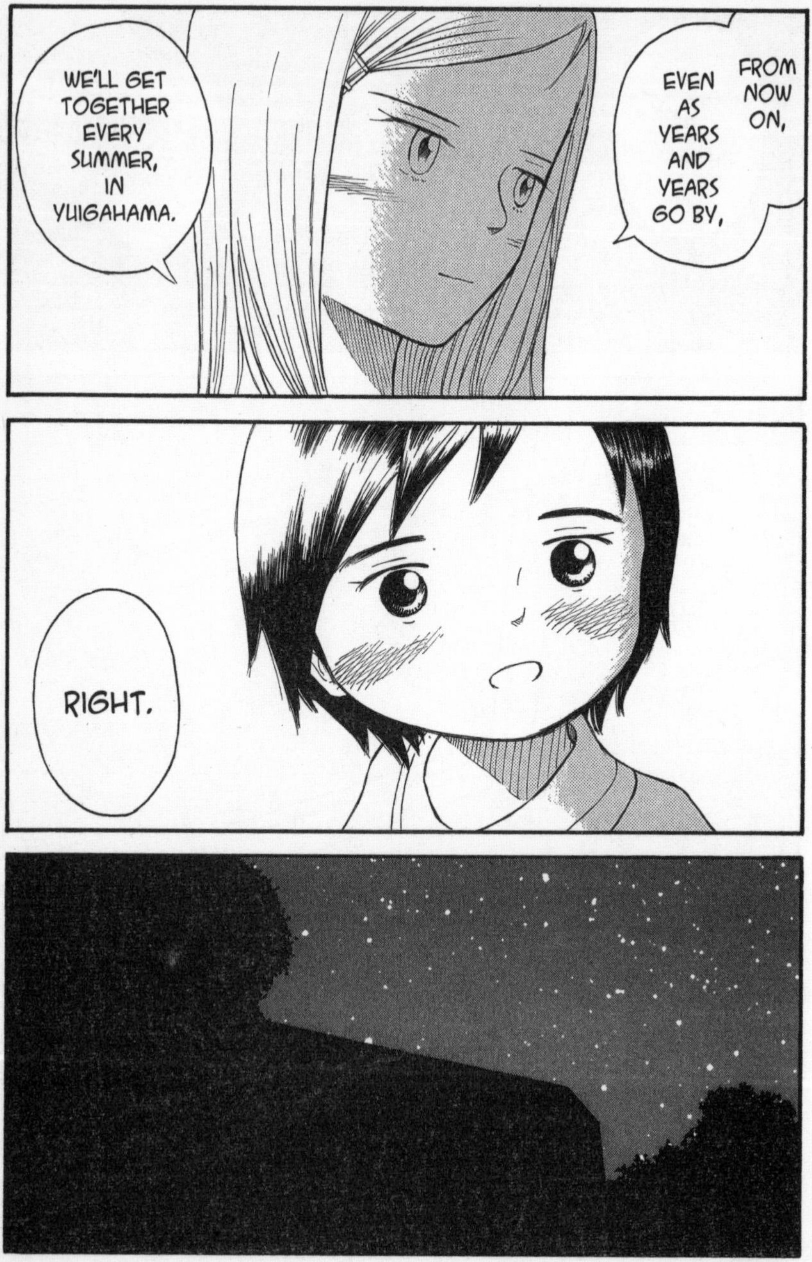
FROM NOW ON, EVEN AS YEARS AND YEARS GO BY,
WE'LL GET TOGETHER EVERY SUMMER, IN YUIGAHAMA.
RIGHT.

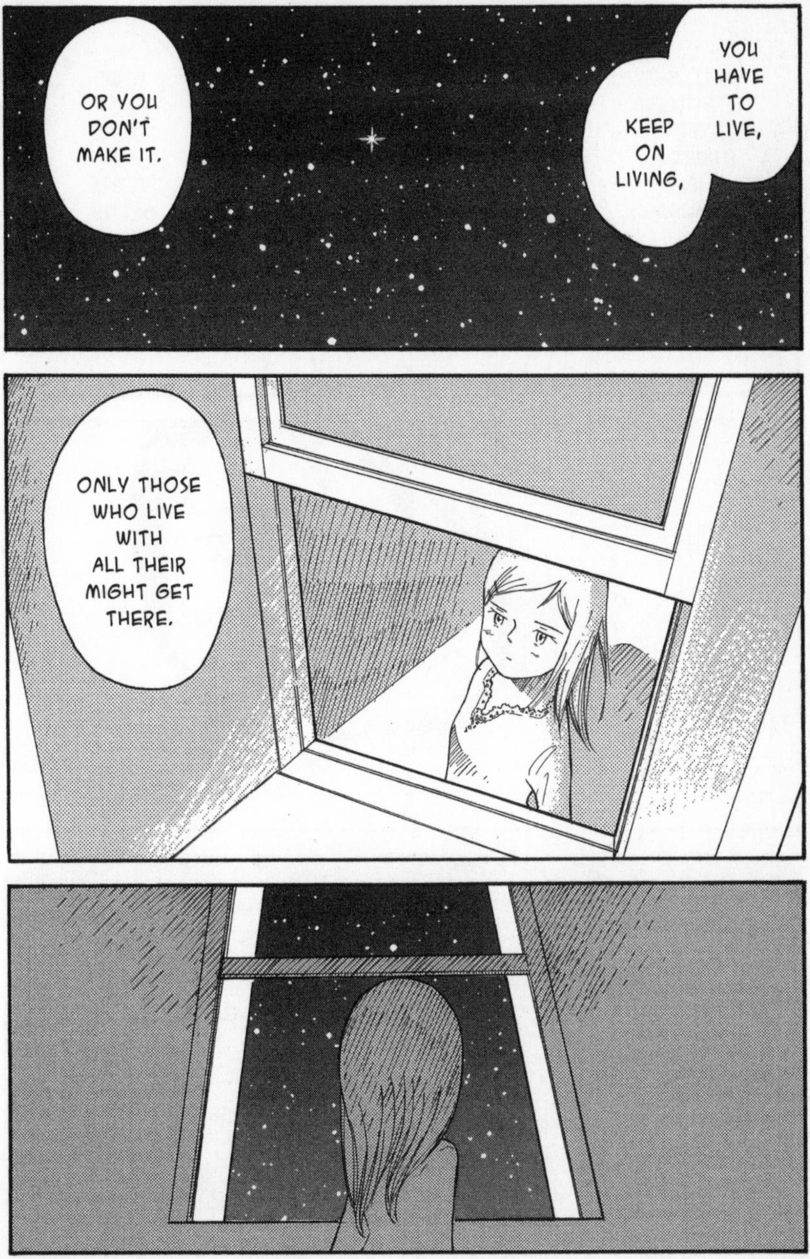
YOU HAVE TO LIVE, KEEP ON LIVING,
OR YOU DON'T MAKE IT.
ONLY THOSE WHO LIVE WITH ALL THEIR MIGHT GET THERE.

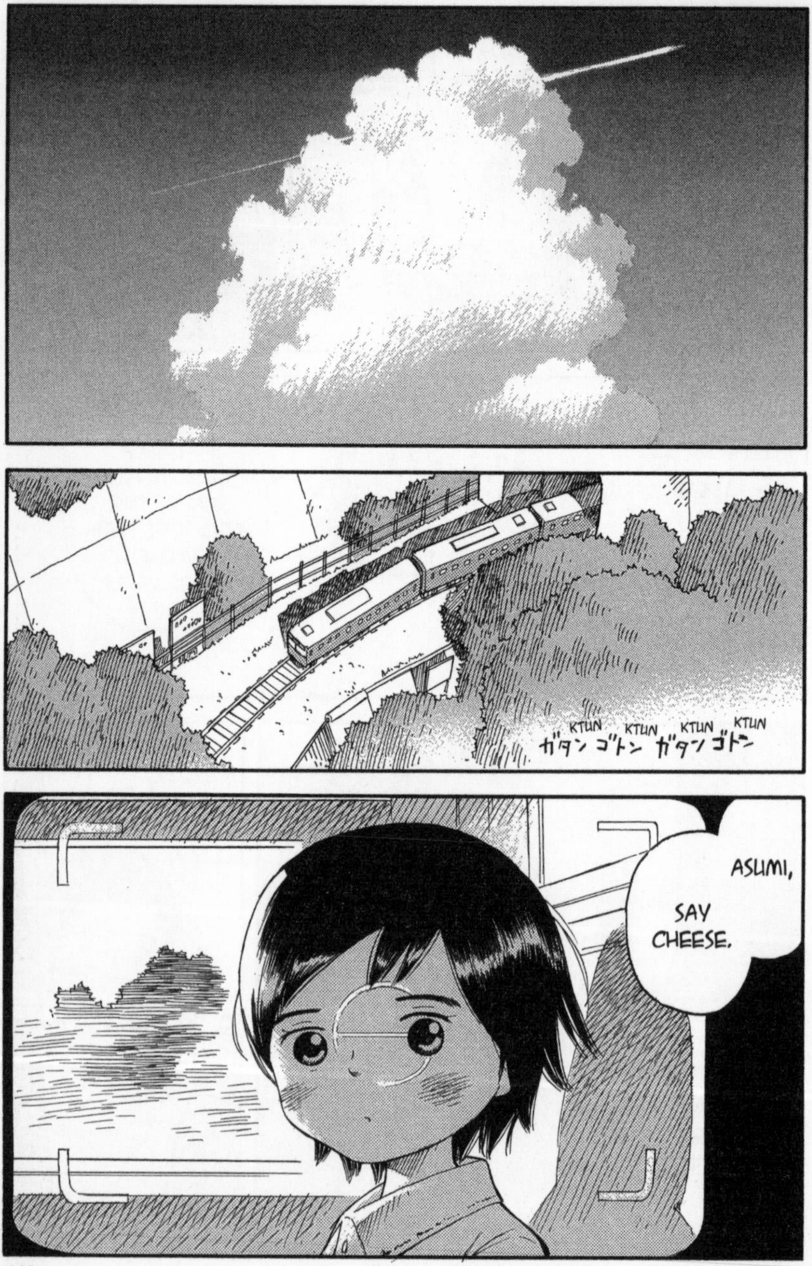
KTUN KTUN KTUN KTUN
ガタン ゴトン ガタン ゴトン
ASUMI,
SAY CHEESE.

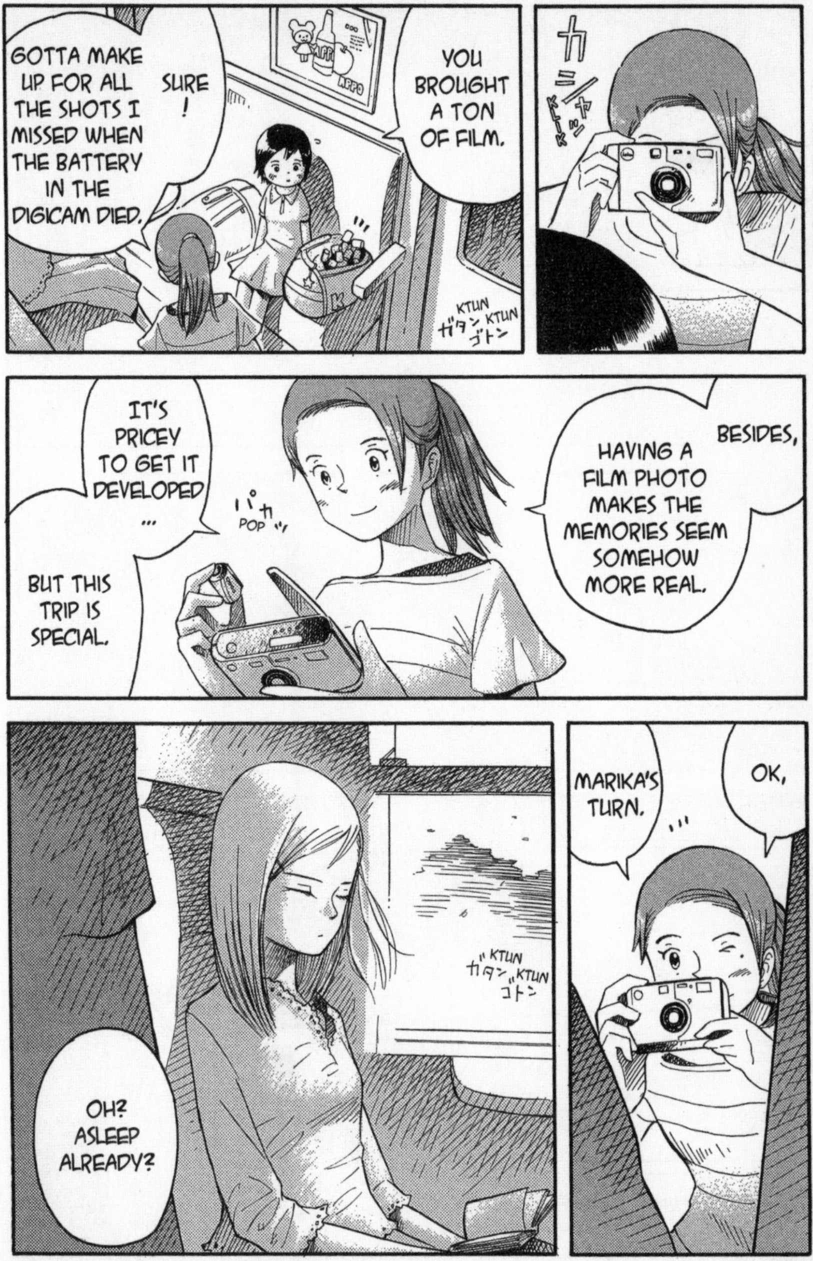
カシャッ
KLIK
YOU BROUGHT A TON OF FILM.
SURE!
GOTTA MAKE UP FOR ALL THE SHOTS I MISSED WHEN THE BATTERY IN THE DIGICAM DIED.
ガタン KTUN
ゴトン KTUN
BESIDES,
HAVING A FILM PHOTO MAKES THE MEMORIES SEEM SOMEHOW MORE REAL.
IT'S PRICEY TO GET IT DEVELOPED...
パカッ
POP
BUT THIS TRIP IS SPECIAL.
OK,
MARIKA'S TURN.
...
ガタン KTUN
ゴトン KTUN
OH? ASLEEP ALREADY?

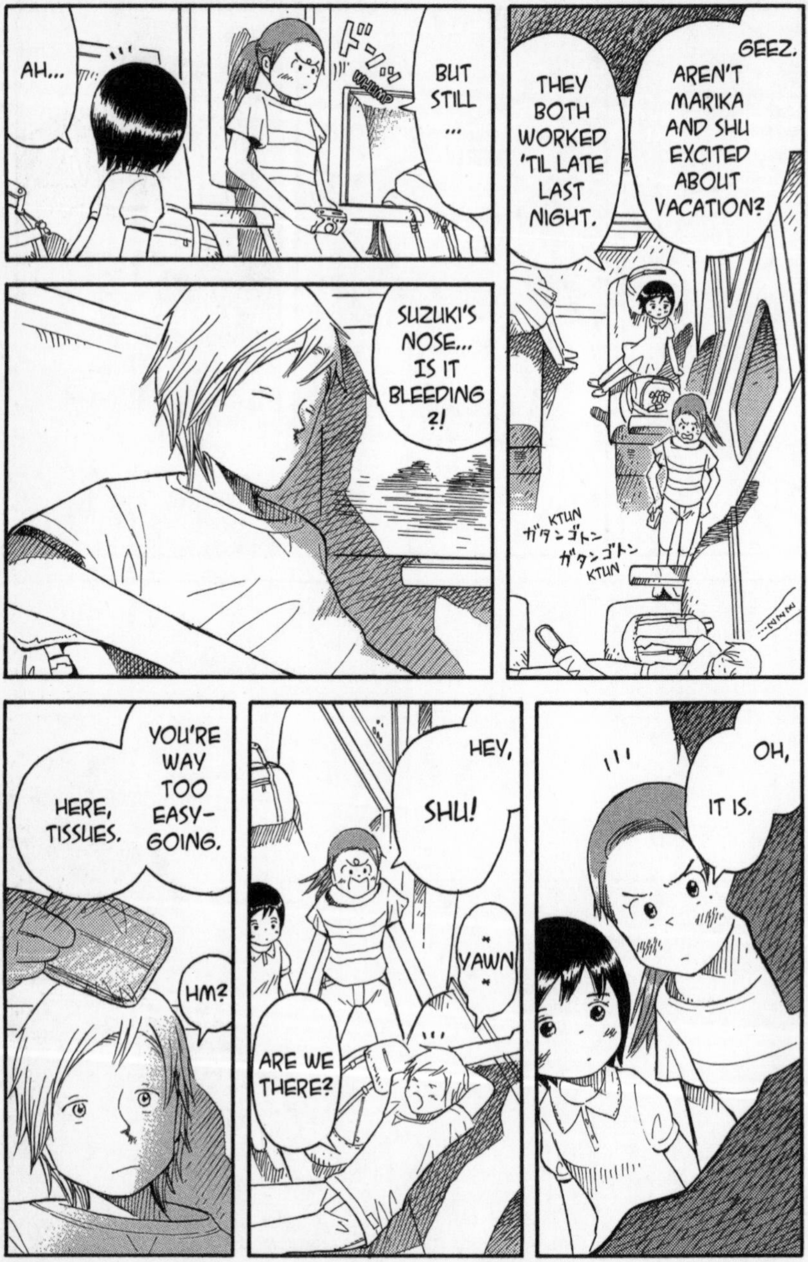
GEEZ. AREN'T MARIKA AND SHU EXCITED ABOUT VACATION?
THEY BOTH WORKED 'TIL LATE LAST NIGHT.
ガタンゴトン KTUN
ガタンゴトン KTUN
BUT STILL ...
ドンッ WHUMP
AH...
SUZUKI'S NOSE... IS IT BLEEDING ?!
OH, IT IS.
HEY, SHU!
YAWN
ARE WE THERE?
YOU'RE WAY TOO EASY-GOING.
HERE, TISSUES.
HM?

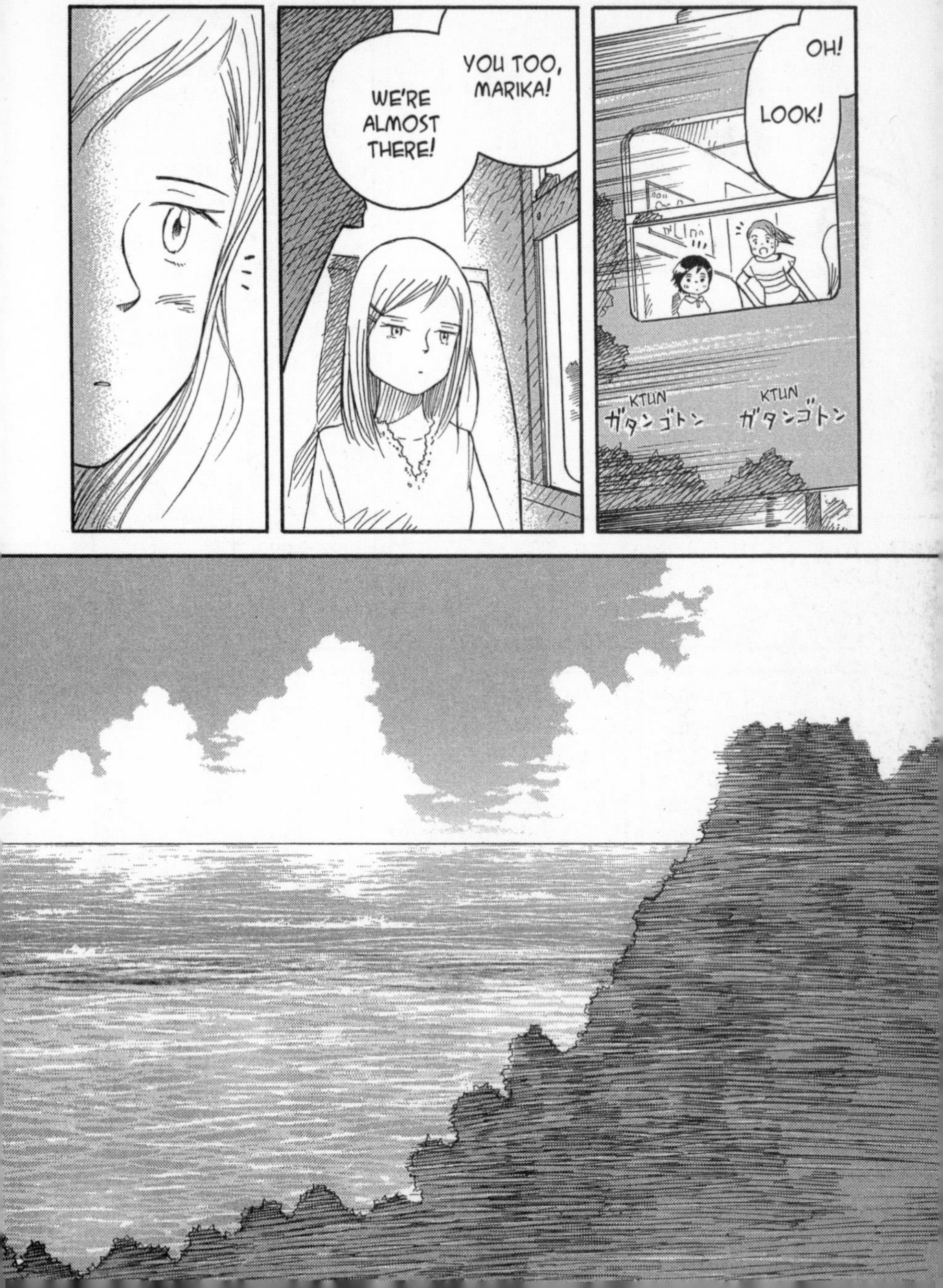
OH!
LOOK!
KTUN
ガタンゴトン
KTUN
ガタンゴトン
YOU TOO, MARIKA!
WE'RE ALMOST THERE!

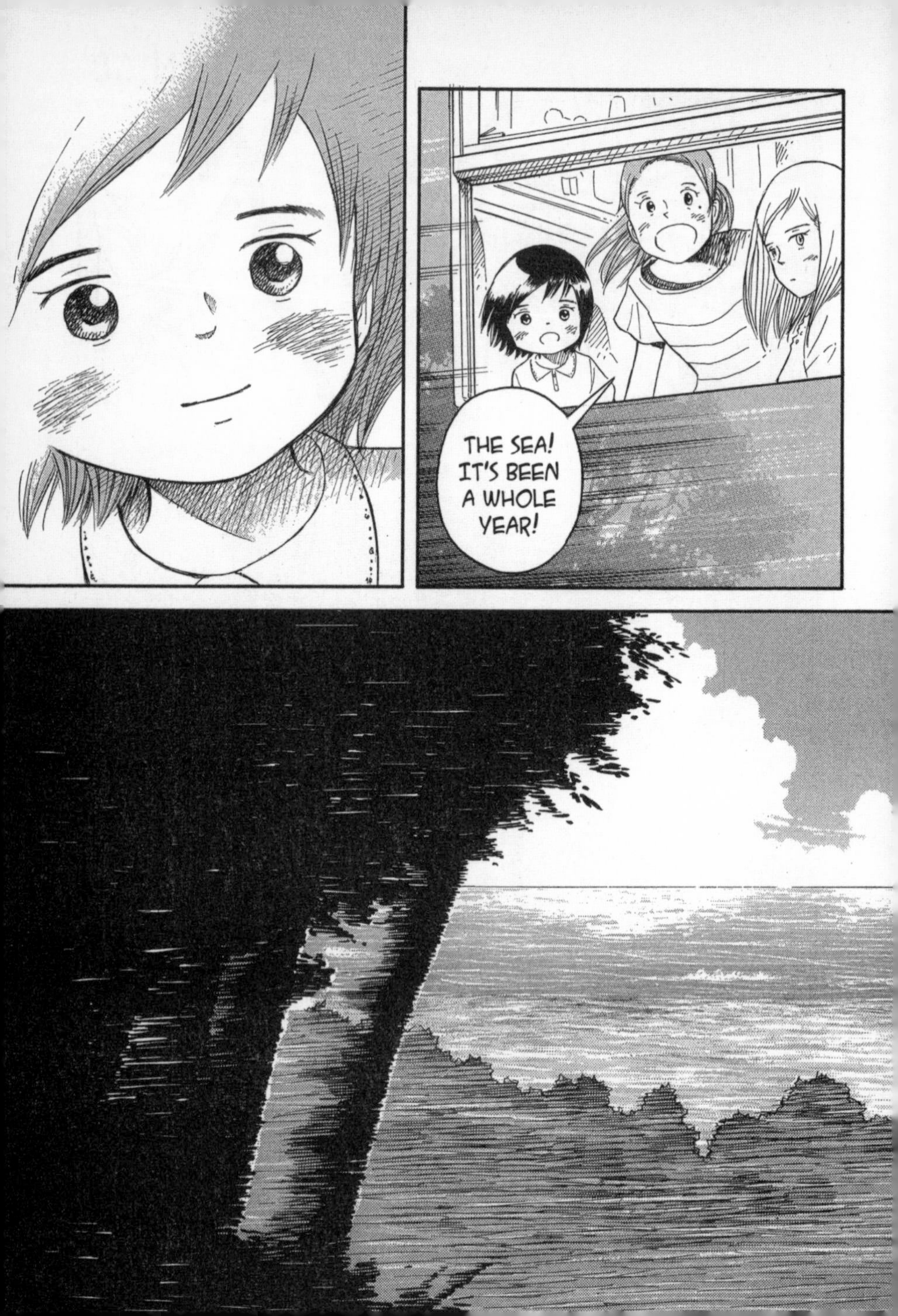
THE SEA! IT'S BEEN A WHOLE YEAR!

MISSION:60

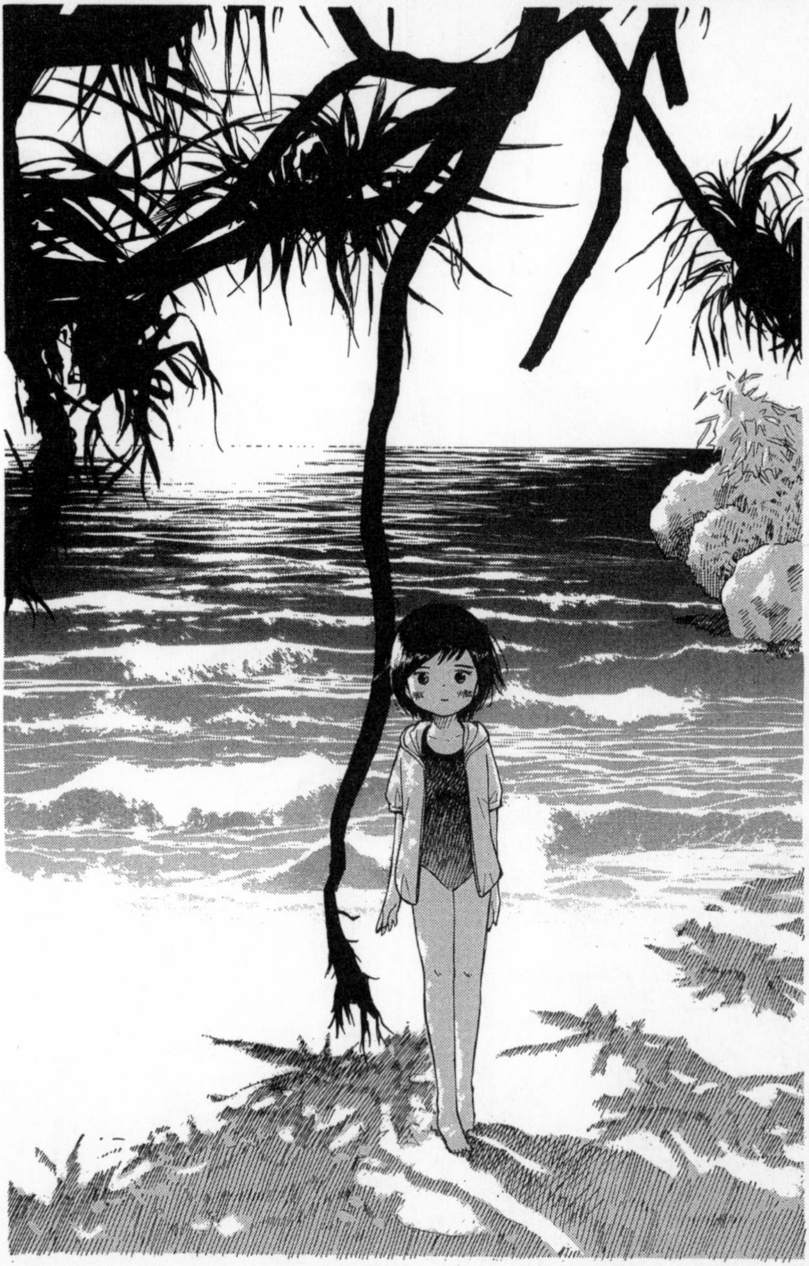

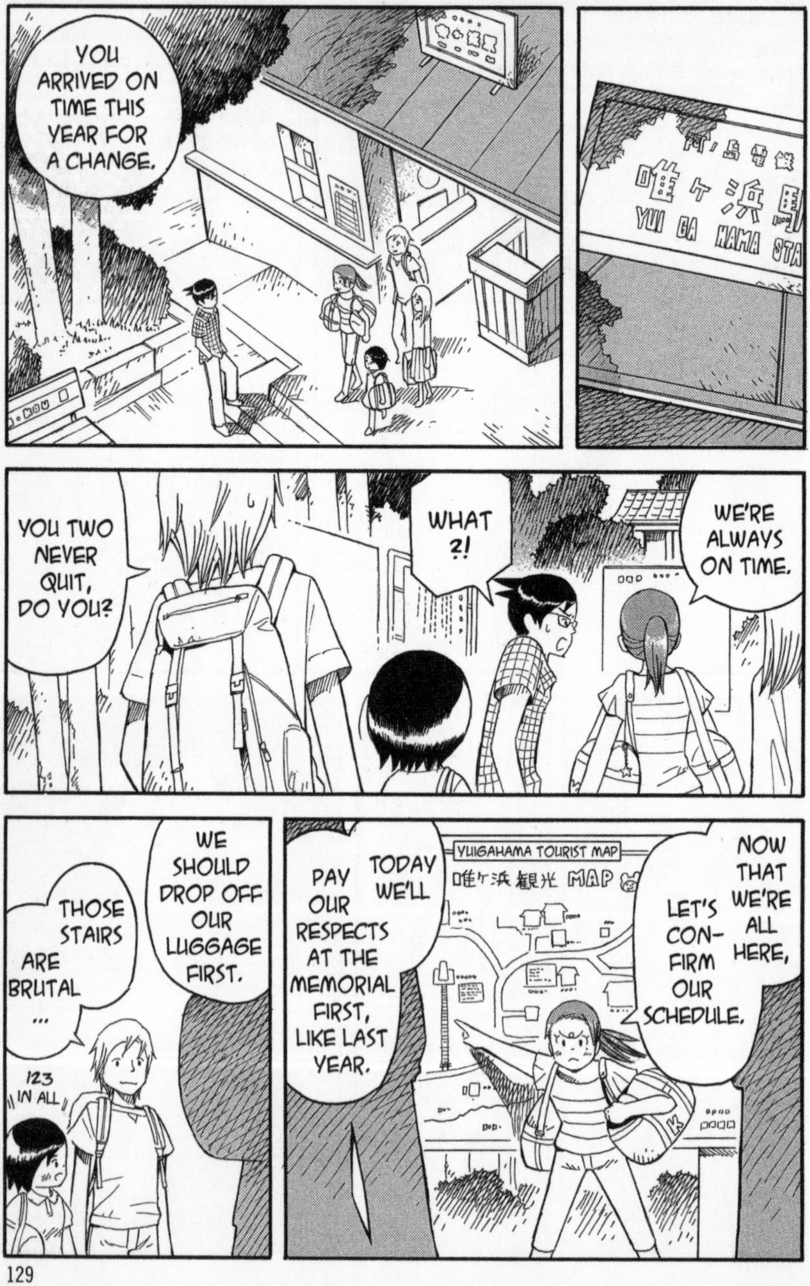
唯ケ浜駅
YUI GA HAMA STA
YOU ARRIVED ON TIME THIS YEAR FOR A CHANGE.
WE'RE ALWAYS ON TIME.
WHAT ?!
YOU TWO NEVER QUIT, DO YOU?
YUIGAHAMA TOURIST MAP
唯ケ浜観光 MAP
NOW THAT WE'RE ALL HERE,
LET'S CON-FIRM OUR SCHEDULE.
TODAY WE'LL PAY OUR RESPECTS AT THE MEMORIAL FIRST, LIKE LAST YEAR.
WE SHOULD DROP OFF OUR LUGGAGE FIRST.
THOSE STAIRS ARE BRUTAL ...
123 IN ALL

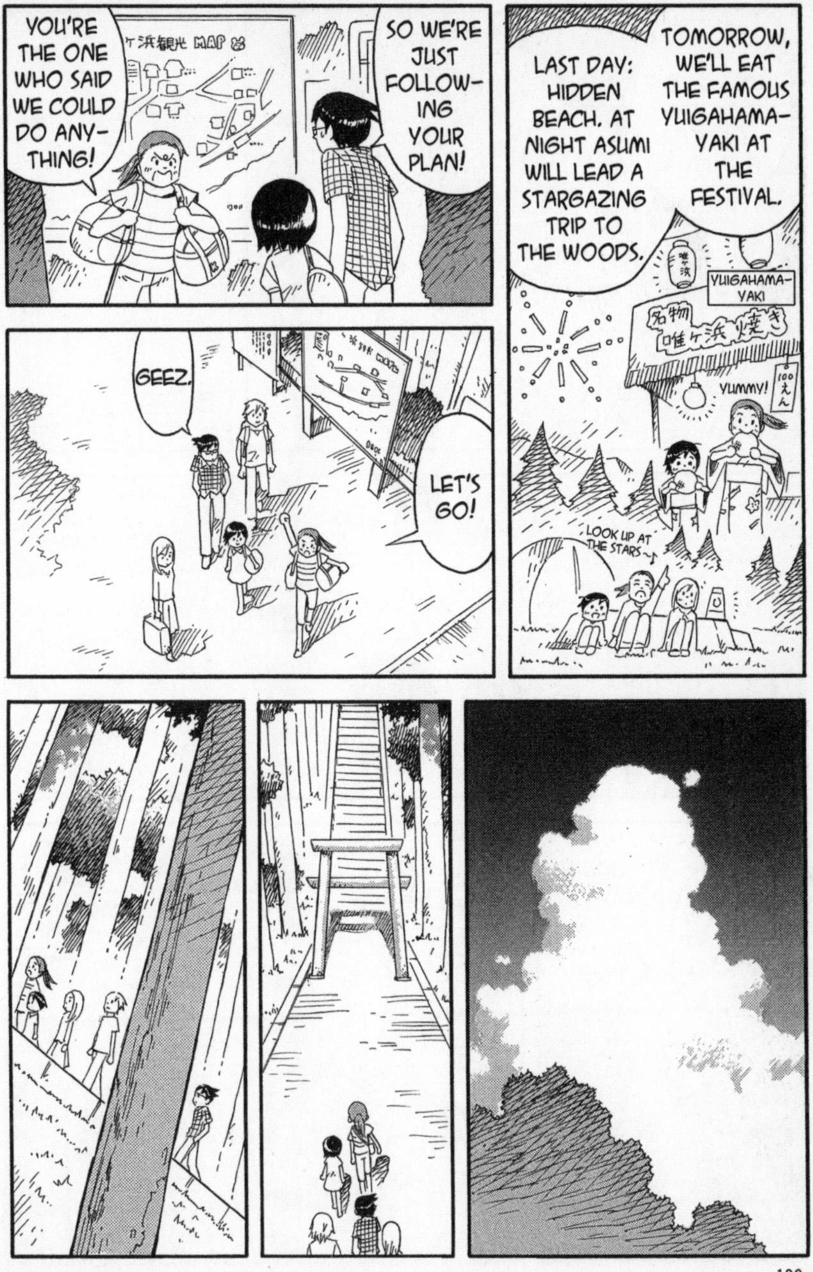
TOMORROW, WE'LL EAT THE FAMOUS YUIGAHAMA-YAKI AT THE FESTIVAL.
LAST DAY: HIDDEN BEACH. AT NIGHT ASUMI WILL LEAD A STARGAZING TRIP TO THE WOODS.
唯ヶ浜
YUIGAHAMA-YAKI
名物 唯ヶ浜焼き
100えん
YUMMY!
LOOK UP AT THE STARS~♪
SO WE'RE JUST FOLLOWING YOUR PLAN!
YOU'RE THE ONE WHO SAID WE COULD DO ANYTHING!
ヶ浜観光 MAP
LET'S GO!
GEEZ.

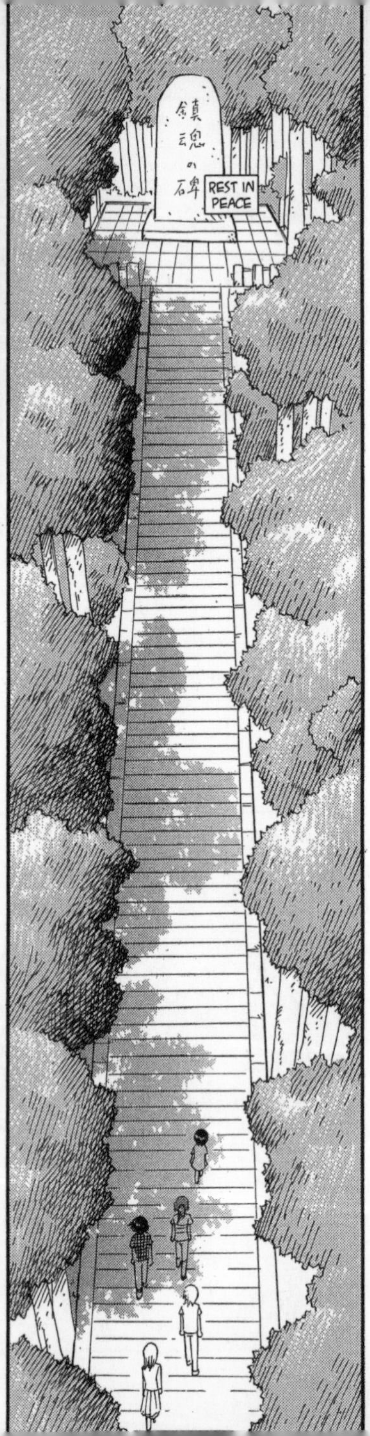
鎮魂の碑
REST IN PEACE

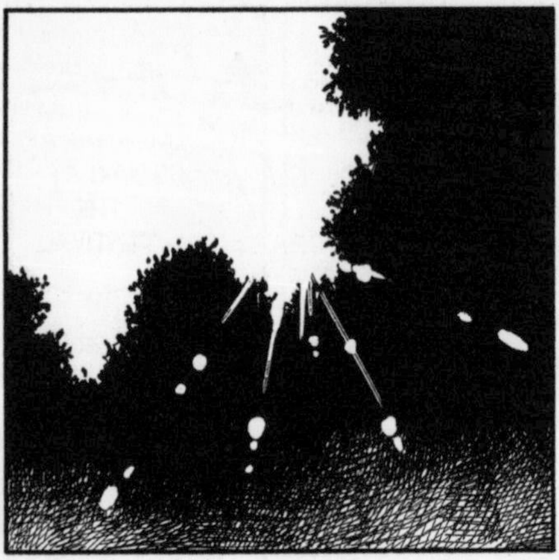

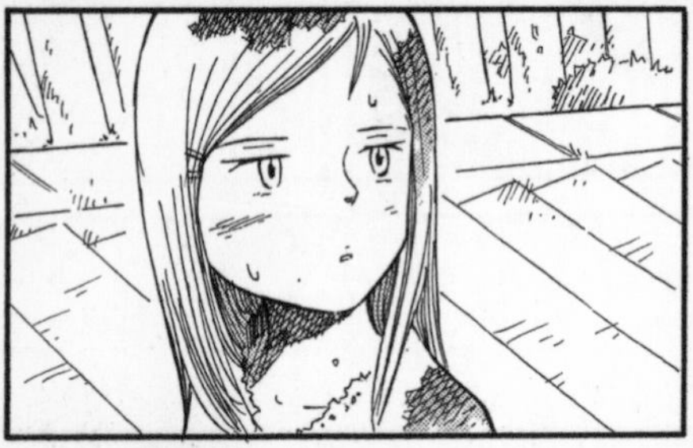

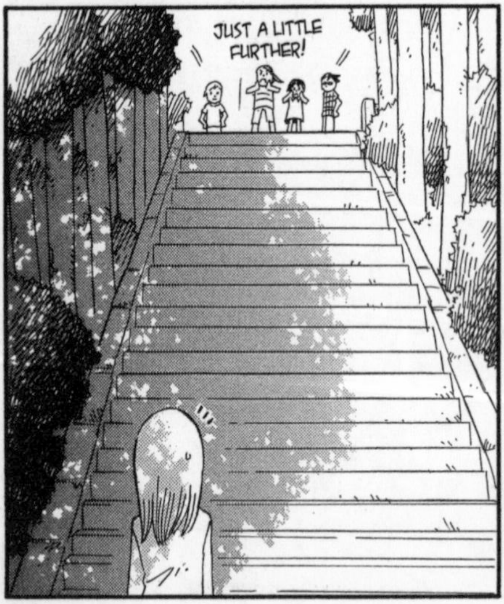
JUST A LITTLE FURTHER!

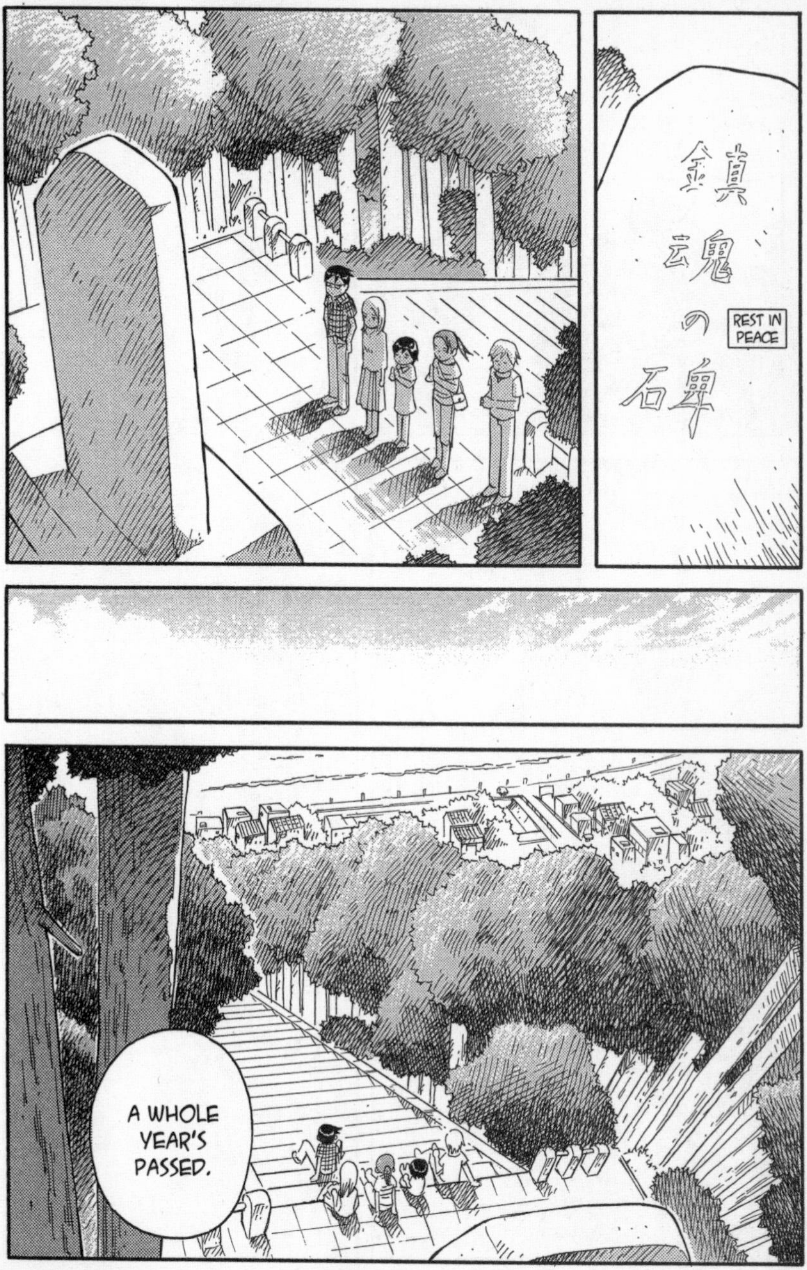
鎮魂の碑
REST IN PEACE
A WHOLE YEAR'S PASSED.

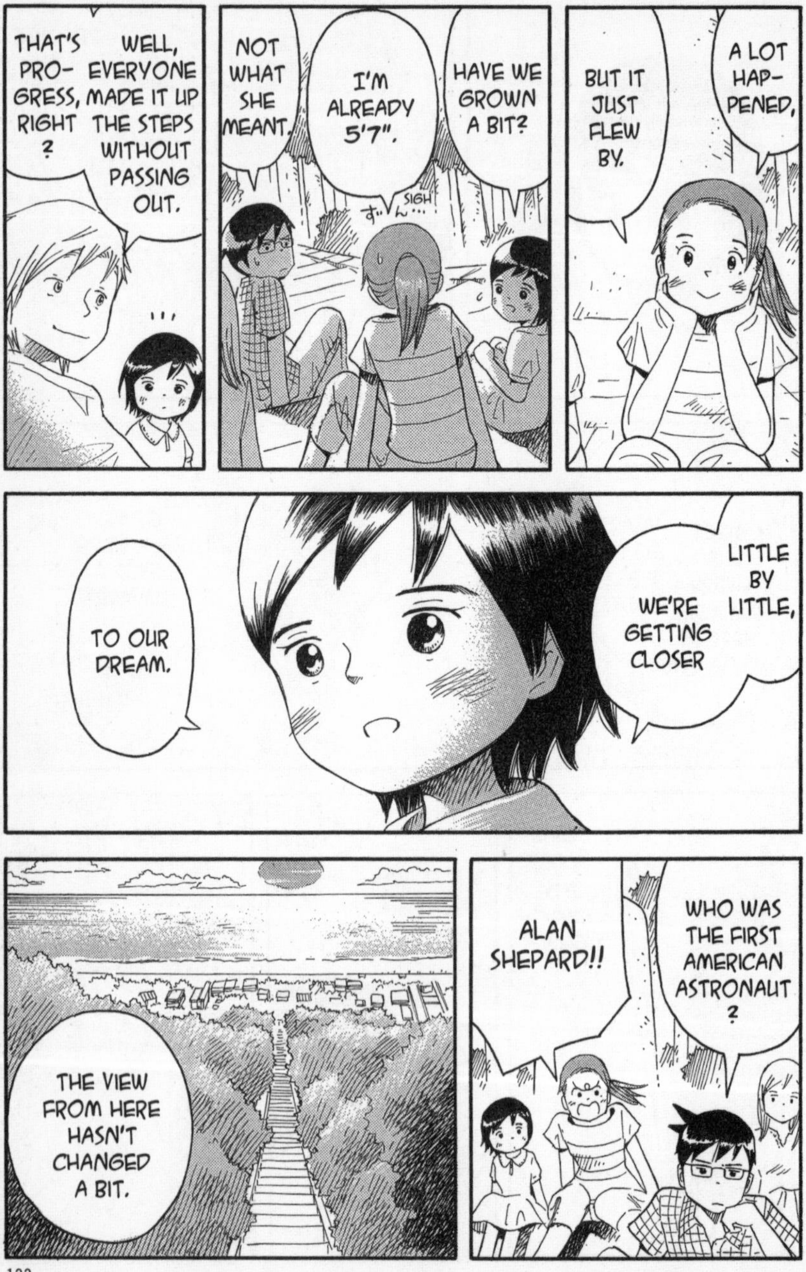
A LOT HAP-PENED,
BUT IT JUST FLEW BY.
HAVE WE GROWN A BIT?
I'M ALREADY 5'7".
SIGH...
NOT WHAT SHE MEANT.
WELL, EVERYONE MADE IT UP THE STEPS WITHOUT PASSING OUT.
THAT'S PRO-GRESS, RIGHT?
LITTLE BY LITTLE,
WE'RE GETTING CLOSER
TO OUR DREAM.
WHO WAS THE FIRST AMERICAN ASTRONAUT?
ALAN SHEPARD!!
THE VIEW FROM HERE HASN'T CHANGED A BIT.

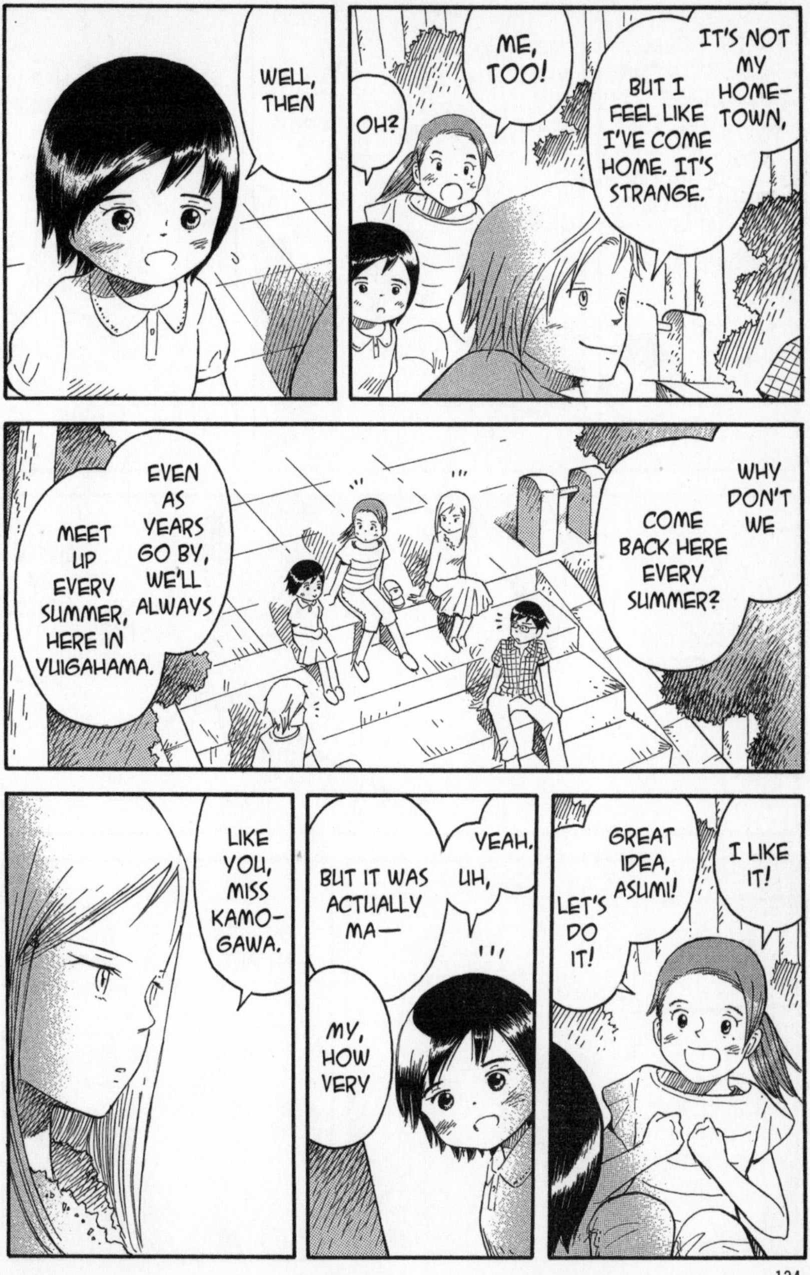
IT'S NOT MY HOME-TOWN,
BUT I FEEL LIKE I'VE COME HOME. IT'S STRANGE.
ME, TOO!
OH?
WELL, THEN
WHY DON'T WE
COME BACK HERE EVERY SUMMER?
EVEN AS YEARS GO BY, WE'LL ALWAYS
MEET UP EVERY SUMMER, HERE IN YUIGAHAMA.
I LIKE IT!
GREAT IDEA, ASUMI!
LET'S DO IT!
YEAH.
UH,
BUT IT WAS ACTUALLY MA—
MY, HOW VERY
LIKE YOU, MISS KAMO-GAWA.

HUH?
...
ポカッ
SMAK
GEEZ
DON'T TURN MY HOME-TOWN INTO A HANG-OUT SPOT.
IT'S EVERY-ONE'S HOME-TOWN, NOW.

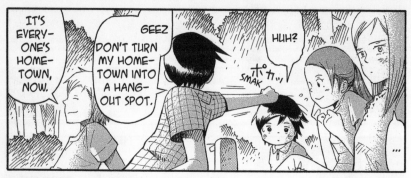

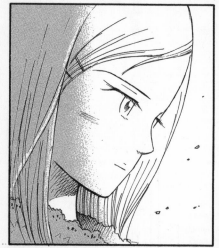

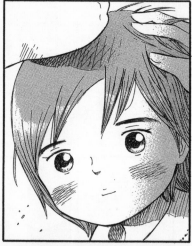

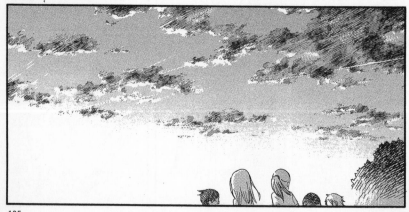

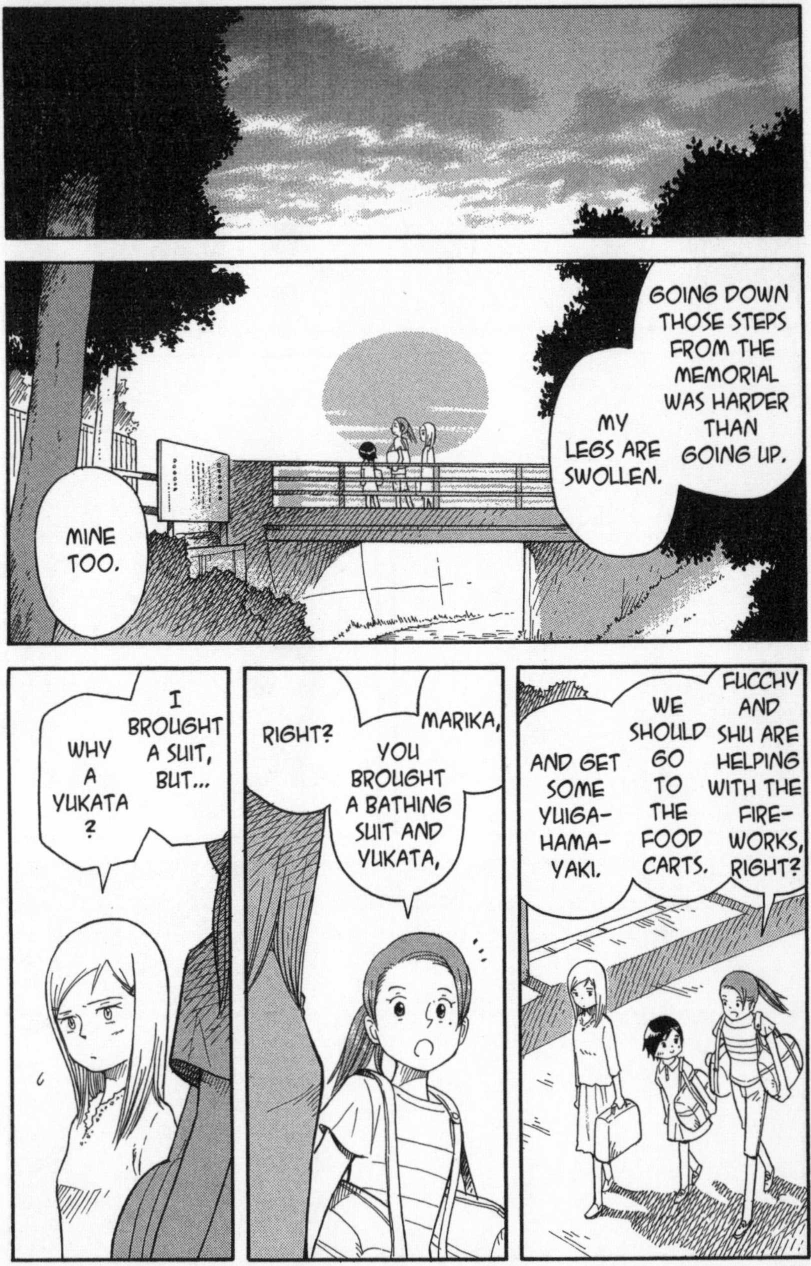
GOING DOWN THOSE STEPS FROM THE MEMORIAL WAS HARDER THAN GOING UP.
MY LEGS ARE SWOLLEN.
MINE TOO.
FUCCHY AND SHU ARE HELPING WITH THE FIRE-WORKS, RIGHT?
WE SHOULD GO TO THE FOOD CARTS.
AND GET SOME YUIGA-HAMA-YAKI.
MARIKA, YOU BROUGHT A BATHING SUIT AND YUKATA, RIGHT?
I BROUGHT A SUIT, BUT...
WHY A YUKATA?

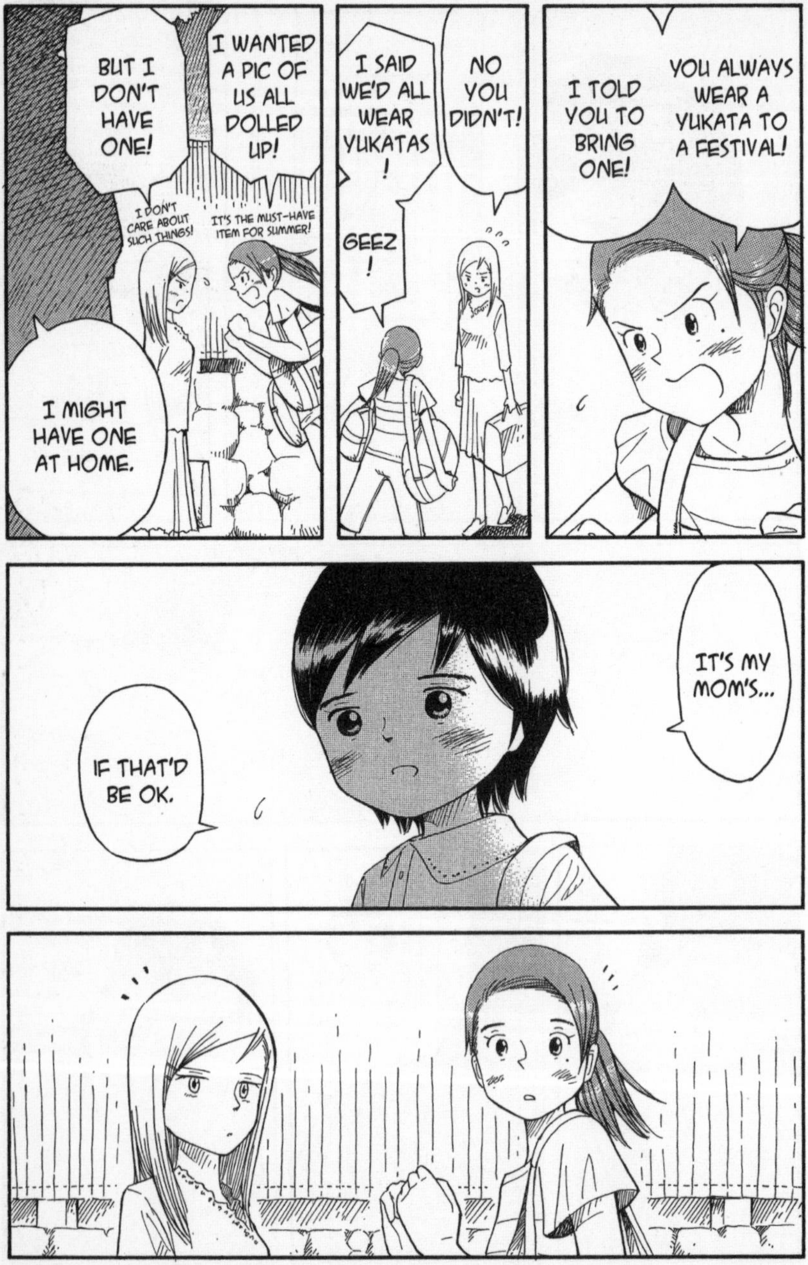
YOU ALWAYS WEAR A YUKATA TO A FESTIVAL!
I TOLD YOU TO BRING ONE!
NO YOU DIDN'T!
I SAID WE'D ALL WEAR YUKATAS!
GEEZ!
I WANTED A PIC OF US ALL DOLLED UP!
BUT I DON'T HAVE ONE!
IT'S THE MUST-HAVE ITEM FOR SUMMER!
I DON'T CARE ABOUT SUCH THINGS!
I MIGHT HAVE ONE AT HOME.
IT'S MY MOM'S...
IF THAT'D BE OK.

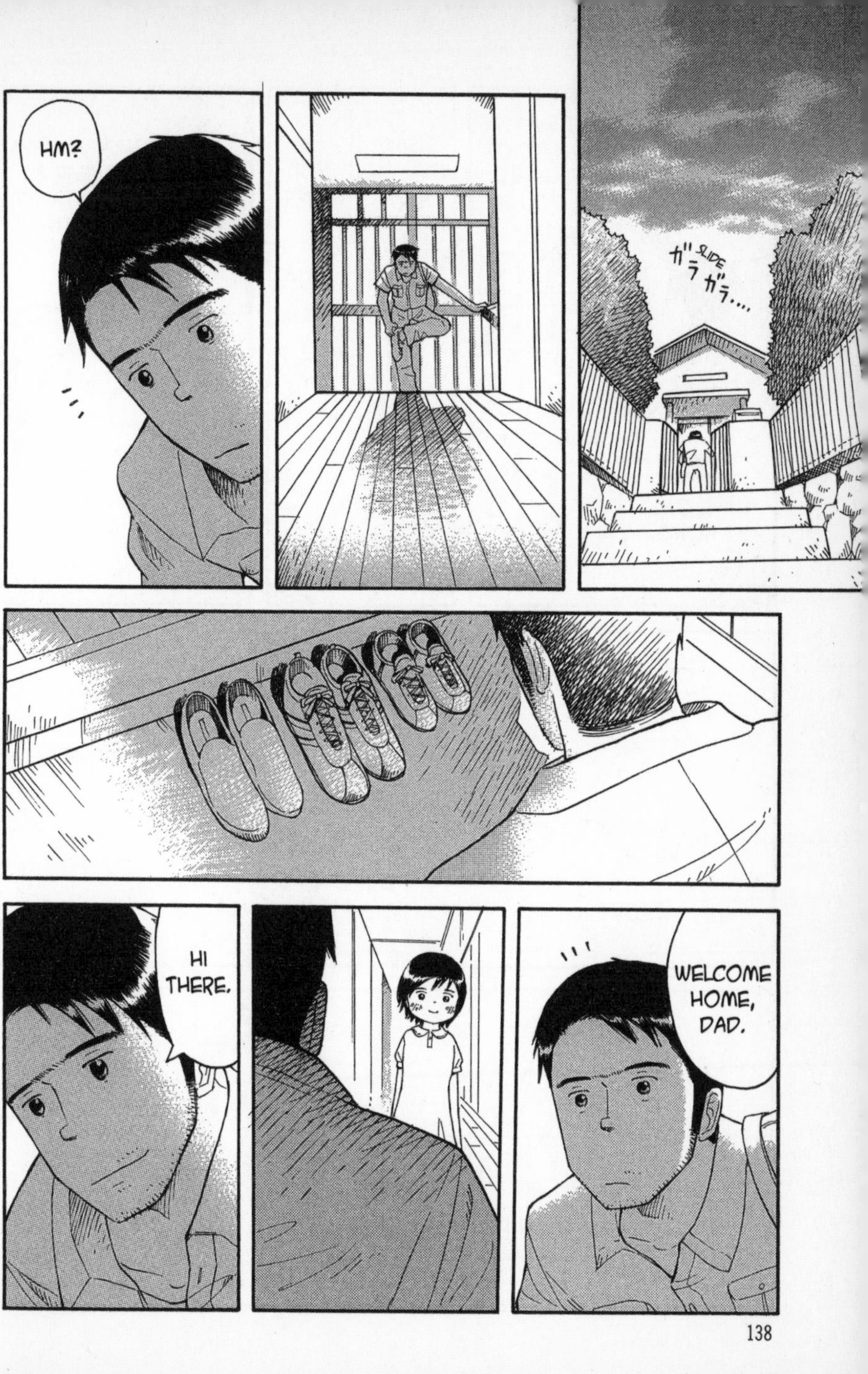
ガラ
SLIDE
ガラ....
HM?
WELCOME HOME, DAD.
HI THERE.

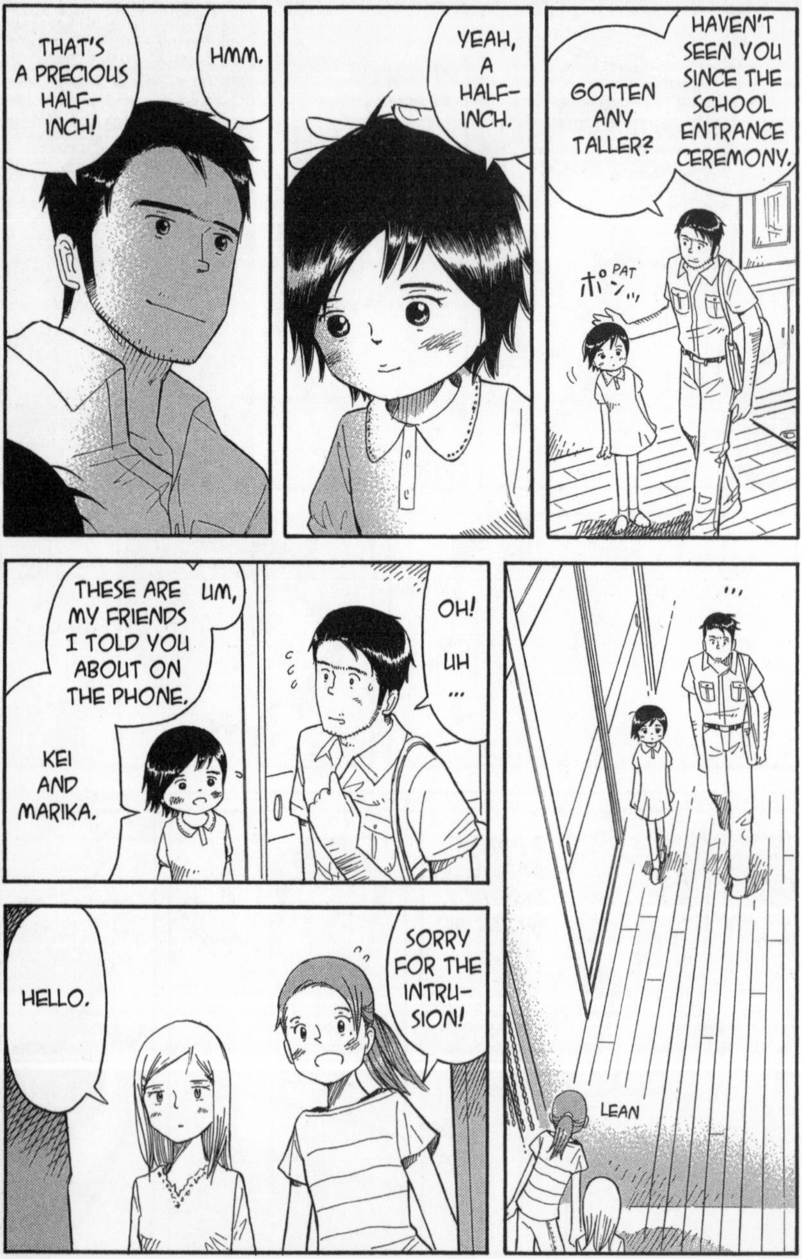
HAVEN'T SEEN YOU SINCE THE SCHOOL ENTRANCE CEREMONY.
GOTTEN ANY TALLER?
ポンッ PAT
YEAH, A HALF-INCH.
HMM.
THAT'S A PRECIOUS HALF-INCH!
...
LEAN
OH!
UH ...
UM,
THESE ARE MY FRIENDS I TOLD YOU ABOUT ON THE PHONE.
KEI AND MARIKA.
SORRY FOR THE INTRUSION!
HELLO.

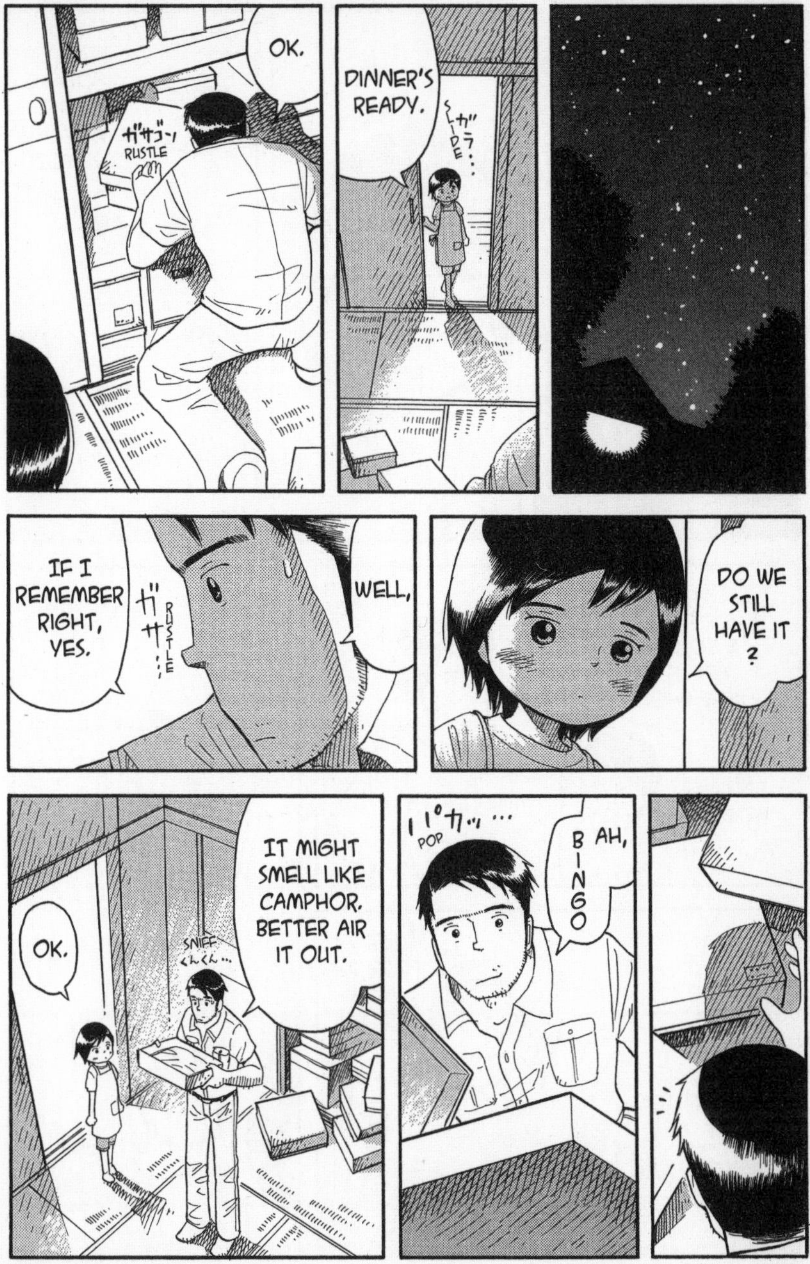
DINNER'S READY.
ガラ… SLIDE
OK.
ガサゴソ RUSTLE
DO WE STILL HAVE IT ?
WELL,
ガサ… RUSTLE
IF I REMEMBER RIGHT, YES.
AH, BINGO
パカッ… POP
IT MIGHT SMELL LIKE CAMPHOR. BETTER AIR IT OUT.
SNIFF くんくん…
OK.

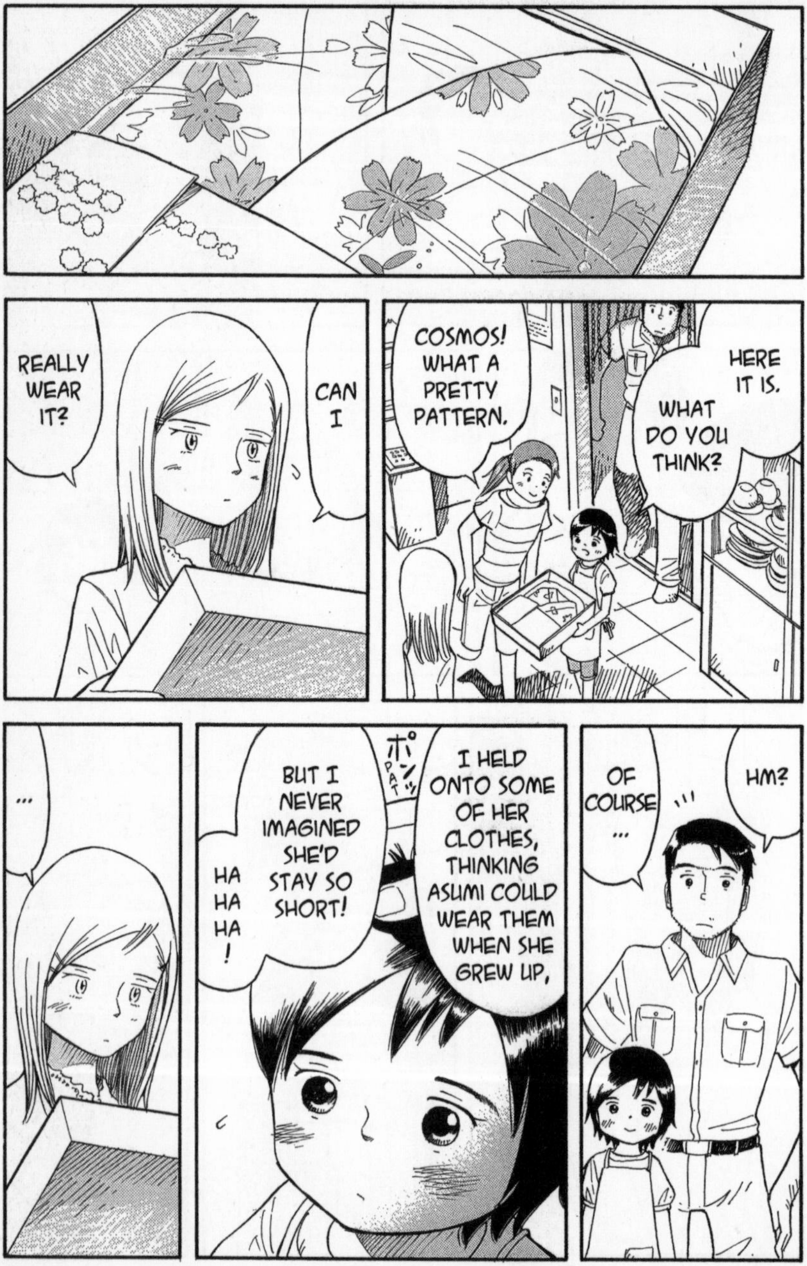
HERE IT IS.
WHAT DO YOU THINK?
COSMOS! WHAT A PRETTY PATTERN.
CAN I
REALLY WEAR IT?
HM?
OF COURSE...
I HELD ONTO SOME OF HER CLOTHES, THINKING ASUMI COULD WEAR THEM WHEN SHE GREW UP,
PAT
BUT I NEVER IMAGINED SHE'D STAY SO SHORT!
HA HA HA!
...

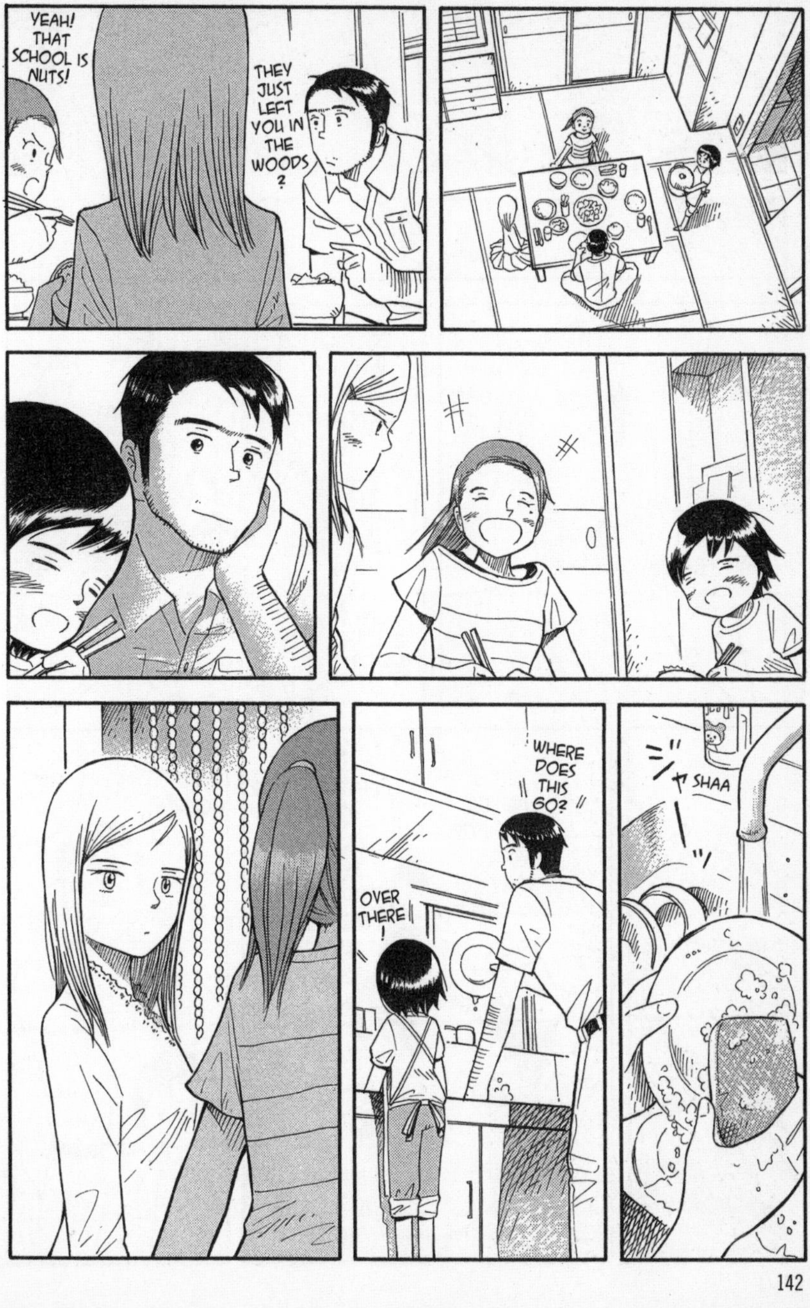
THEY JUST LEFT YOU IN THE WOODS?
YEAH! THAT SCHOOL IS NUTS!
SHAA
WHERE DOES THIS GO?
OVER THERE!

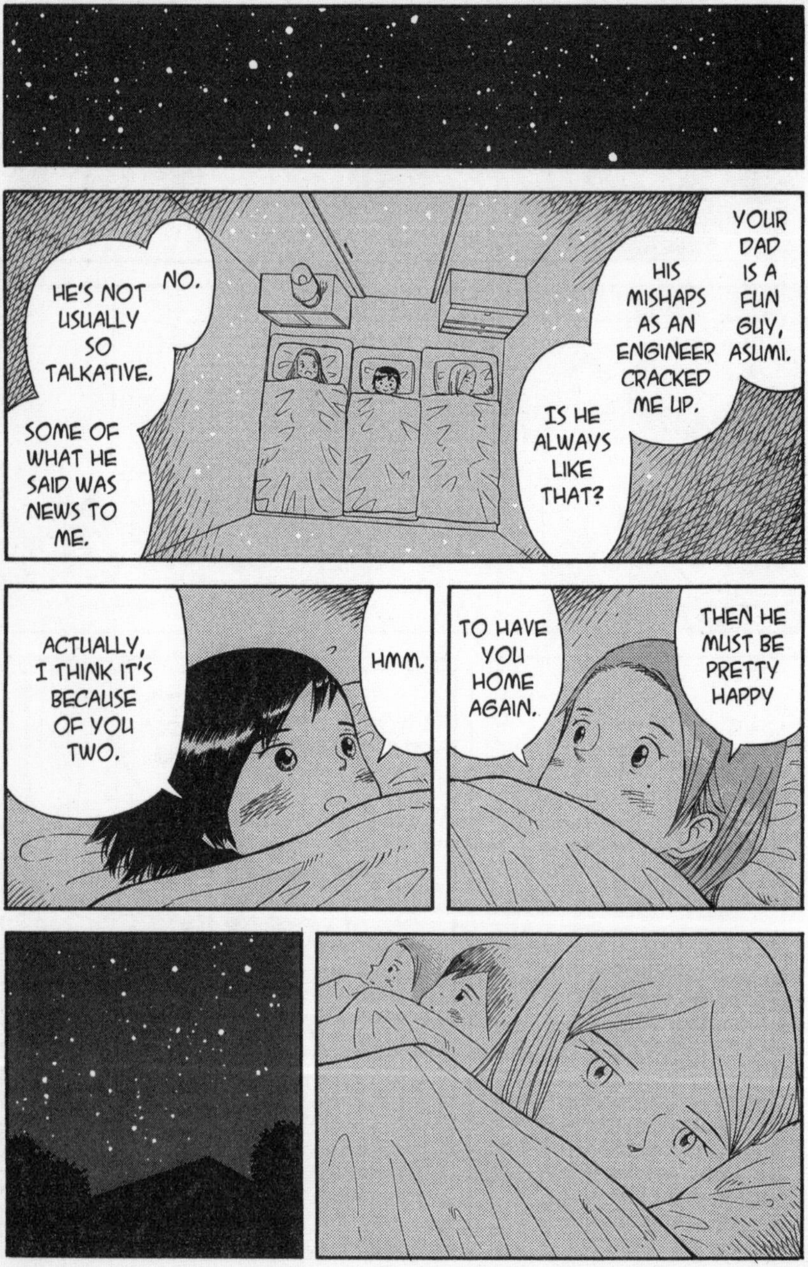
YOUR DAD IS A FUN GUY, ASUMI.
HIS MISHAPS AS AN ENGINEER CRACKED ME UP.
IS HE ALWAYS LIKE THAT?
NO.
HE'S NOT USUALLY SO TALKATIVE.
SOME OF WHAT HE SAID WAS NEWS TO ME.
THEN HE MUST BE PRETTY HAPPY
TO HAVE YOU HOME AGAIN.
HMM.
ACTUALLY, I THINK IT'S BECAUSE OF YOU TWO.

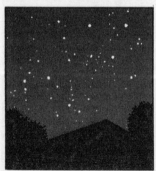

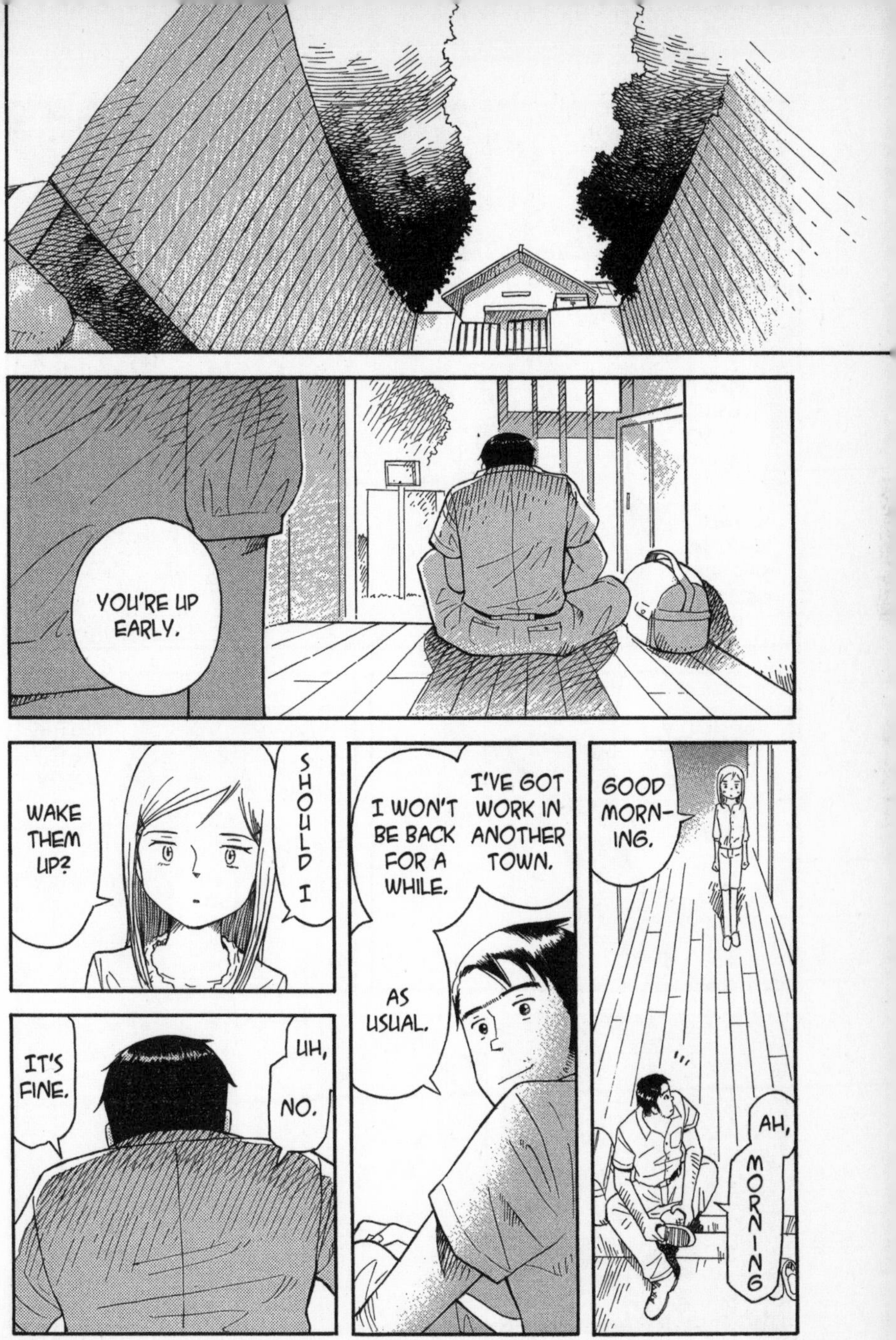
YOU'RE UP EARLY.
GOOD MORN-ING.
AH, MORNING
I'VE GOT WORK IN ANOTHER TOWN.
I WON'T BE BACK FOR A WHILE.
AS USUAL.
SHOULD I
WAKE THEM UP?
UH,
NO.
IT'S FINE.

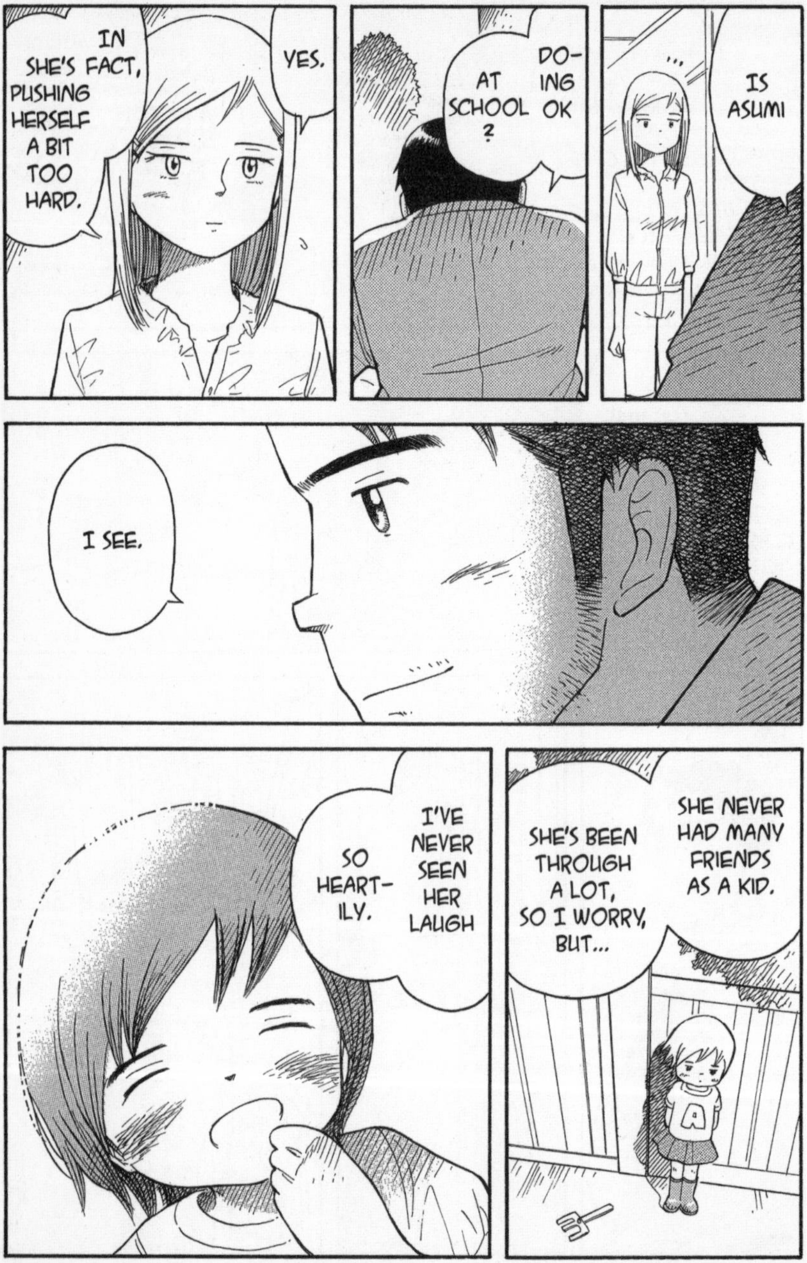
...
IS ASUMI
DOING OK AT SCHOOL?
YES.
IN FACT, SHE'S PUSHING HERSELF A BIT TOO HARD.
I SEE.
SHE NEVER HAD MANY FRIENDS AS A KID.
SHE'S BEEN THROUGH A LOT, SO I WORRY, BUT...
I'VE NEVER SEEN HER LAUGH
SO HEART-ILY.

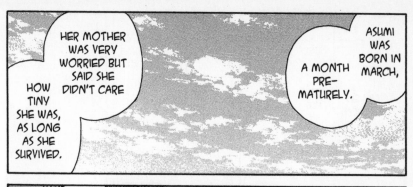

ASUMI WAS BORN IN MARCH,

A MONTH PRE- MATURELY.

HER MOTHER WAS VERY WORRIED BUT SAID SHE DIDN'T CARE

HOW TINY SHE WAS, AS LONG AS SHE SURVIVED.

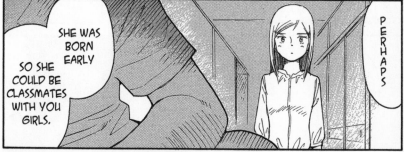

SHE WAS BORN EARLY

SO SHE COULD BE CLASSMATES WITH YOU GIRLS.

PERHAPS

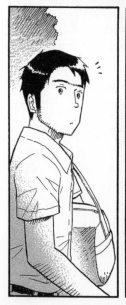

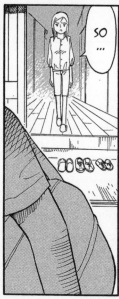

SO ...

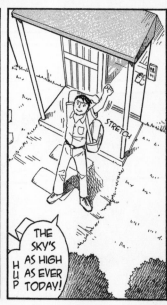

STRETCH

THE SKY'S AS HIGH AS EVER TODAY!

HUP

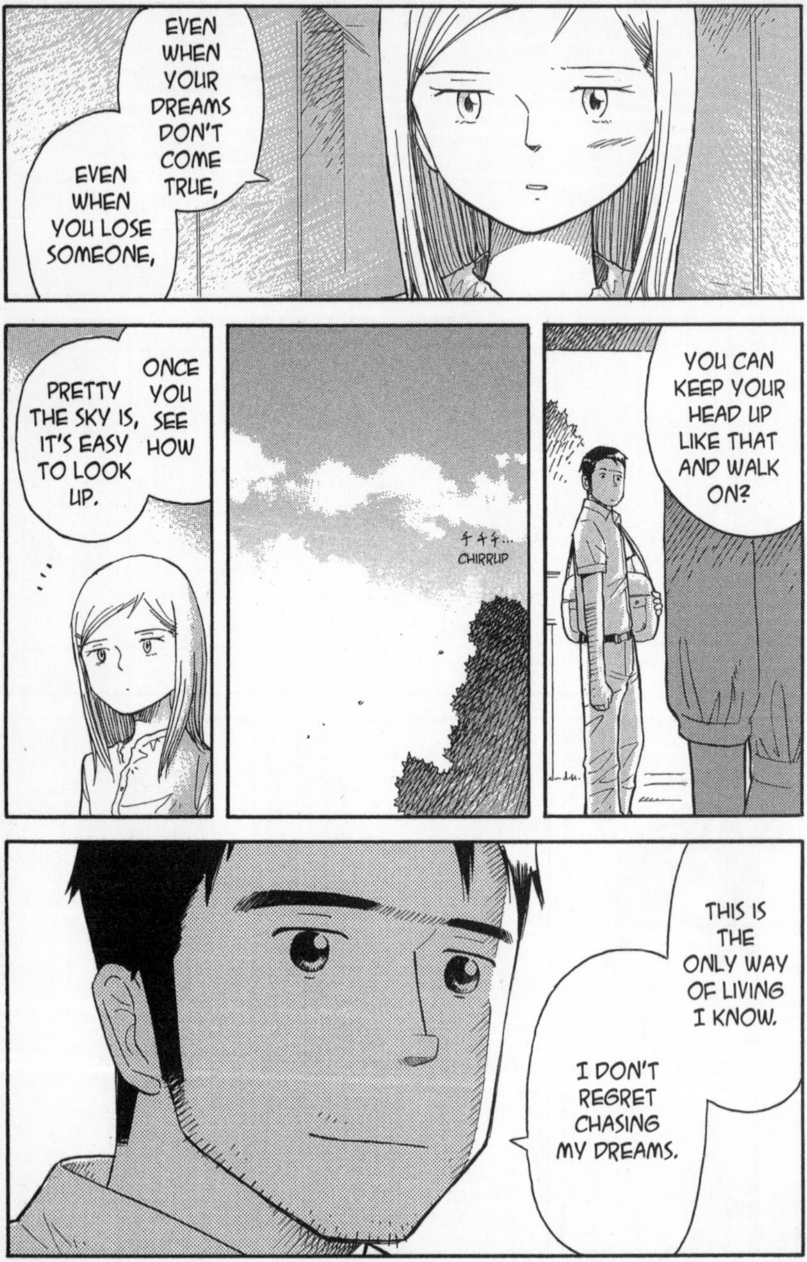
EVEN WHEN YOUR DREAMS DON'T COME TRUE,
EVEN WHEN YOU LOSE SOMEONE,
YOU CAN KEEP YOUR HEAD UP LIKE THAT AND WALK ON?
チチチ... CHIRRUP
ONCE YOU SEE HOW PRETTY THE SKY IS, IT'S EASY TO LOOK UP.
THIS IS THE ONLY WAY OF LIVING I KNOW.
I DON'T REGRET CHASING MY DREAMS.

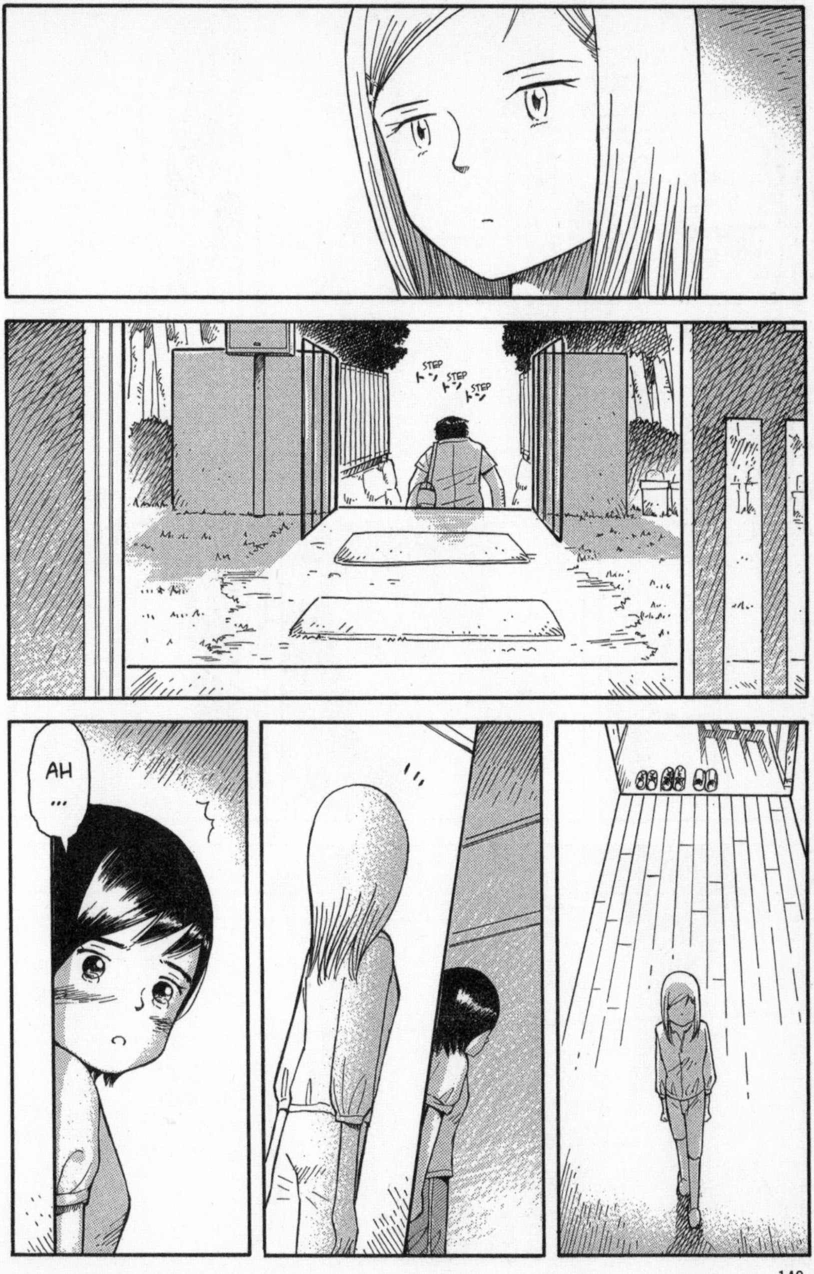

STEP
トン
STEP
トン
STEP
トン
AH ...

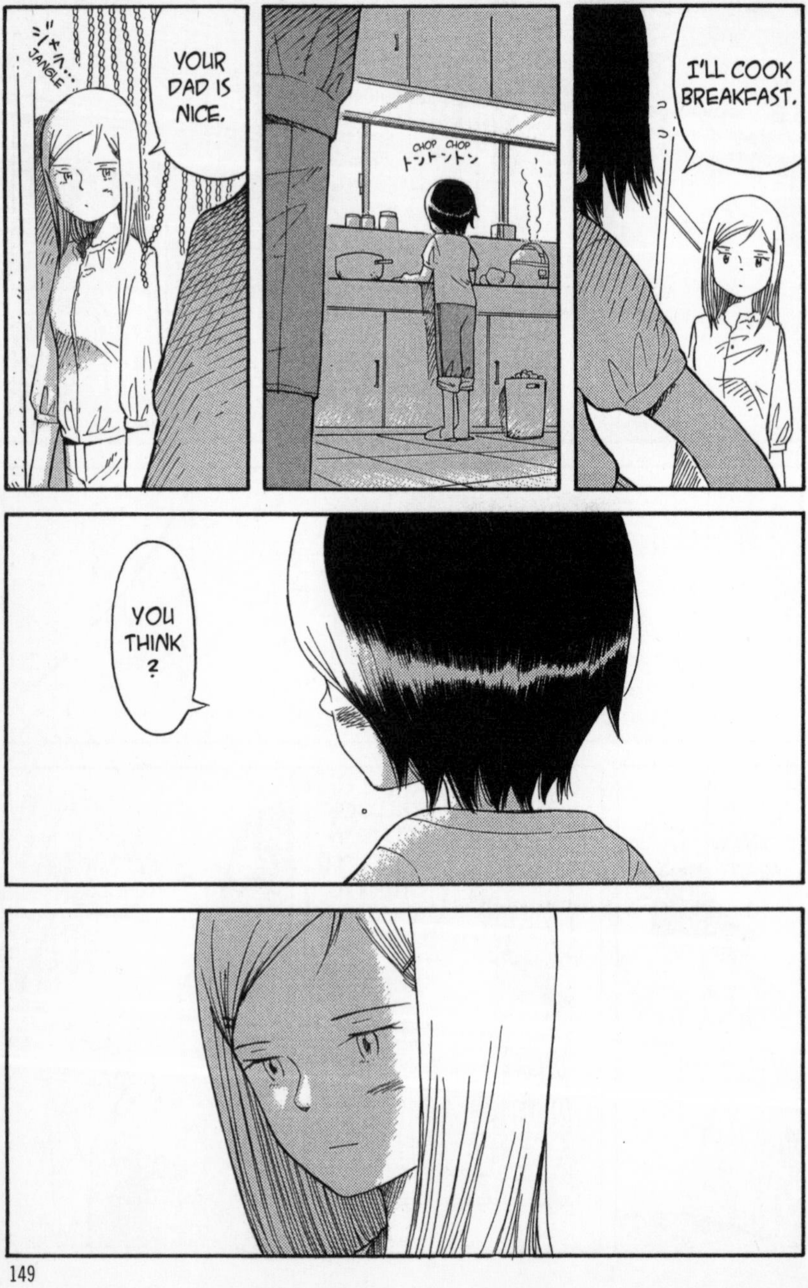
I'LL COOK BREAKFAST.
CHOP CHOP
トントントン
ジャラ…
JANGLE
YOUR DAD IS NICE.
YOU THINK?

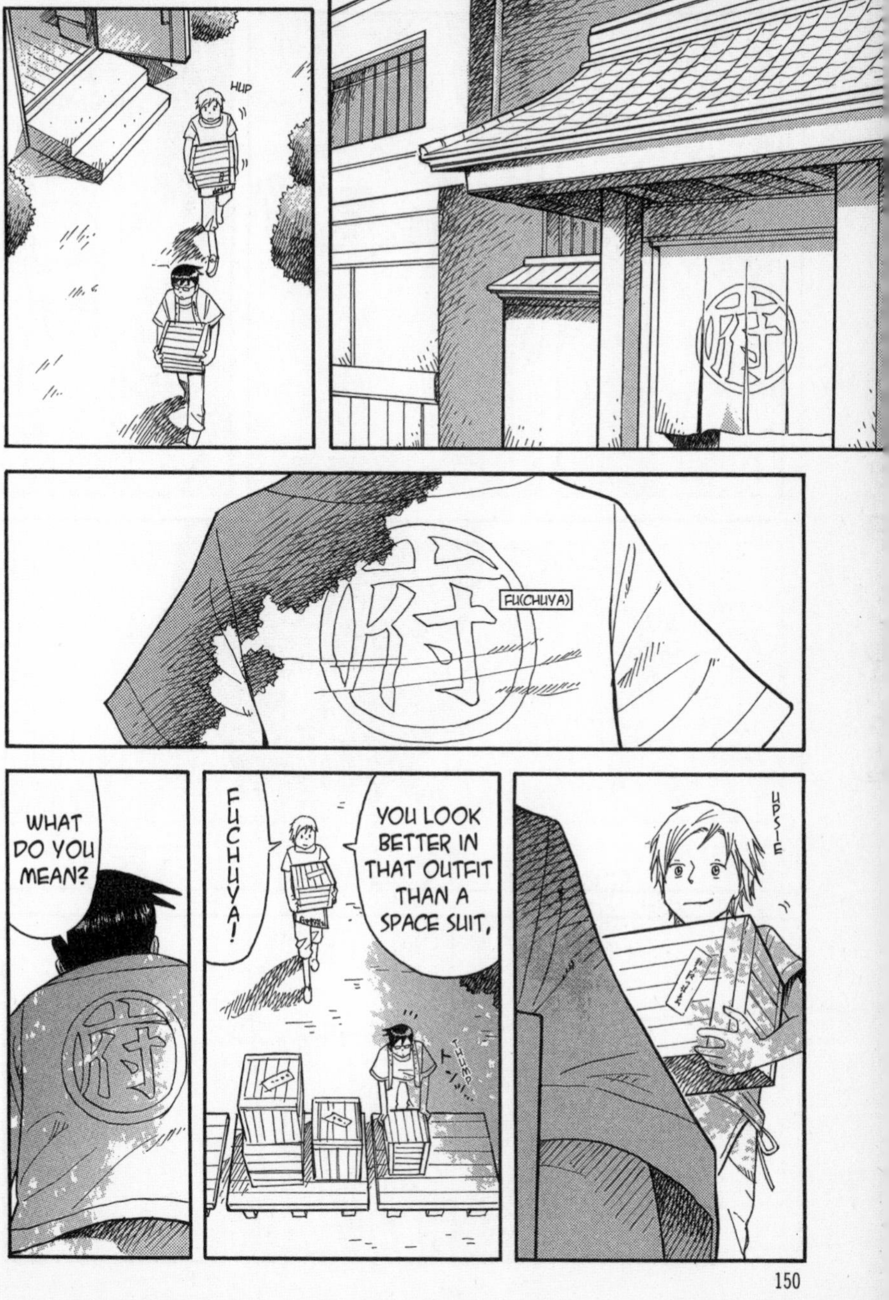
HUP
FU(CHUYA)
UPSIE
YOU LOOK BETTER IN THAT OUTFIT THAN A SPACE SUIT,
FUCHUYA!
THUMP
WHAT DO YOU MEAN?

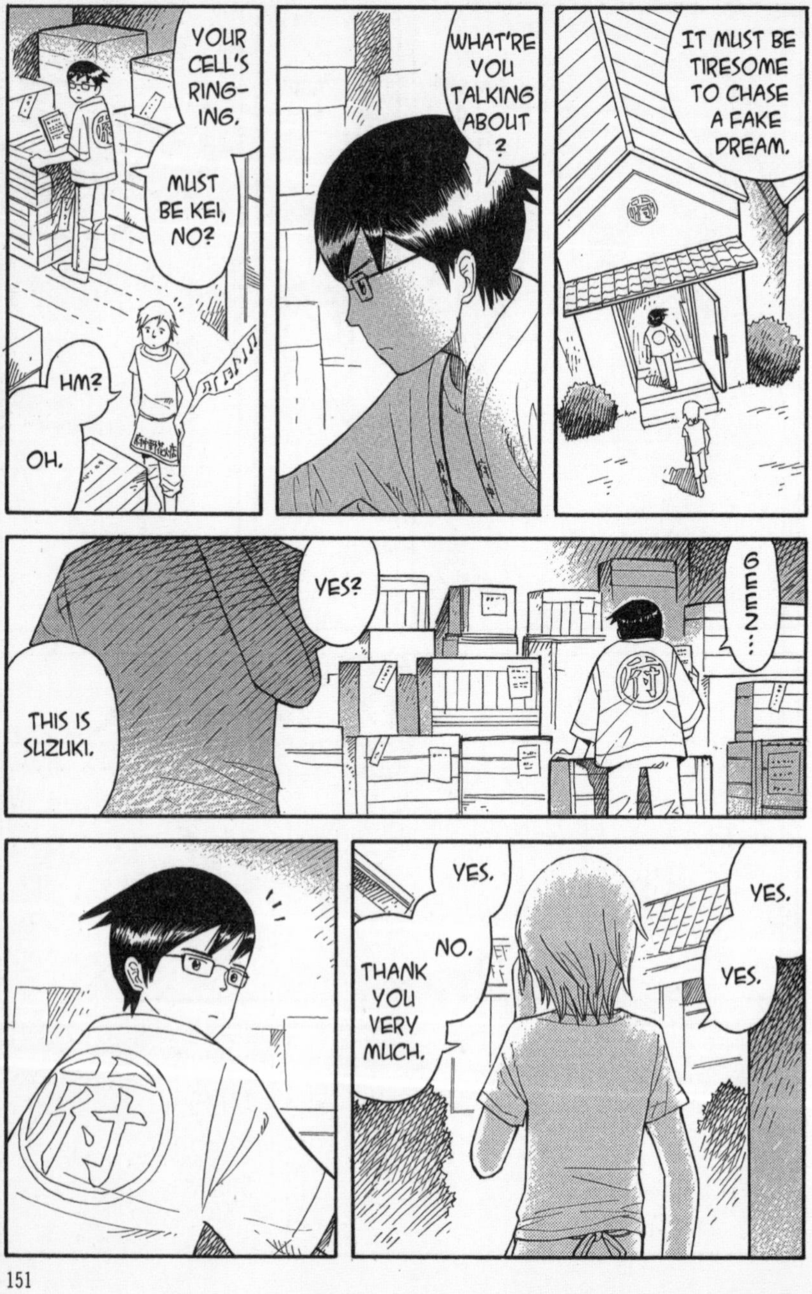
IT MUST BE TIRESOME TO CHASE A FAKE DREAM.
WHAT'RE YOU TALKING ABOUT?
YOUR CELL'S RINGING.
MUST BE KEI, NO?
HM?
OH.
GEEZ...
YES?
THIS IS SUZUKI.
YES.
YES.
NO.
YES.
THANK YOU VERY MUCH.

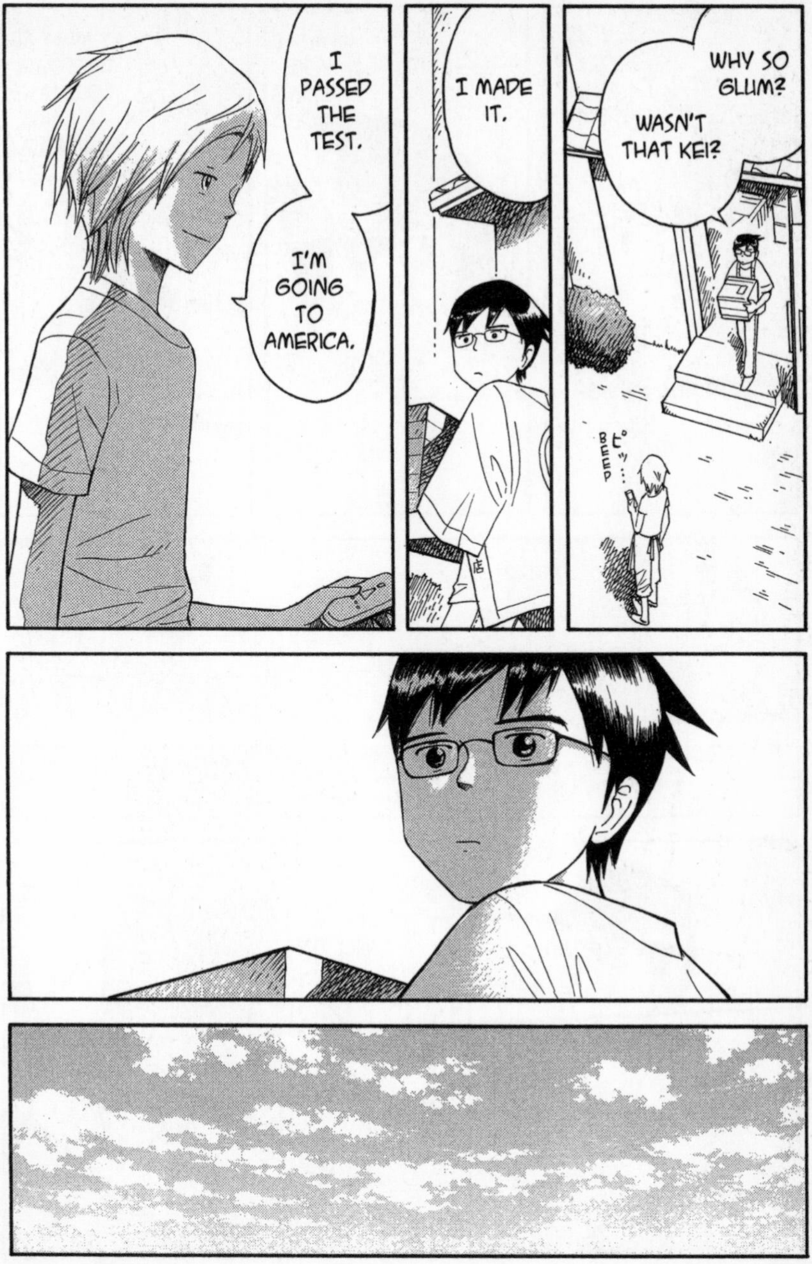
WHY SO GLUM?
WASN'T THAT KEI?
ピッ… BEEP
I MADE IT.
I PASSED THE TEST.
I'M GOING TO AMERICA.

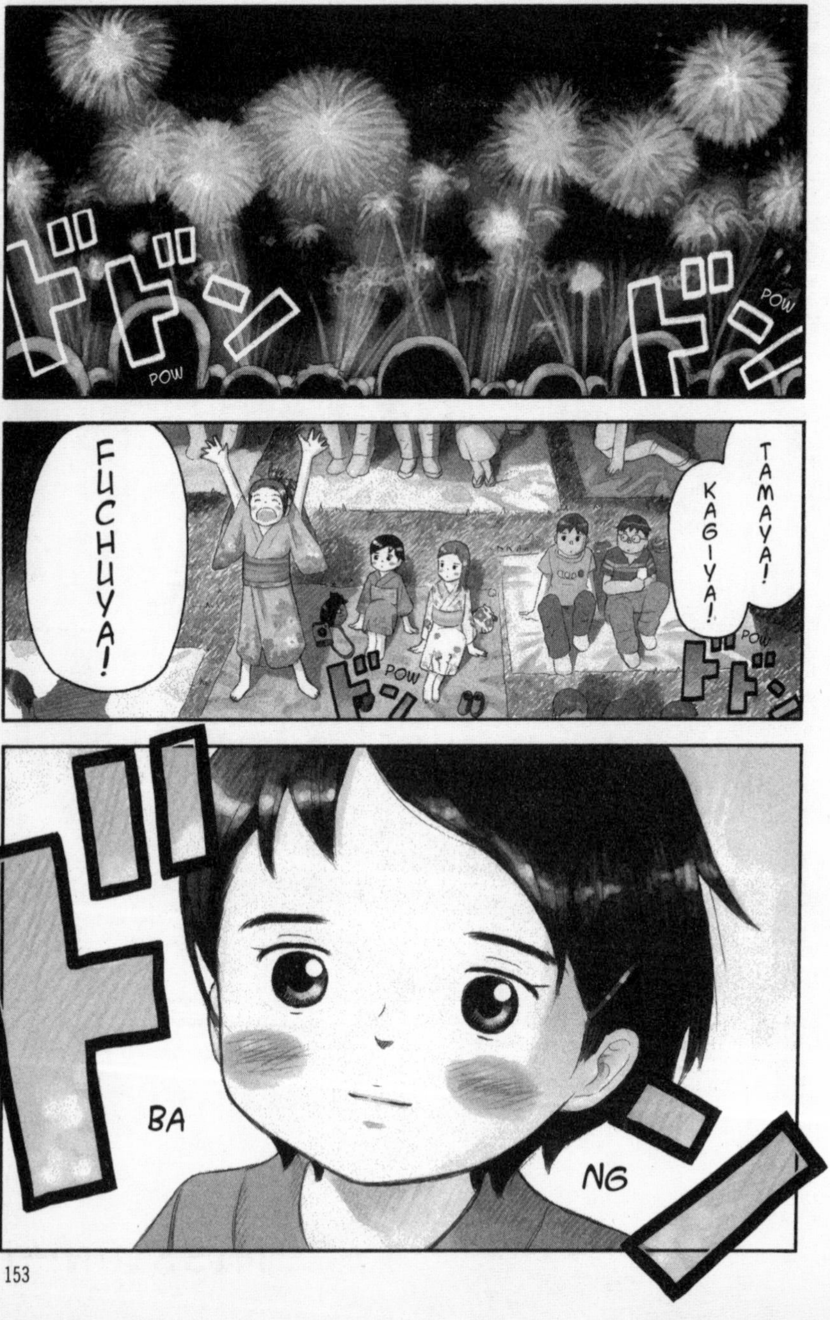
ドドーン
POW
ドドーン
POW
TAMAYA!
KAGIYA!
POW
POW
FUCHUYA!
ドーン
BA
NG

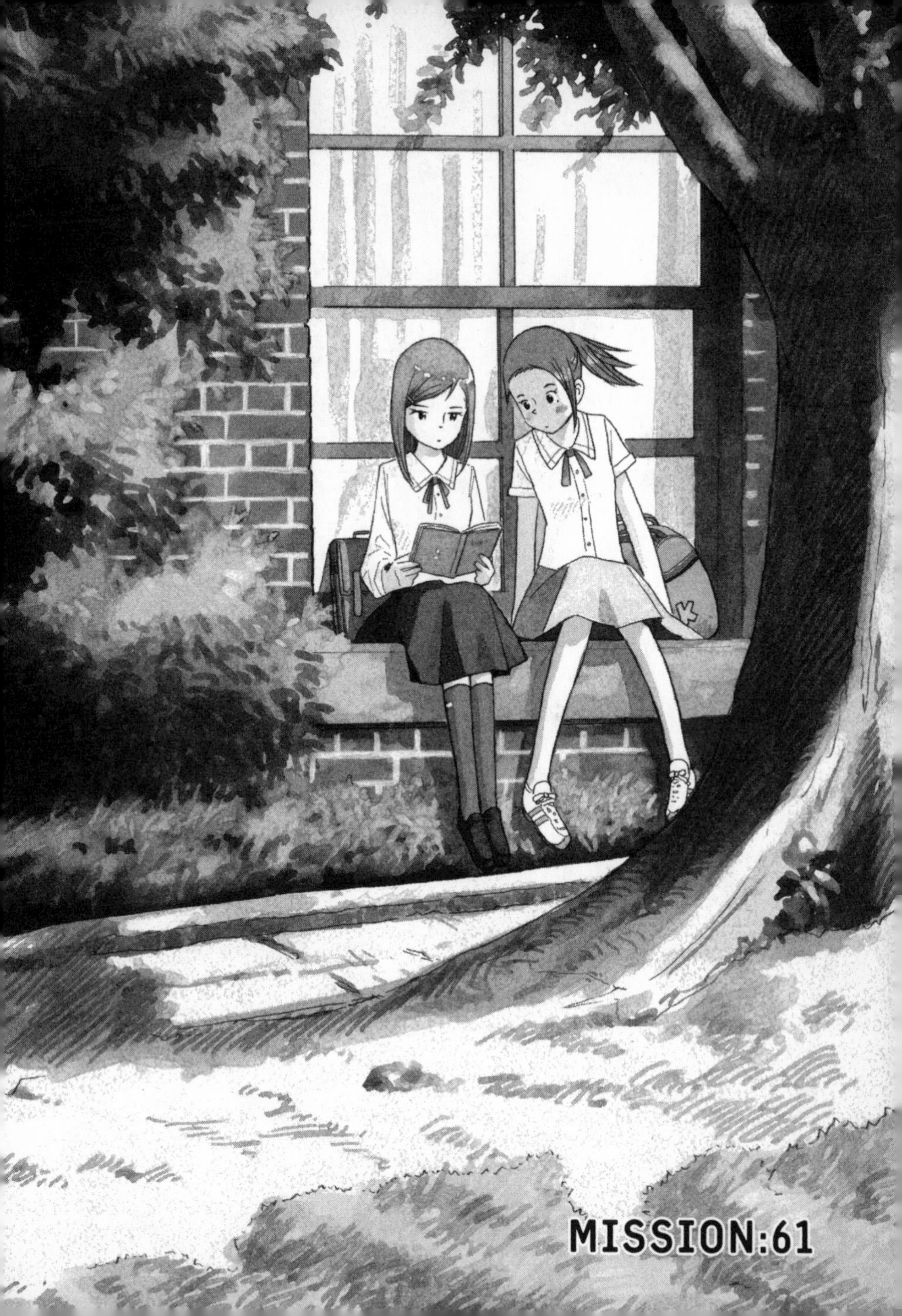
MISSION:61

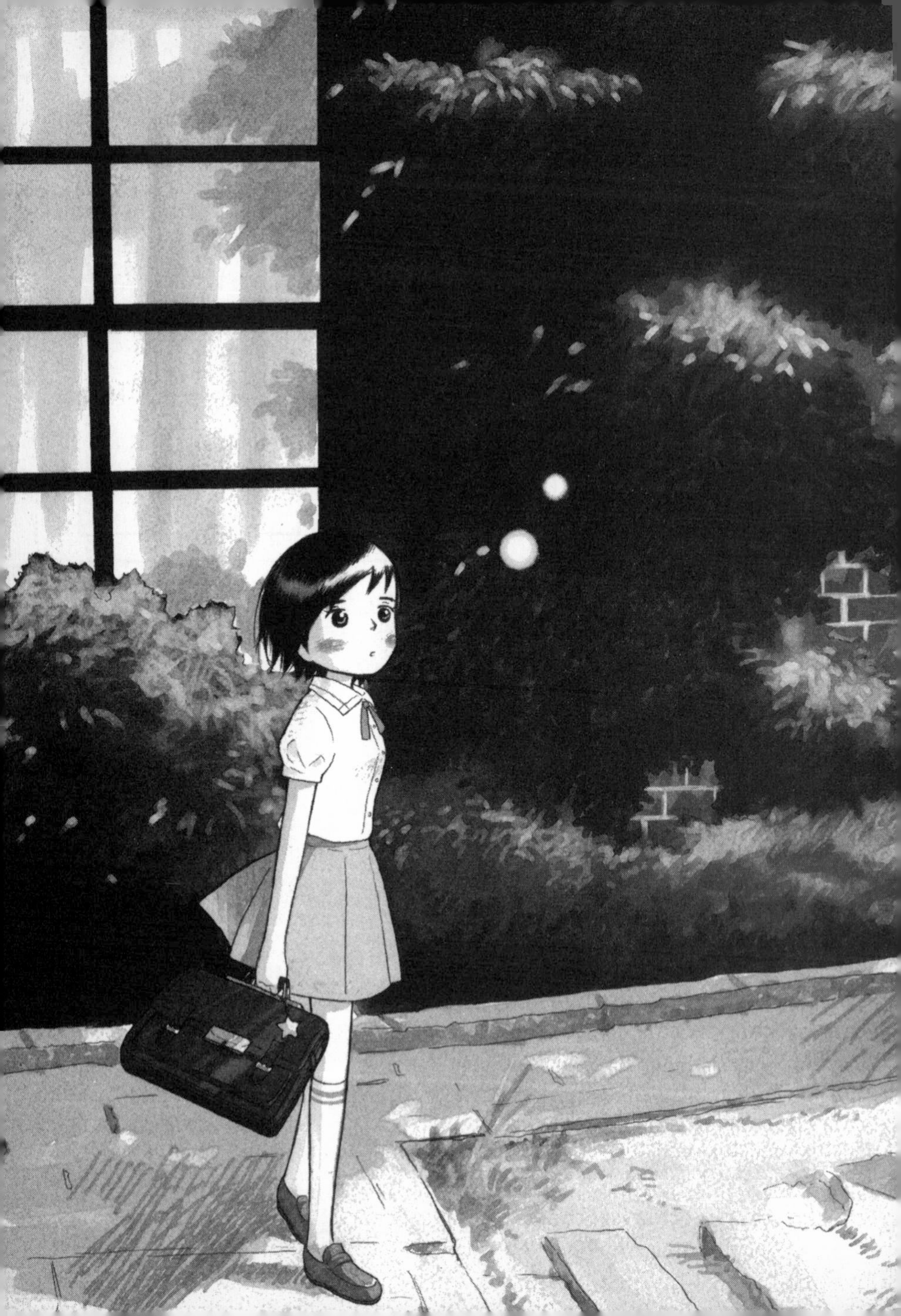

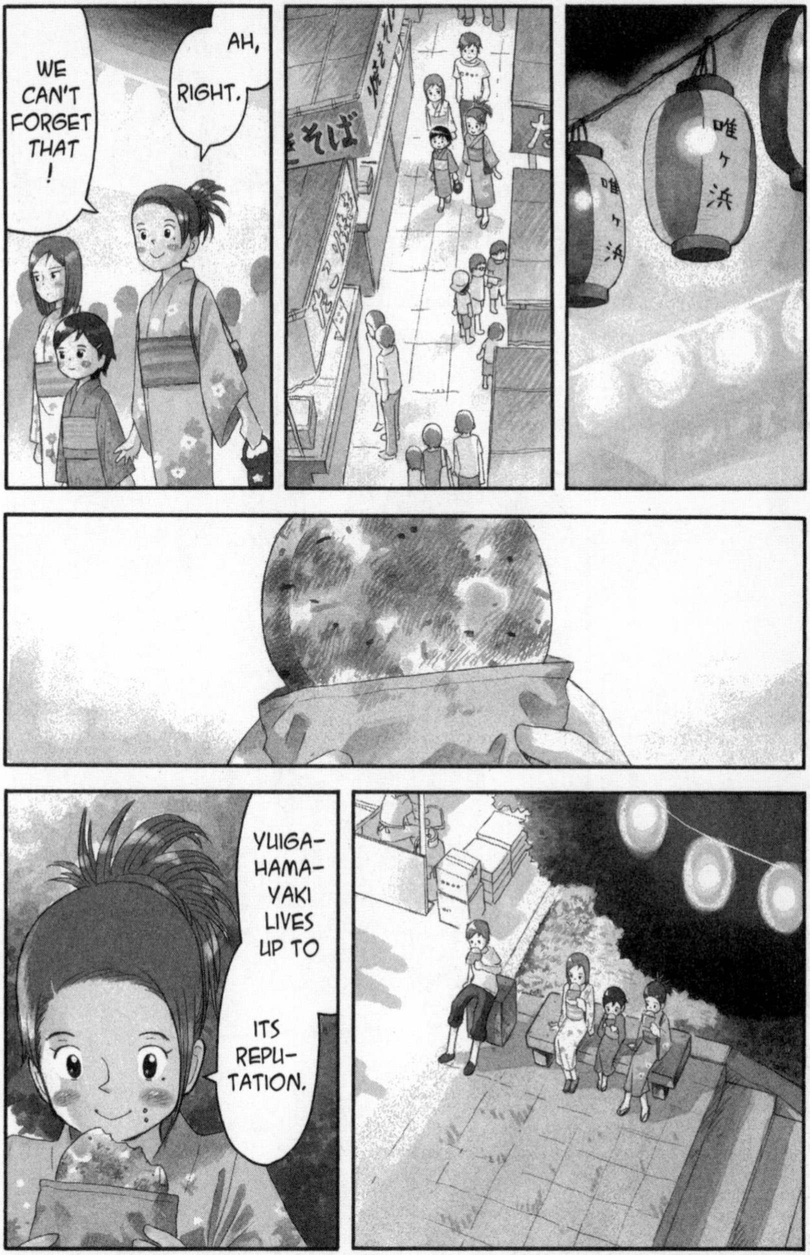
唯ヶ浜
唯ヶ浜
AH, RIGHT.
WE CAN'T FORGET THAT!
YUIGA-HAMA-YAKI LIVES UP TO ITS REPUTATION.

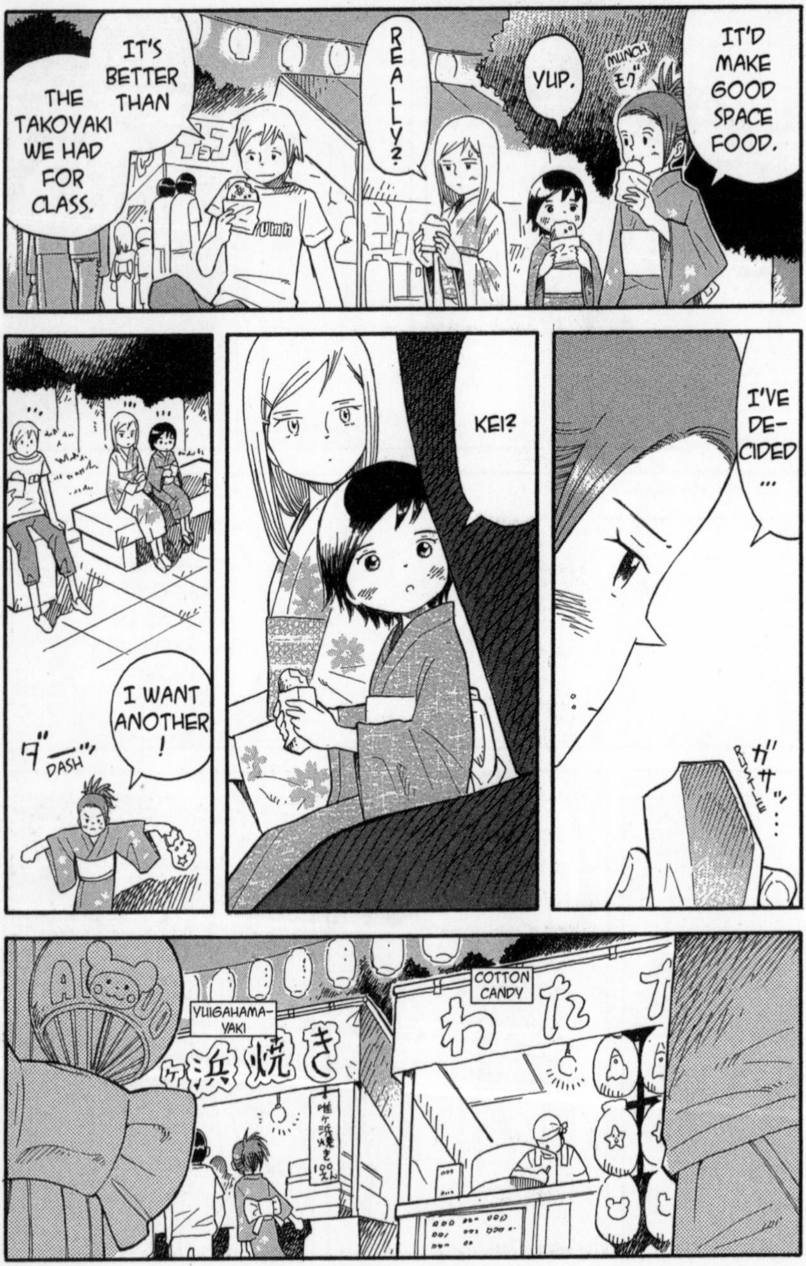
IT'D MAKE GOOD SPACE FOOD.
MUNCH
モグ
YUP.
REALLY?
IT'S BETTER THAN THE TAKOYAKI WE HAD FOR CLASS.
I'VE DE-CIDED ...
ガサッ…
RUSTLE
KEI?
I WANT ANOTHER!
ダーッ
DASH
COTTON CANDY
わた
YUIGAHAMA-YAKI
ケ浜焼き

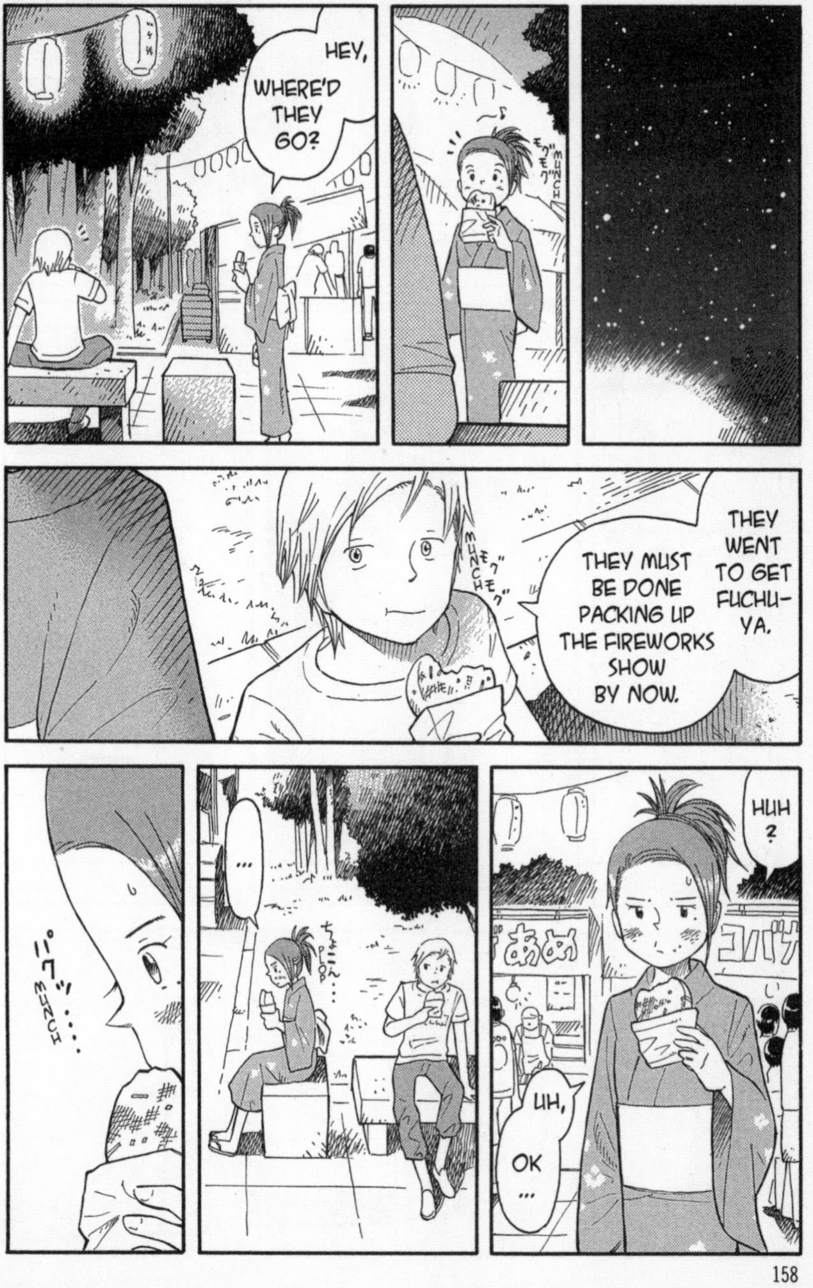
モグモグ
MUNCH
HEY,
WHERE'D THEY GO?
THEY WENT TO GET FUCHU-YA.
THEY MUST BE DONE PACKING UP THE FIREWORKS SHOW BY NOW.
モグモグ
MUNCH
HUH?
UH, OK ...
...
ちょこん...
PLOP
パクッ....
MUNCH

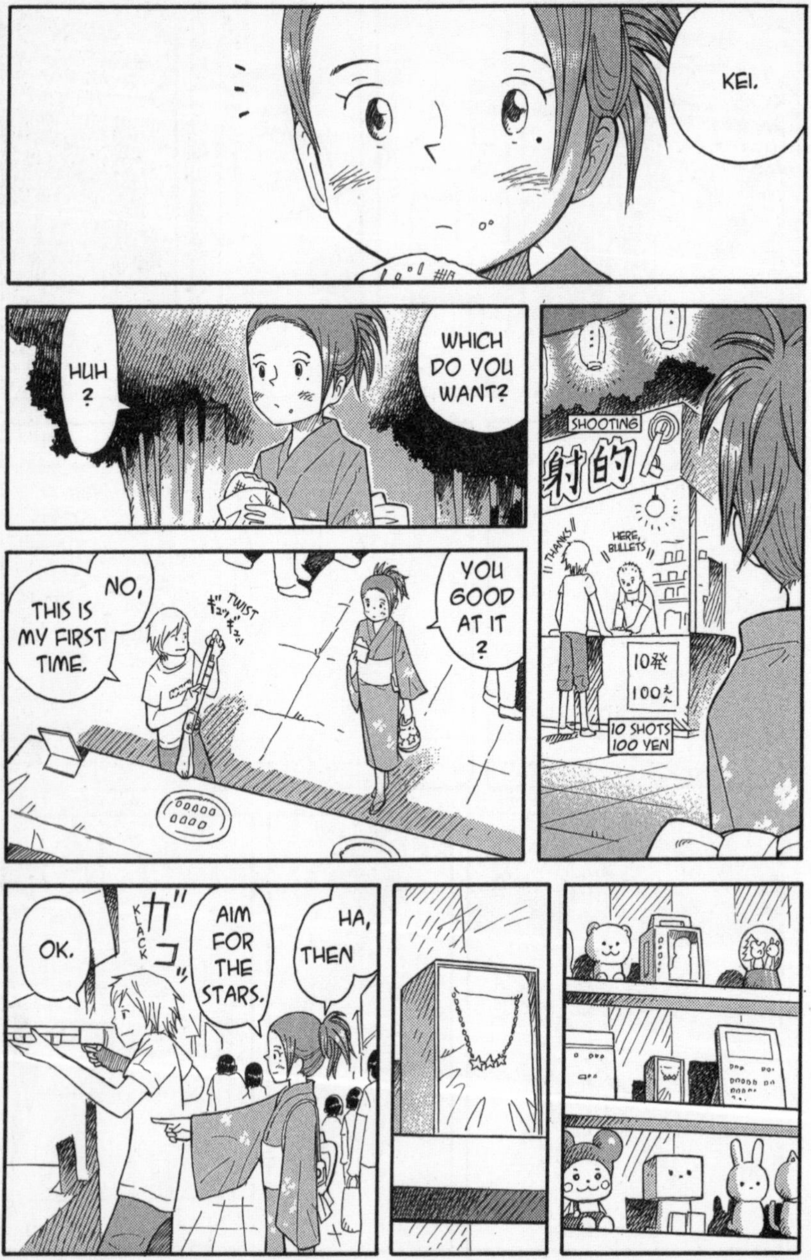
KEI.
SHOOTING
射的
THANKS
HERE, BULLETS
10発
100えん
10 SHOTS 100 YEN
WHICH DO YOU WANT?
HUH ?
YOU GOOD AT IT ?
TWIST ギュッギュッ
NO, THIS IS MY FIRST TIME.
HA, THEN
AIM FOR THE STARS.
KLACK ガコ
OK.

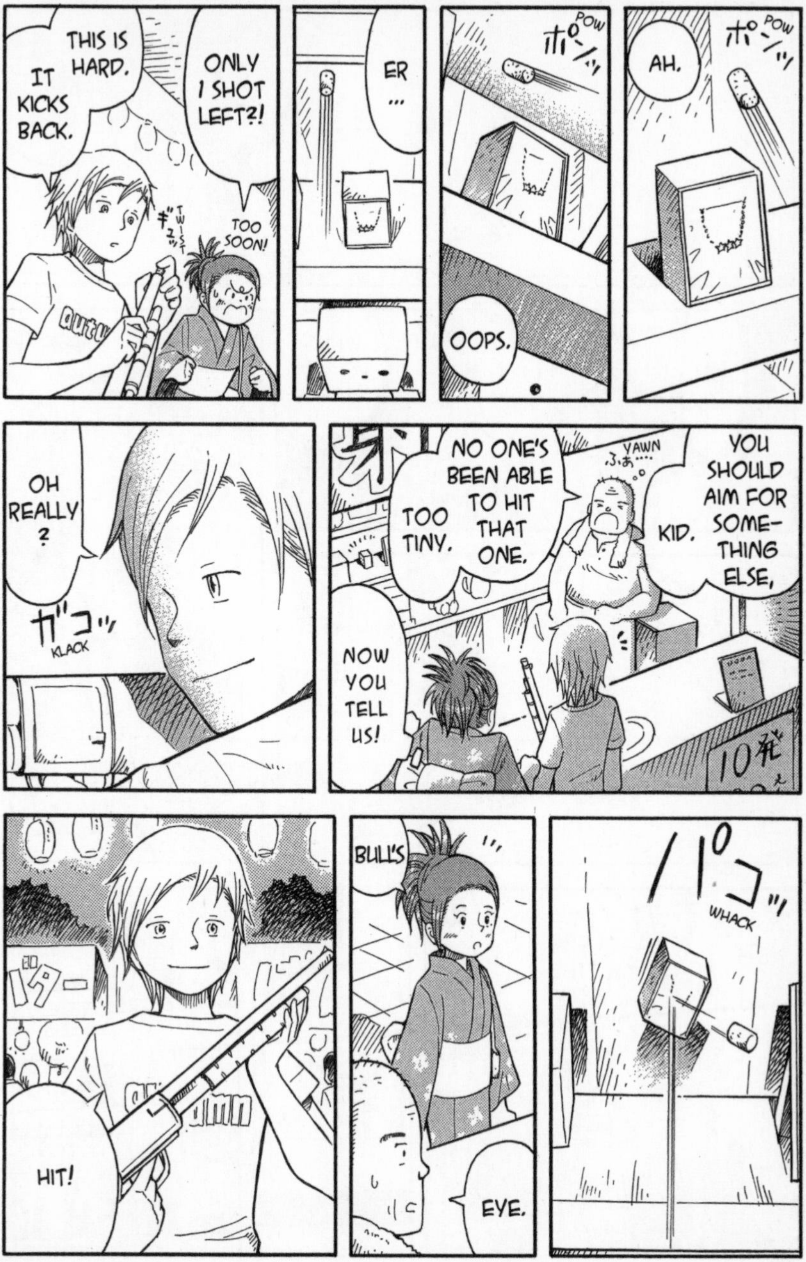
POW
ポンッ
AH.
POW
ポンッ
OOPS.
ER ...
ONLY 1 SHOT LEFT?!
THIS IS HARD.
IT KICKS BACK.
TOO SOON!
ギュッ TWIST
YOU SHOULD AIM FOR SOME-THING ELSE,
KID.
ふあ… YAWN
NO ONE'S BEEN ABLE TO HIT THAT ONE.
TOO TINY.
NOW YOU TELL US!
10発
OH REALLY?
ガコッ KLACK
パコッ WHACK
BULL'S
EYE.
HIT!

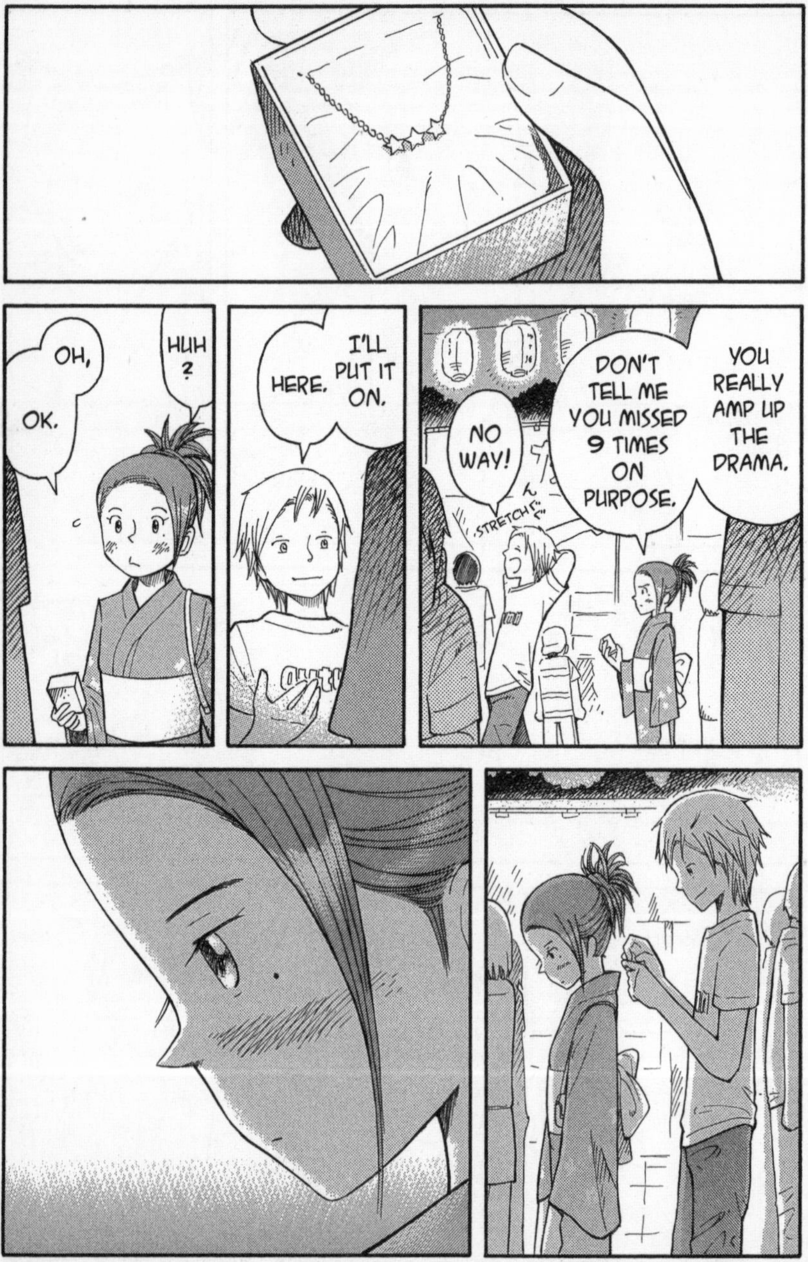
YOU REALLY AMP UP THE DRAMA.
DON'T TELL ME YOU MISSED 9 TIMES ON PURPOSE.
NO WAY!
STRETCH
I'LL PUT IT ON.
HERE.
HUH?
OH, OK.

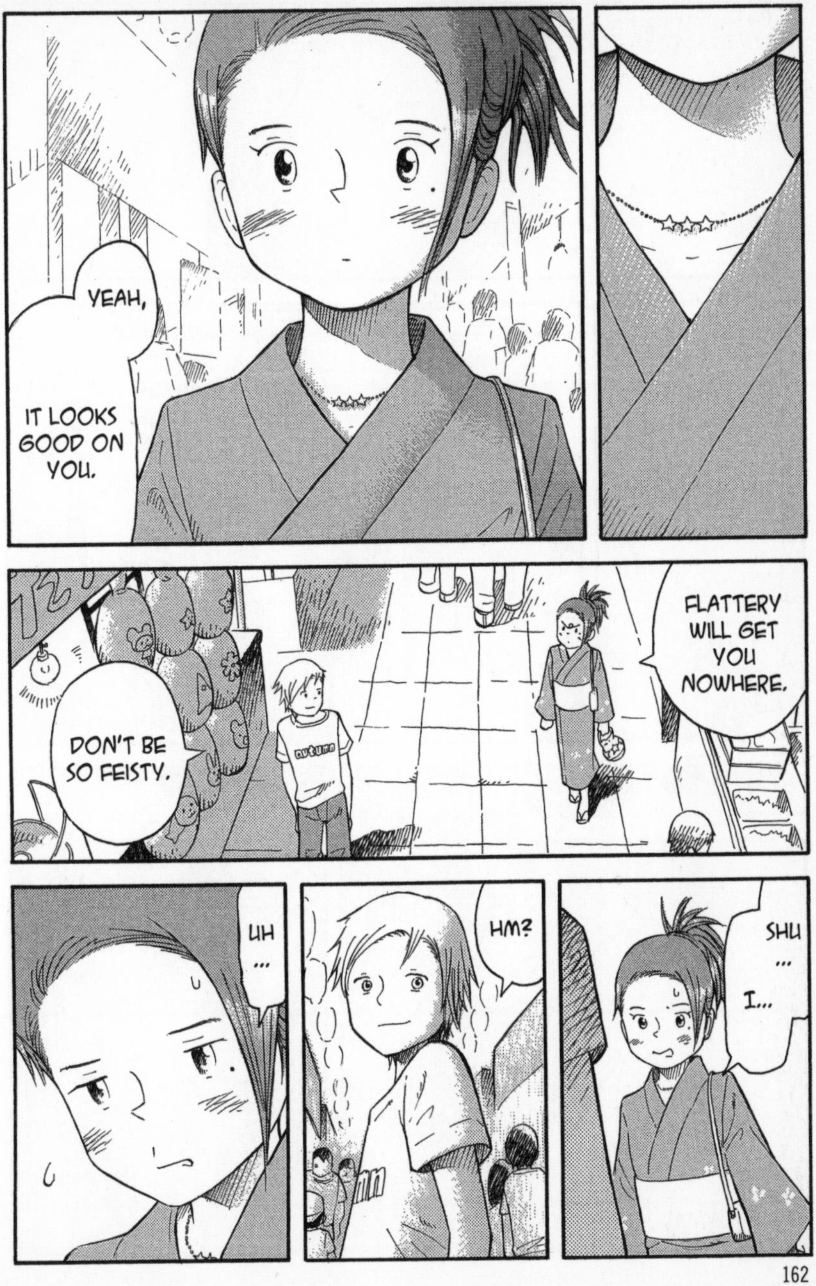
YEAH,
IT LOOKS GOOD ON YOU.
FLATTERY WILL GET YOU NOWHERE.
DON'T BE SO FEISTY.
SHU ... I...
HM?
UH ...

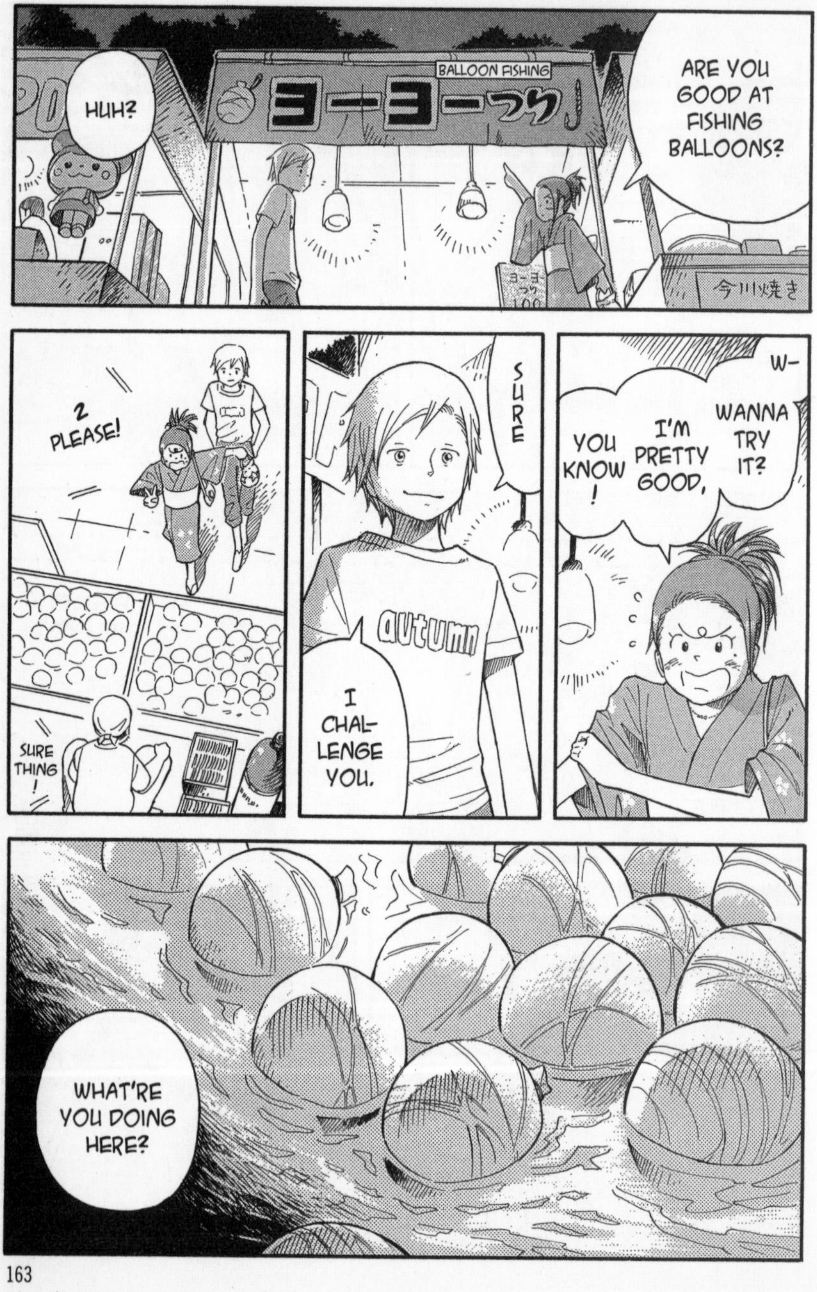
ARE YOU GOOD AT FISHING BALLOONS?
BALLOON FISHING
ヨーヨーつり
HUH?
今川焼き
W- WANNA TRY IT?
I'M PRETTY GOOD, YOU KNOW!
SURE
I CHALLENGE YOU.
2 PLEASE!
SURE THING!
WHAT'RE YOU DOING HERE?

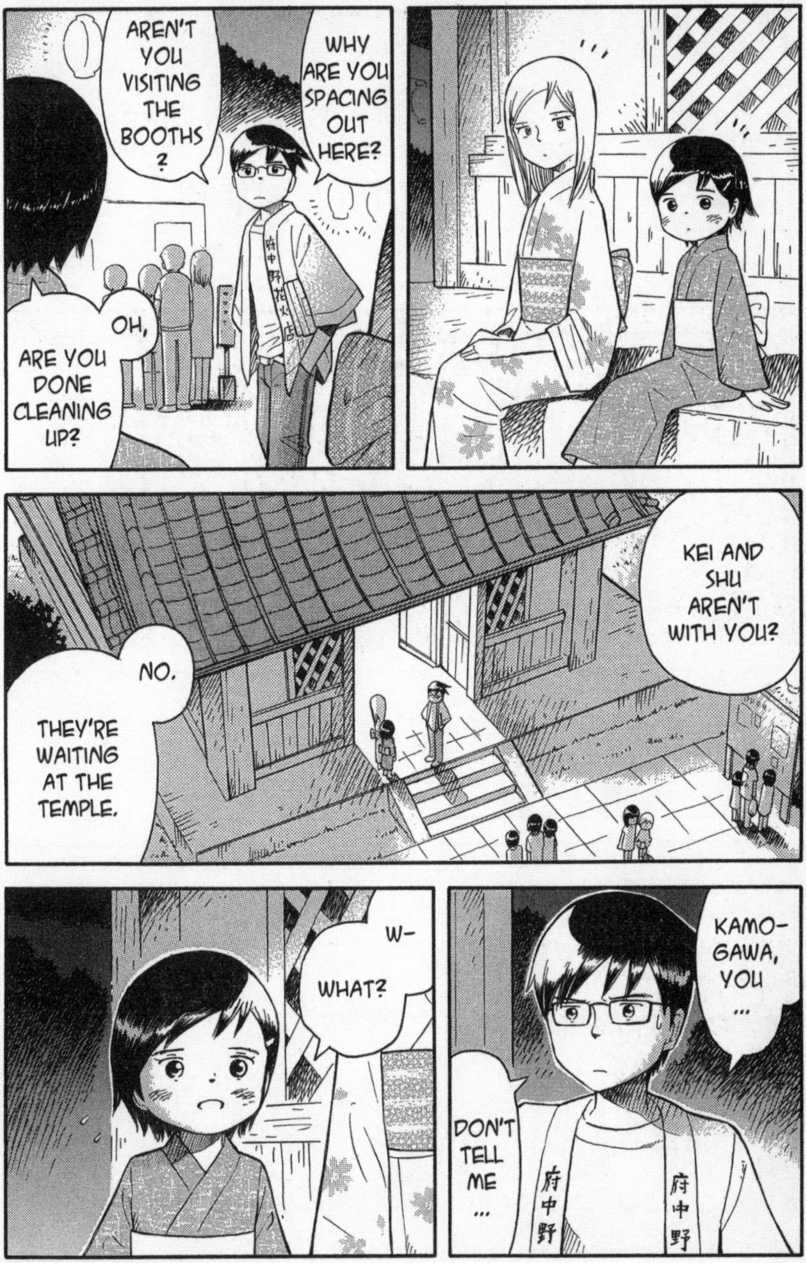
WHY ARE YOU SPACING OUT HERE?
AREN'T YOU VISITING THE BOOTHS?
府中野花火店
OH, ARE YOU DONE CLEANING UP?
KEI AND SHU AREN'T WITH YOU?
NO.
THEY'RE WAITING AT THE TEMPLE.
KAMOGAWA, YOU ...
府中野
府中野
DON'T TELL ME ...
W-
WHAT?

THAT'S THE SAME YUKATA YOU WORE IN GRADE SCHOOL?
?!

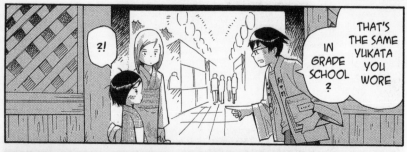

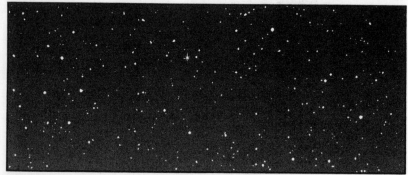

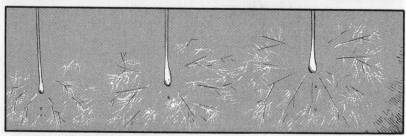

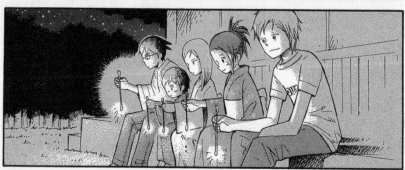

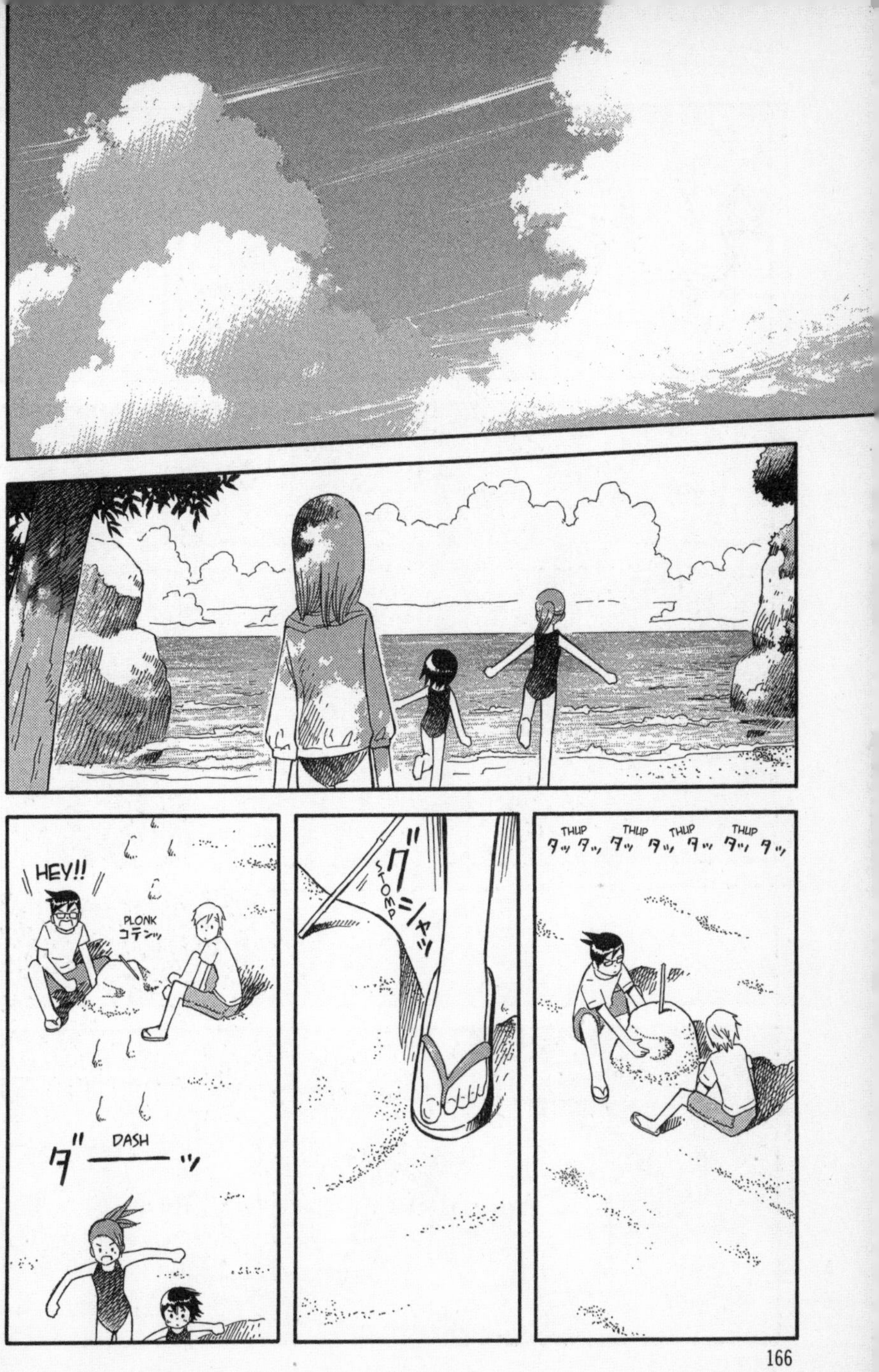
THUP THUP THUP THUP
タッタッタッタッタッタッタッ
STOMP
グニャッ
HEY!!
PLONK
コテンッ
DASH
ダーーッ

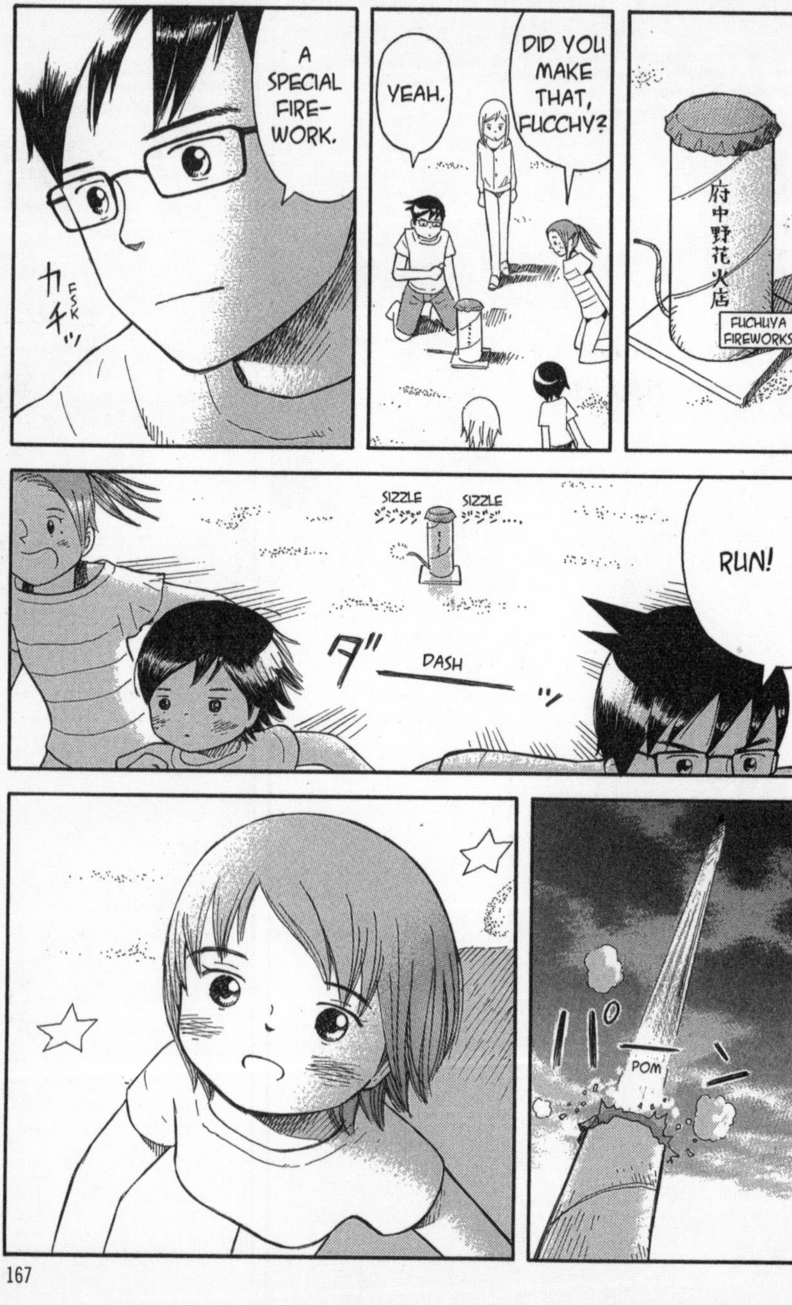
府中野花火店
FUCHUYA FIREWORKS
DID YOU MAKE THAT, FUCCHY?
YEAH.
A SPECIAL FIRE-WORK.
カチッ
FSK
RUN!
SIZZLE
ジジジジ
SIZZLE
ジジジ…
ダーッ
DASH
パ
POM

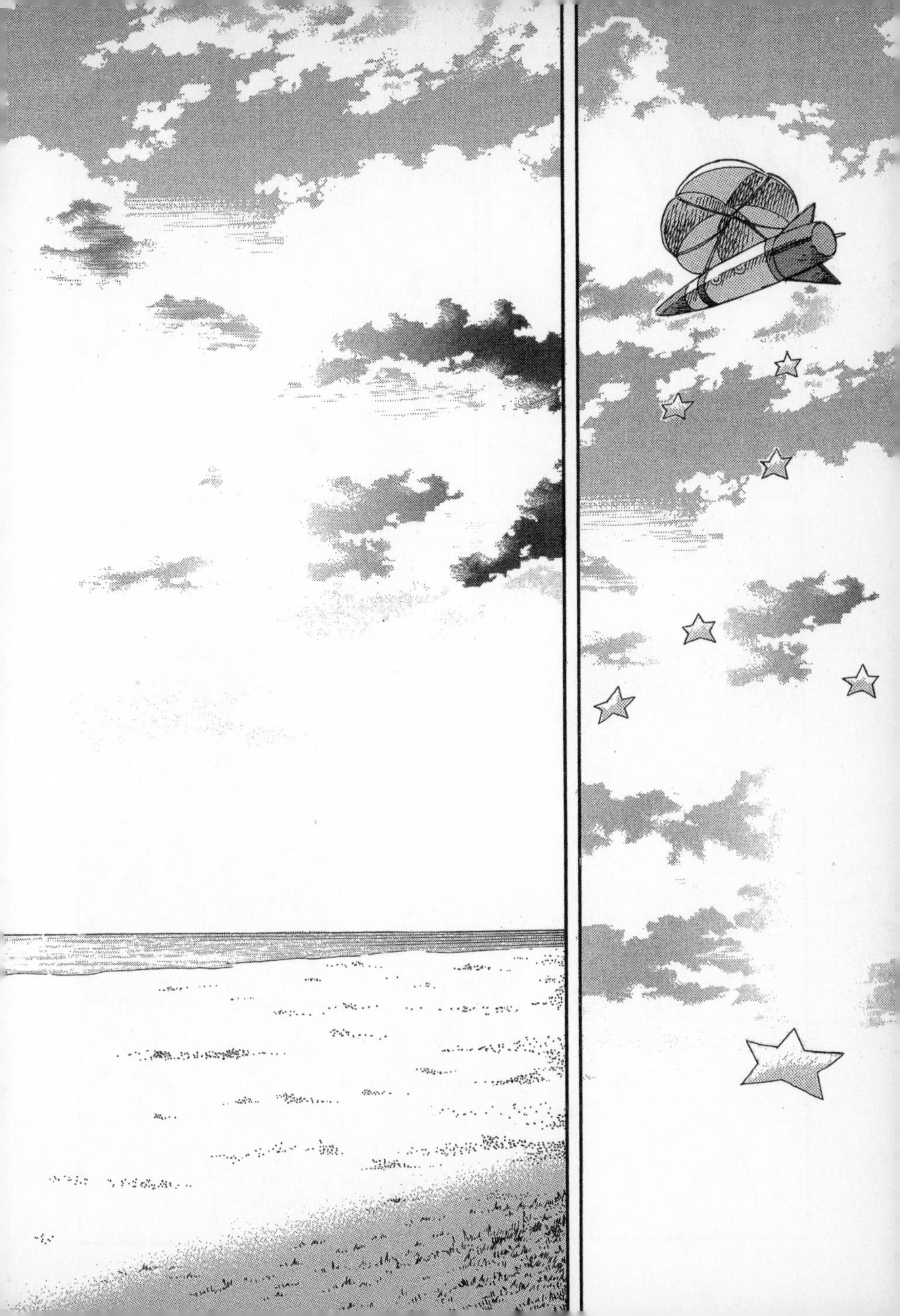

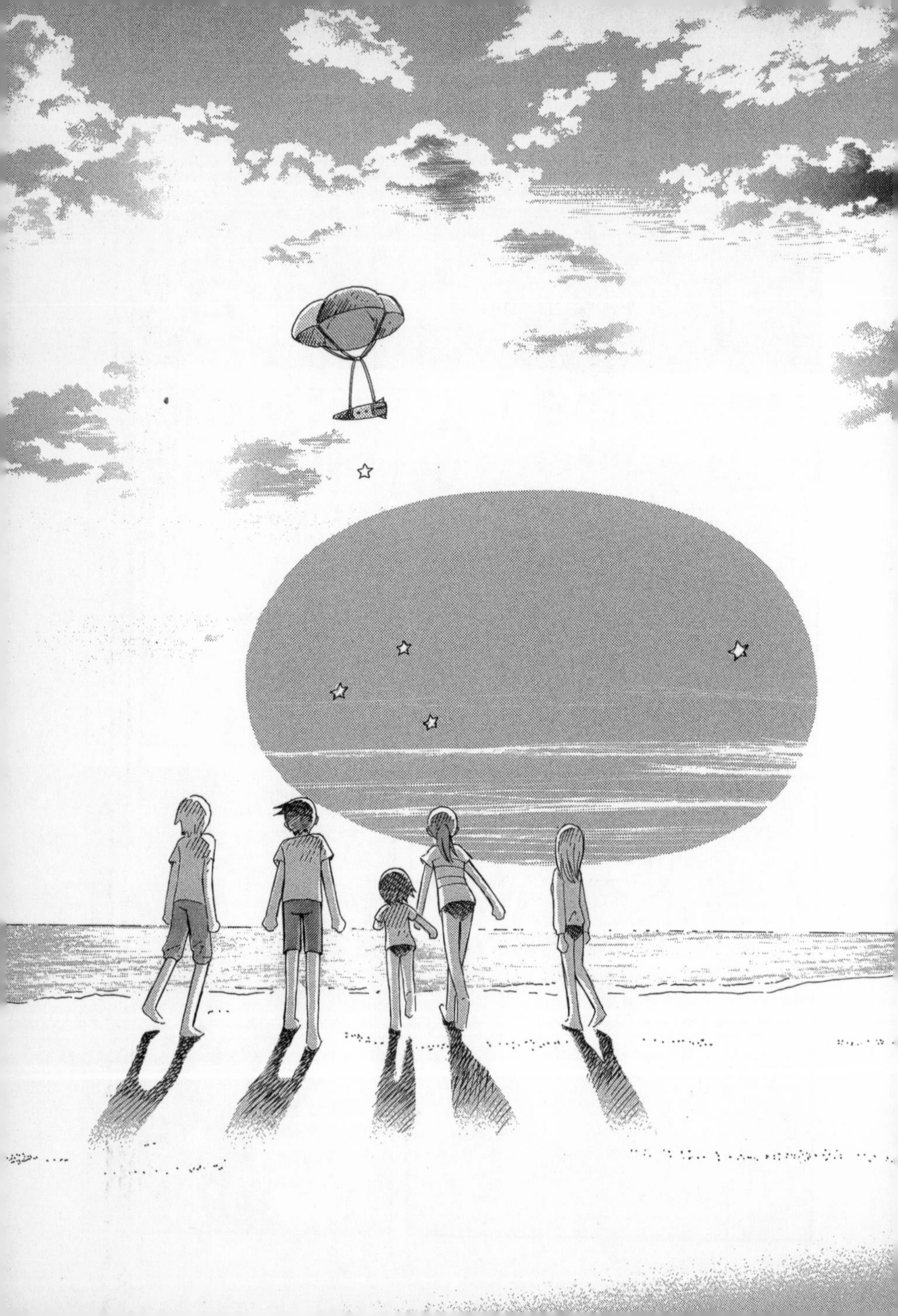

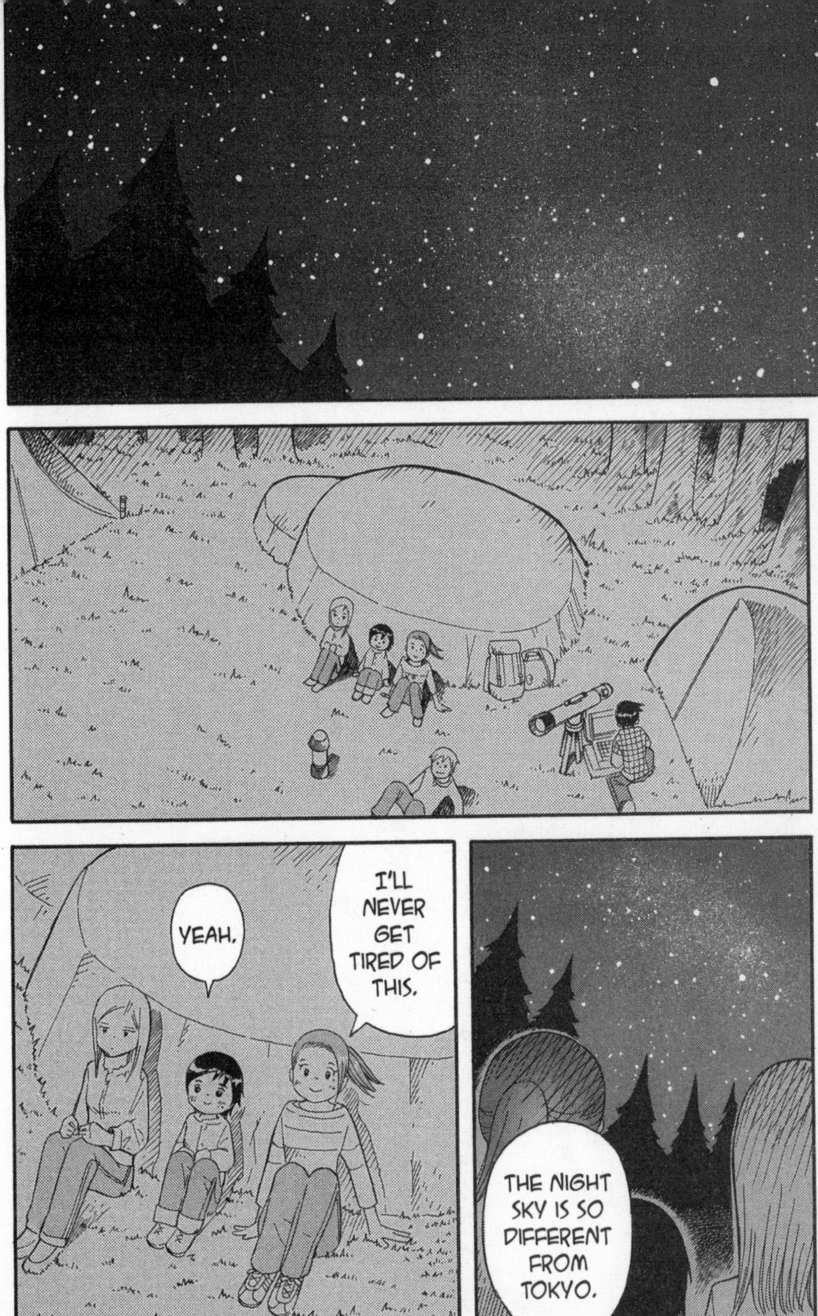
THE NIGHT SKY IS SO DIFFERENT FROM TOKYO.
I'LL NEVER GET TIRED OF THIS.
YEAH.

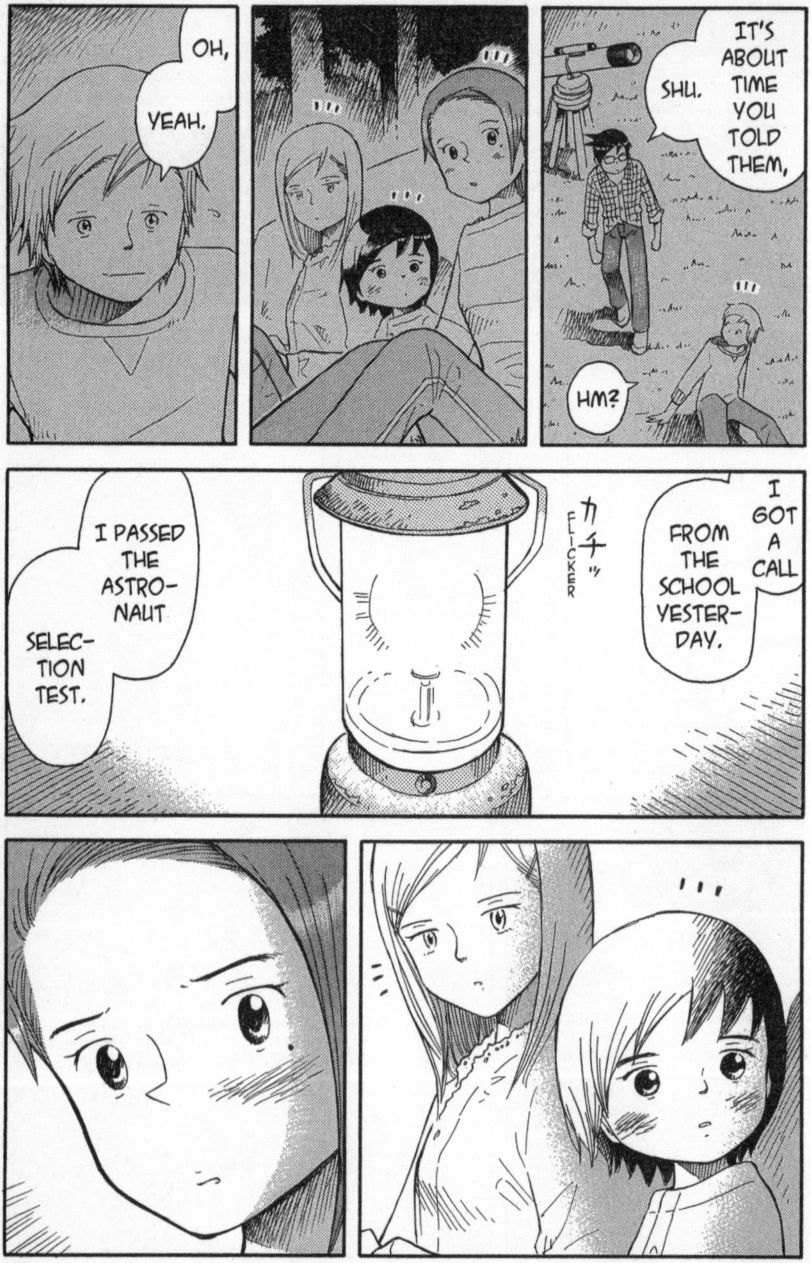
IT'S ABOUT TIME YOU TOLD THEM,
SHU.
HM?
OH,
YEAH.
I GOT A CALL
FROM THE SCHOOL YESTER-DAY.
カチッ
FLICKER
I PASSED THE ASTRO-NAUT
SELEC-TION TEST.

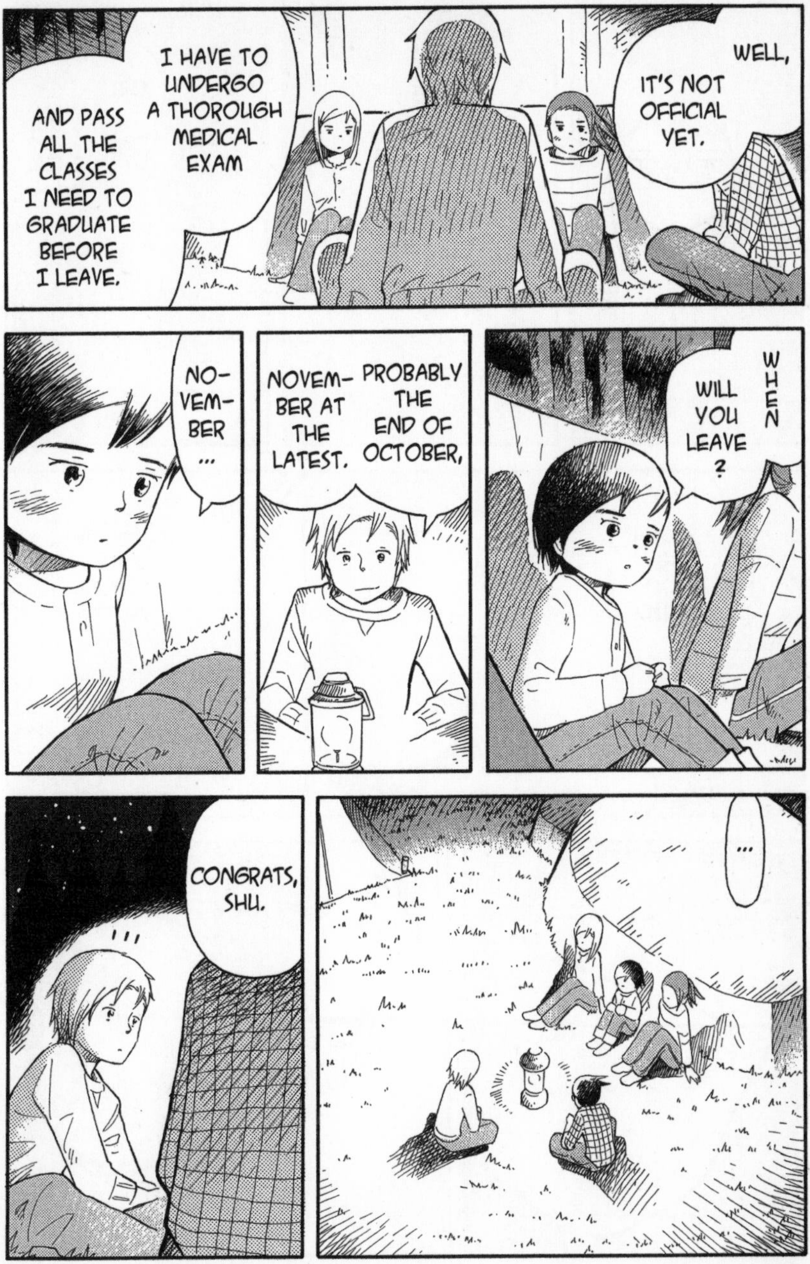
WELL, IT'S NOT OFFICIAL YET.
I HAVE TO UNDERGO A THOROUGH MEDICAL EXAM
AND PASS ALL THE CLASSES I NEED TO GRADUATE BEFORE I LEAVE.
WHEN WILL YOU LEAVE?
PROBABLY THE END OF OCTOBER,
NOVEMBER AT THE LATEST.
NO-VEMBER ...
...
CONGRATS, SHU.

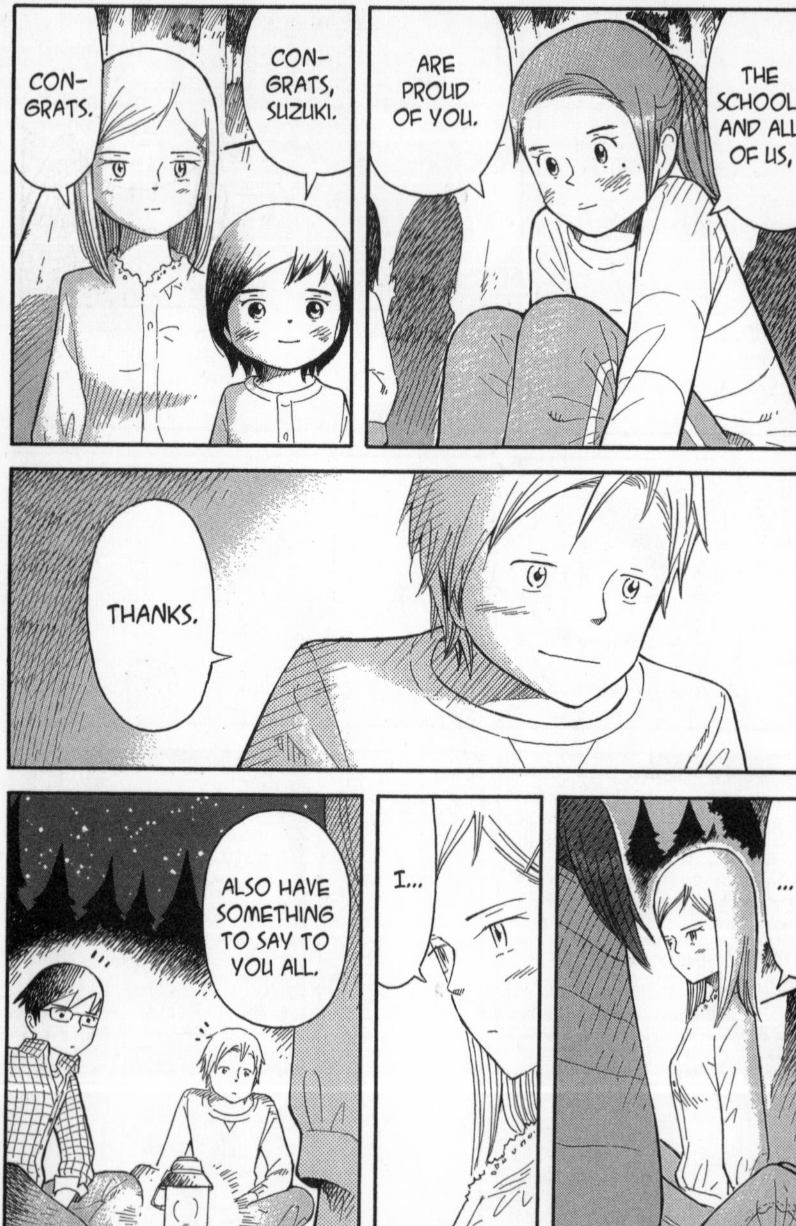
THE SCHOOL, AND ALL OF US,
ARE PROUD OF YOU.
CON-GRATS, SUZUKI.
CON-GRATS.
THANKS.
...
I...
ALSO HAVE SOMETHING TO SAY TO YOU ALL.

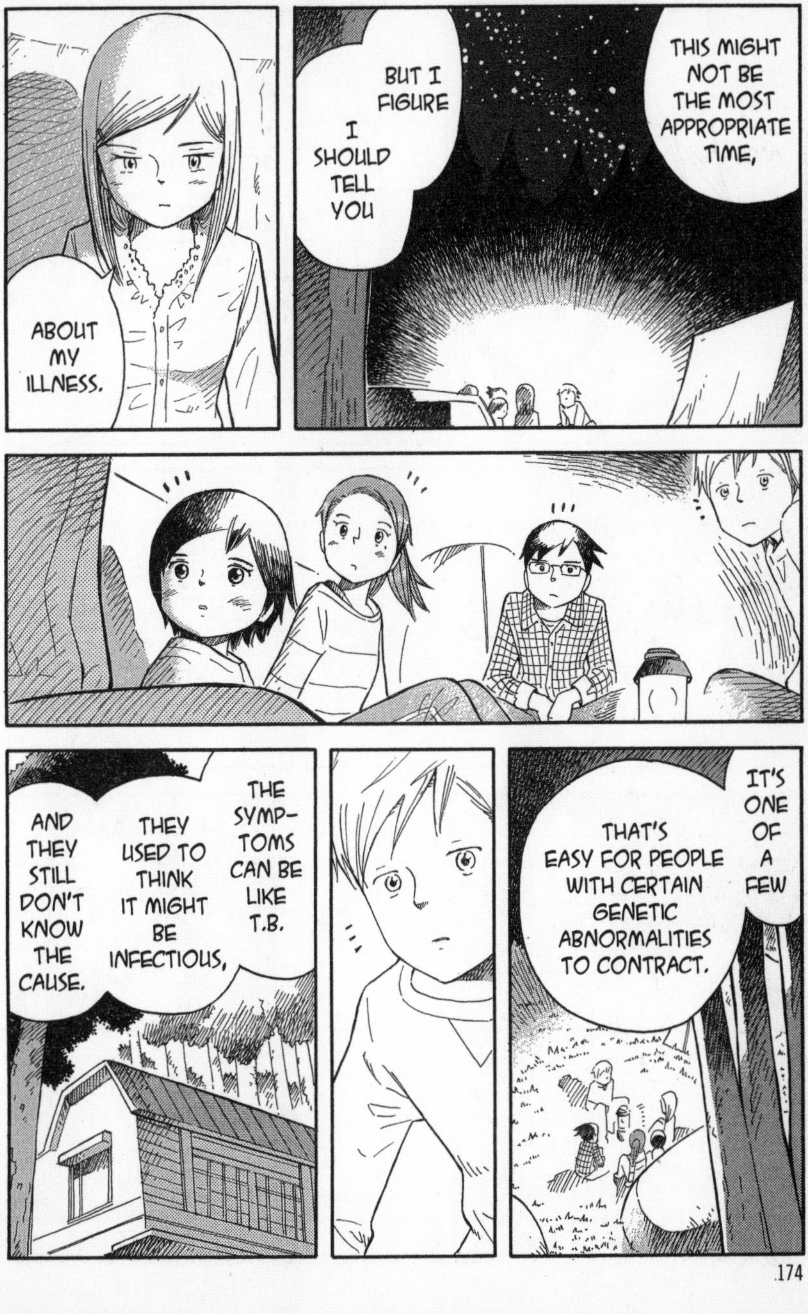
THIS MIGHT NOT BE THE MOST APPROPRIATE TIME,
BUT I FIGURE
I SHOULD TELL YOU
ABOUT MY ILLNESS.
IT'S ONE OF A FEW
THAT'S EASY FOR PEOPLE WITH CERTAIN GENETIC ABNORMALITIES TO CONTRACT.
THE SYMP-TOMS CAN BE LIKE T.B.
THEY USED TO THINK IT MIGHT BE INFECTIOUS,
AND THEY STILL DON'T KNOW THE CAUSE.

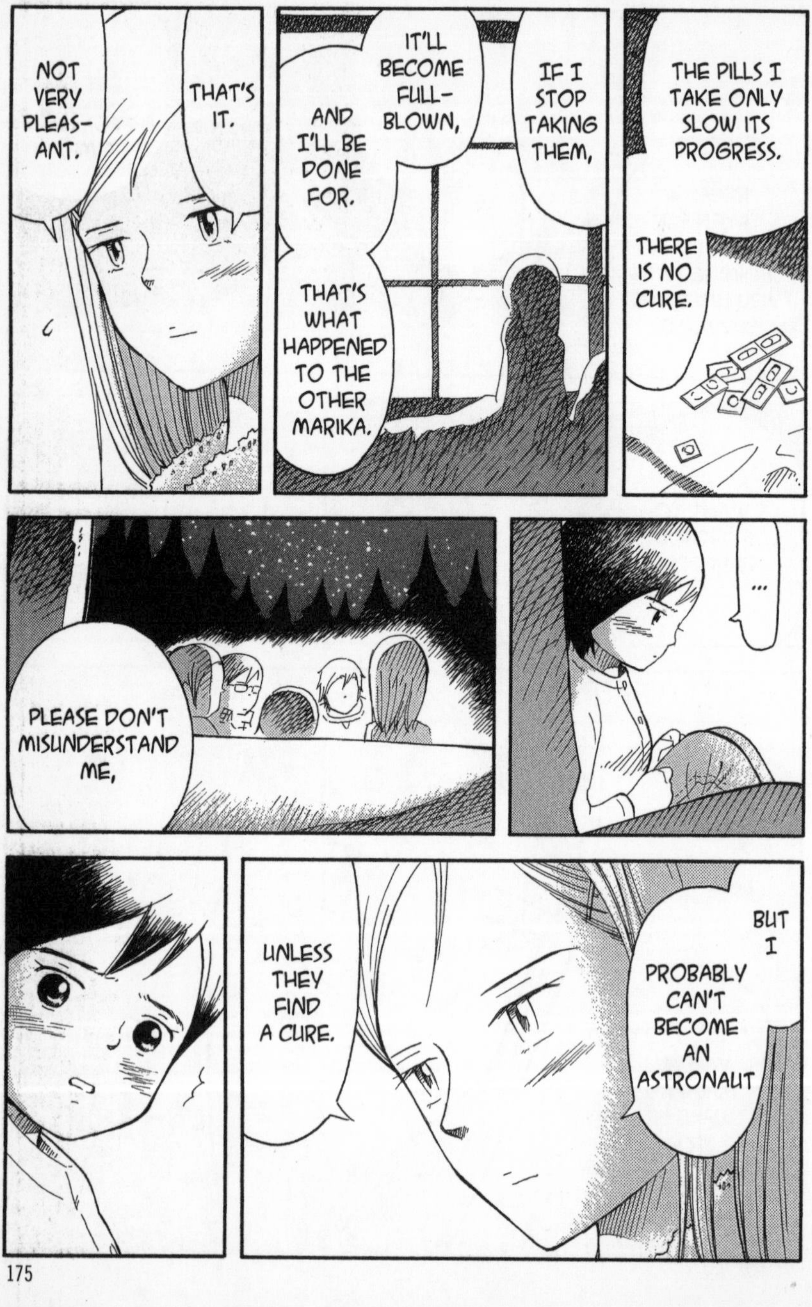
THE PILLS I TAKE ONLY SLOW ITS PROGRESS.
THERE IS NO CURE.
IF I STOP TAKING THEM,
IT'LL BECOME FULL-BLOWN,
AND I'LL BE DONE FOR.
THAT'S WHAT HAPPENED TO THE OTHER MARIKA.
THAT'S IT.
NOT VERY PLEASANT.
...
PLEASE DON'T MISUNDERSTAND ME,
BUT I PROBABLY CAN'T BECOME AN ASTRONAUT
UNLESS THEY FIND A CURE.

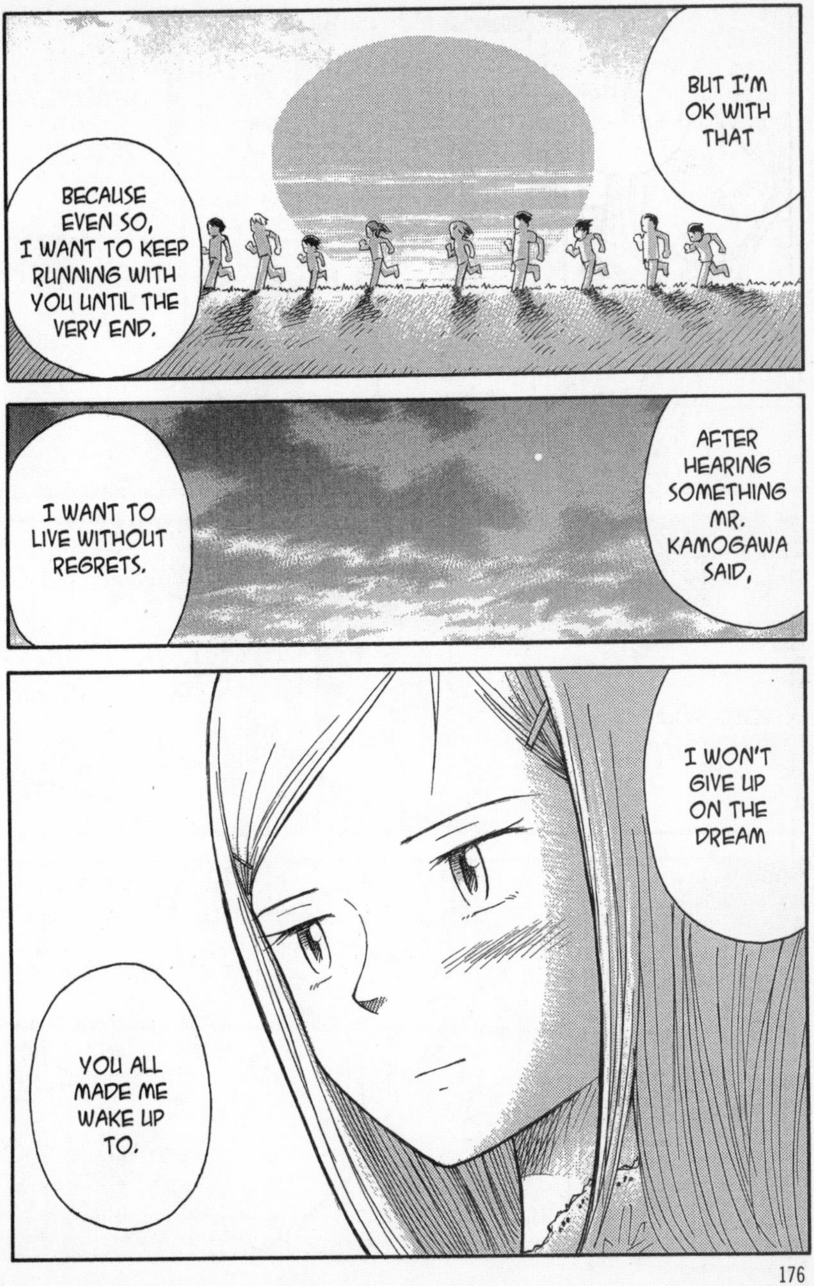
BUT I'M OK WITH THAT
BECAUSE EVEN SO, I WANT TO KEEP RUNNING WITH YOU UNTIL THE VERY END.
AFTER HEARING SOMETHING MR. KAMOGAWA SAID,
I WANT TO LIVE WITHOUT REGRETS.
I WON'T GIVE UP ON THE DREAM
YOU ALL MADE ME WAKE UP TO.

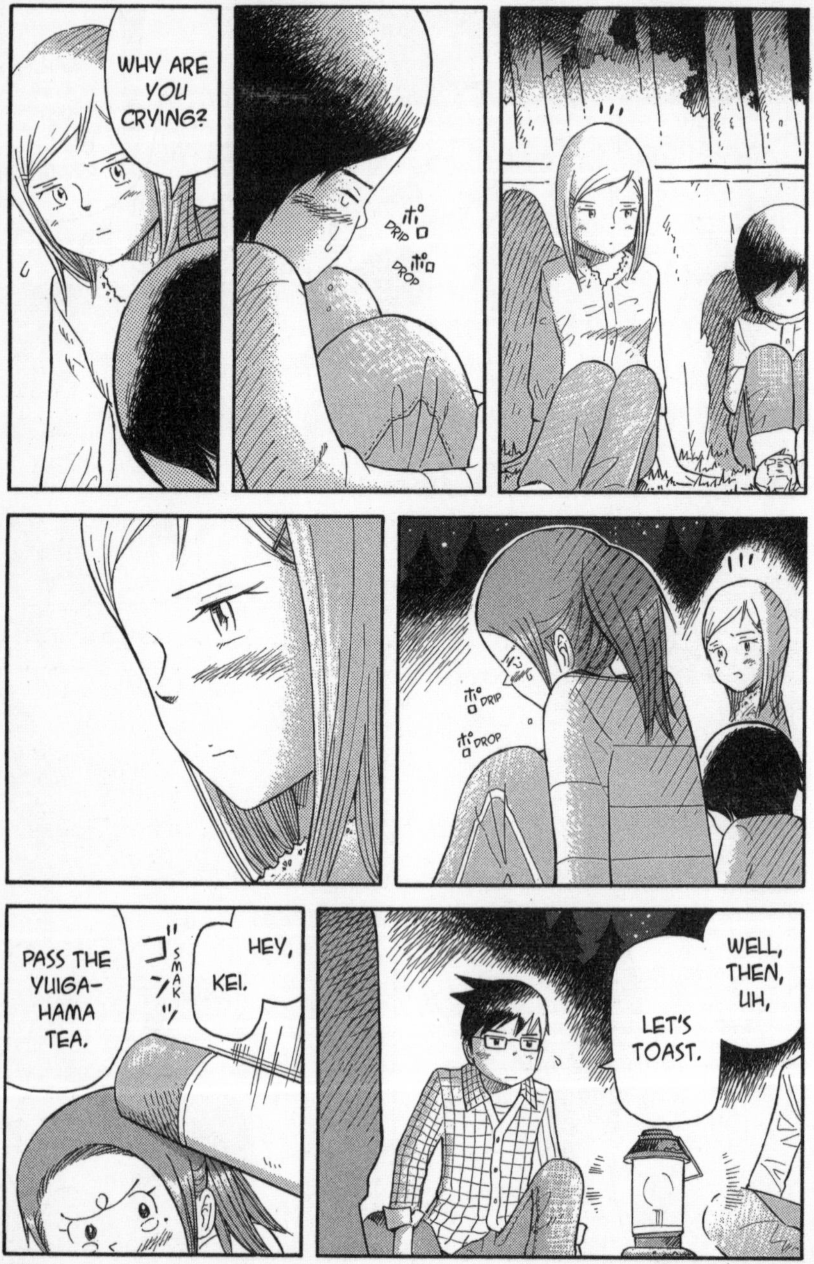
ポロ DRIP
ポロ DROP
WHY ARE YOU CRYING?
ポロ DRIP
ポロ DROP
WELL, THEN, UH,
LET'S TOAST.
HEY, KEI.
ゴンッ SMAK
PASS THE YUIGA-HAMA TEA.

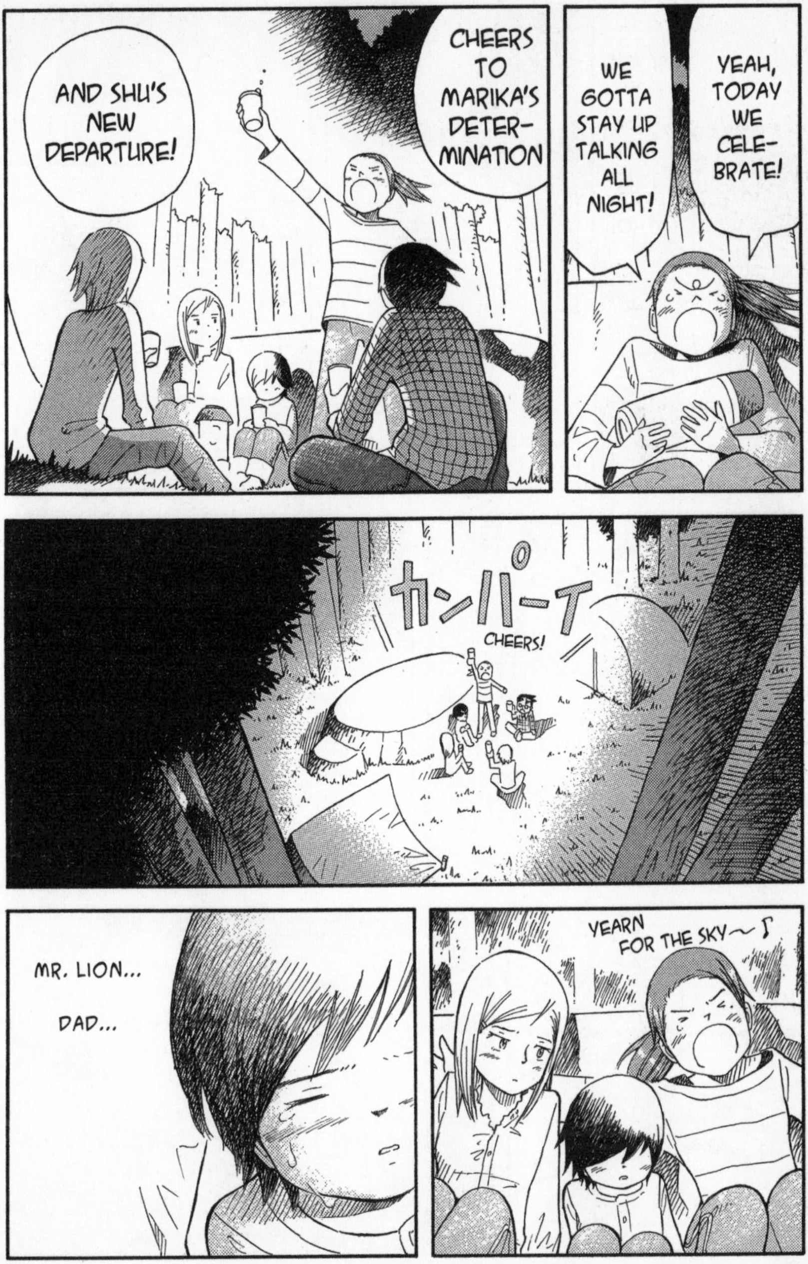
YEAH, TODAY WE CELEBRATE!
WE GOTTA STAY UP TALKING ALL NIGHT!
CHEERS TO MARIKA'S DETERMINATION
AND SHU'S NEW DEPARTURE!
カンパーイ
CHEERS!
YEARN FOR THE SKY~♪
MR. LION...
DAD...

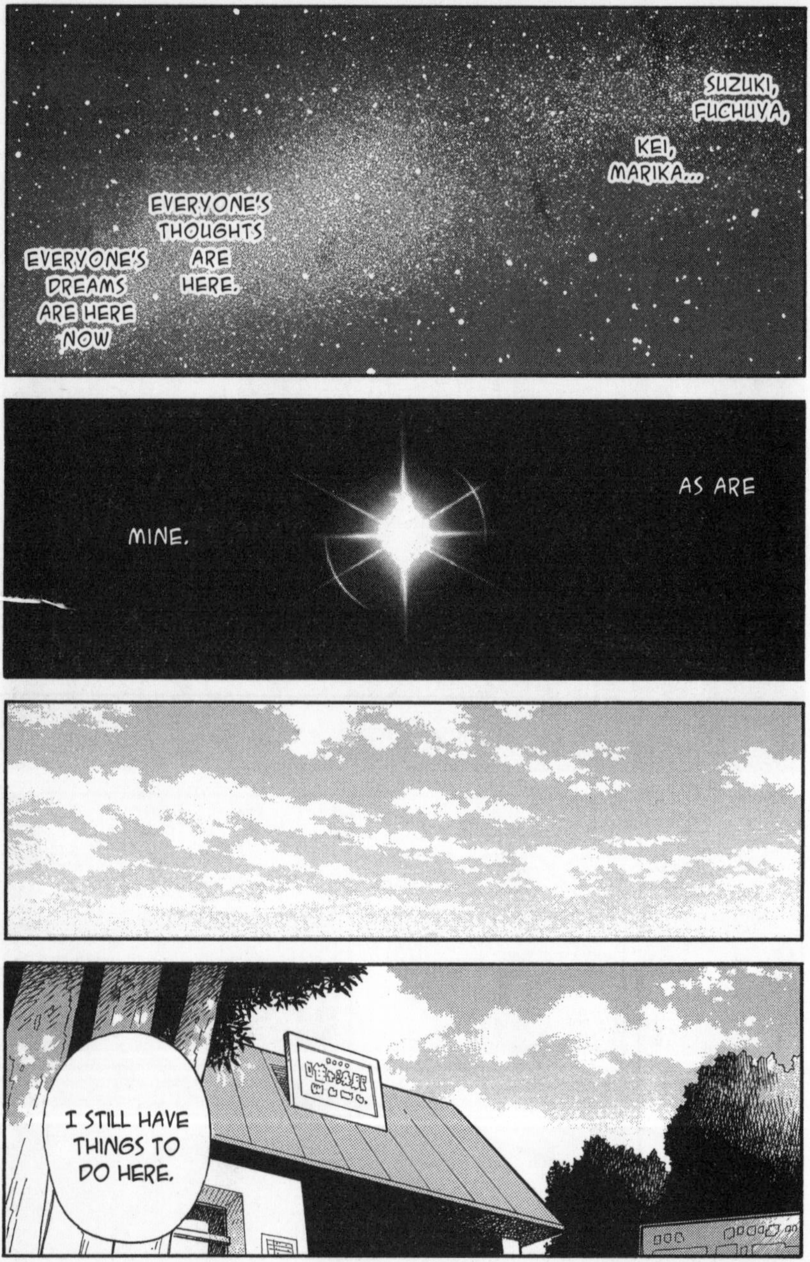
SUZUKI, FUCHUYA,
KEI, MARIKA...
EVERYONE'S THOUGHTS ARE HERE.
EVERYONE'S DREAMS ARE HERE NOW
AS ARE
MINE.
I STILL HAVE THINGS TO DO HERE.

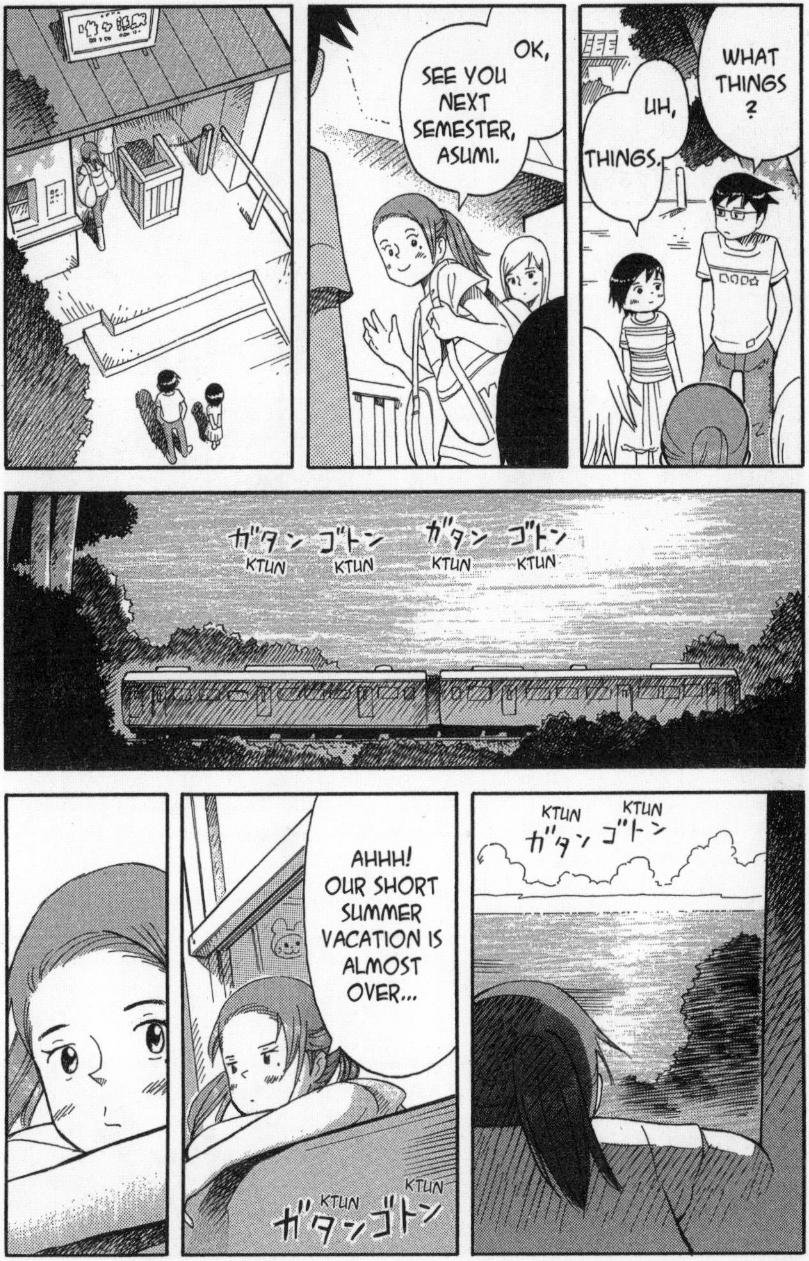
WHAT THINGS?
UH, THINGS.
OK, SEE YOU NEXT SEMESTER, ASUMI.
ガタン KTUN ゴトン KTUN ガタン KTUN ゴトン KTUN
ガタン KTUN ゴトン KTUN
AHHH! OUR SHORT SUMMER VACATION IS ALMOST OVER...
ガタンゴトン KTUN KTUN

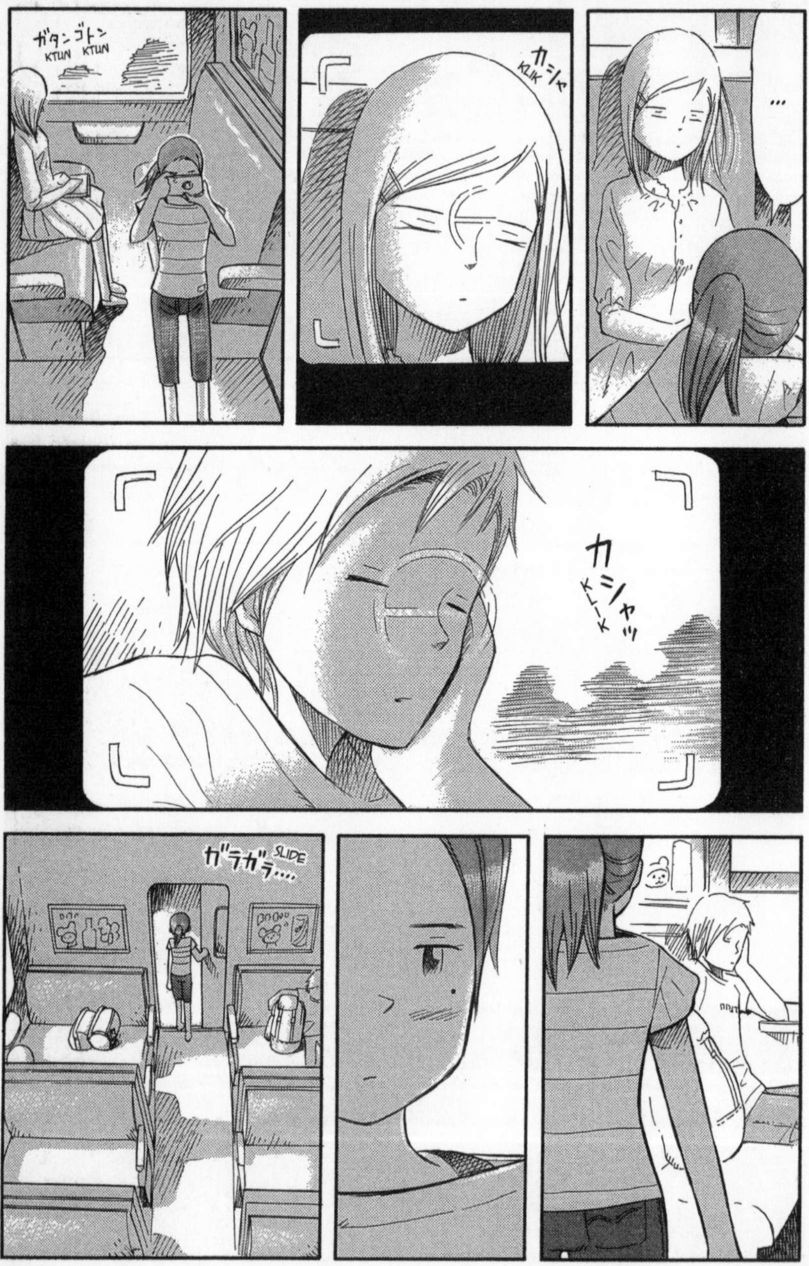
...
カシャ
KLIK
ガタンゴトン
KTUN KTUN
カシャッ
KLIK
ガラガラ…
SLIDE

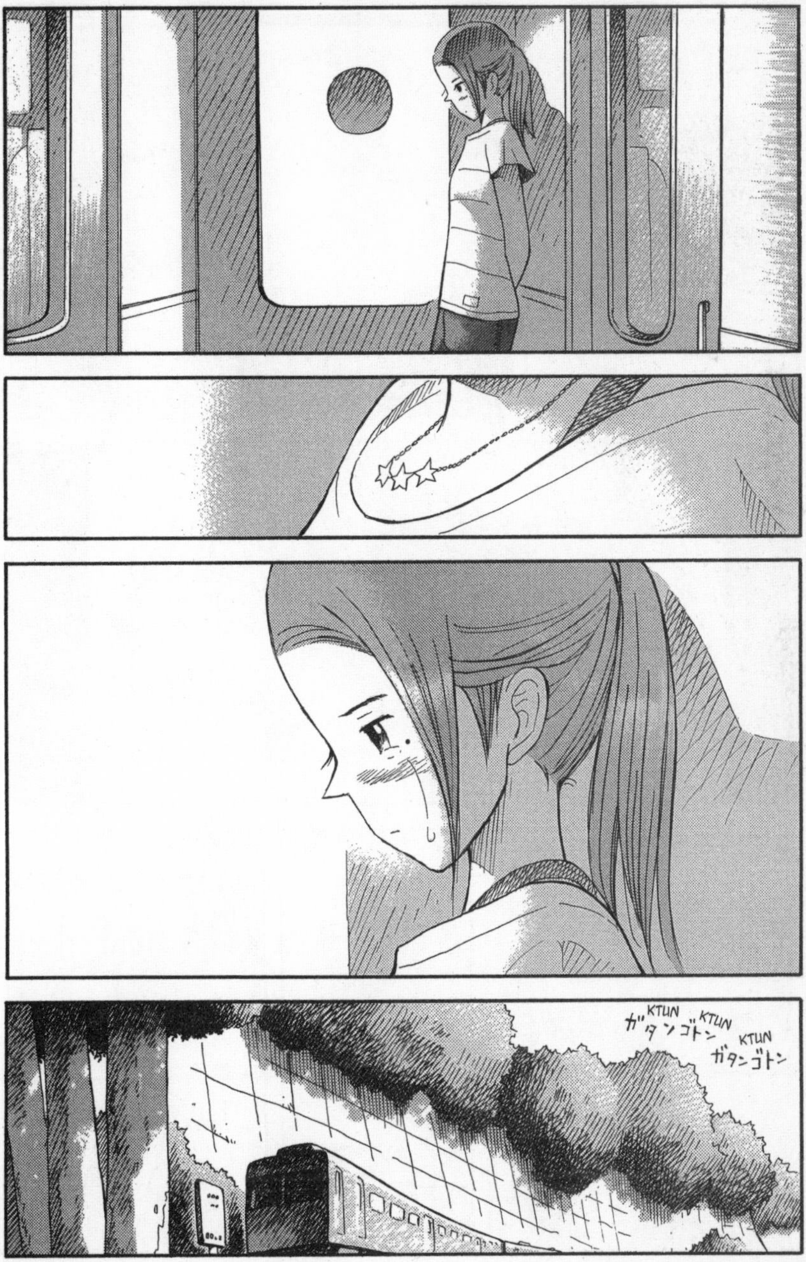
KTUN KTUN
ガタンゴトン
KTUN
ガタンゴトン

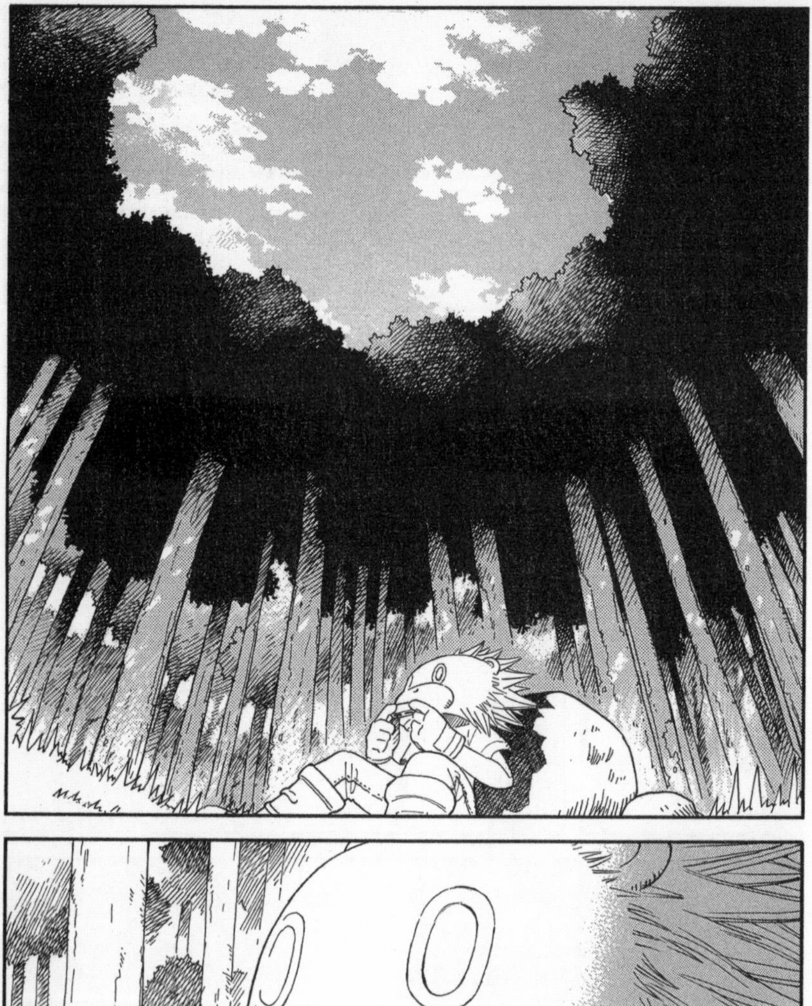

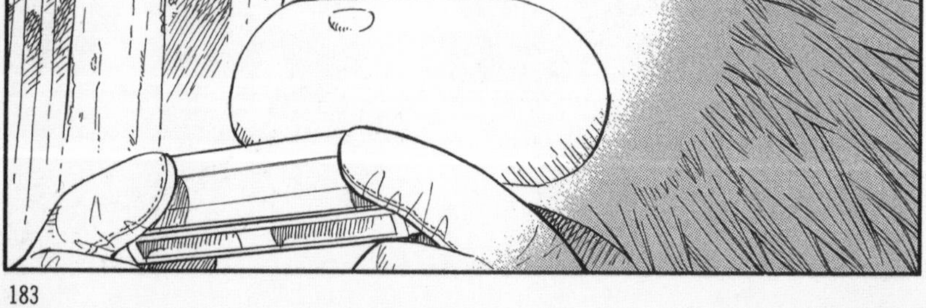

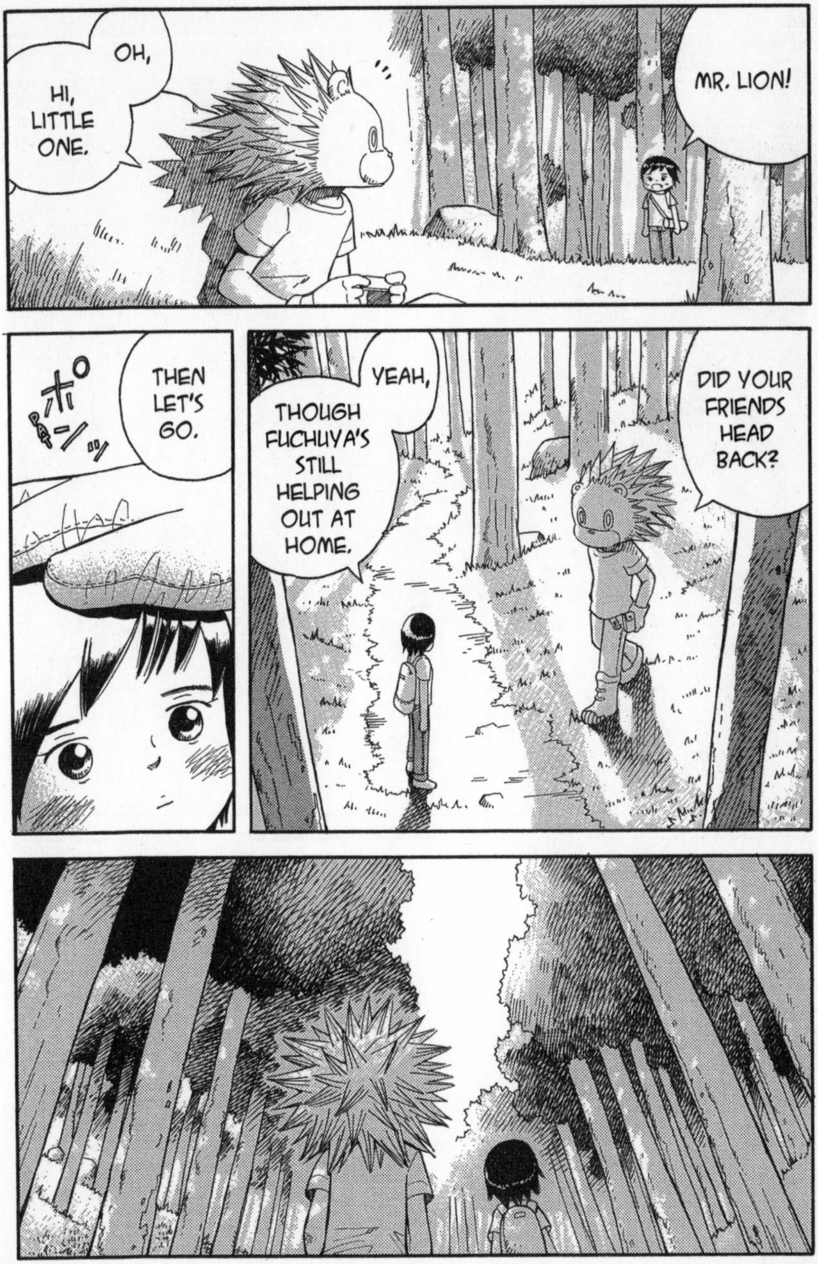
MR. LION!
OH,
HI, LITTLE ONE.
DID YOUR FRIENDS HEAD BACK?
YEAH,
THOUGH FUCHUYA'S STILL HELPING OUT AT HOME.
THEN LET'S GO.
PAT

MISSION:62

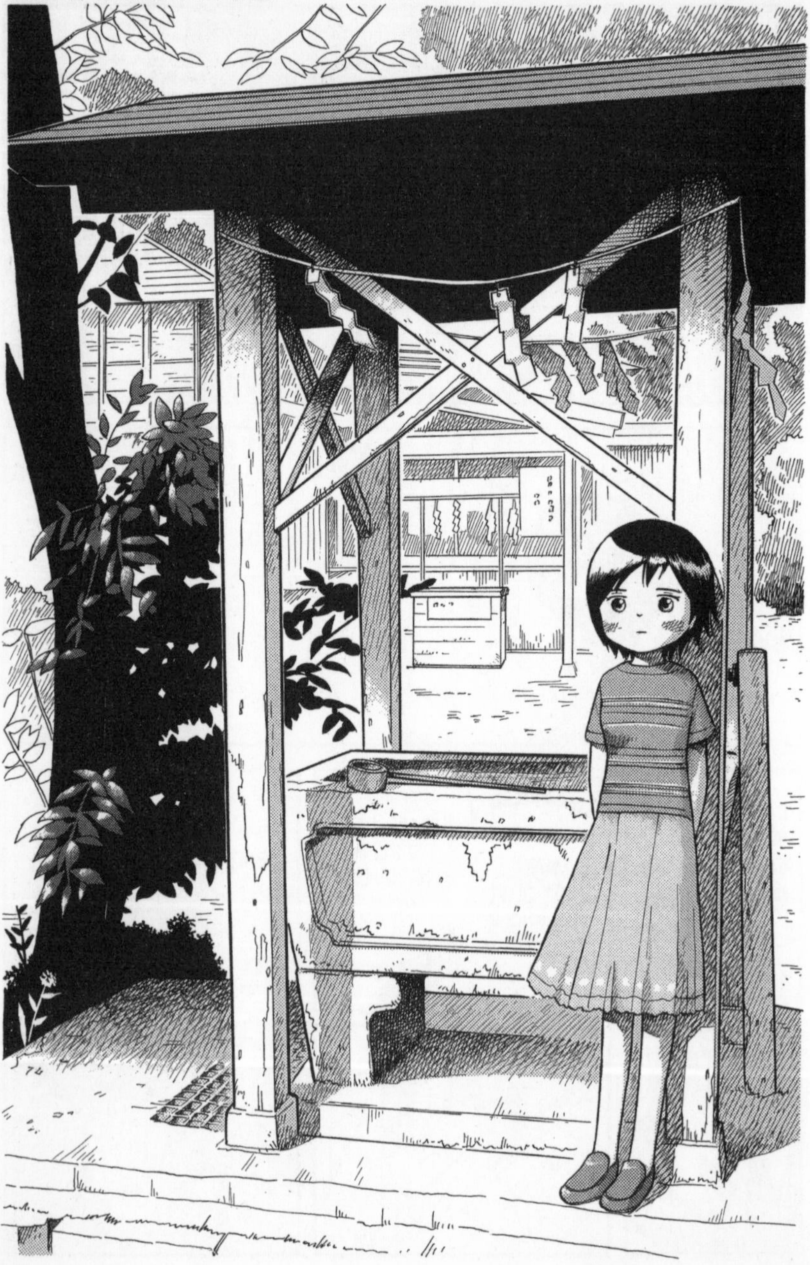

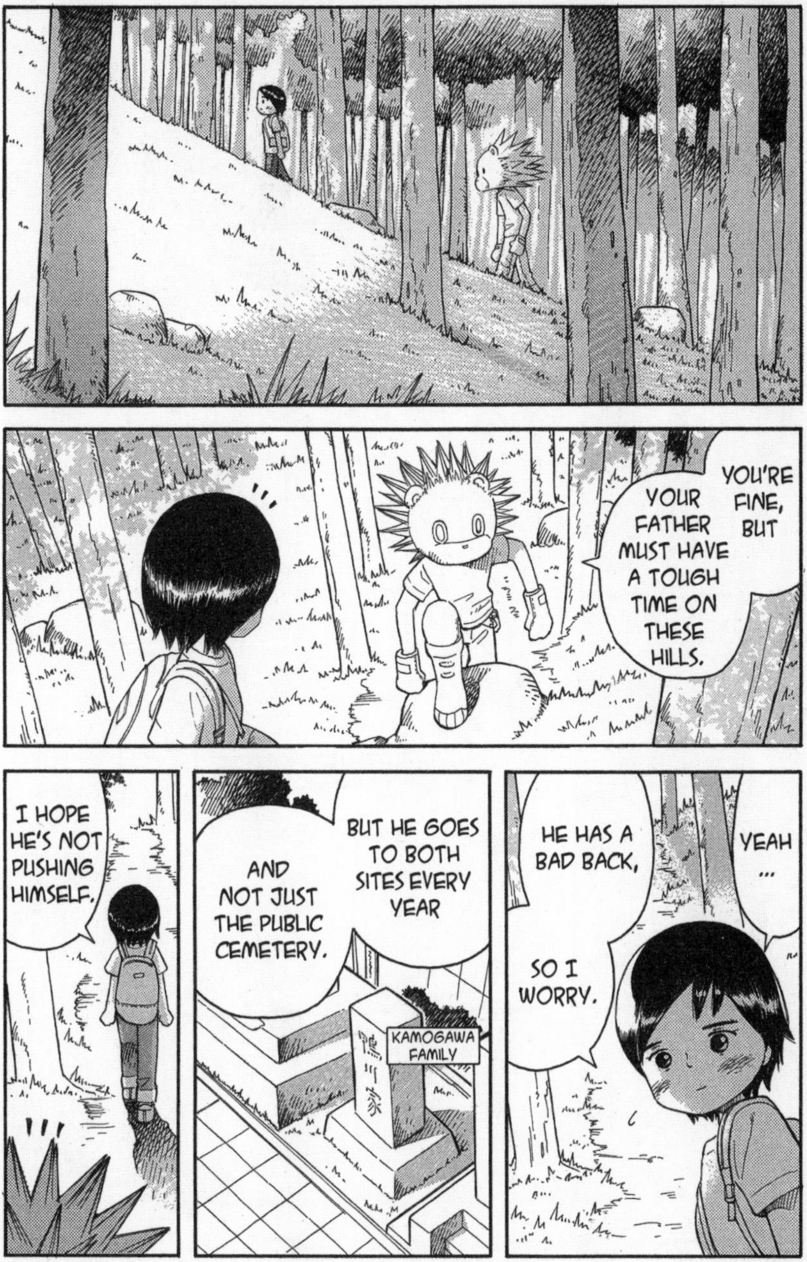
YOU'RE FINE, BUT YOUR FATHER MUST HAVE A TOUGH TIME ON THESE HILLS.
YEAH ...
HE HAS A BAD BACK,
SO I WORRY.
BUT HE GOES TO BOTH SITES EVERY YEAR
AND NOT JUST THE PUBLIC CEMETERY.
KAMOGAWA FAMILY
I HOPE HE'S NOT PUSHING HIMSELF.

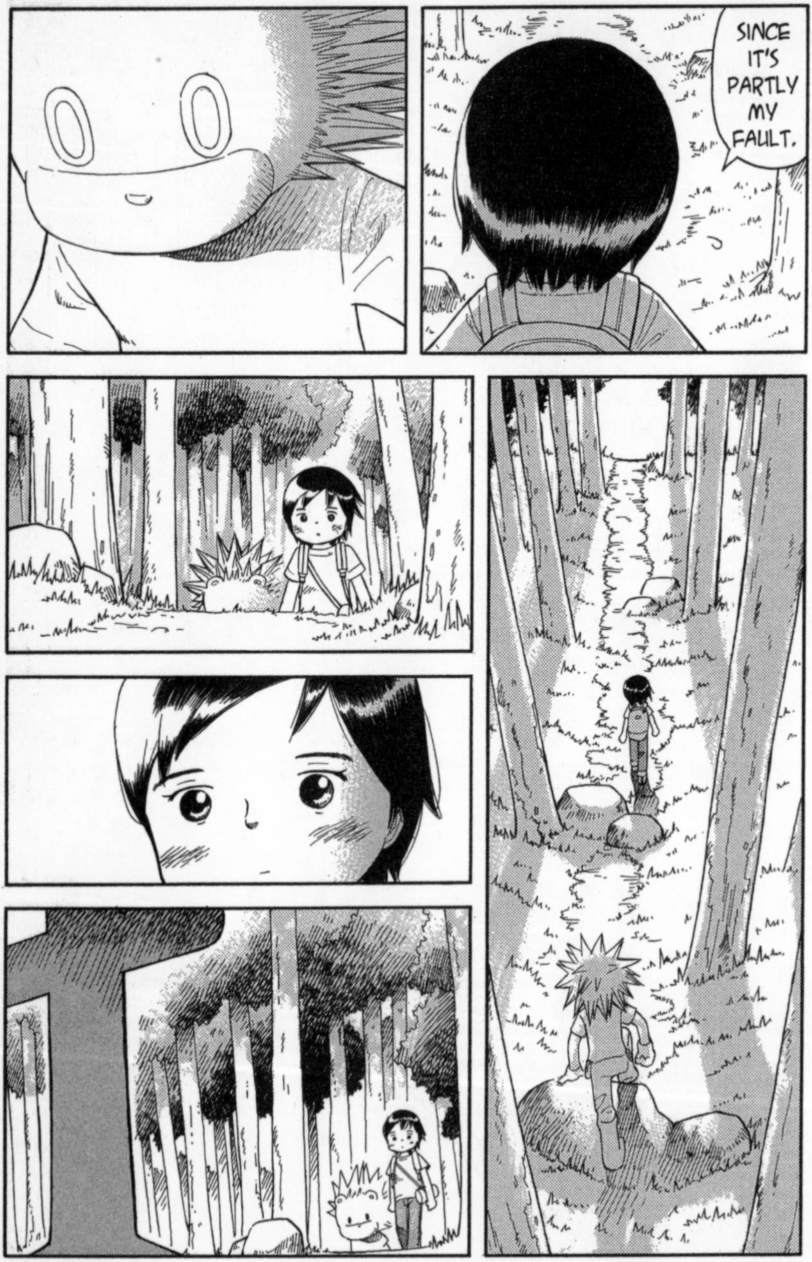
SINCE IT'S PARTLY MY FAULT.

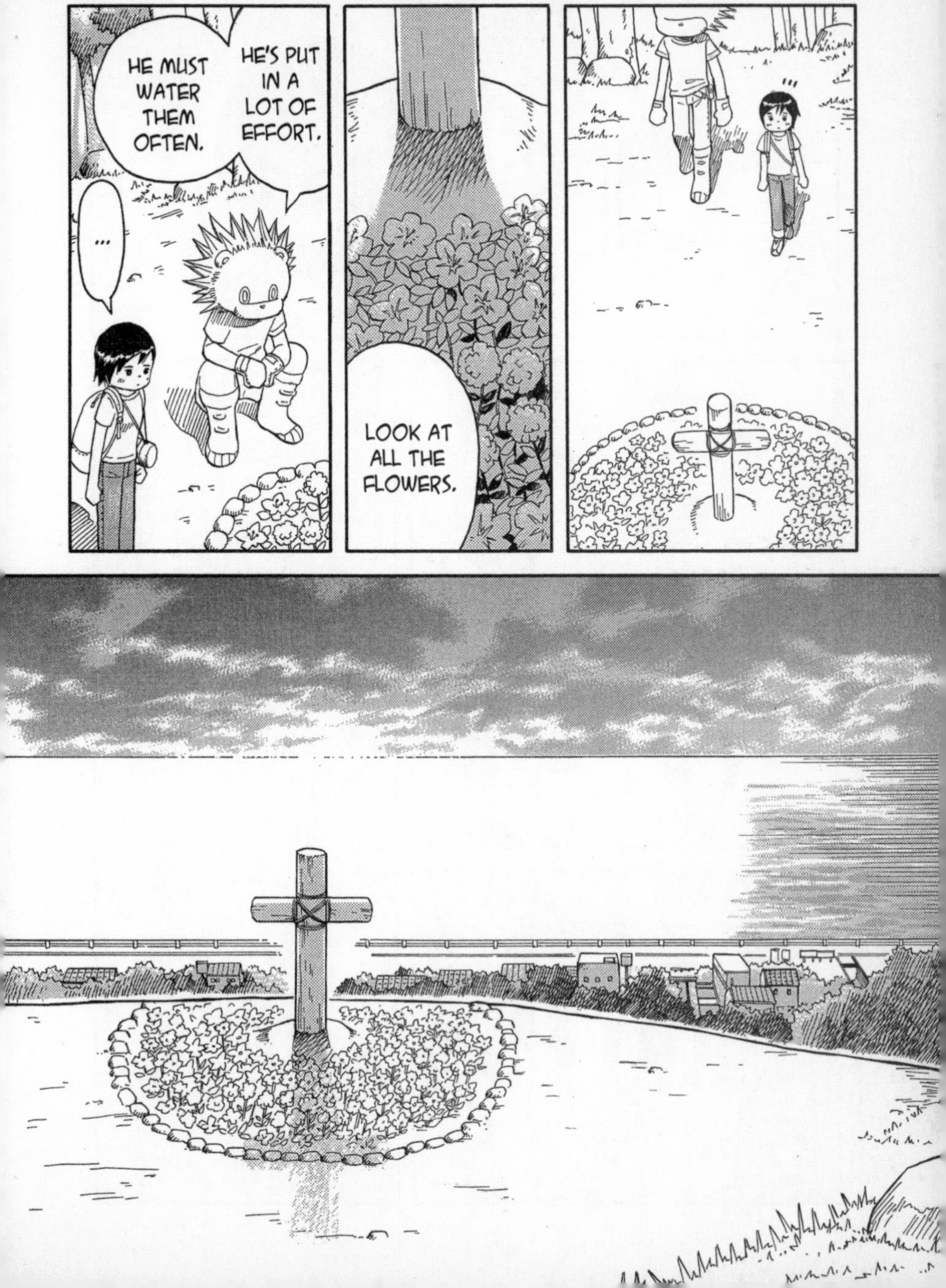
LOOK AT ALL THE FLOWERS.
HE'S PUT IN A LOT OF EFFORT.
HE MUST WATER THEM OFTEN.
...

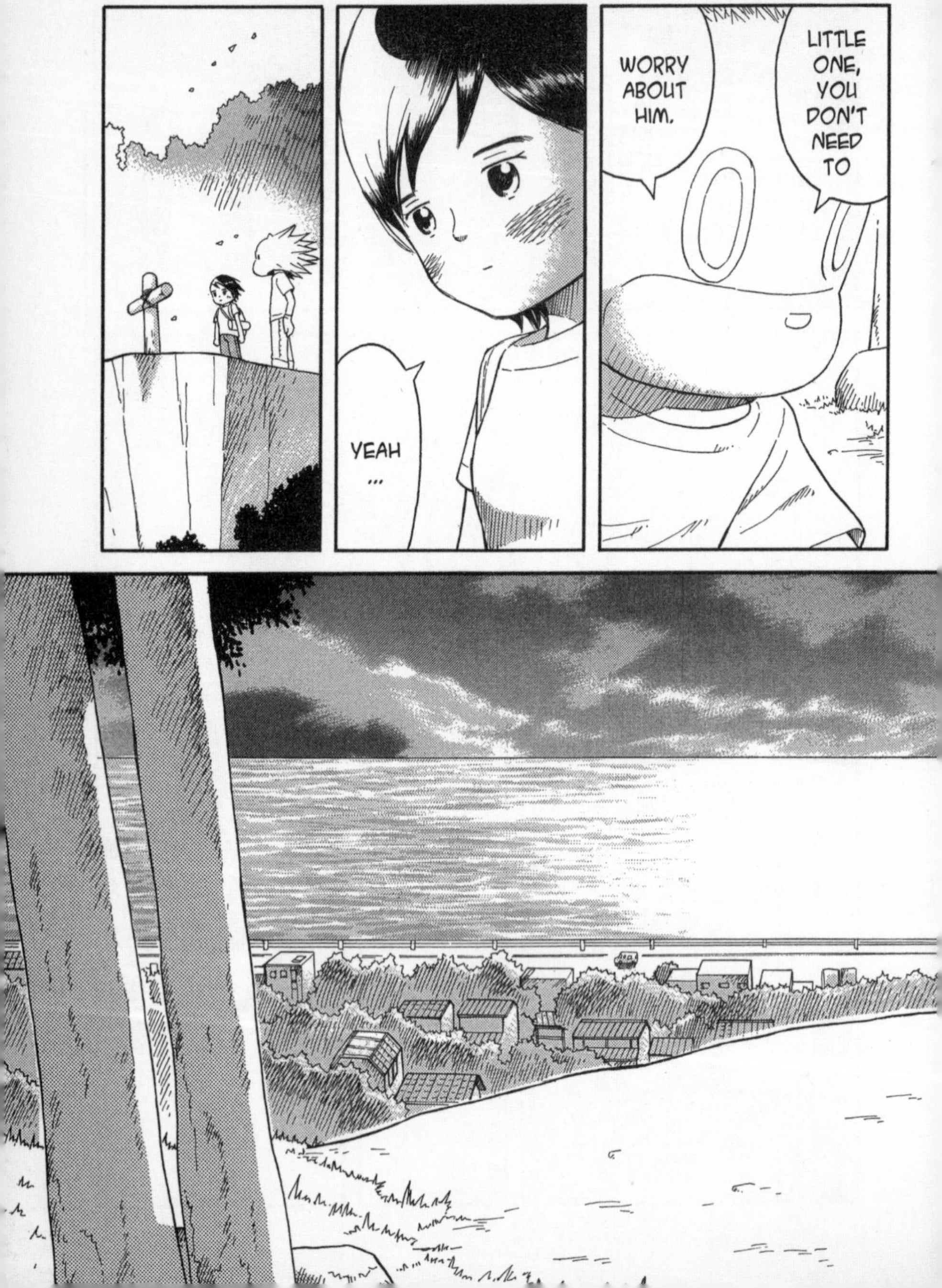
LITTLE ONE, YOU DON'T NEED TO
WORRY ABOUT HIM.
YEAH ...

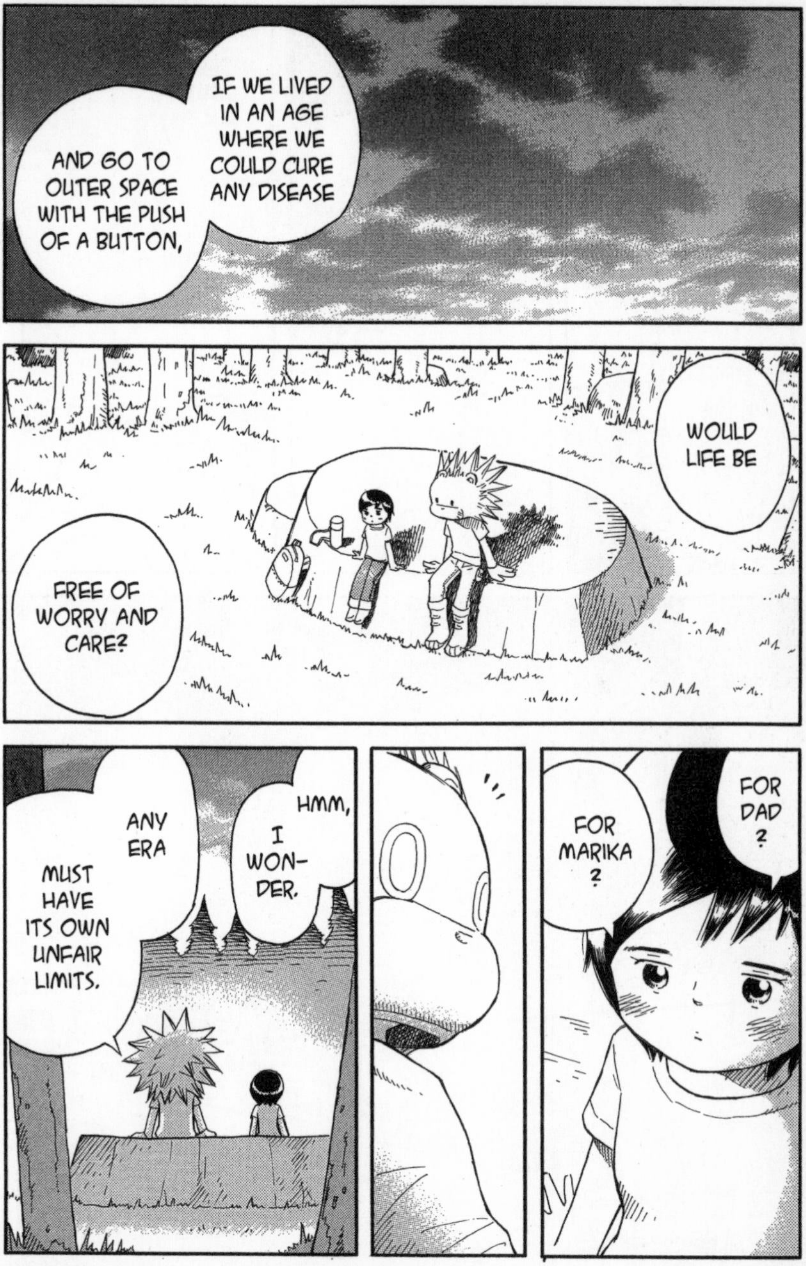
IF WE LIVED IN AN AGE WHERE WE COULD CURE ANY DISEASE
AND GO TO OUTER SPACE WITH THE PUSH OF A BUTTON,
WOULD LIFE BE
FREE OF WORRY AND CARE?
FOR DAD?
FOR MARIKA?
HMM, I WON-DER.
ANY ERA MUST HAVE ITS OWN UNFAIR LIMITS.

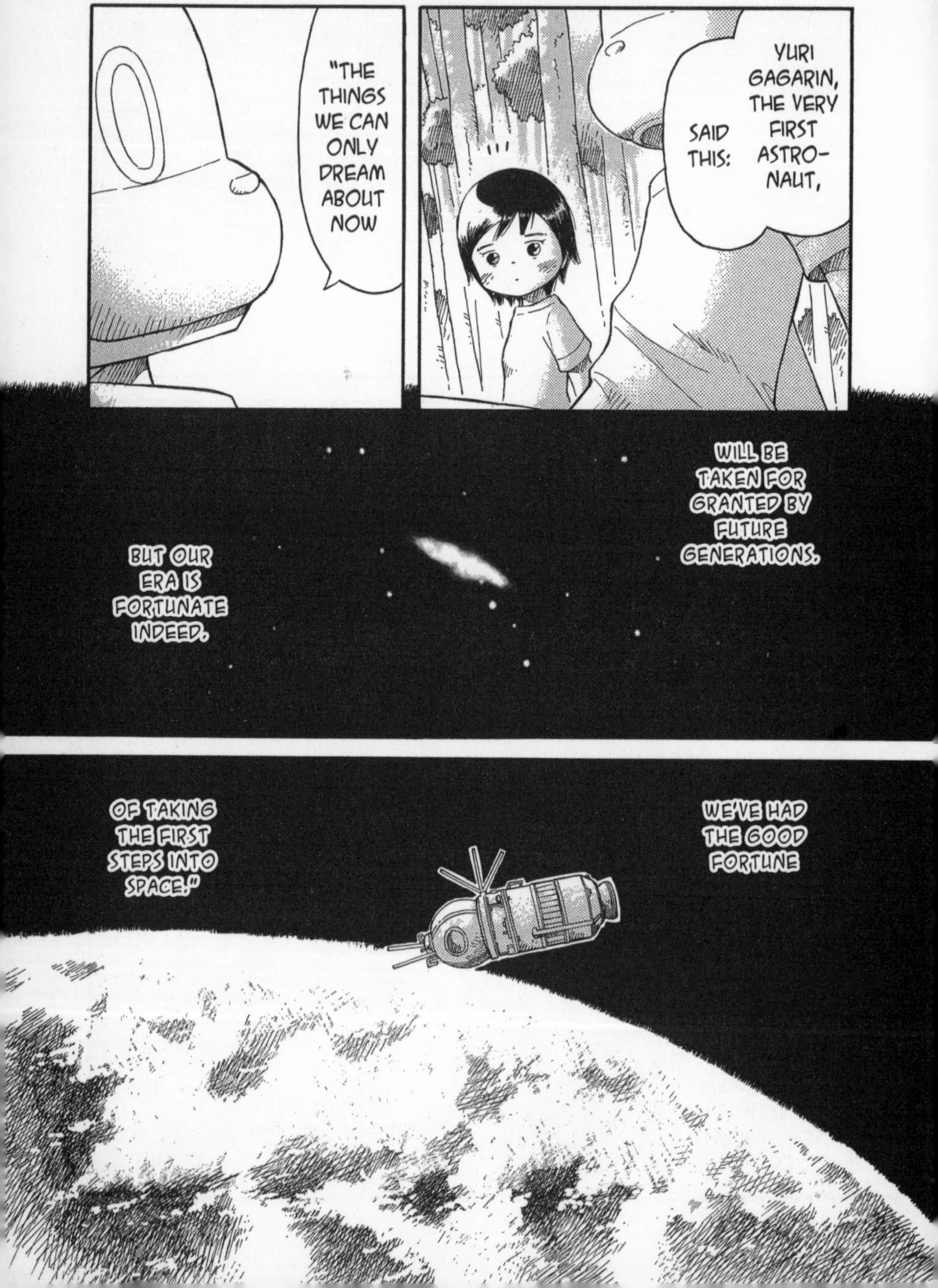
YURI GAGARIN, THE VERY FIRST ASTRONAUT,
SAID THIS:
"THE THINGS WE CAN ONLY DREAM ABOUT NOW
WILL BE TAKEN FOR GRANTED BY FUTURE GENERATIONS.
BUT OUR ERA IS FORTUNATE INDEED.
WE'VE HAD THE GOOD FORTUNE
OF TAKING THE FIRST STEPS INTO SPACE."

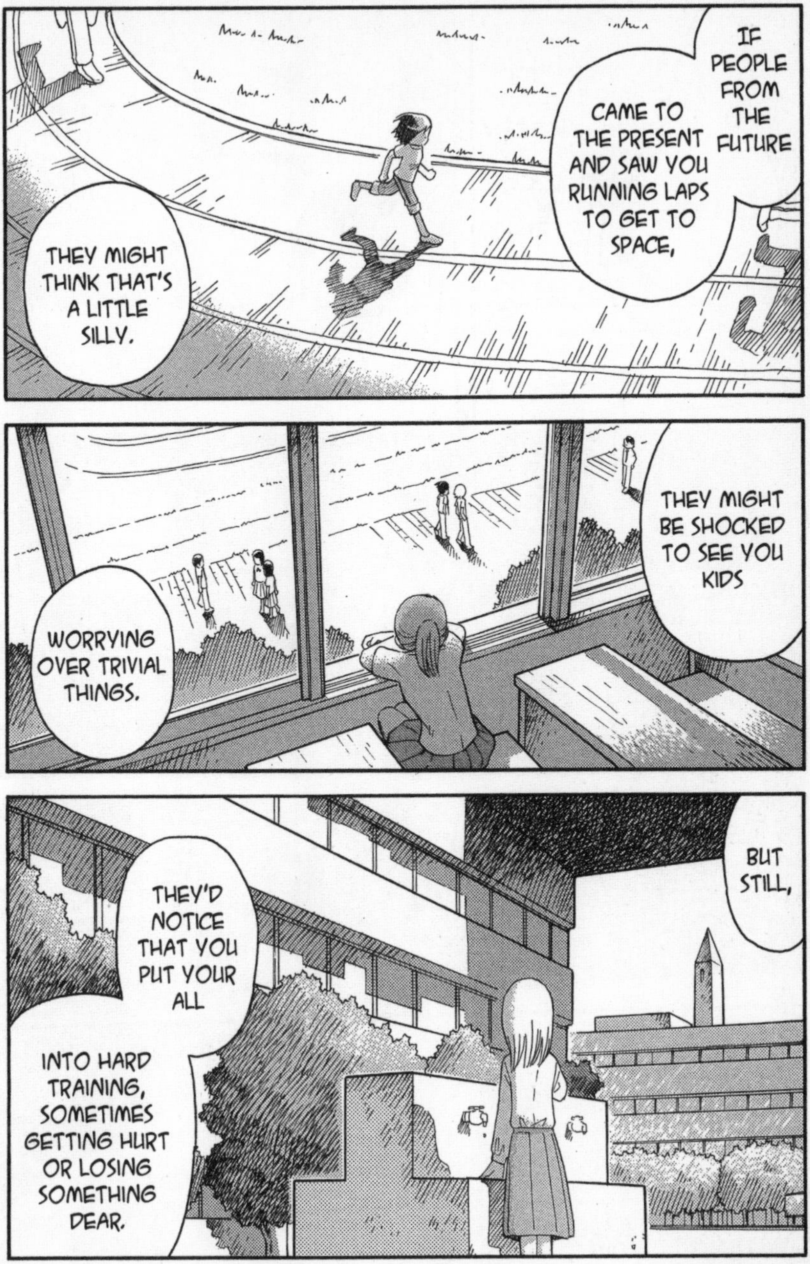
IF PEOPLE FROM THE FUTURE
CAME TO THE PRESENT AND SAW YOU RUNNING LAPS TO GET TO SPACE,
THEY MIGHT THINK THAT'S A LITTLE SILLY.
THEY MIGHT BE SHOCKED TO SEE YOU KIDS
WORRYING OVER TRIVIAL THINGS.
BUT STILL,
THEY'D NOTICE THAT YOU PUT YOUR ALL
INTO HARD TRAINING, SOMETIMES GETTING HURT OR LOSING SOMETHING DEAR.

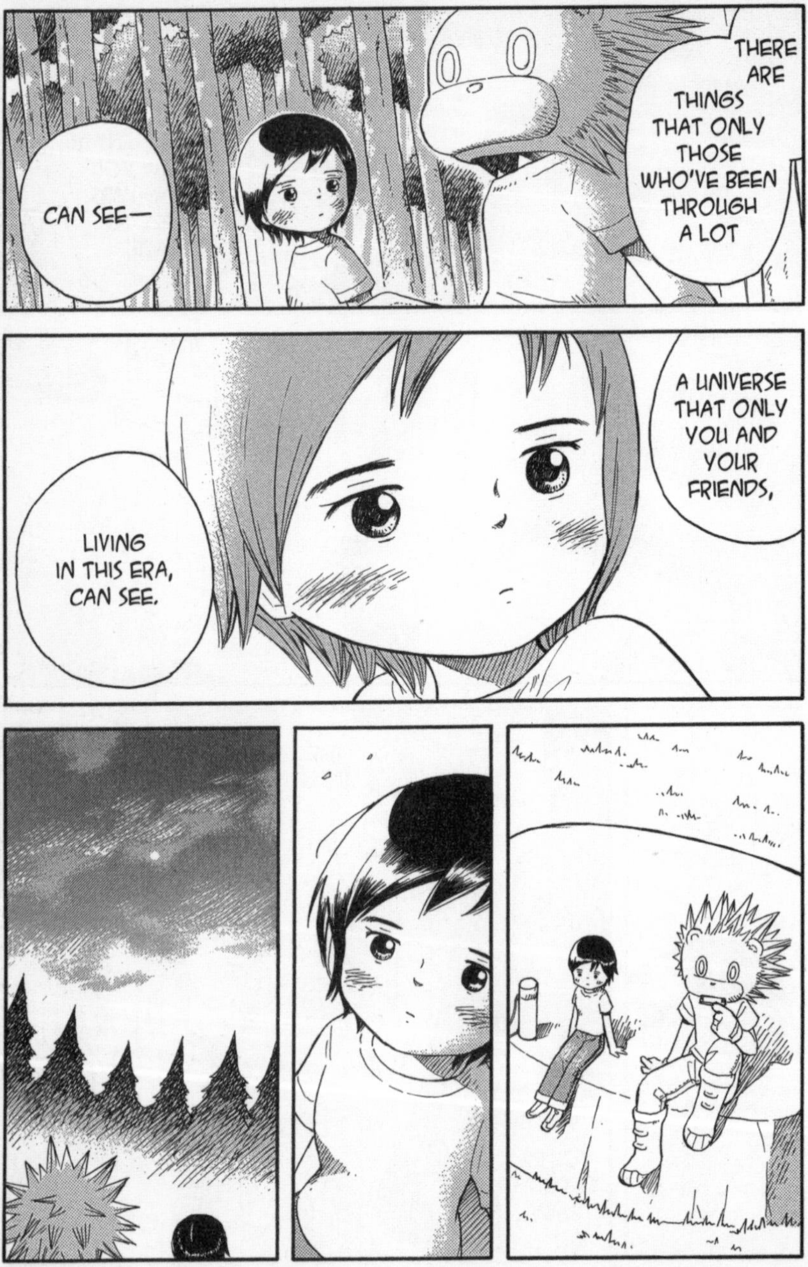
THERE ARE THINGS THAT ONLY THOSE WHO'VE BEEN THROUGH A LOT
CAN SEE—
A UNIVERSE THAT ONLY YOU AND YOUR FRIENDS,
LIVING IN THIS ERA, CAN SEE.

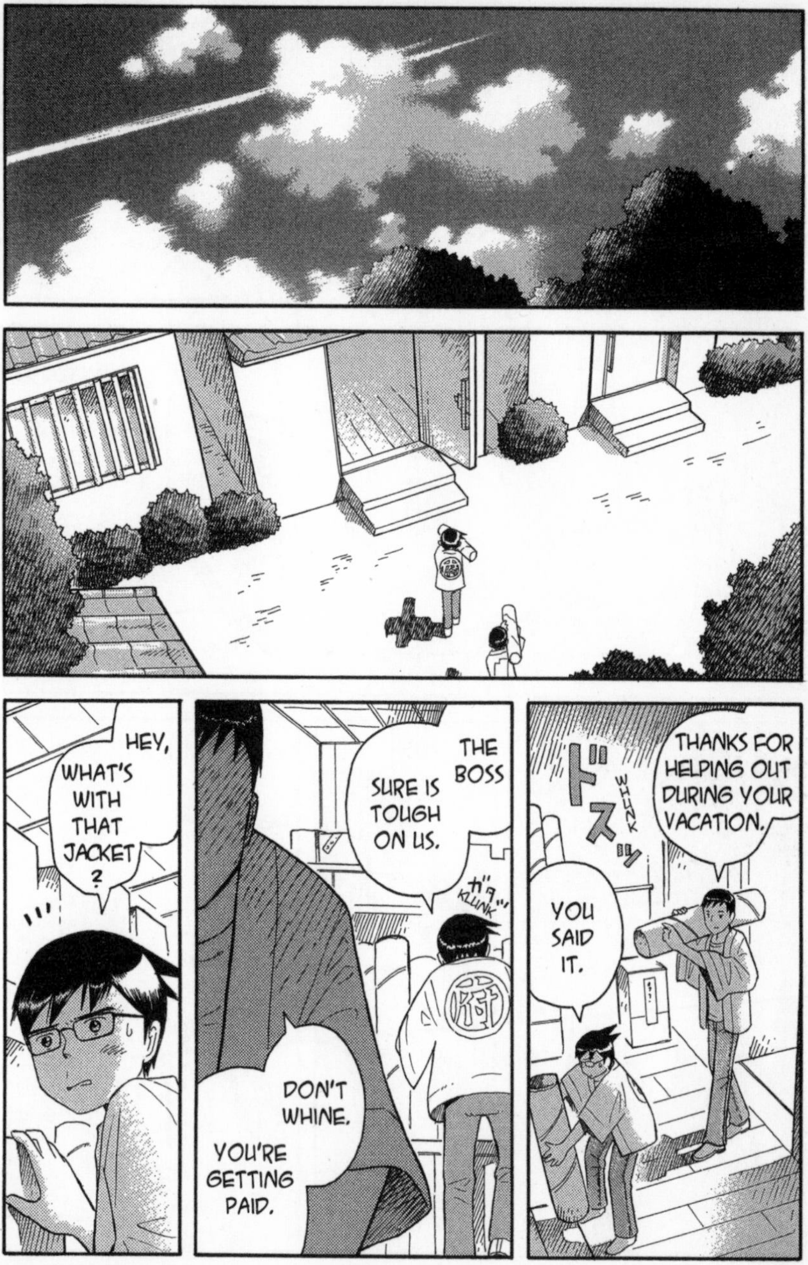

THANKS FOR HELPING OUT DURING YOUR VACATION.
ドスッ
WHUNK
YOU SAID IT.
THE BOSS SURE IS TOUGH ON US.
ガタッ
KLUNK
DON'T WHINE.
YOU'RE GETTING PAID.
HEY, WHAT'S WITH THAT JACKET?

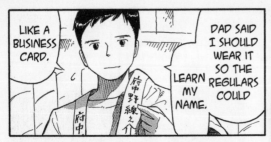

HM?
AH.
府中野 線之介 二十七代目
FUCHUYA THE 27TH SENNOSUKE
DAD SAID I SHOULD WEAR IT SO THE REGULARS COULD
LEARN MY NAME.
LIKE A BUSINESS CARD.
IT'S NOT EASY BEING THE ONE WHO HAS TO TAKE OVER THE FAMILY BIZ.
UH ...
MAYBE REBEL A LITTLE MORE?
ドスン
THUNK
WHEW.
LAST ONE.
SO ARE YOU REALLY GOING TO SPACE?

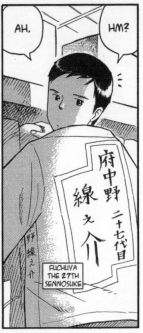

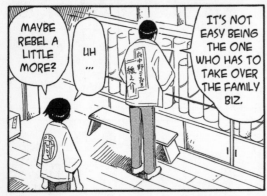

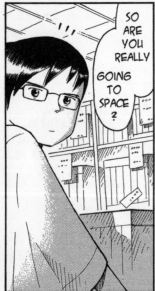

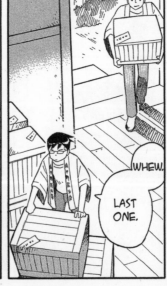

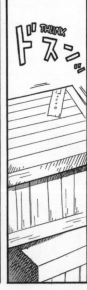

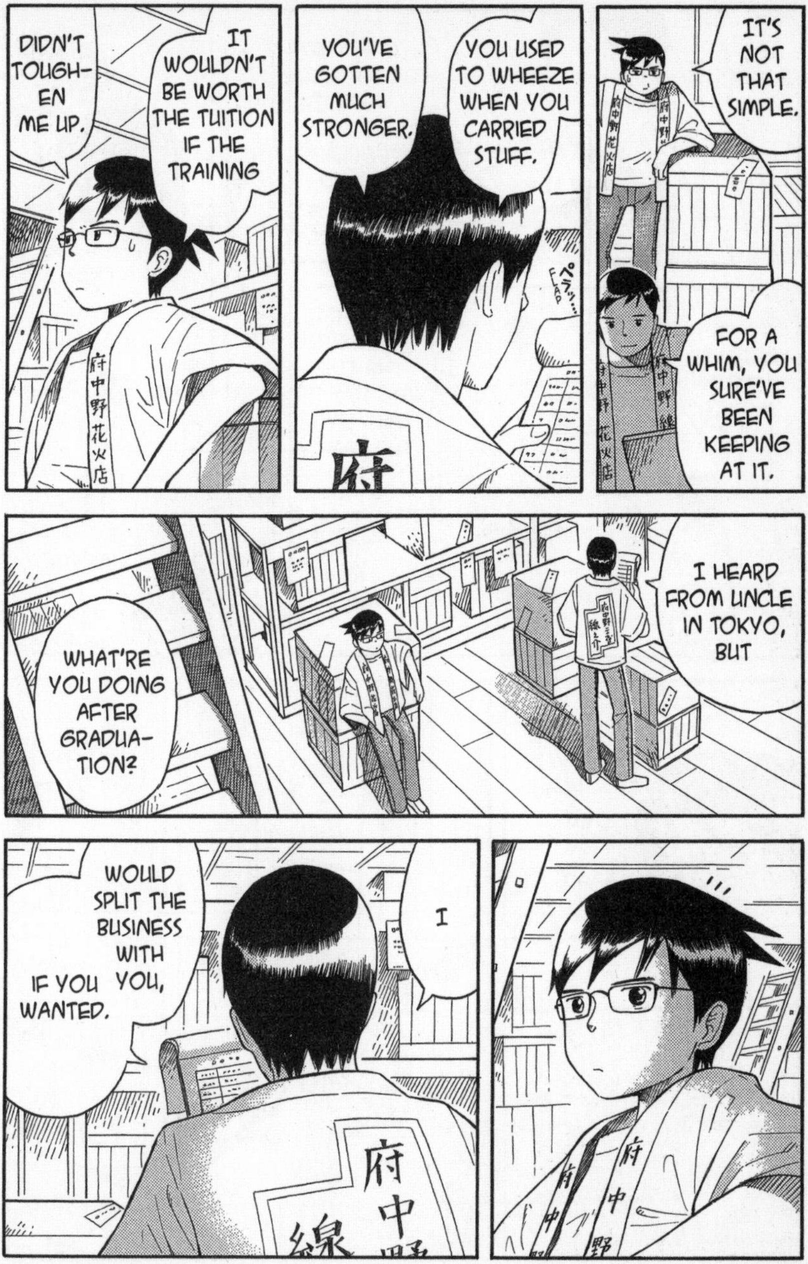
IT'S NOT THAT SIMPLE.
FOR A WHIM, YOU SURE'VE BEEN KEEPING AT IT.
YOU USED TO WHEEZE WHEN YOU CARRIED STUFF.
YOU'VE GOTTEN MUCH STRONGER.
ペラッ… FLAP
IT WOULDN'T BE WORTH THE TUITION IF THE TRAINING
DIDN'T TOUGHEN ME UP.
I HEARD FROM UNCLE IN TOKYO, BUT
WHAT'RE YOU DOING AFTER GRADUATION?
!!
I
WOULD SPLIT THE BUSINESS WITH YOU, IF YOU WANTED.

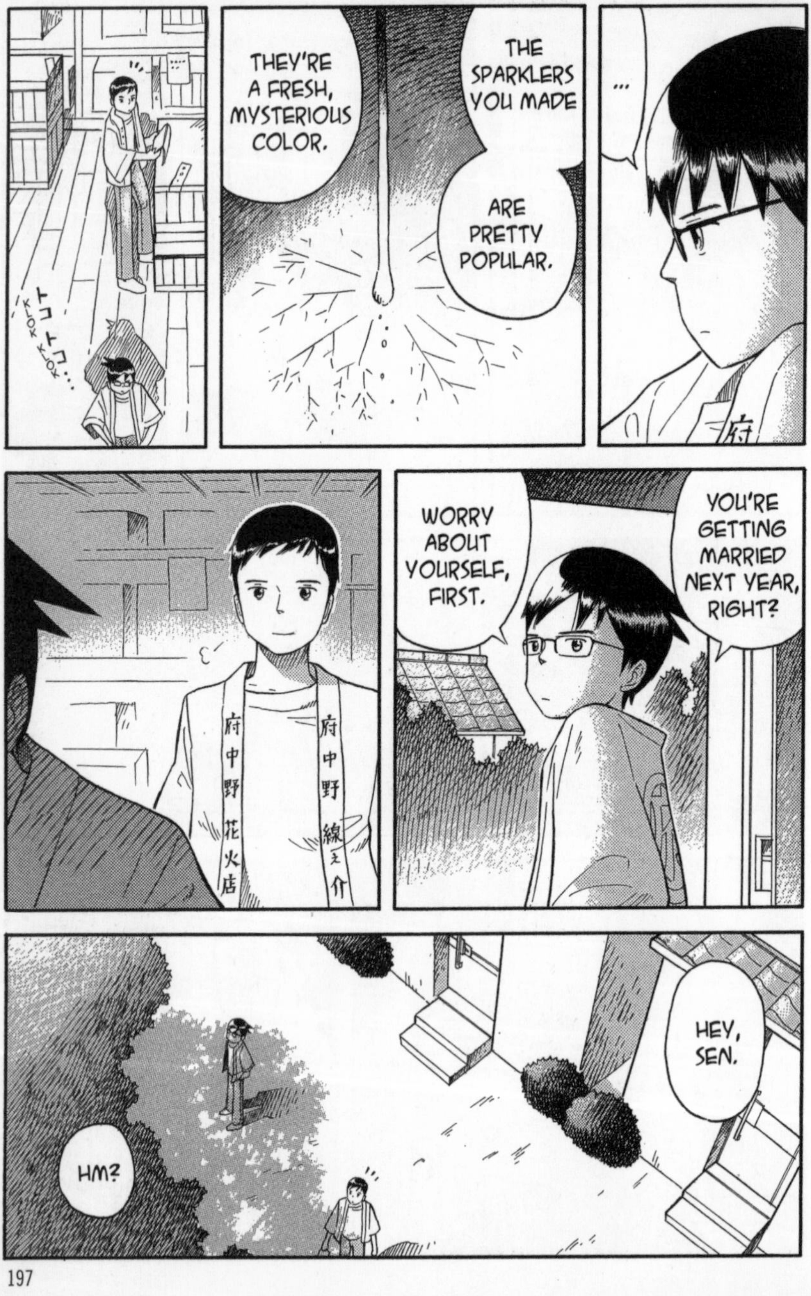
...
THE SPARKLERS YOU MADE
ARE PRETTY POPULAR.
THEY'RE A FRESH, MYSTERIOUS COLOR.
トコトコ
KLOK KLOK...
YOU'RE GETTING MARRIED NEXT YEAR, RIGHT?
WORRY ABOUT YOURSELF, FIRST.
府中野花火店
HEY, SEN.
HM?

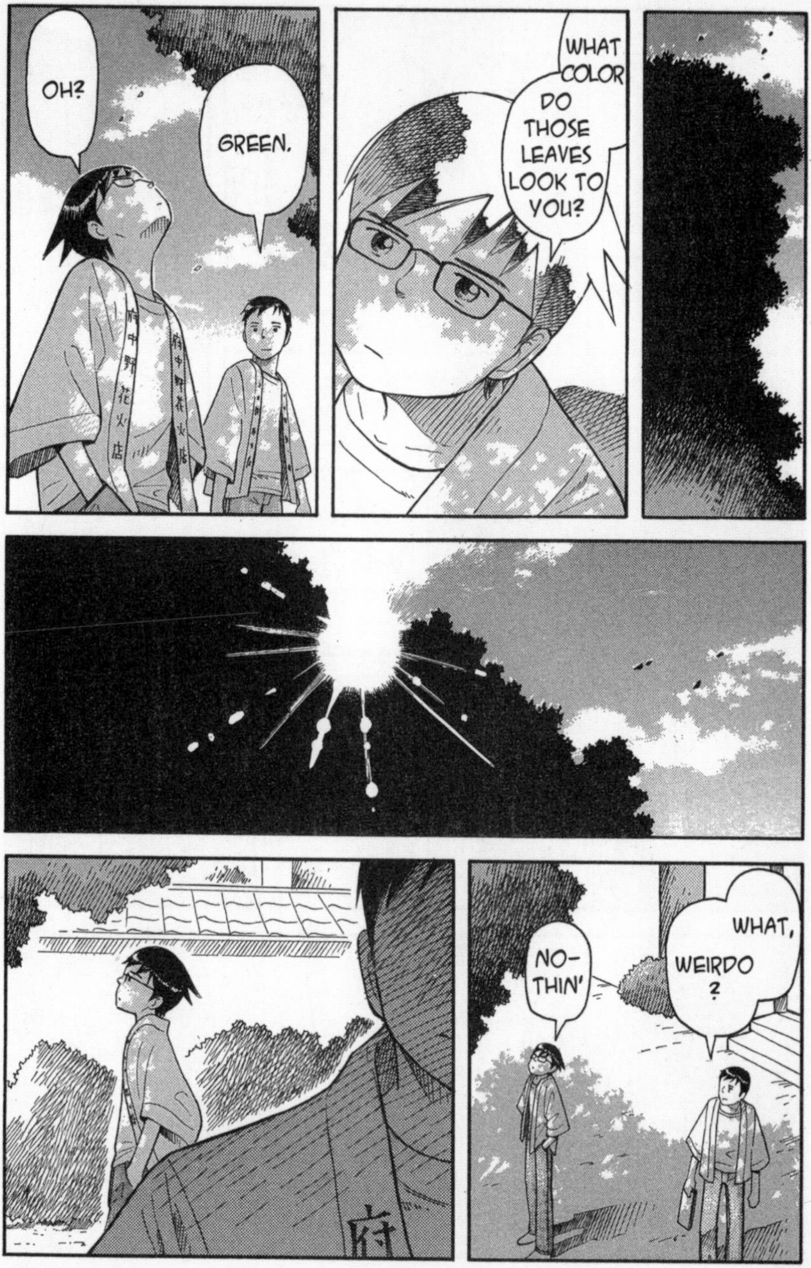
WHAT COLOR DO THOSE LEAVES LOOK TO YOU?
GREEN.
OH?
WHAT, WEIRDO?
NO-THIN'

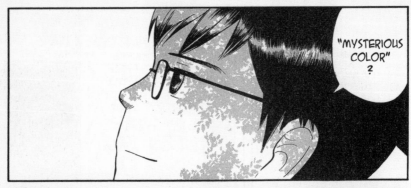

"MYSTERIOUS
COLOR"
?

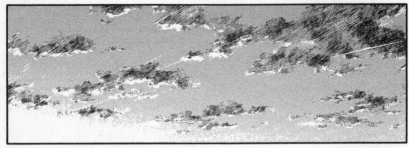

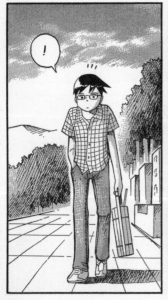

!

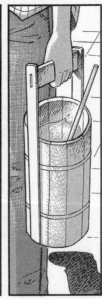

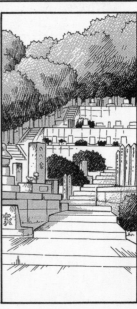

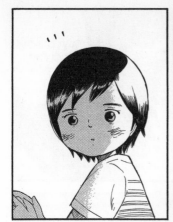

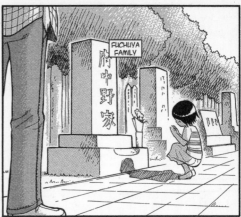

FUCHUYA FAMILY

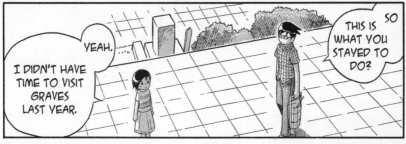

SO THIS IS WHAT YOU STAYED TO DO?

YEAH. I DIDN'T HAVE TIME TO VISIT GRAVES LAST YEAR.

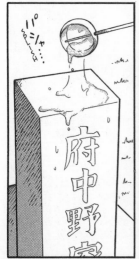

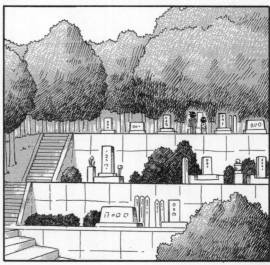

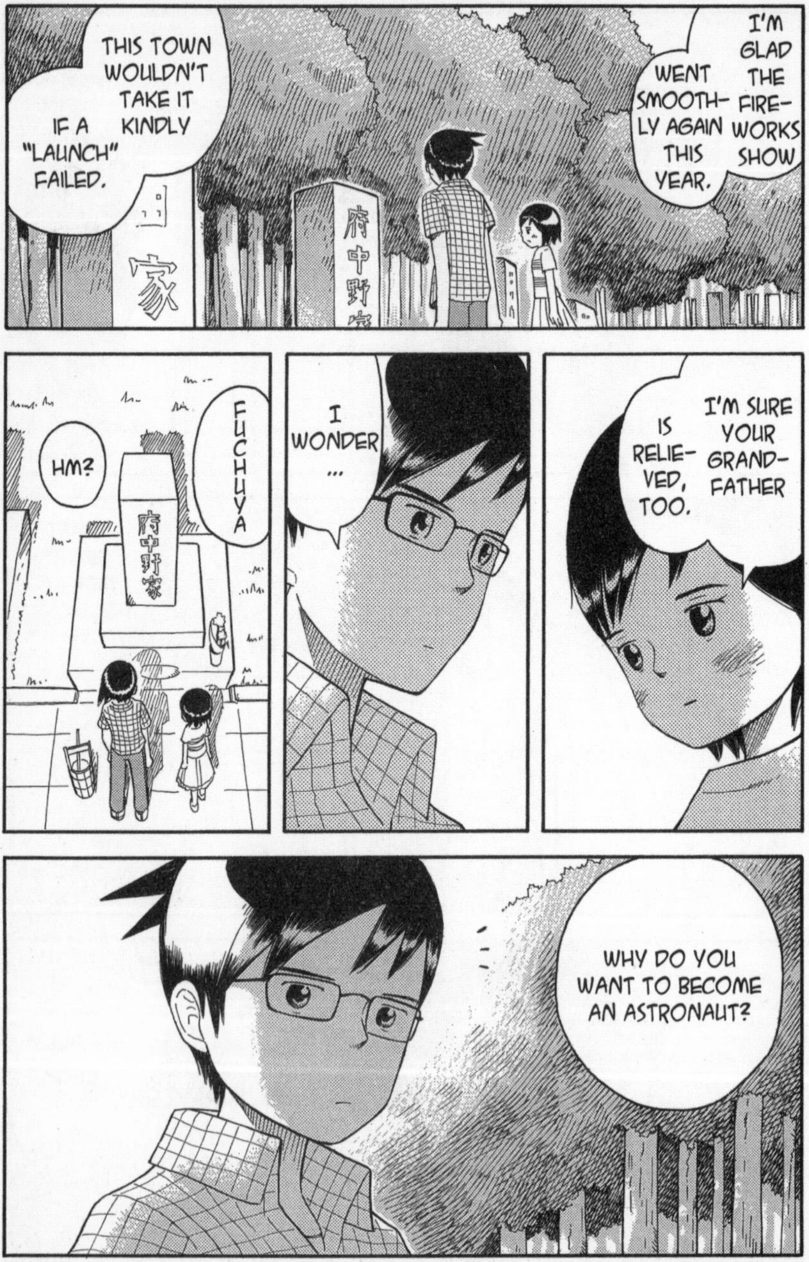
I'M GLAD THE FIREWORKS SHOW WENT SMOOTHLY AGAIN THIS YEAR.
THIS TOWN WOULDN'T TAKE IT KINDLY IF A "LAUNCH" FAILED.
家
I'M SURE YOUR GRANDFATHER IS RELIEVED, TOO.
I WONDER...
FUCHUYA
HM?
府中野家
WHY DO YOU WANT TO BECOME AN ASTRONAUT?

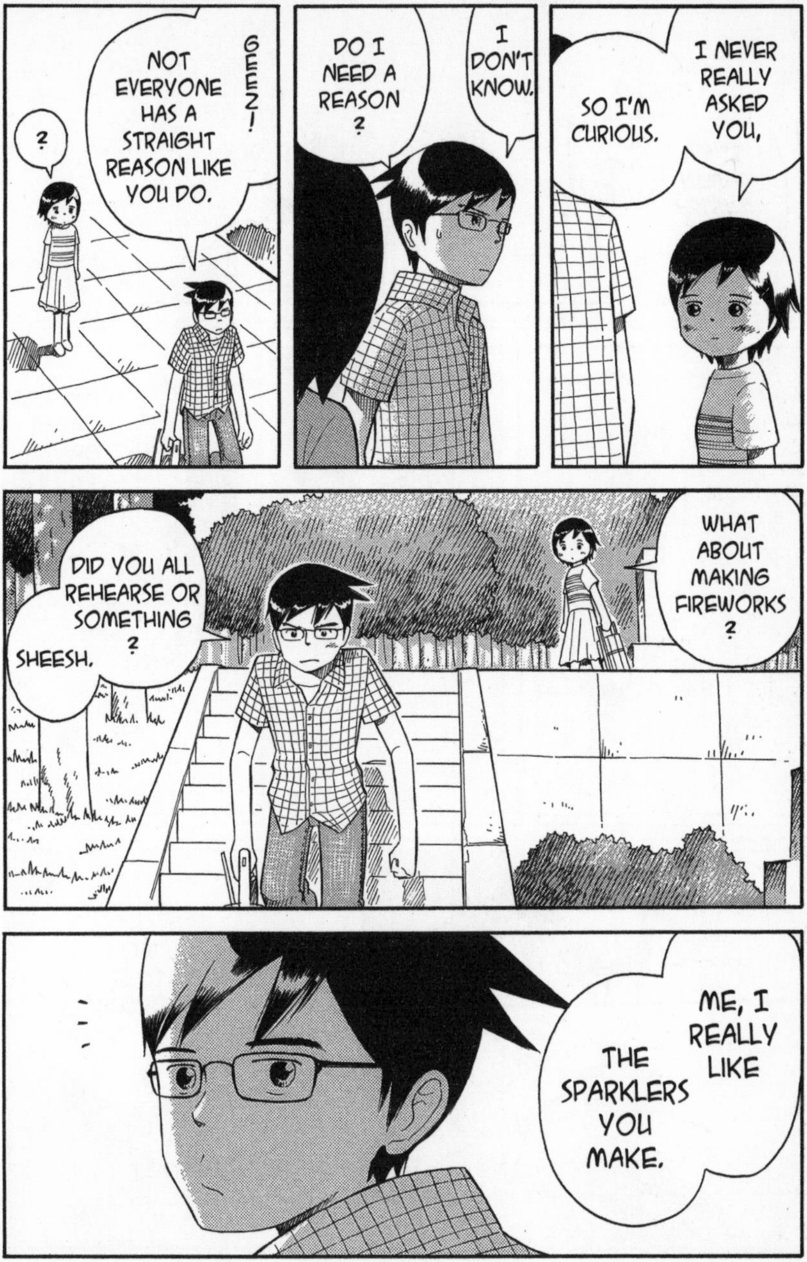
I NEVER REALLY ASKED YOU,
SO I'M CURIOUS.
I DON'T KNOW.
DO I NEED A REASON?
GEEZ!
NOT EVERYONE HAS A STRAIGHT REASON LIKE YOU DO.
?
WHAT ABOUT MAKING FIREWORKS?
DID YOU ALL REHEARSE OR SOMETHING? SHEESH.
ME, I REALLY LIKE THE SPARKLERS YOU MAKE.
...

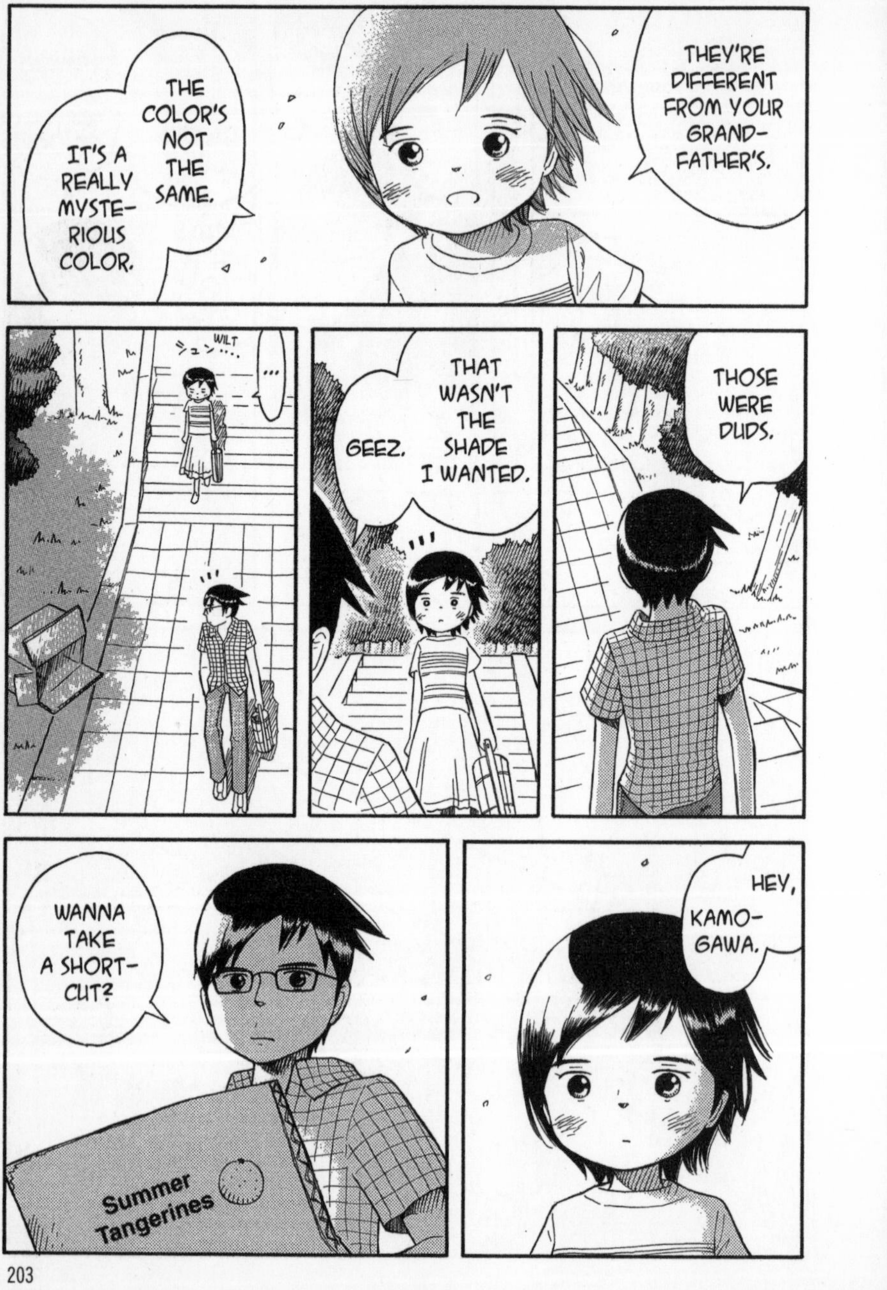
THEY'RE DIFFERENT FROM YOUR GRAND-FATHER'S.
THE COLOR'S NOT THE SAME.
IT'S A REALLY MYSTE-RIOUS COLOR.
THOSE WERE DUDS.
THAT WASN'T THE SHADE I WANTED.
GEEZ.
シュン… WILT
...
HEY, KAMO-GAWA.
WANNA TAKE A SHORT-CUT?
Summer Tangerines

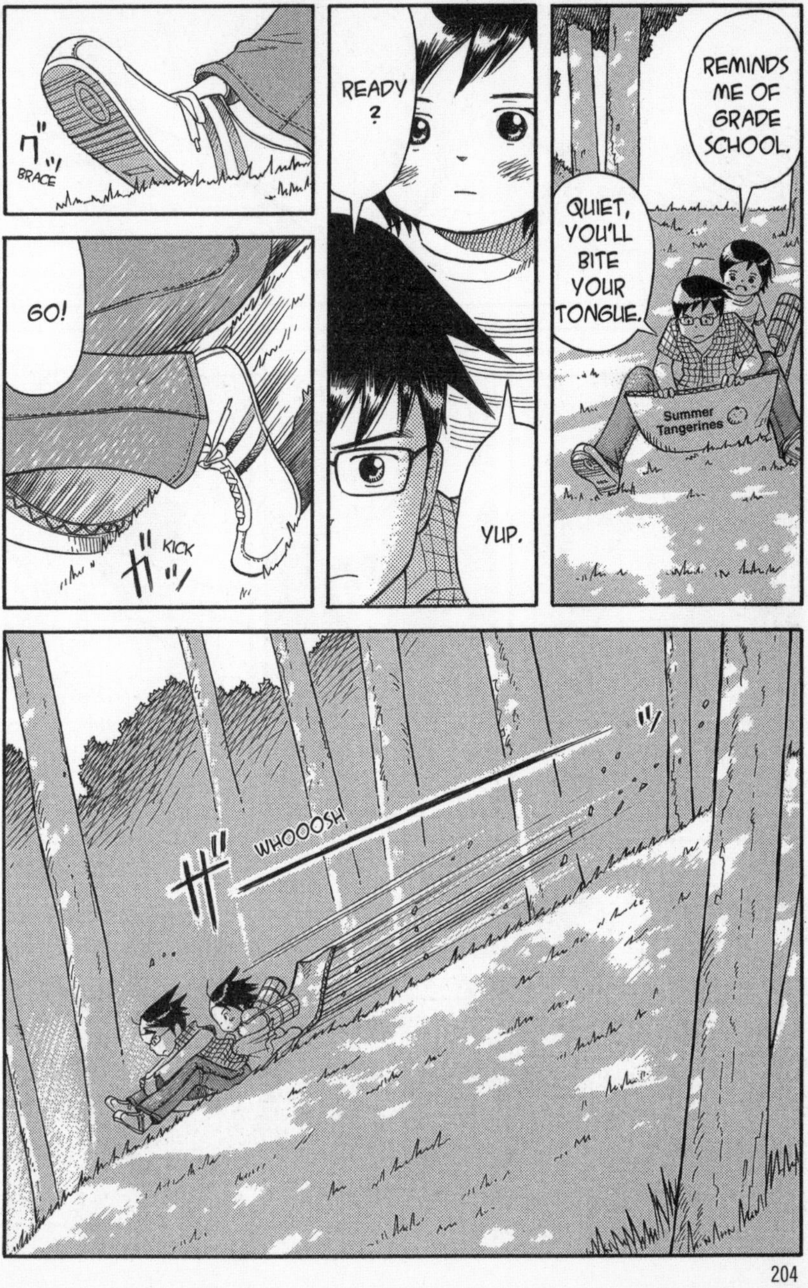
REMINDS ME OF GRADE SCHOOL.
QUIET, YOU'LL BITE YOUR TONGUE.
Summer Tangerines
READY?
YUP.
BRACE
GO!
KICK
WHOOOSH

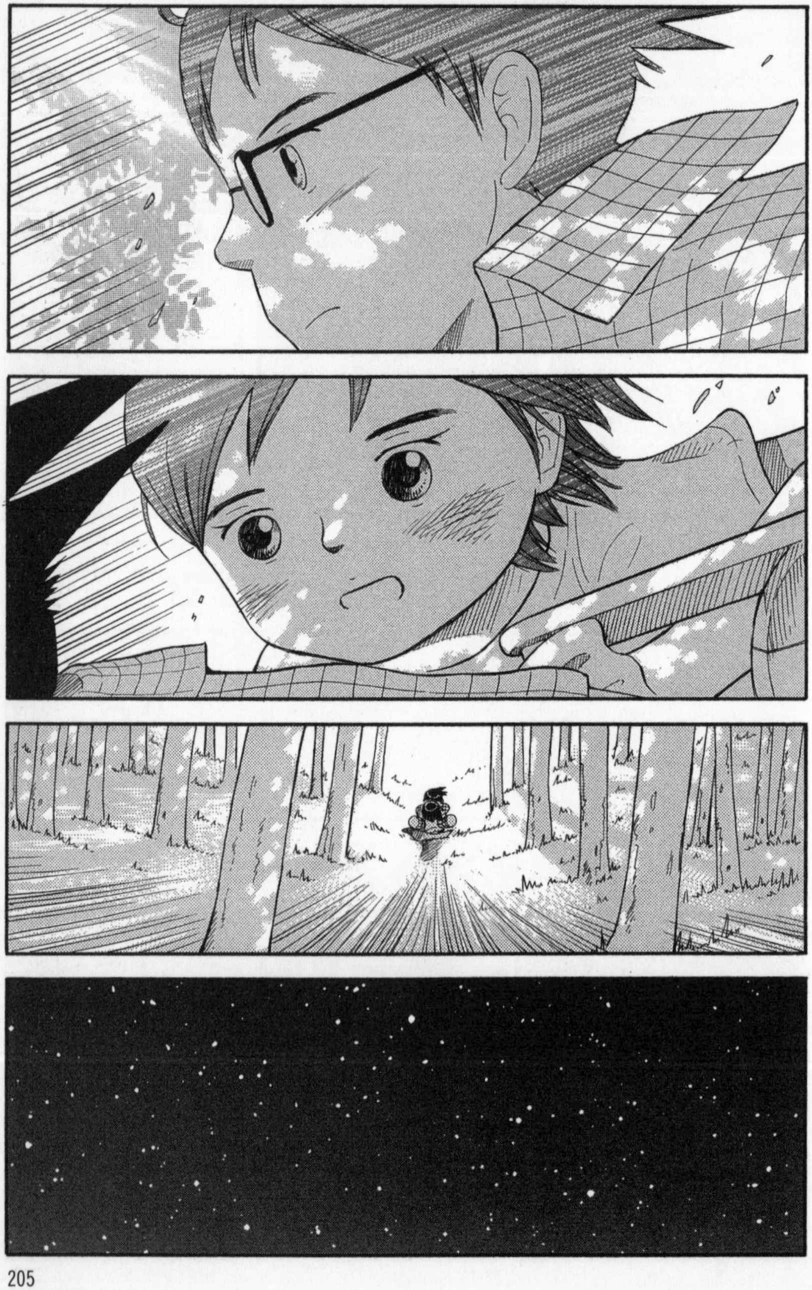

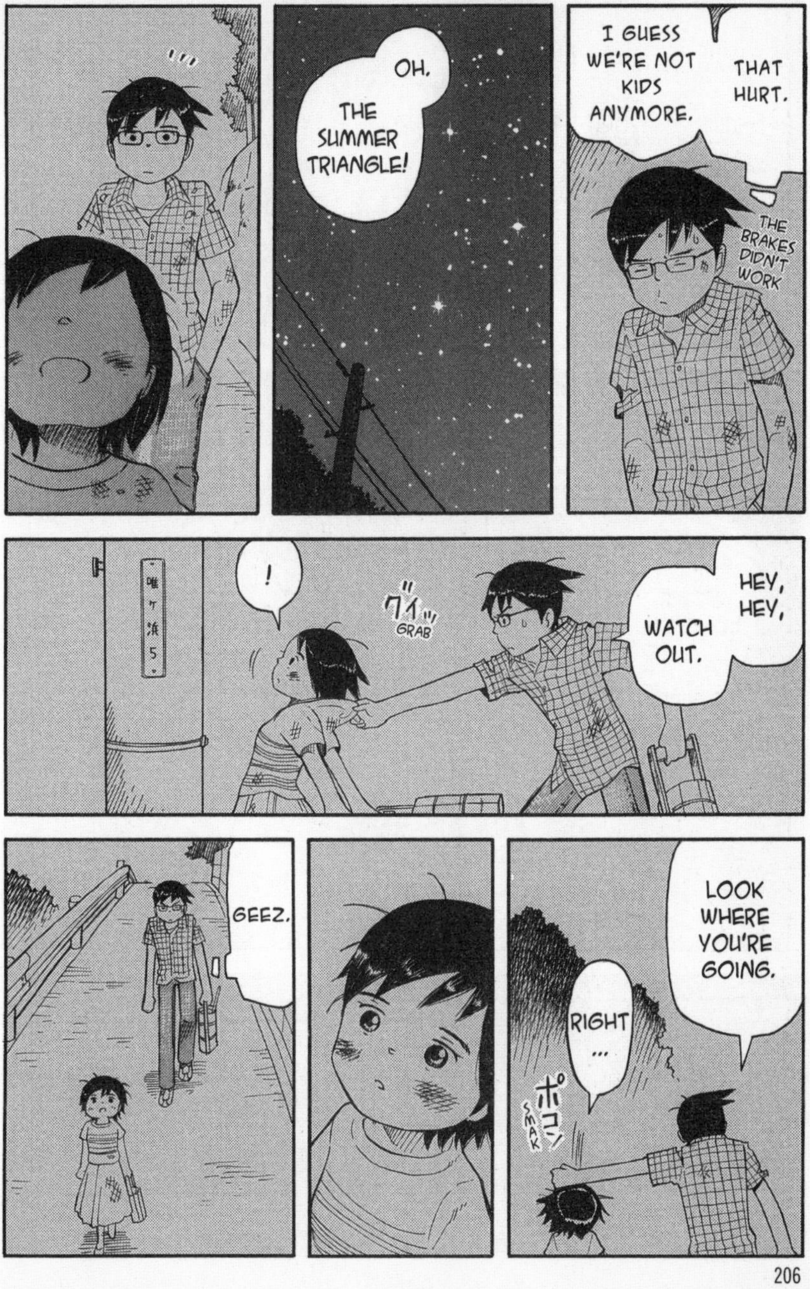
THAT HURT.
I GUESS WE'RE NOT KIDS ANYMORE.
THE BRAKES DIDN'T WORK
OH. THE SUMMER TRIANGLE!
HEY, HEY, WATCH OUT.
グイッ
GRAB
!
LOOK WHERE YOU'RE GOING.
RIGHT ...
ポコン
SMAK
GEEZ.

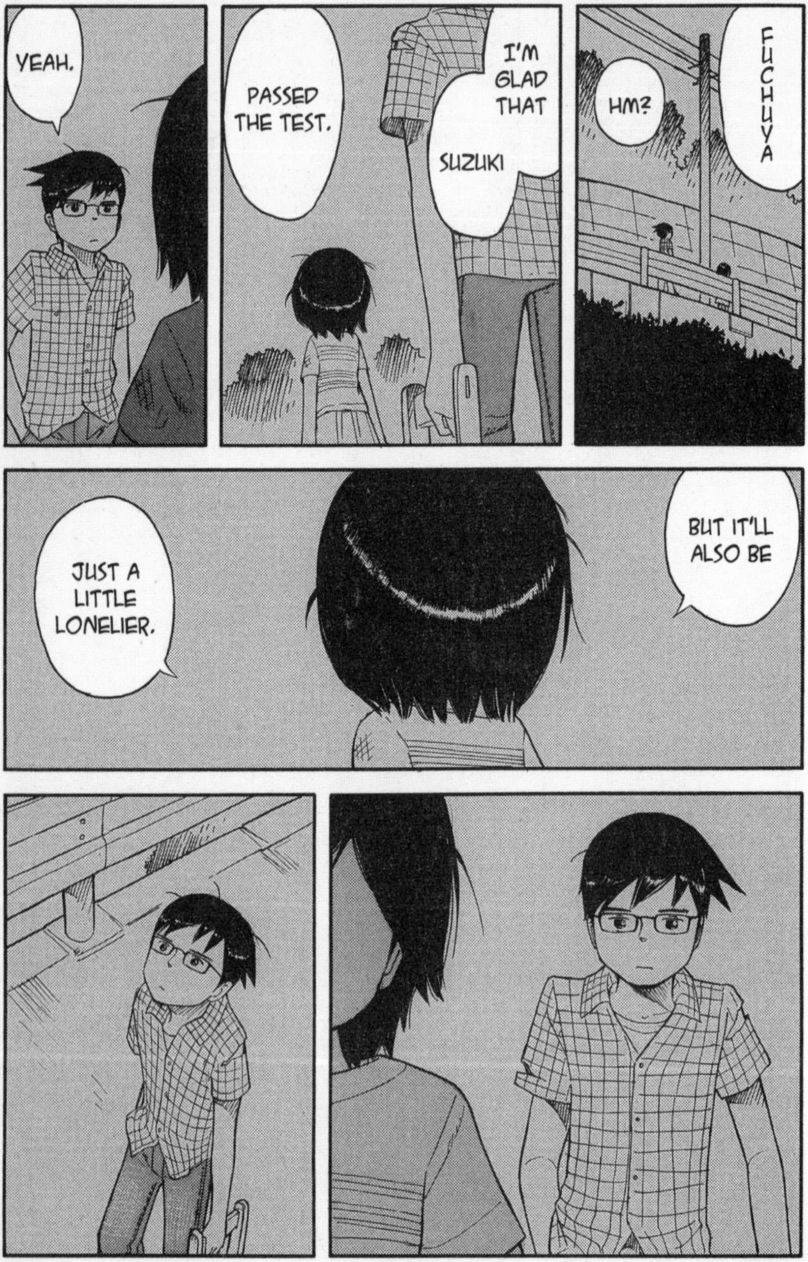
FUCHUYA
HM?
I'M GLAD THAT
SUZUKI
PASSED THE TEST.
YEAH.
BUT IT'LL ALSO BE
JUST A LITTLE LONELIER.

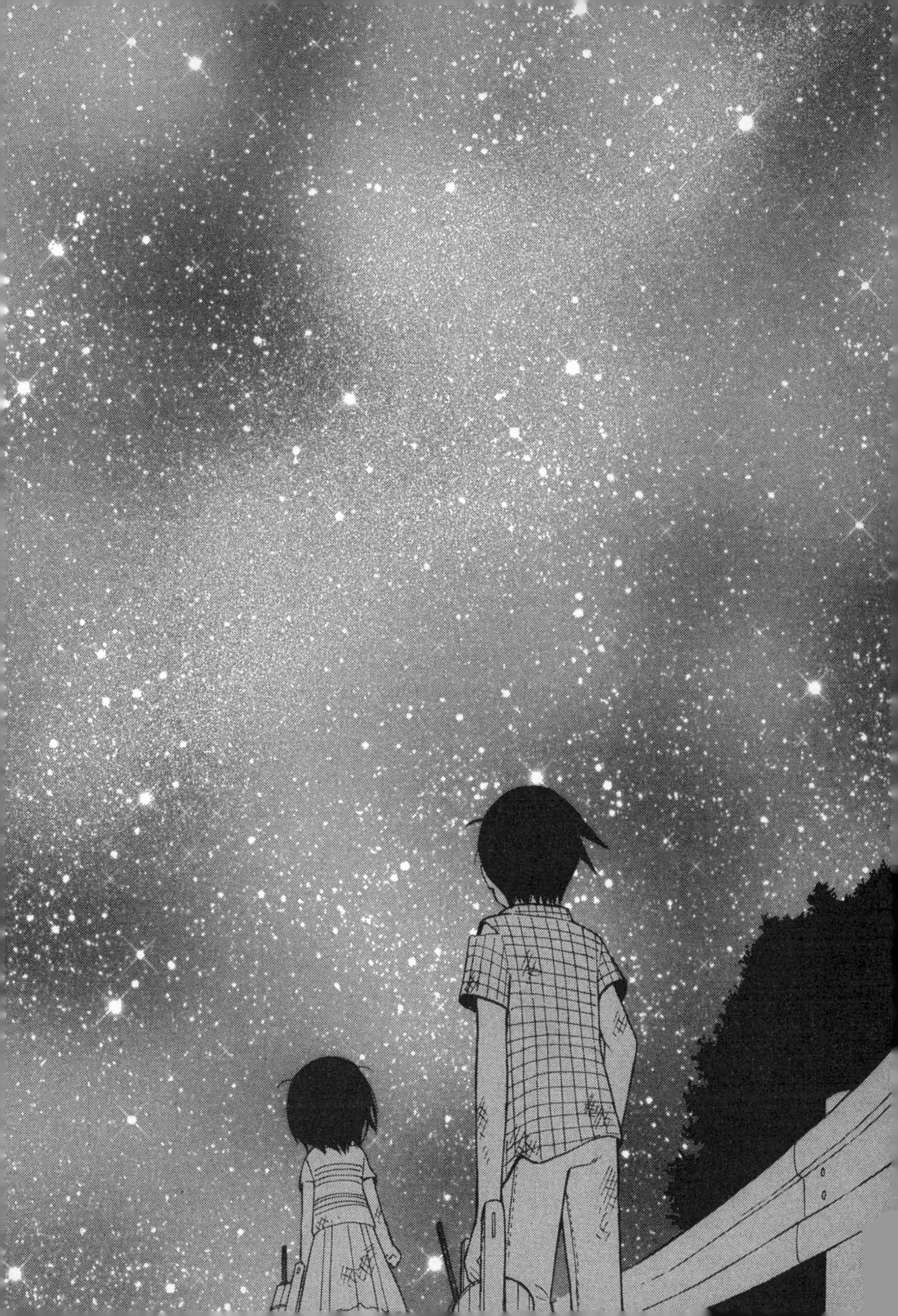

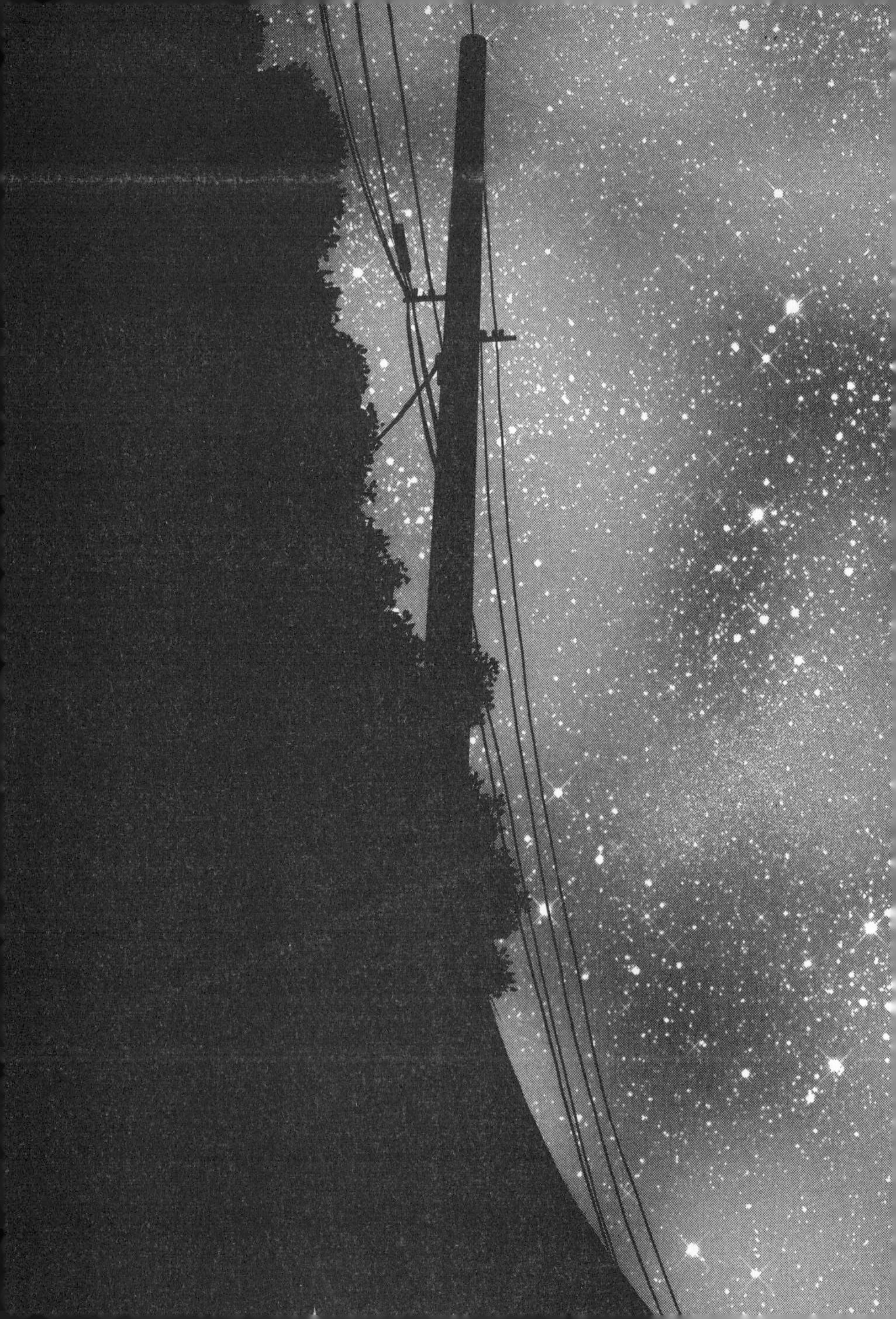

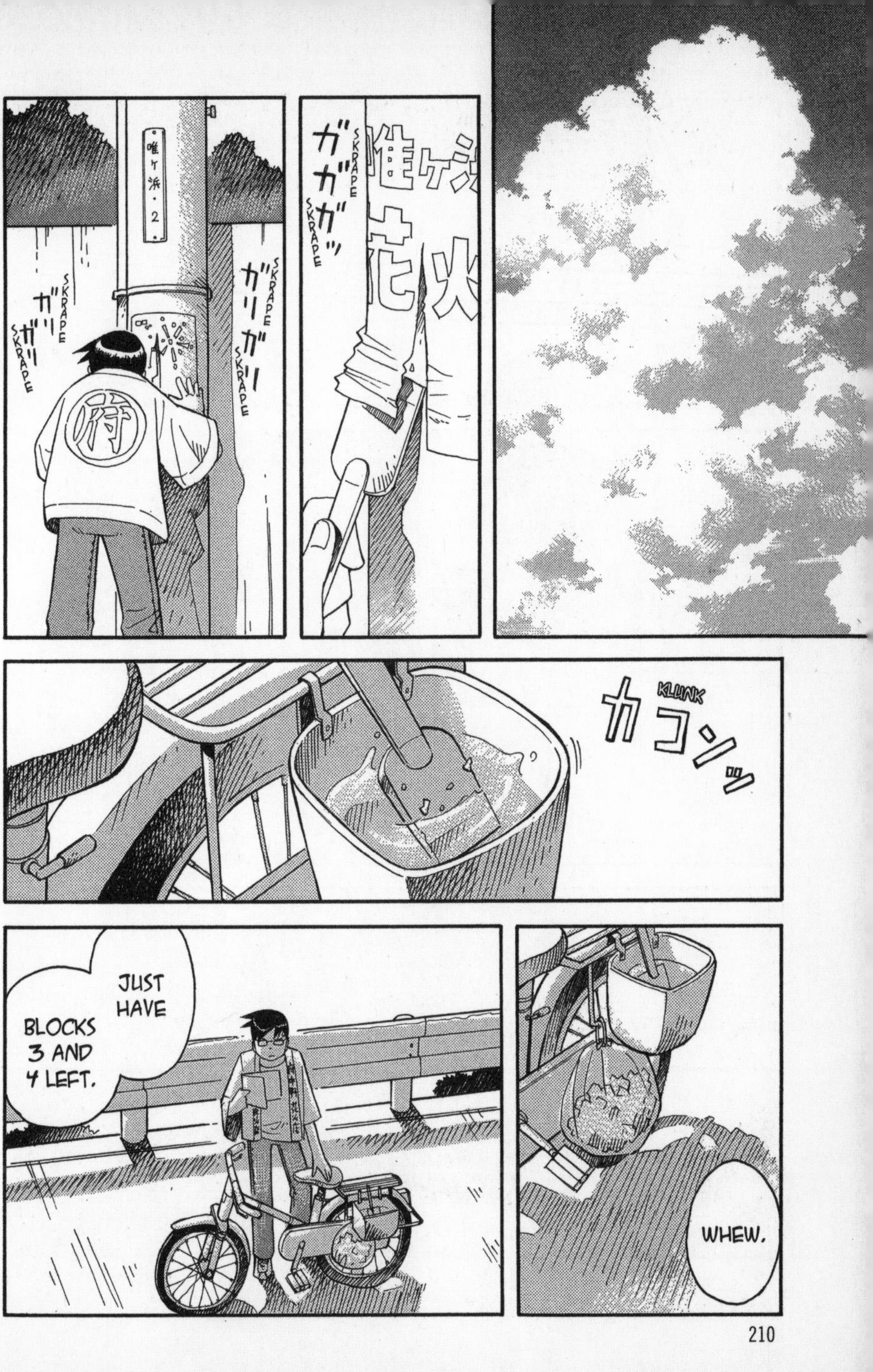
ガガガッ
SKRAPE
SKRAPE
花火
唯ヶ浜・2
ガリガリ
SKRAPE
SKRAPE
ガリガリ
SKRAPE
SKRAPE
カコンッ
KLUNK
WHEW.
JUST HAVE BLOCKS 3 AND 4 LEFT.

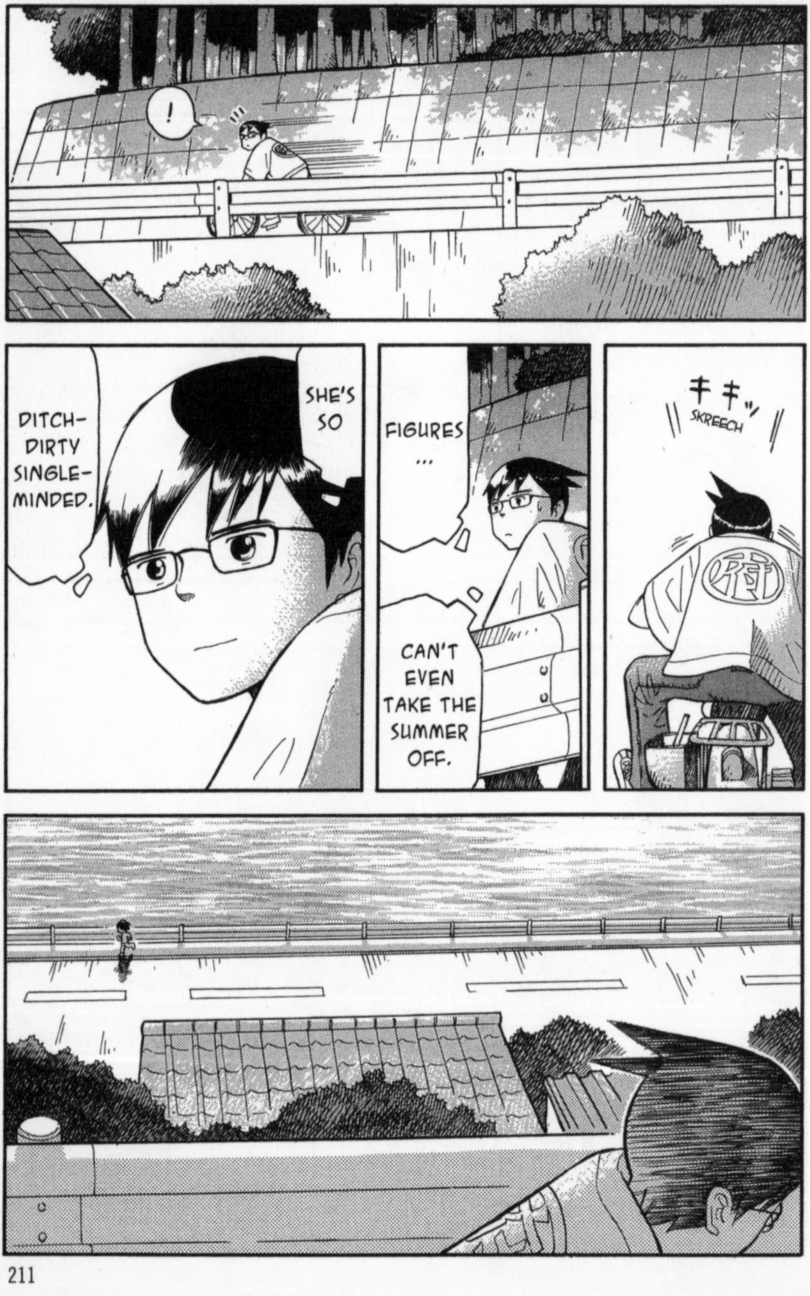
!
キキッ
SKREECH
FIGURES ...
CAN'T EVEN TAKE THE SUMMER OFF.
SHE'S SO
DITCH-DIRTY SINGLE-MINDED.

HUFF
HUFF
HUFF

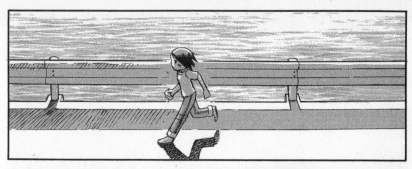

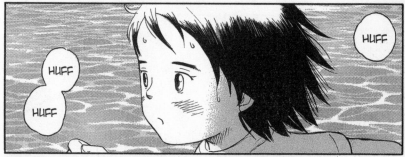

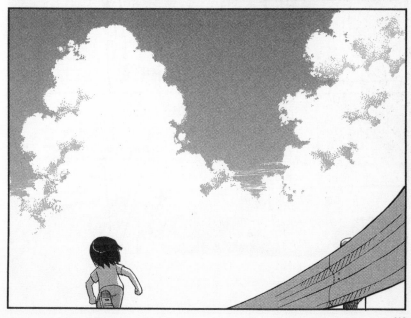

MISSION:63

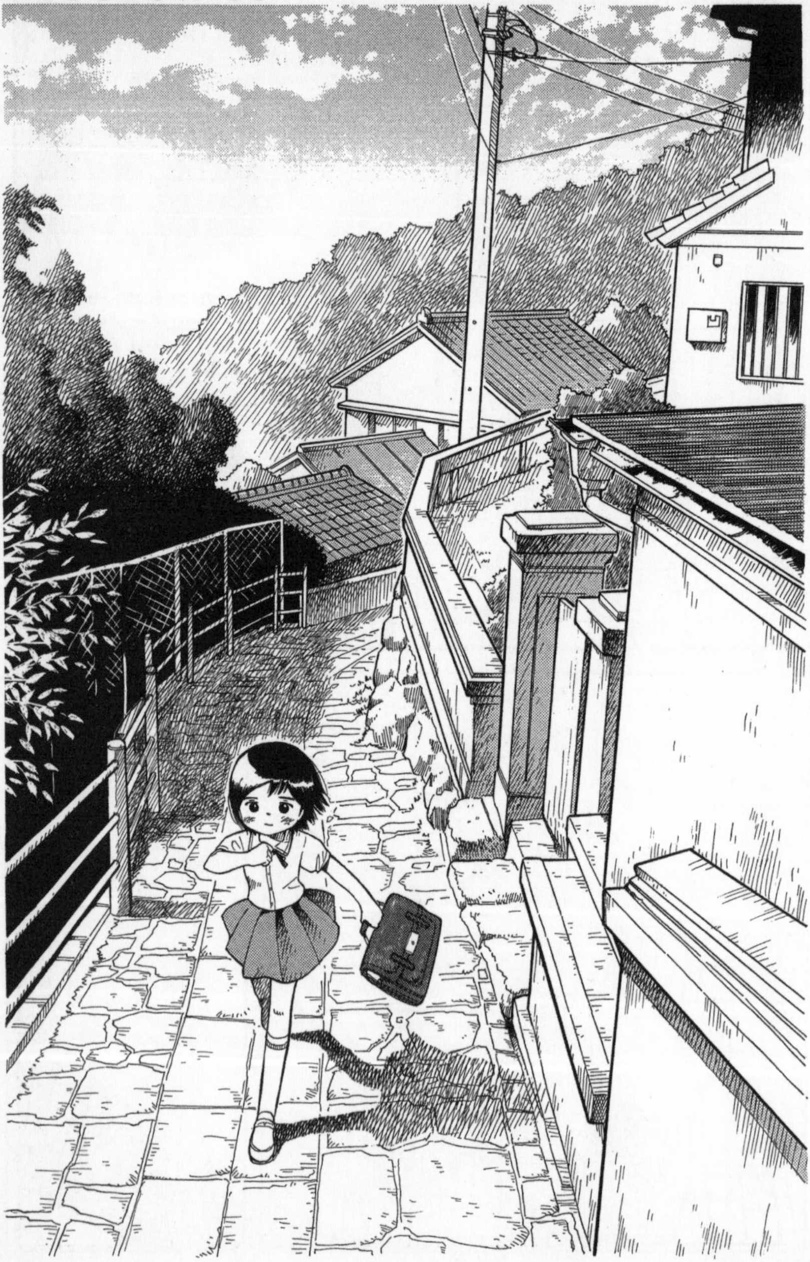

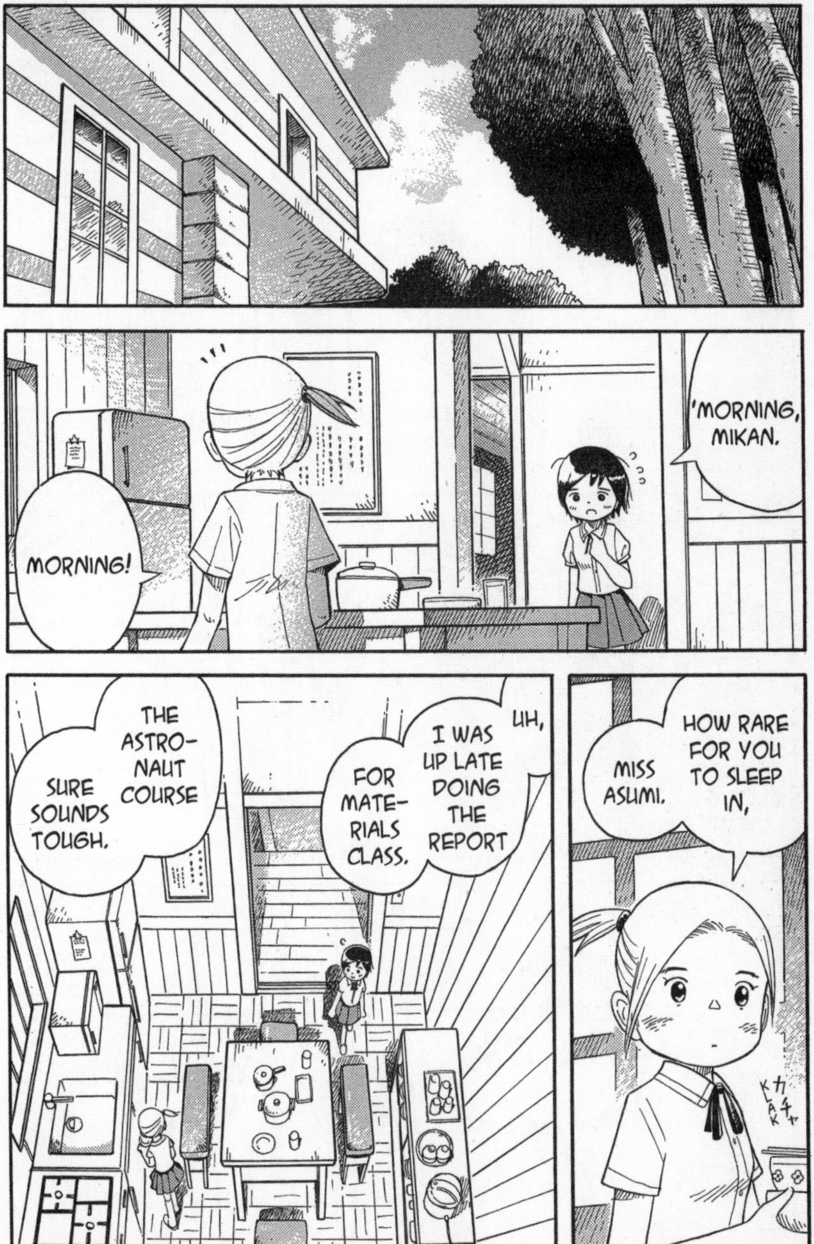
'MORNING, MIKAN.
MORNING!
HOW RARE FOR YOU TO SLEEP IN,
MISS ASUMI.
KLAK
カチャ
UH,
I WAS UP LATE DOING THE REPORT
FOR MATE-RIALS CLASS.
THE ASTRO-NAUT COURSE
SURE SOUNDS TOUGH.

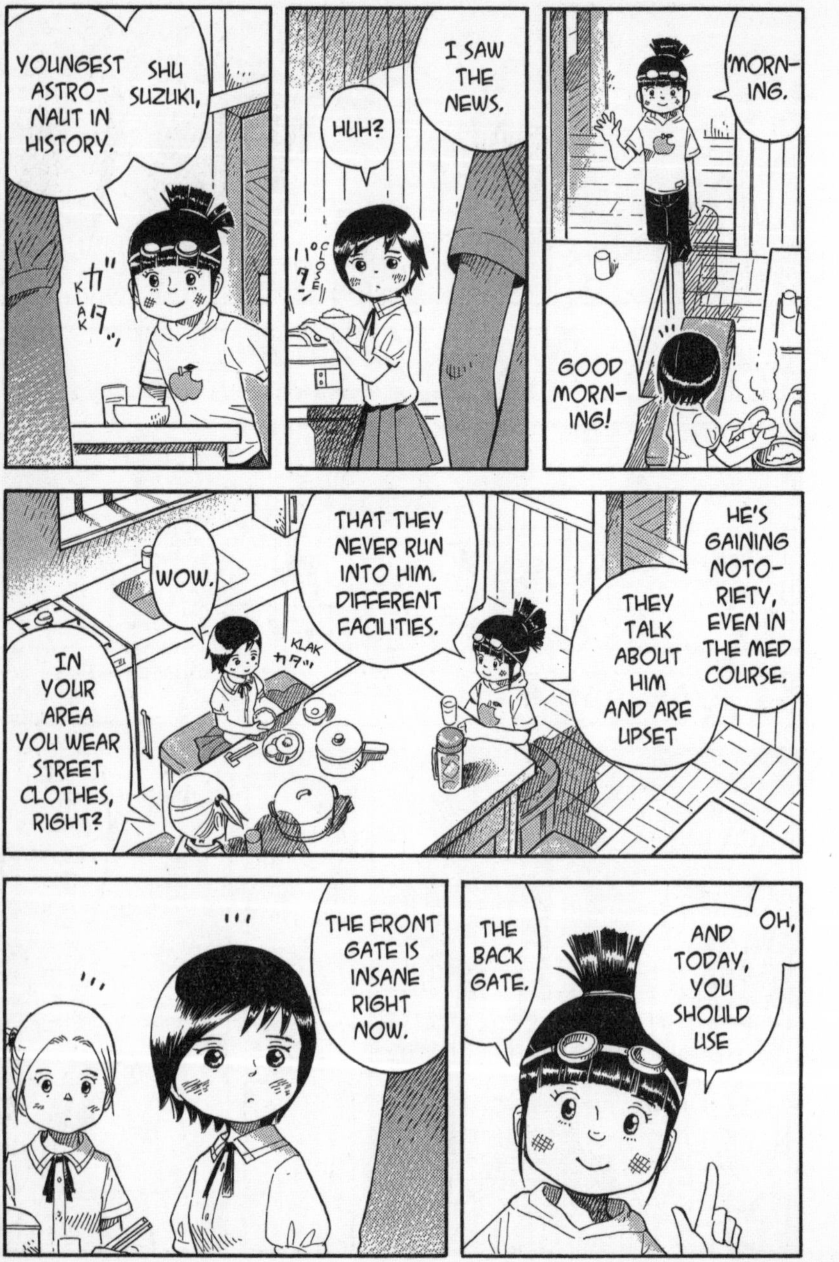
'MORNING.
GOOD MORNING!
I SAW THE NEWS.
HUH?
CLOSE
SHU SUZUKI,
YOUNGEST ASTRONAUT IN HISTORY.
KLAK
HE'S GAINING NOTORIETY, EVEN IN THE MED COURSE.
THEY TALK ABOUT HIM AND ARE UPSET
THAT THEY NEVER RUN INTO HIM. DIFFERENT FACILITIES.
KLAK
WOW.
IN YOUR AREA YOU WEAR STREET CLOTHES, RIGHT?
OH,
AND TODAY, YOU SHOULD USE
THE BACK GATE.
THE FRONT GATE IS INSANE RIGHT NOW.
...
...

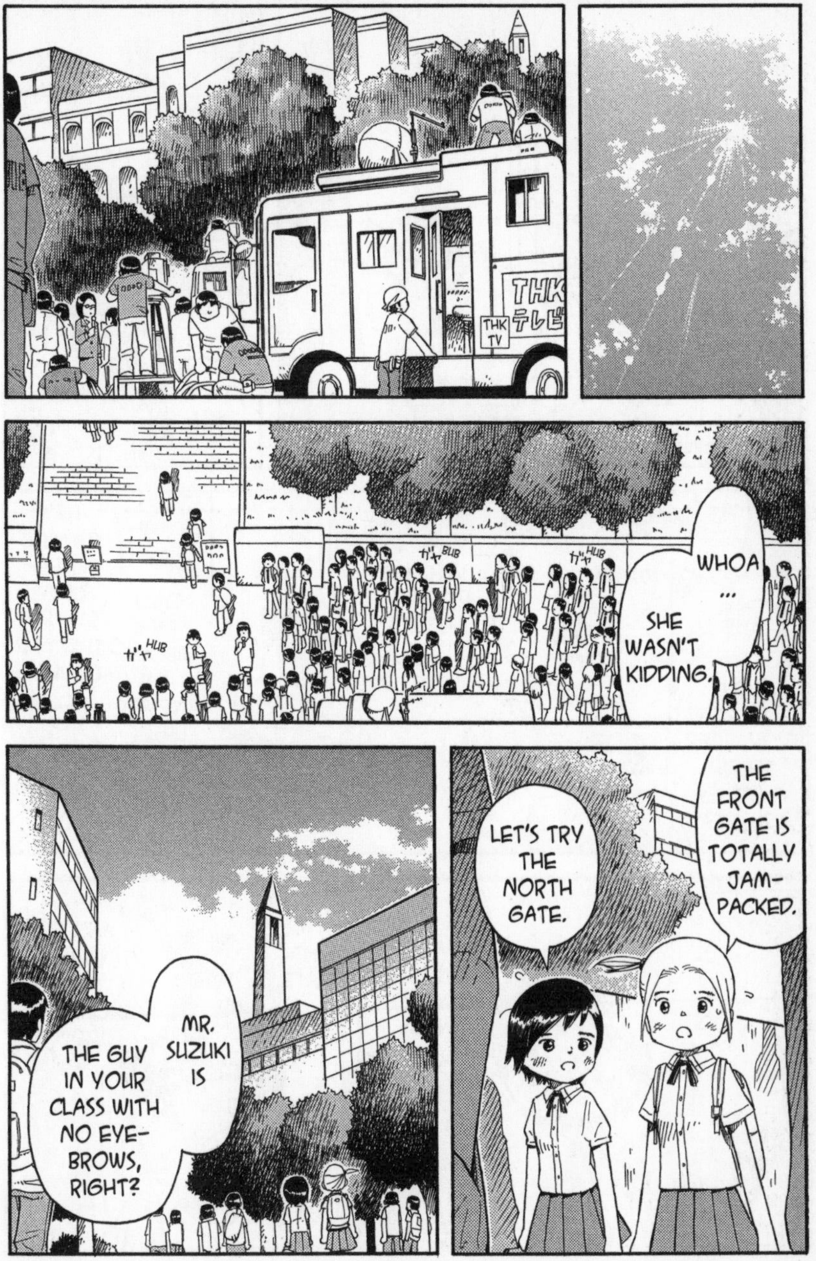
THK
テレビ
THK
TV
ガヤ HUB
ガヤ HUB
ガヤ HUB
WHOA ... SHE WASN'T KIDDING.
THE FRONT GATE IS TOTALLY JAM-PACKED.
LET'S TRY THE NORTH GATE.
MR. SUZUKI IS
THE GUY IN YOUR CLASS WITH NO EYE-BROWS, RIGHT?

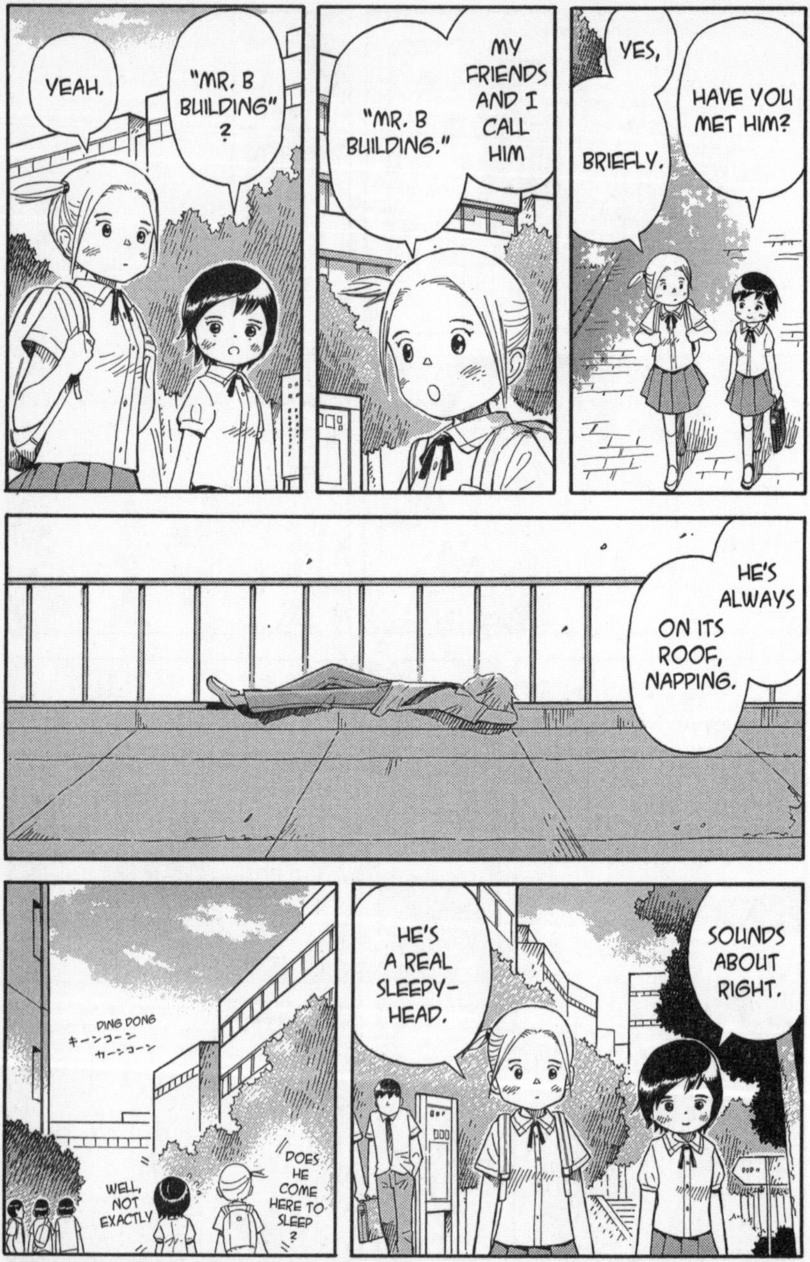
HAVE YOU MET HIM?
YES, BRIEFLY.
MY FRIENDS AND I CALL HIM
"MR. B BUILDING."
"MR. B BUILDING"?
YEAH.
HE'S ALWAYS ON ITS ROOF, NAPPING.
SOUNDS ABOUT RIGHT.
HE'S A REAL SLEEPY-HEAD.
DING DONG
キーンコーン
カーンコーン
DOES HE COME HERE TO SLEEP?
WELL, NOT EXACTLY

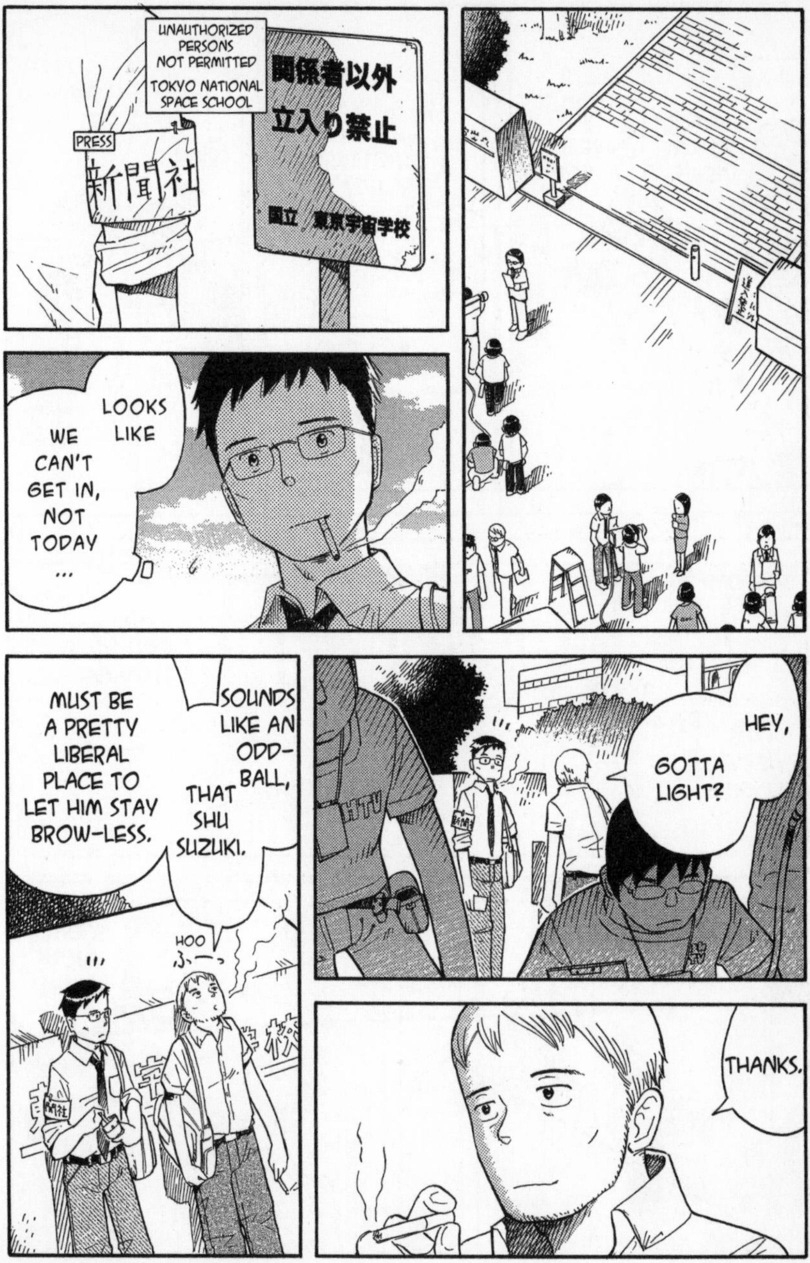
関係者以外
立入り禁止
国立 東京宇宙学校
UNAUTHORIZED PERSONS NOT PERMITTED
TOKYO NATIONAL SPACE SCHOOL
PRESS
新聞社
LOOKS LIKE WE CAN'T GET IN, NOT TODAY ...
HEY, GOTTA LIGHT?
THANKS.
SOUNDS LIKE AN ODD-BALL, THAT SHU SUZUKI.
MUST BE A PRETTY LIBERAL PLACE TO LET HIM STAY BROW-LESS.
HOO
ふーっ

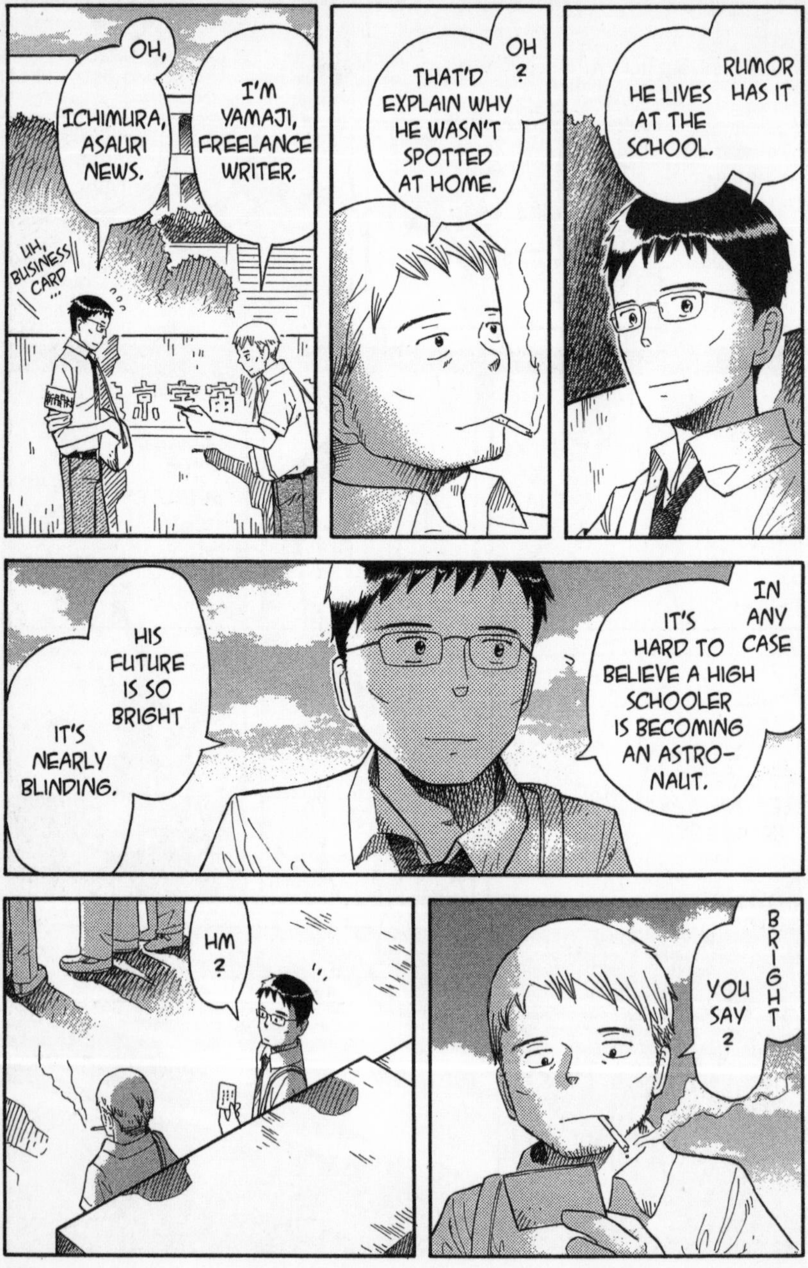
RUMOR HAS IT HE LIVES AT THE SCHOOL.
OH?
THAT'D EXPLAIN WHY HE WASN'T SPOTTED AT HOME.
I'M YAMAJI, FREELANCE WRITER.
OH, ICHIMURA, ASAURI NEWS.
UH, BUSINESS CARD ...
IN ANY CASE IT'S HARD TO BELIEVE A HIGH SCHOOLER IS BECOMING AN ASTRO-NAUT.
HIS FUTURE IS SO BRIGHT IT'S NEARLY BLINDING.
BRIGHT YOU SAY?
HM?

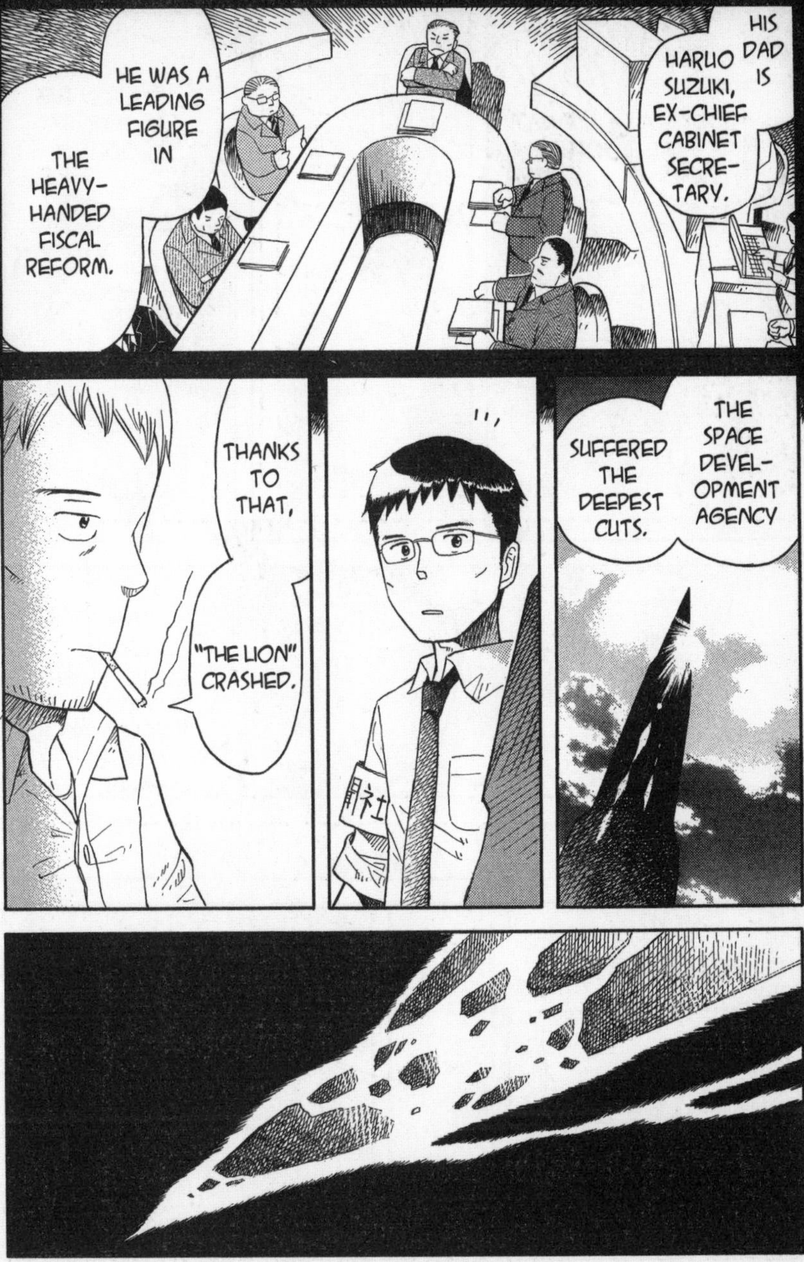
HIS DAD IS HARUO SUZUKI, EX-CHIEF CABINET SECRETARY.
HE WAS A LEADING FIGURE IN THE HEAVY-HANDED FISCAL REFORM.
THE SPACE DEVELOPMENT AGENCY SUFFERED THE DEEPEST CUTS.
THANKS TO THAT, "THE LION" CRASHED.

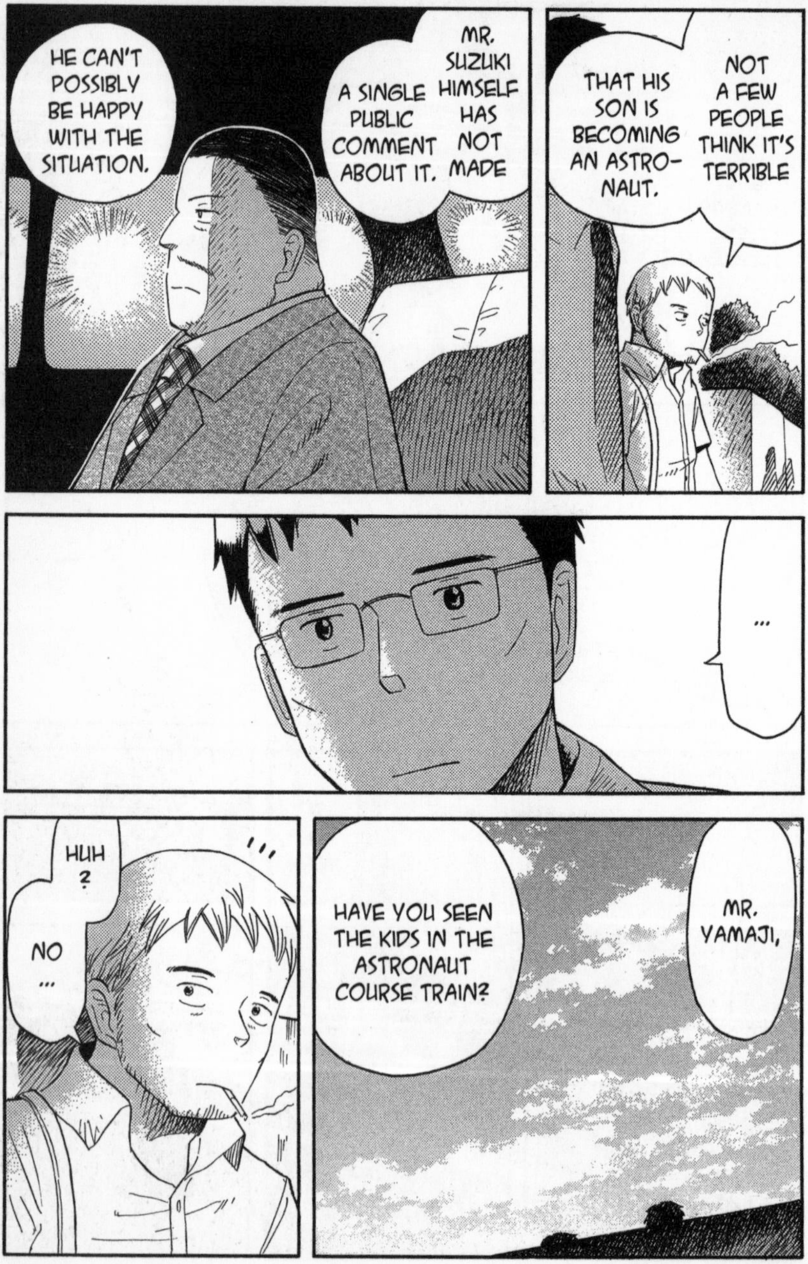
NOT A FEW PEOPLE THINK IT'S TERRIBLE
THAT HIS SON IS BECOMING AN ASTRONAUT.
MR. SUZUKI HIMSELF HAS NOT MADE
A SINGLE PUBLIC COMMENT ABOUT IT.
HE CAN'T POSSIBLY BE HAPPY WITH THE SITUATION.
...
MR. YAMAJI,
HAVE YOU SEEN THE KIDS IN THE ASTRONAUT COURSE TRAIN?
HUH?
NO ...

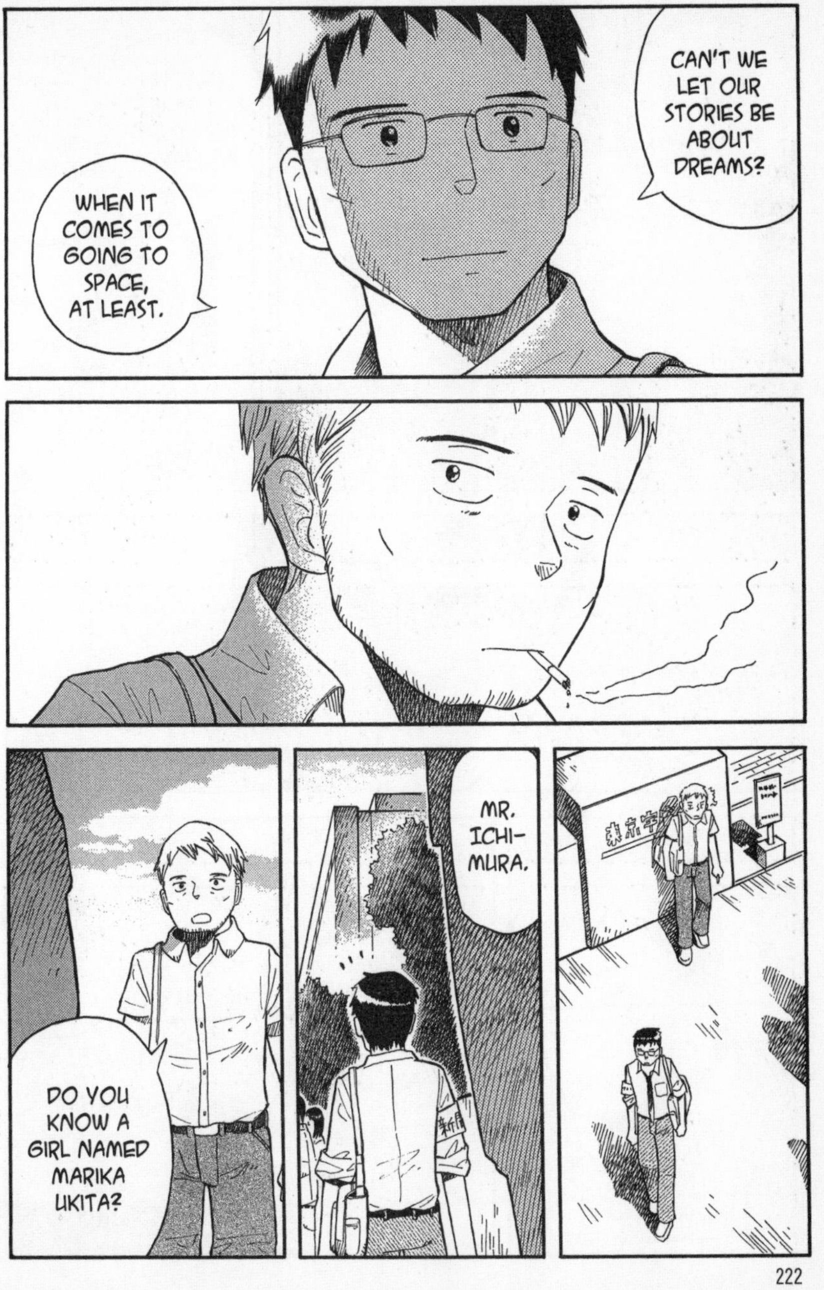
CAN'T WE LET OUR STORIES BE ABOUT DREAMS?
WHEN IT COMES TO GOING TO SPACE, AT LEAST.
MR. ICHI-MURA.
DO YOU KNOW A GIRL NAMED MARIKA UKITA?

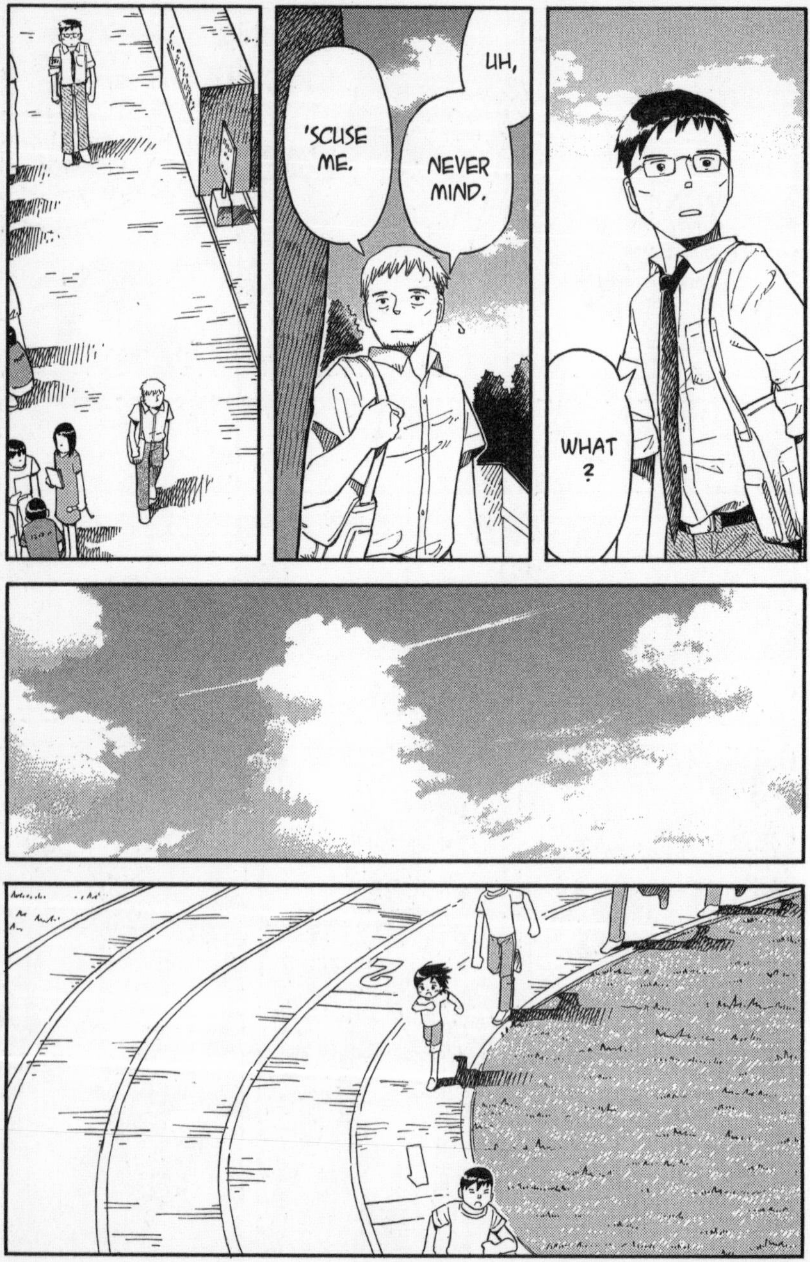
WHAT?
UH,
NEVER MIND.
'SCUSE ME.

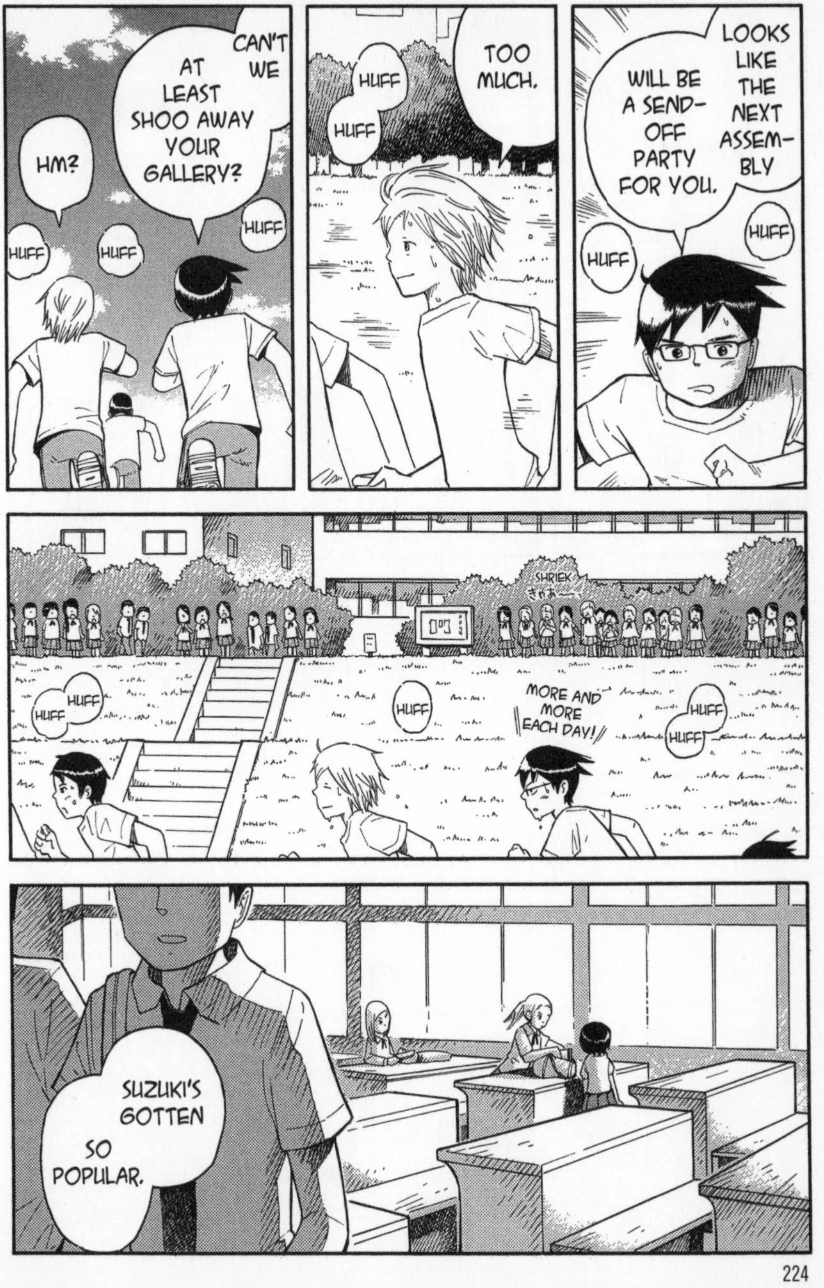
LOOKS LIKE THE NEXT ASSEM-BLY WILL BE A SEND-OFF PARTY FOR YOU.
HUFF
HUFF
TOO MUCH.
HUFF
HUFF
CAN'T WE AT LEAST SHOO AWAY YOUR GALLERY?
HM?
HUFF
HUFF
HUFF
SHRIEK
きゃあ〜〜
HUFF
HUFF
MORE AND MORE EACH DAY!
HUFF
HUFF
HUFF
SUZUKI'S GOTTEN SO POPULAR.

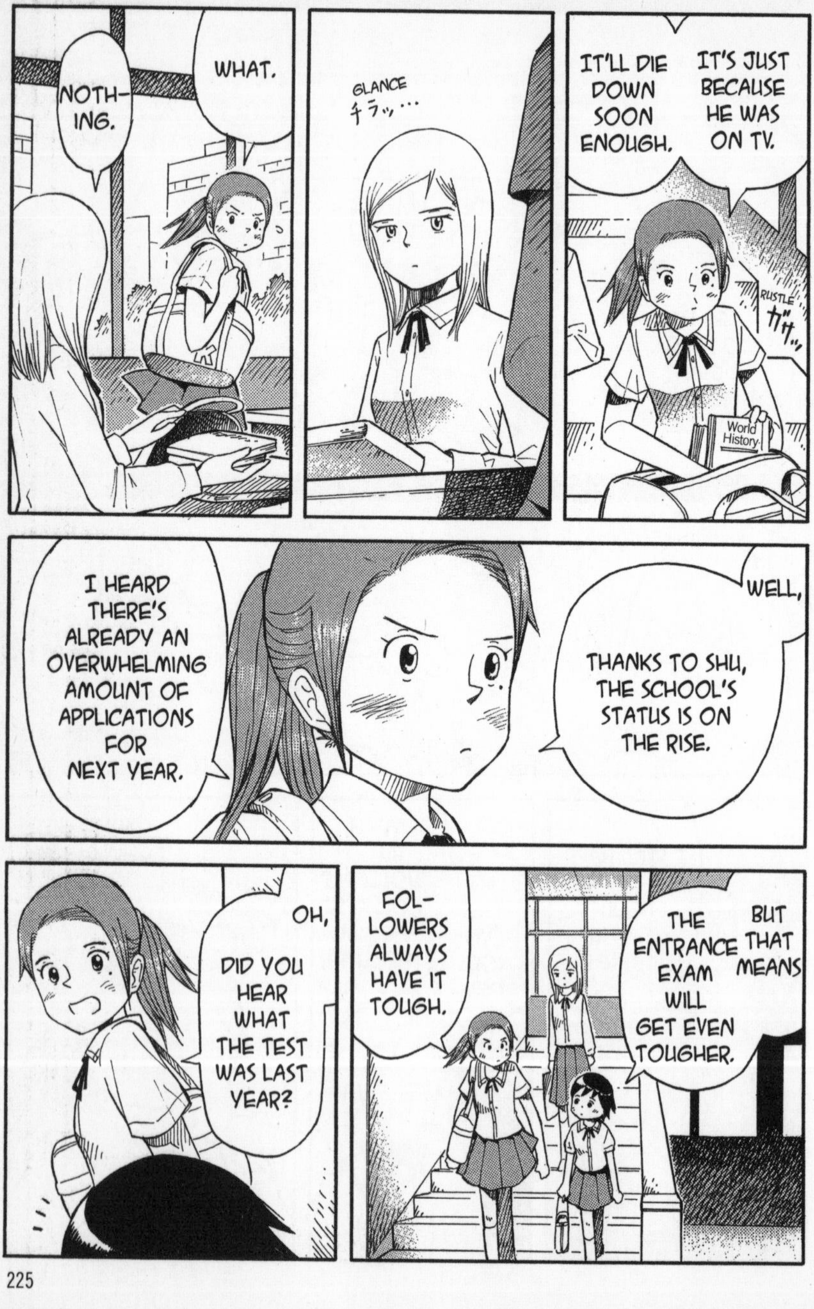
IT'S JUST BECAUSE HE WAS ON TV.
IT'LL DIE DOWN SOON ENOUGH.
World History
RUSTLE
ガサッ
GLANCE
チラッ…
WHAT.
NOTH-ING.
WELL,
THANKS TO SHU, THE SCHOOL'S STATUS IS ON THE RISE.
I HEARD THERE'S ALREADY AN OVERWHELMING AMOUNT OF APPLICATIONS FOR NEXT YEAR.
BUT THAT MEANS
THE ENTRANCE EXAM WILL GET EVEN TOUGHER.
FOL-LOWERS ALWAYS HAVE IT TOUGH.
OH,
DID YOU HEAR WHAT THE TEST WAS LAST YEAR?

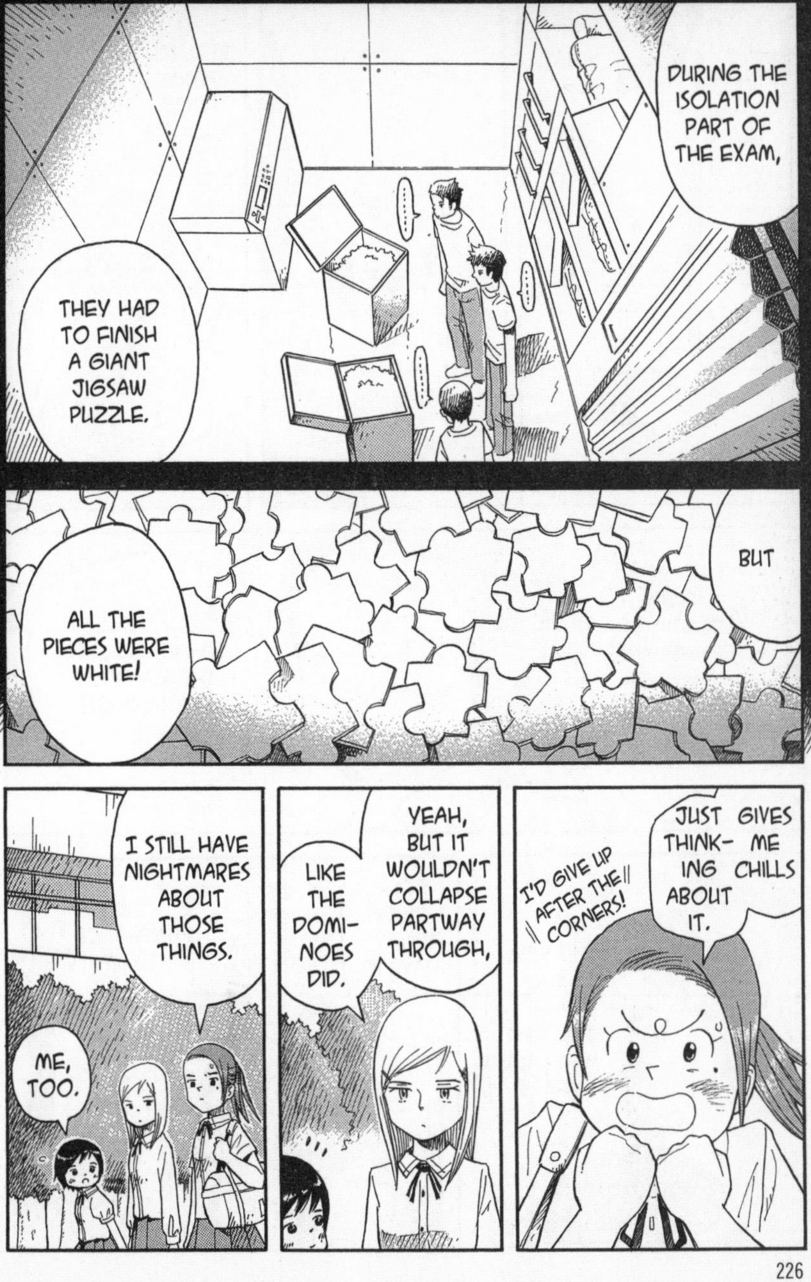
DURING THE ISOLATION PART OF THE EXAM,
THEY HAD TO FINISH A GIANT JIGSAW PUZZLE.
……
……
……
BUT
ALL THE PIECES WERE WHITE!
JUST THINKING ABOUT IT. GIVES ME CHILLS
I'D GIVE UP AFTER THE CORNERS!
YEAH, BUT IT WOULDN'T COLLAPSE PARTWAY THROUGH,
LIKE THE DOMINOES DID.
I STILL HAVE NIGHTMARES ABOUT THOSE THINGS.
ME, TOO.

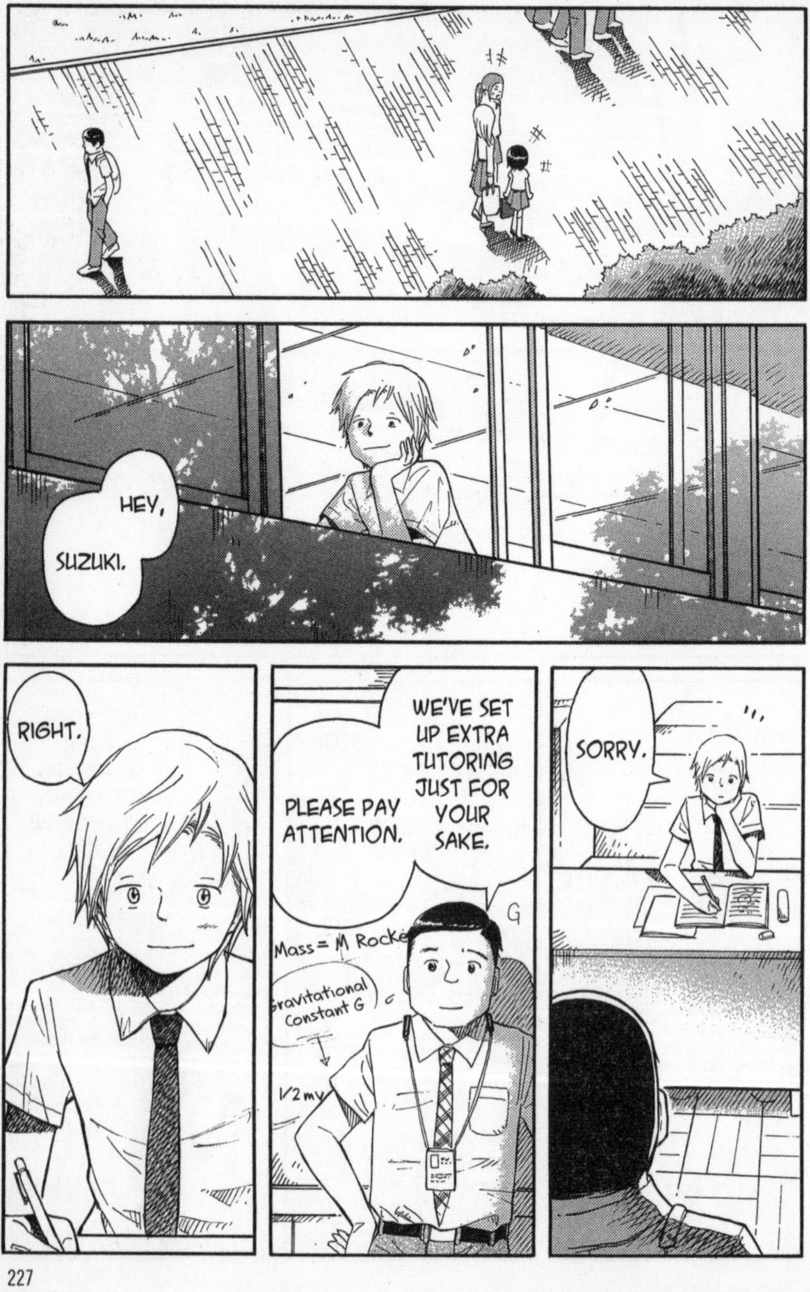
HEY,
SUZUKI.
SORRY.
WE'VE SET UP EXTRA TUTORING JUST FOR YOUR SAKE.
PLEASE PAY ATTENTION.
G
Mass = M Rocke
Gravitational Constant G
1/2mv
RIGHT.

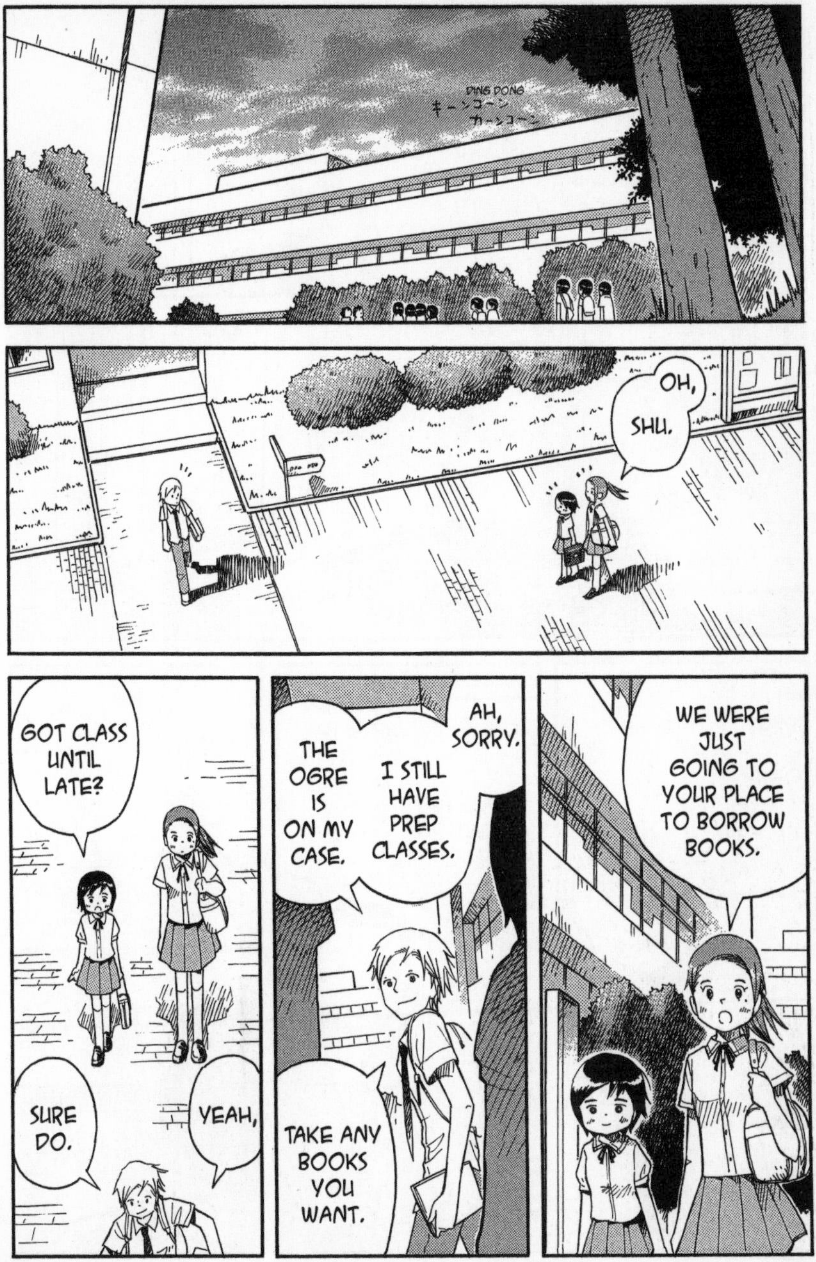
DING DONG
キーンコーン
カーンコーン
OH, SHU.
WE WERE JUST GOING TO YOUR PLACE TO BORROW BOOKS.
AH, SORRY.
I STILL HAVE PREP CLASSES.
THE OGRE IS ON MY CASE.
TAKE ANY BOOKS YOU WANT.
GOT CLASS UNTIL LATE?
YEAH,
SURE DO.

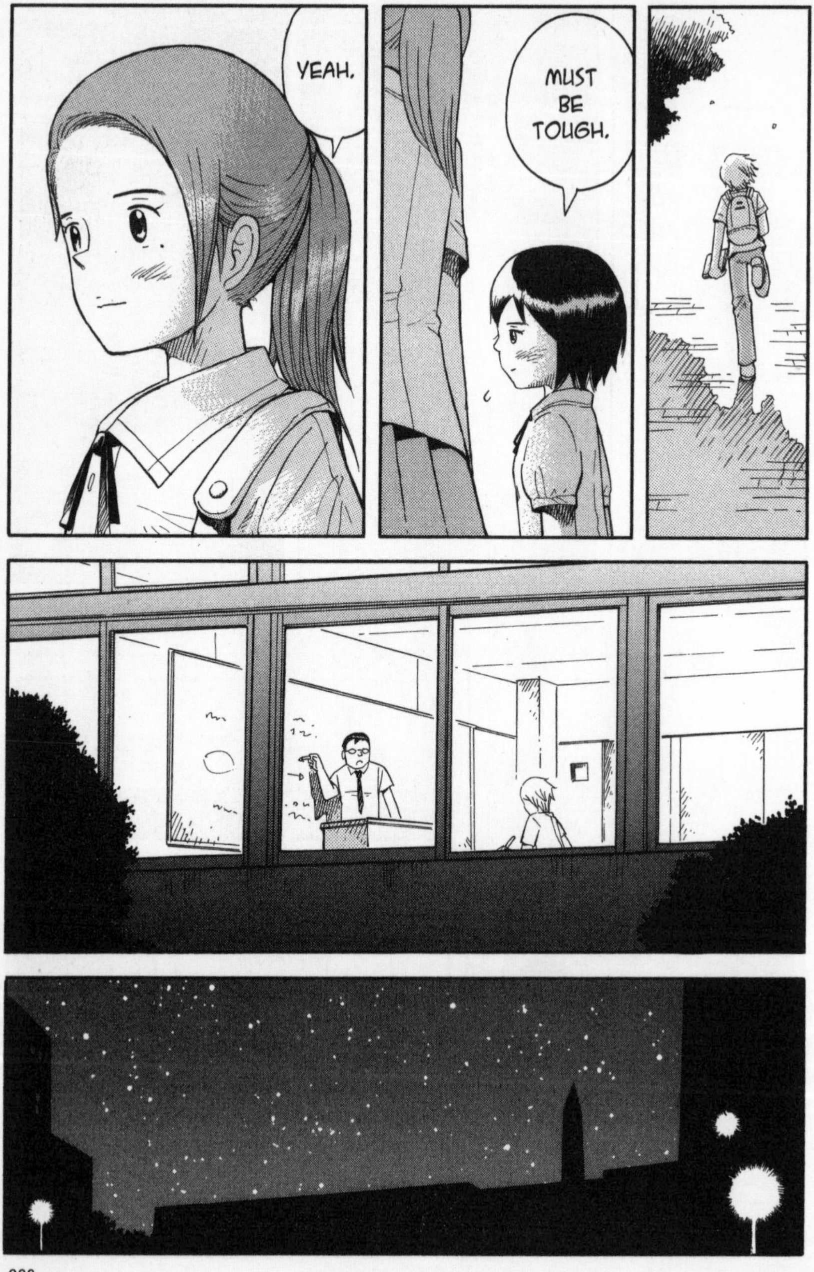
MUST BE TOUGH.
YEAH.

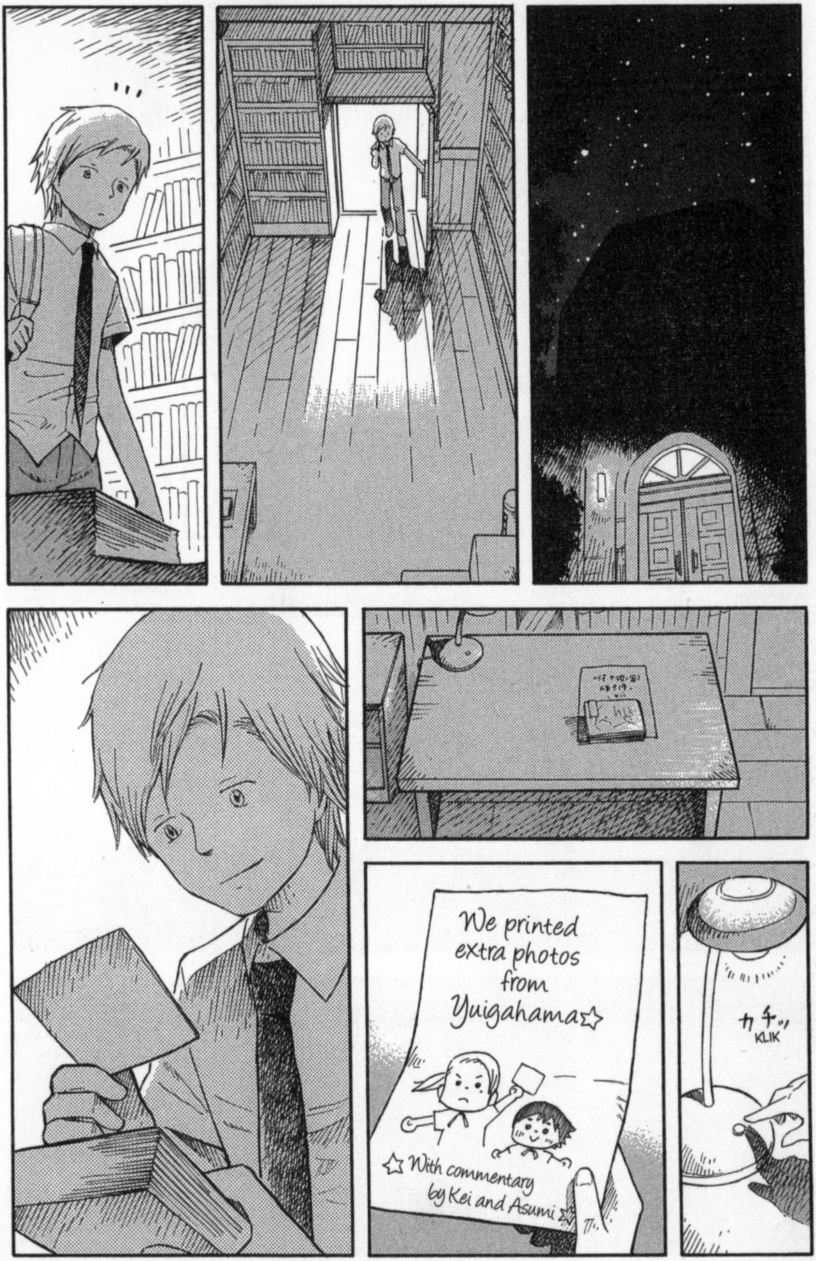
カチッ
KLIK
We printed extra photos from Yuigahama☆
☆With commentary by Kei and Asumi☆

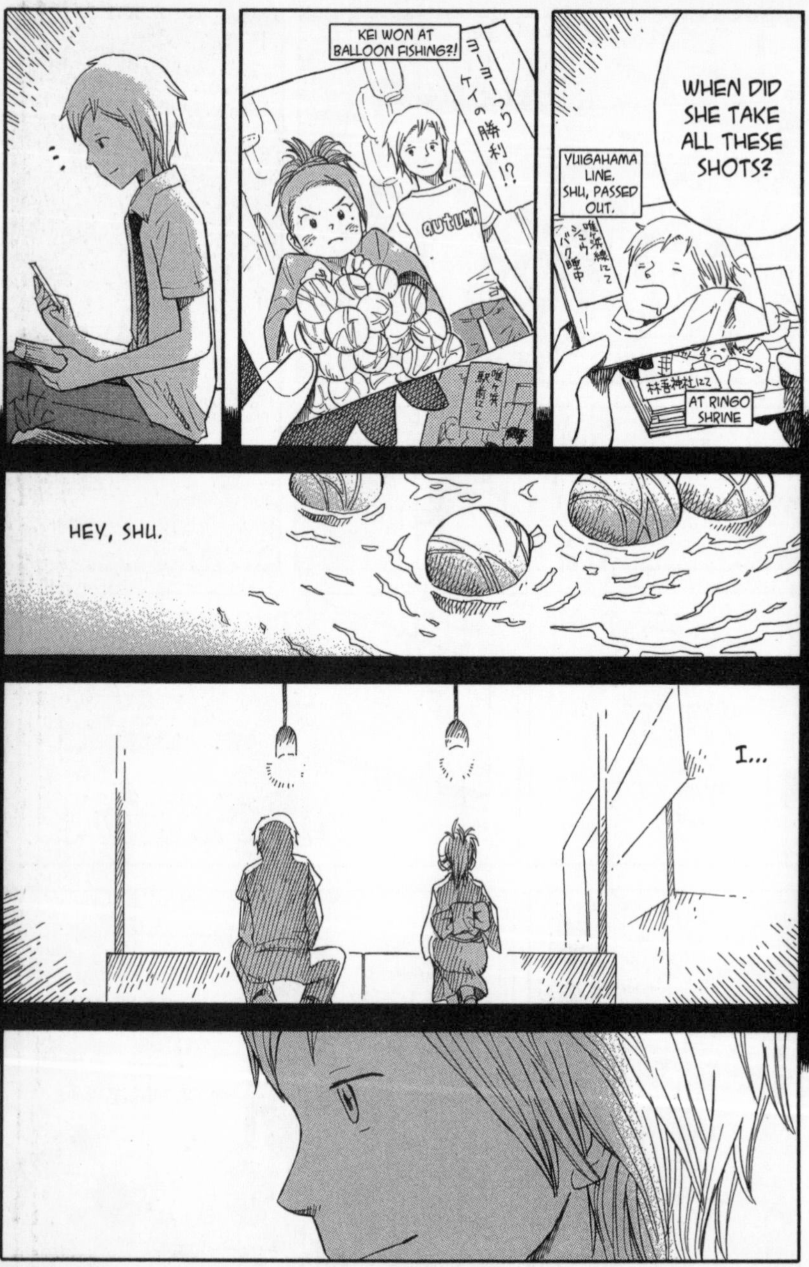
WHEN DID SHE TAKE ALL THESE SHOTS?
YUIGAHAMA LINE. SHU, PASSED OUT.
唯ヶ浜線にて シュウ バク睡中
林香神社にて
AT RINGO SHRINE
KEI WON AT BALLOON FISHING?!
ヨーヨーつり ケイの勝利!?
唯ヶ浜駅前にて
...
HEY, SHU.
I...

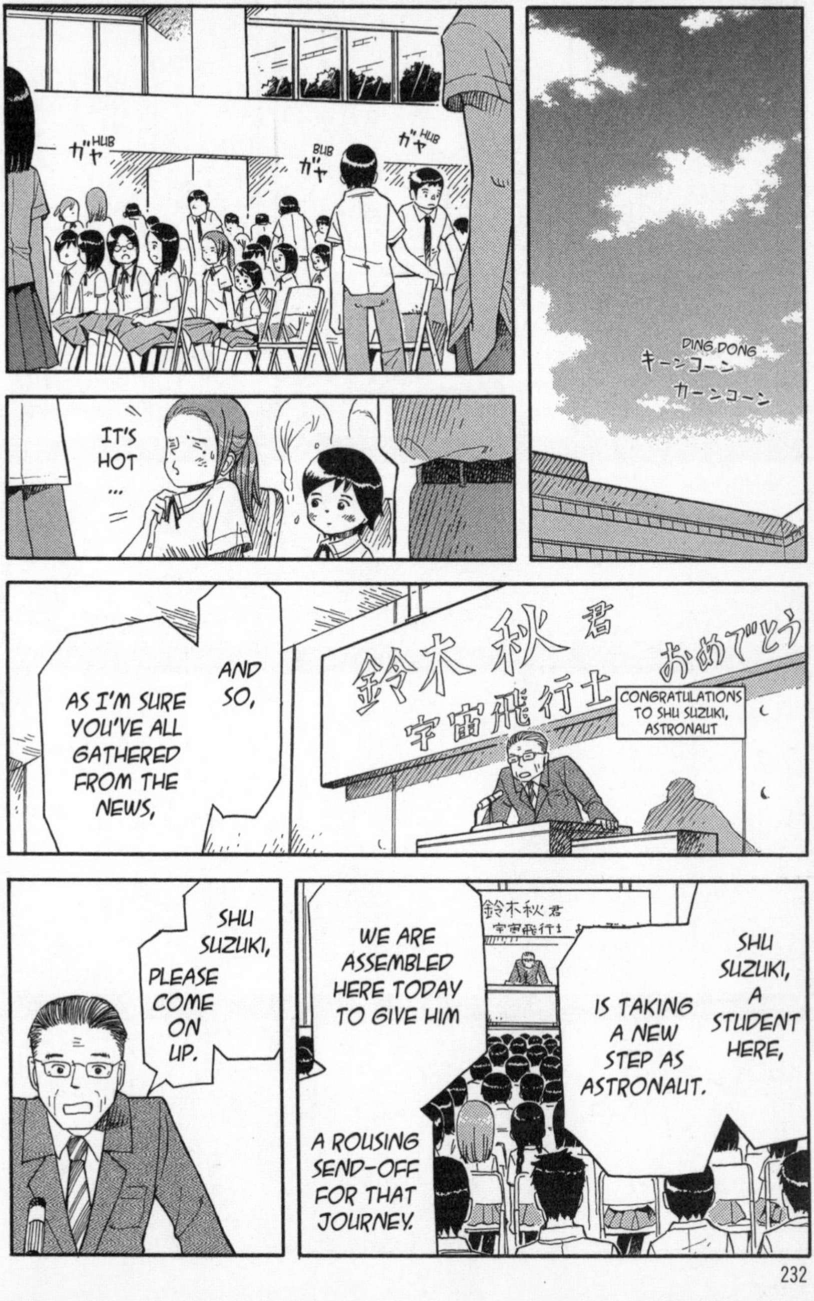
DING DONG
キーンコーン
カーンコーン
HUB
ガヤ
BUB
ガヤ
HUB
ガヤ
IT'S HOT ...
AND SO,
AS I'M SURE YOU'VE ALL GATHERED FROM THE NEWS,
鈴木秋君
宇宙飛行士
おめでとう
CONGRATULATIONS TO SHU SUZUKI, ASTRONAUT
SHU SUZUKI, A STUDENT HERE,
IS TAKING A NEW STEP AS ASTRONAUT.
WE ARE ASSEMBLED HERE TODAY TO GIVE HIM
A ROUSING SEND-OFF FOR THAT JOURNEY.
SHU SUZUKI,
PLEASE COME ON UP.

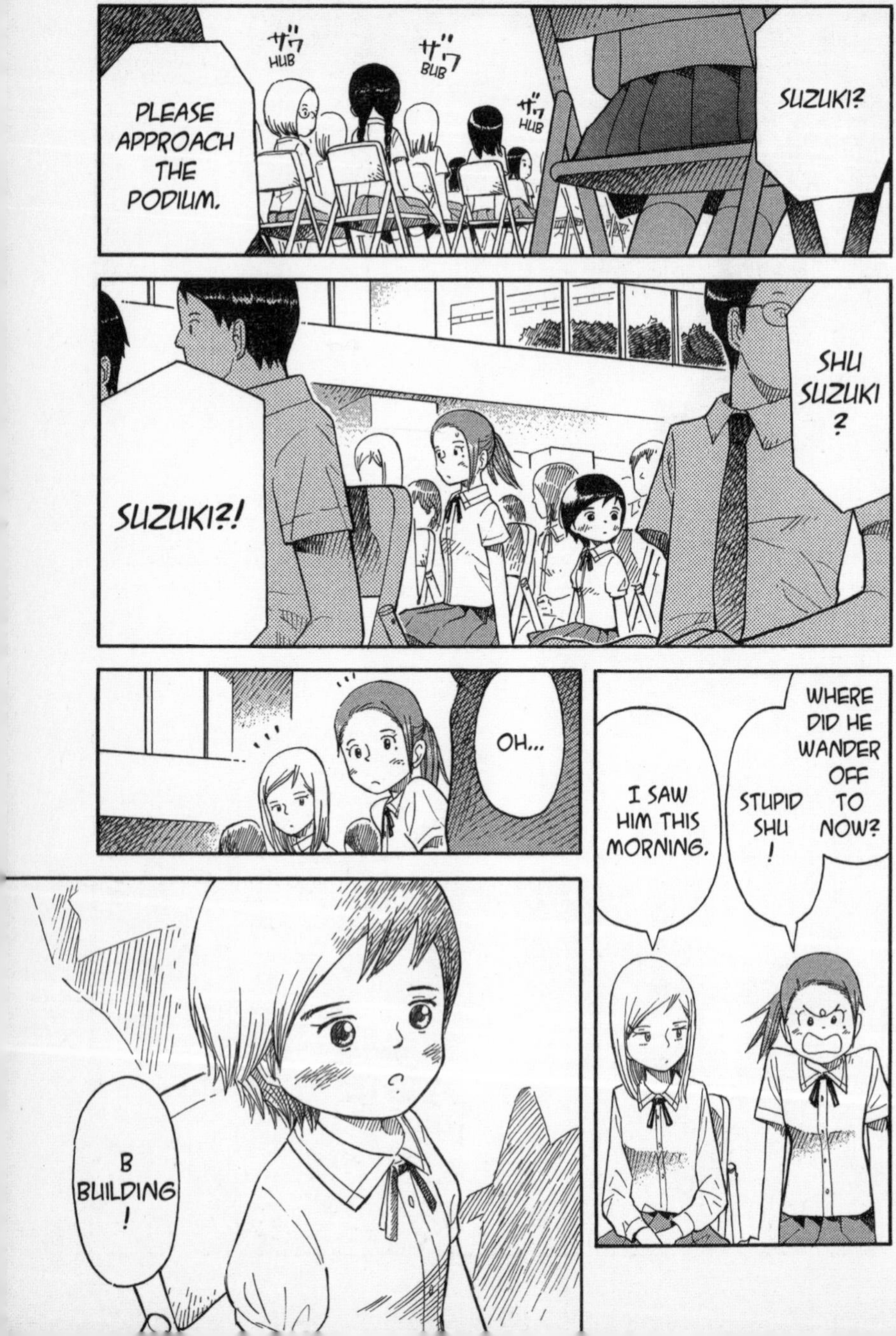
SUZUKI?
ザワ HUB
ザワ BUB
ザワ HUB
PLEASE APPROACH THE PODIUM.
SHU SUZUKI?
SUZUKI?!
WHERE DID HE WANDER OFF TO NOW?
STUPID SHU!
I SAW HIM THIS MORNING.
OH...
B BUILDING!

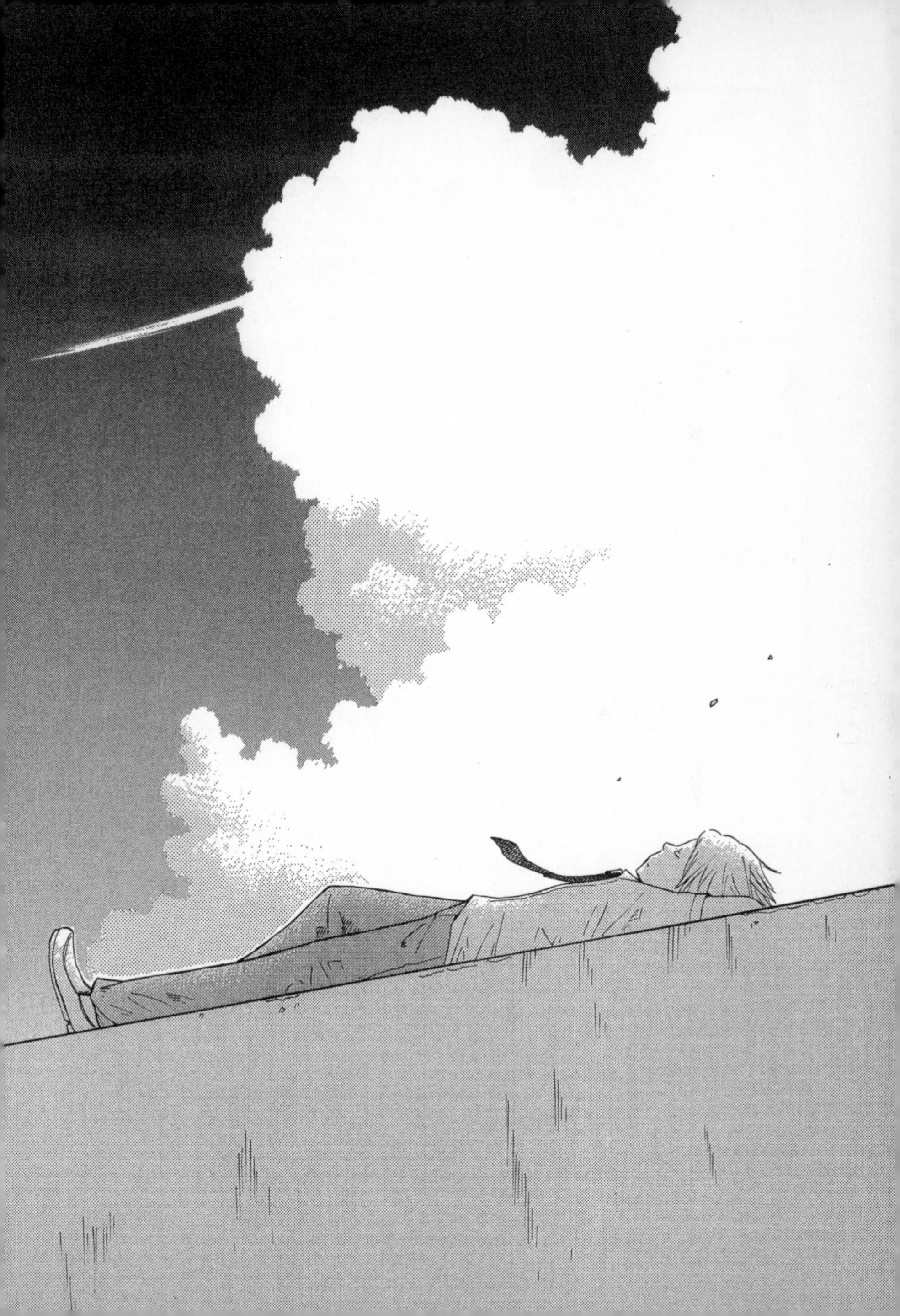

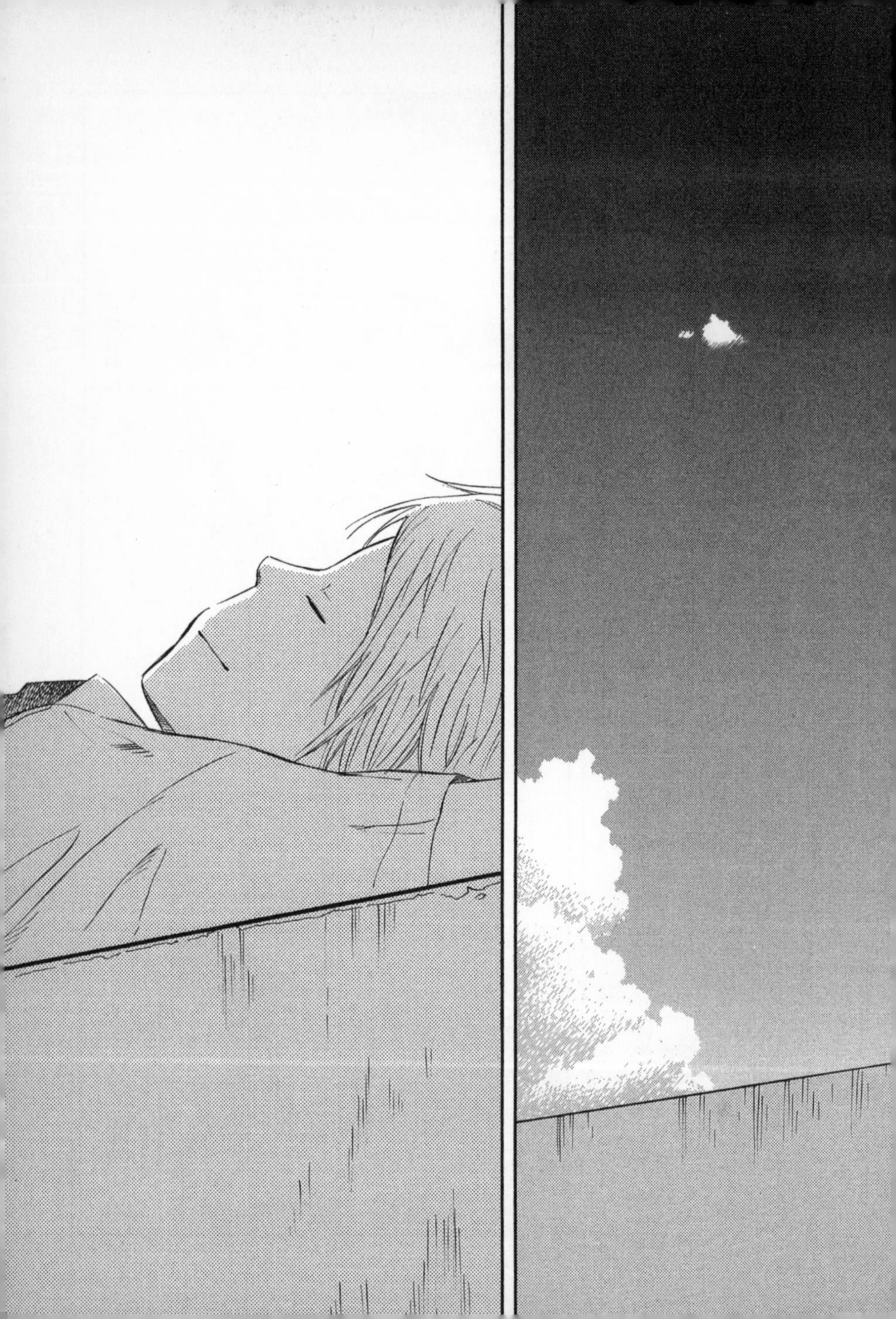

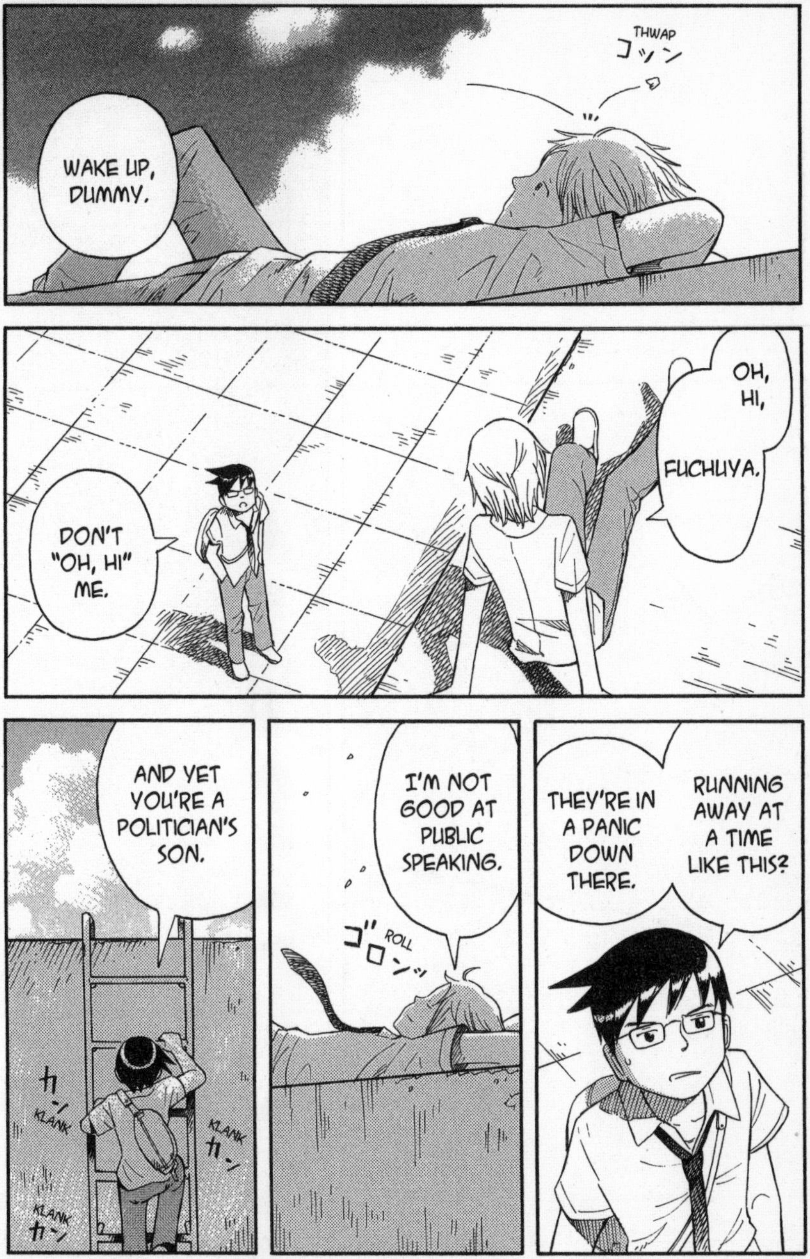
THWAP
コッン
WAKE UP, DUMMY.
OH, HI, FUCHUYA.
DON'T "OH, HI" ME.
RUNNING AWAY AT A TIME LIKE THIS?
THEY'RE IN A PANIC DOWN THERE.
I'M NOT GOOD AT PUBLIC SPEAKING.
ROLL
ゴロンッ
AND YET YOU'RE A POLITICIAN'S SON.
KLANK
カーン
KLANK
カーン
KLANK
カーン

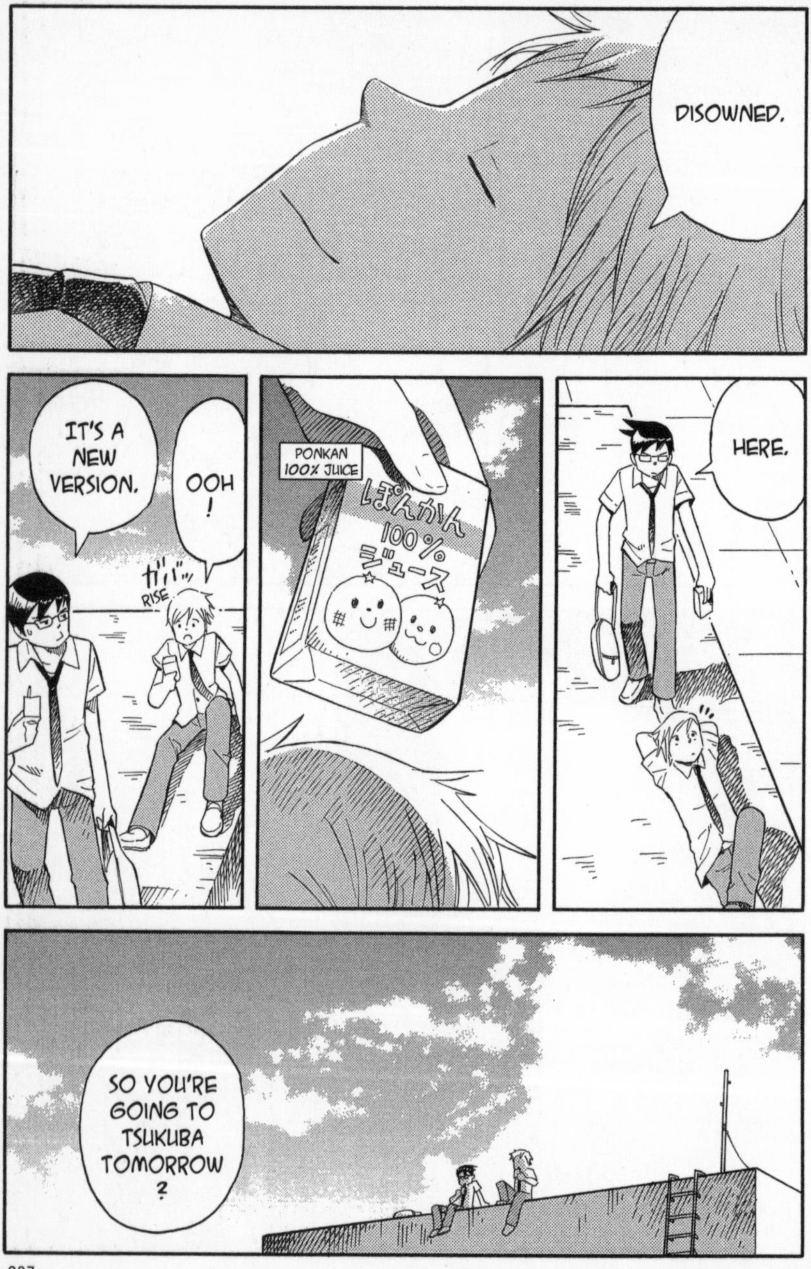
DISOWNED.
HERE.
PONKAN 100% JUICE
ぽんかん 100% ジュース
OOH !
IT'S A NEW VERSION.
ガバッ
RISE
SO YOU'RE GOING TO TSUKUBA TOMORROW ?

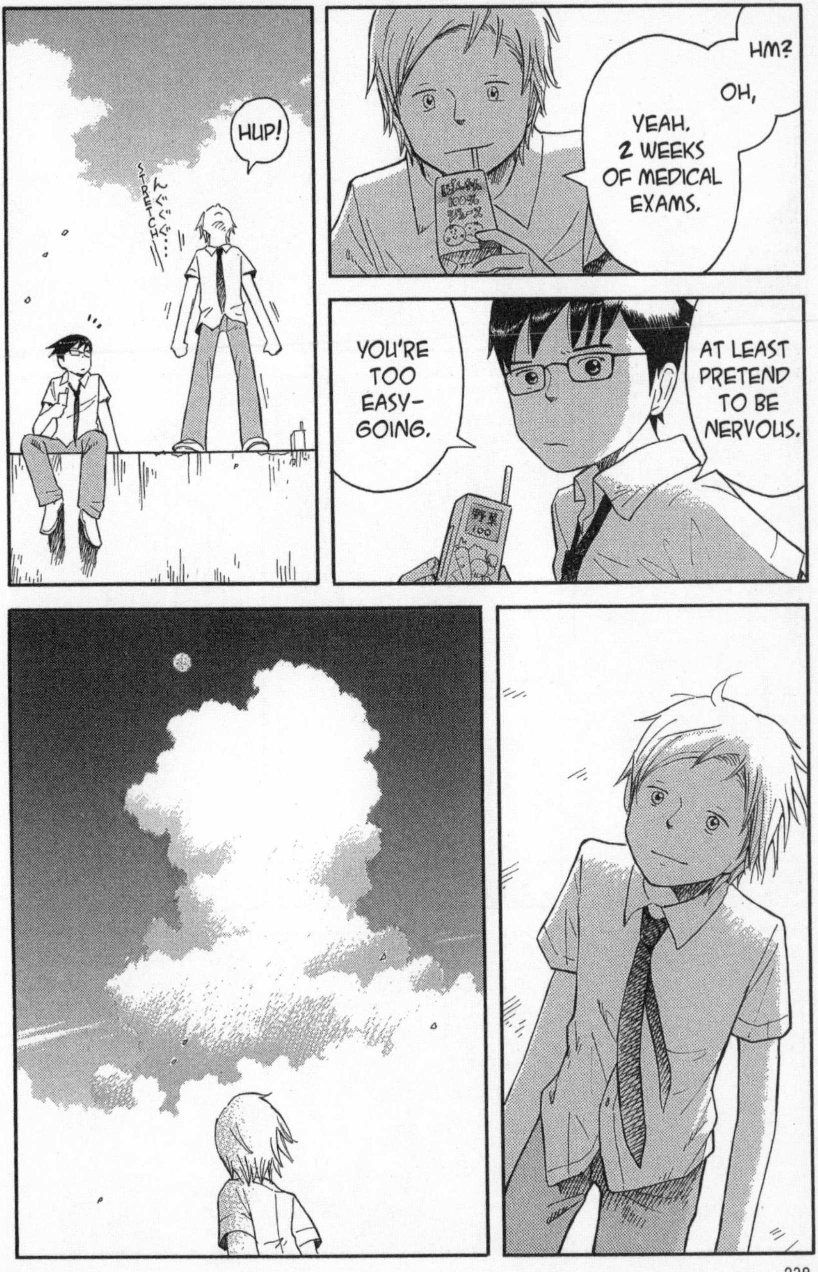
HM? OH,
YEAH. 2 WEEKS OF MEDICAL EXAMS.
AT LEAST PRETEND TO BE NERVOUS.
YOU'RE TOO EASY-GOING.
HUP!
STRETCH
んぐぐぐ…

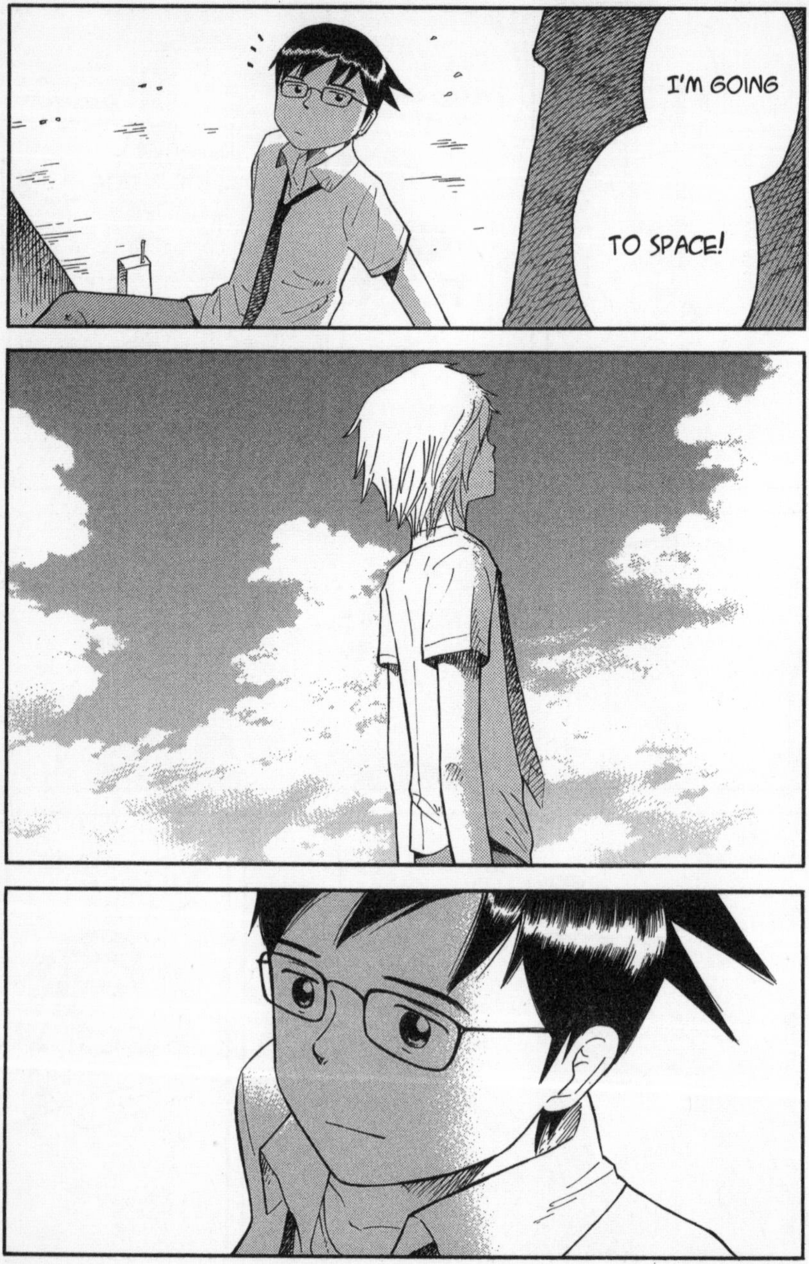
I'M GOING
TO SPACE!

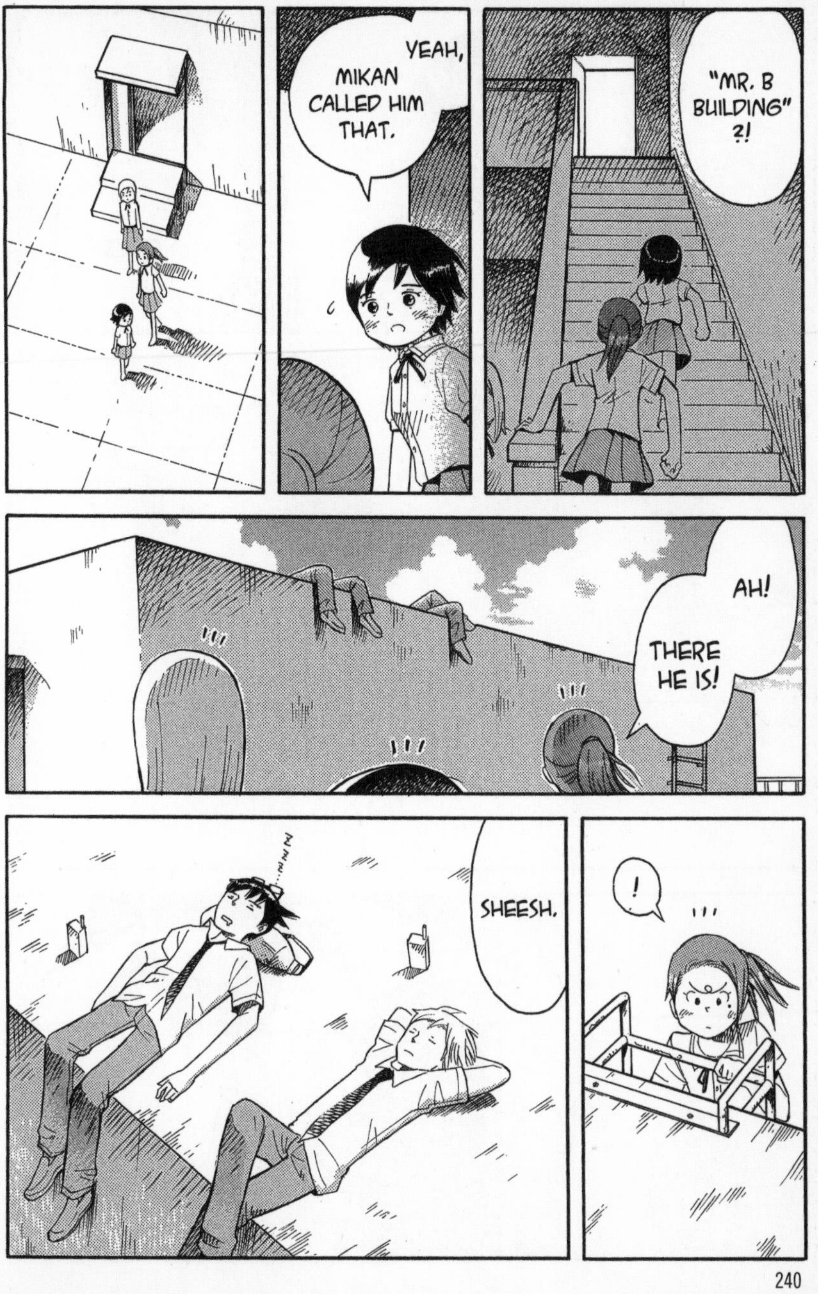
"MR. B BUILDING" ?!
YEAH, MIKAN CALLED HIM THAT.
AH! THERE HE IS!
!
SHEESH.

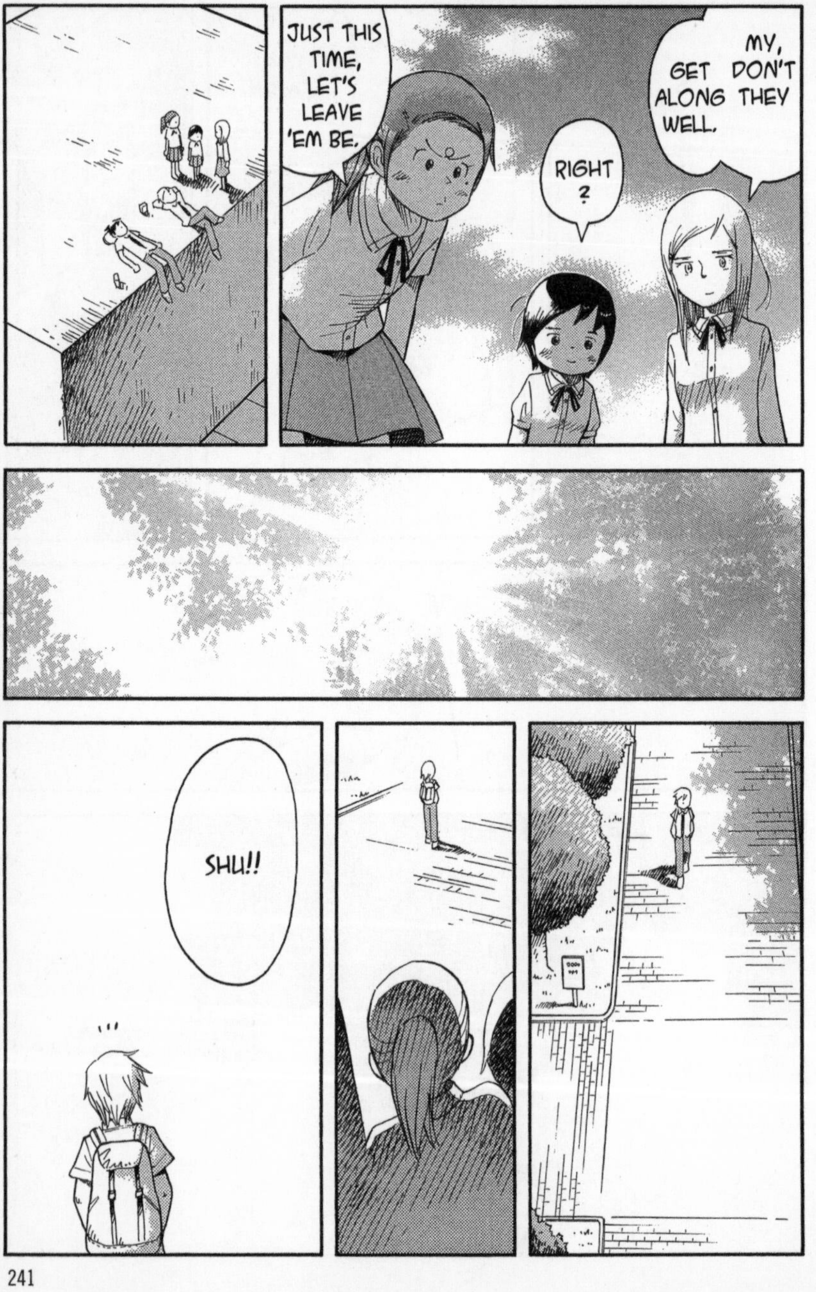
MY,
GET DON'T
ALONG THEY
WELL.
RIGHT ?
JUST THIS TIME, LET'S LEAVE 'EM BE.
SHU!!

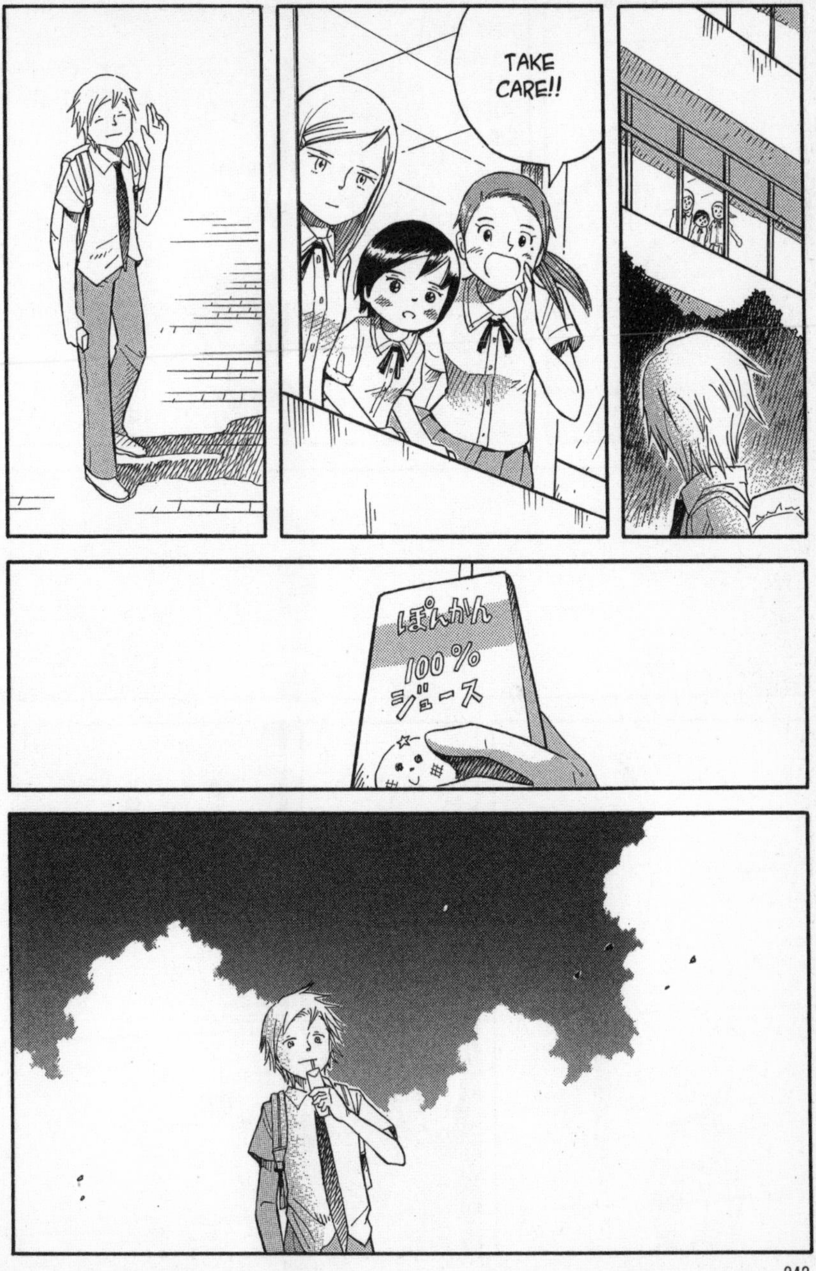
TAKE CARE!!
ぽんかん
100%
ジュース

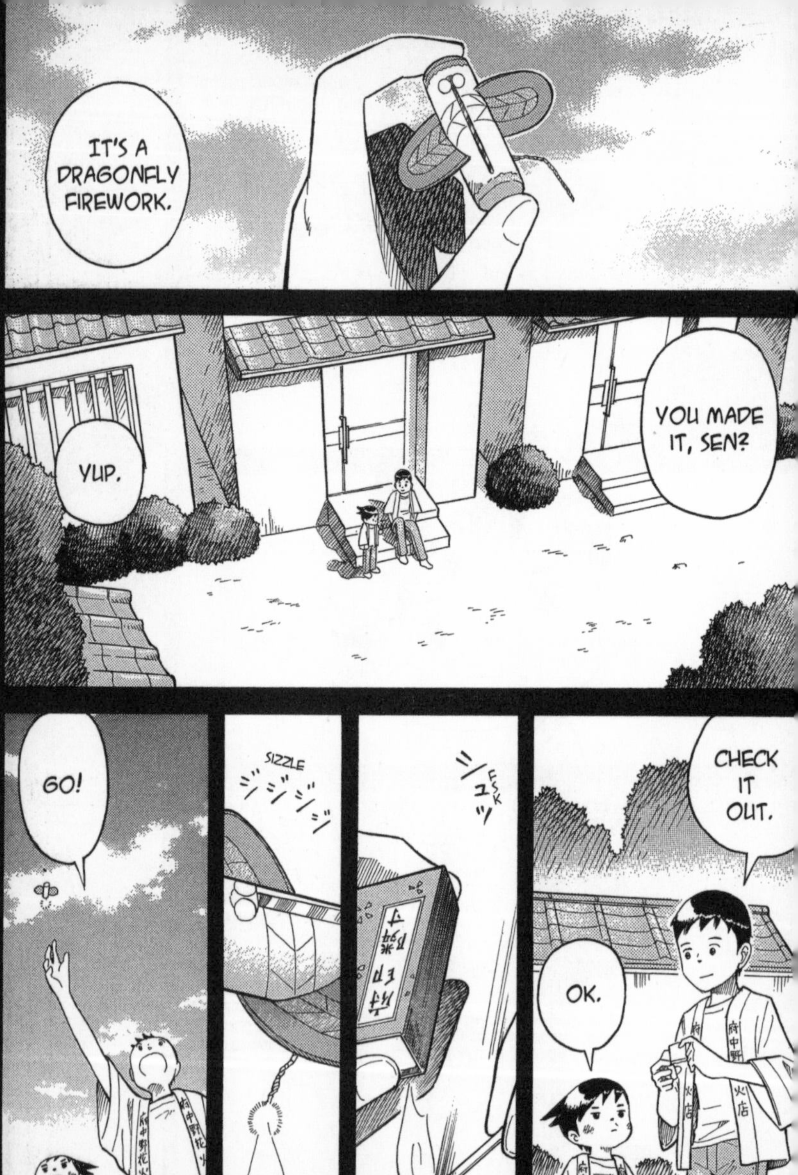
IT'S A DRAGONFLY FIREWORK.
YOU MADE IT, SEN?
YUP.
CHECK IT OUT.
OK.
ジュッ
FSK
ジジジジ
SIZZLE
GO!

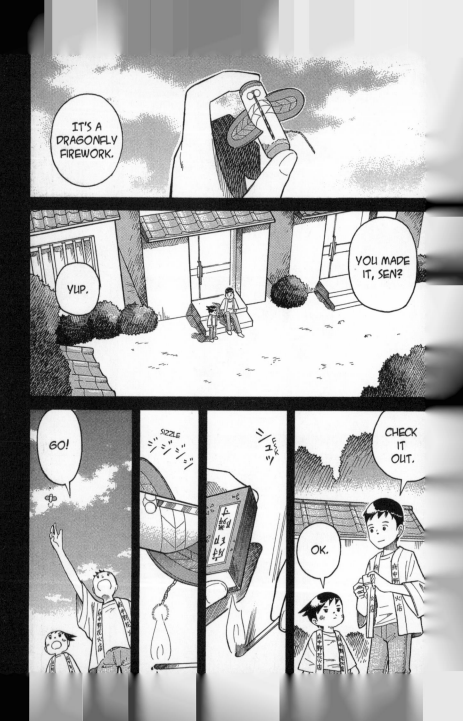

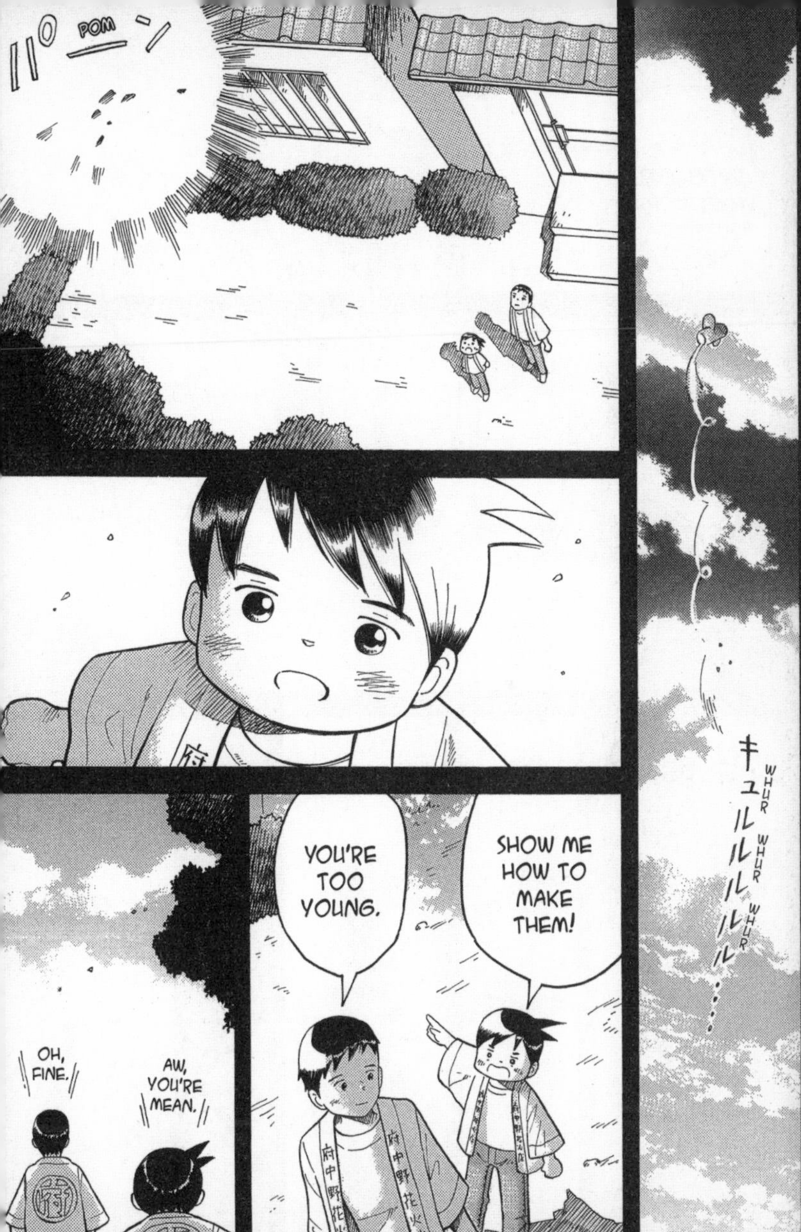
キュルルルル・・・・
WHUR WHUR WHUR
POM
SHOW ME HOW TO MAKE THEM!
YOU'RE TOO YOUNG.
AW, YOU'RE MEAN.
OH, FINE.

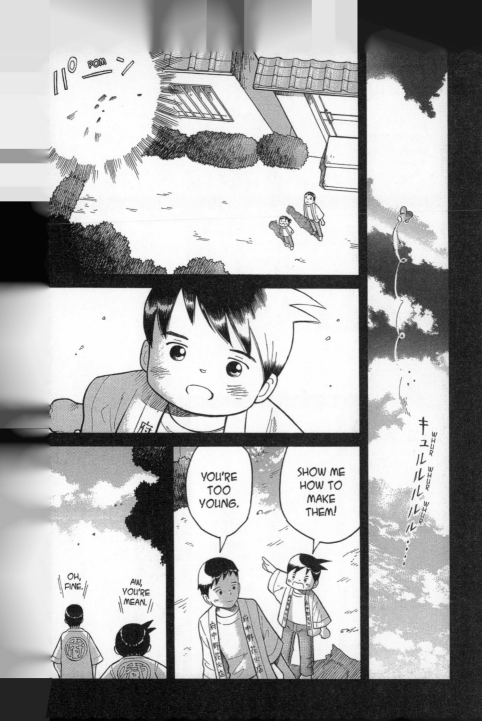

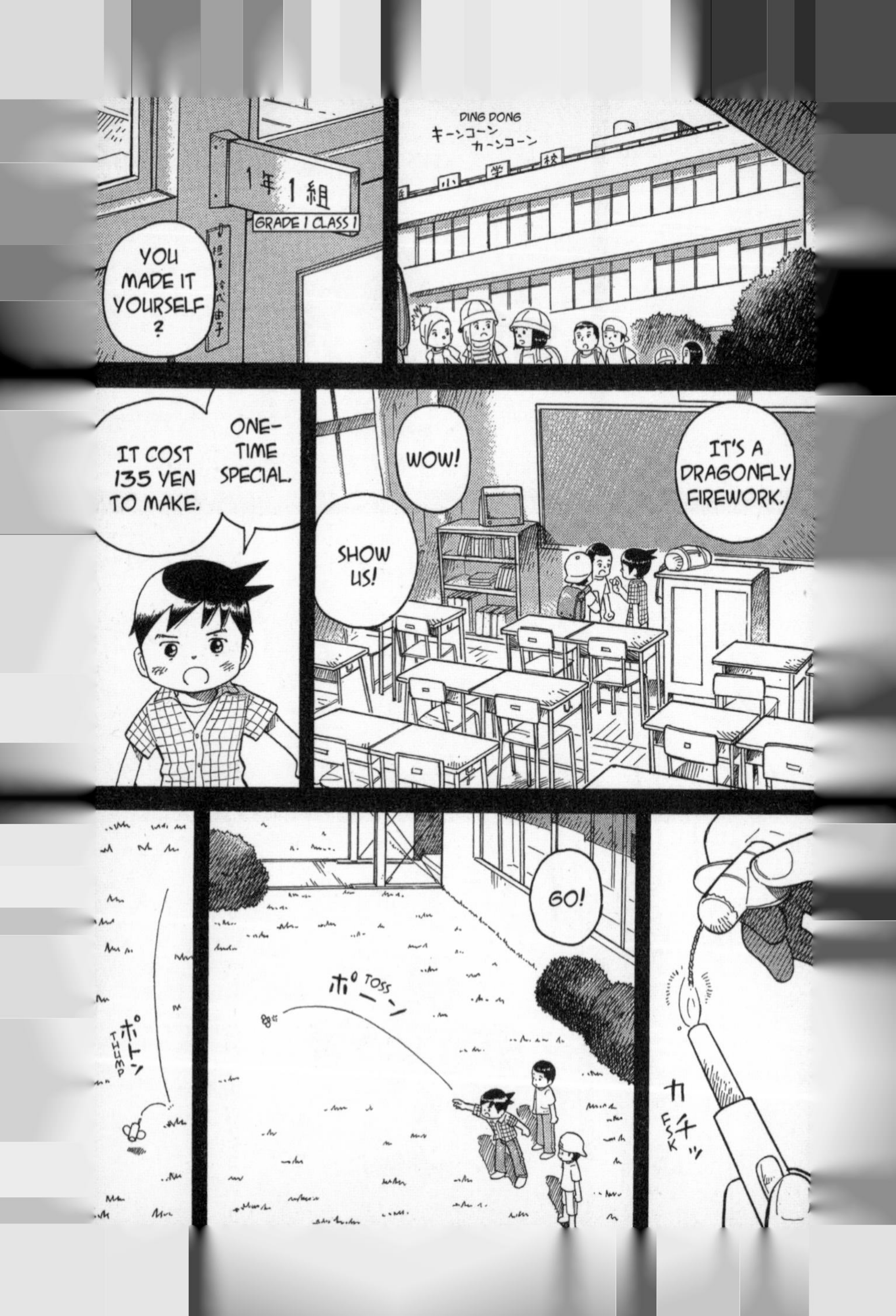
DING DONG
キーンコーン カーンコーン
小学校
1年1組
GRADE 1 CLASS 1
YOU MADE IT YOURSELF?
IT'S A DRAGONFLY FIREWORK.
WOW!
SHOW US!
ONE-TIME SPECIAL.
IT COST 135 YEN TO MAKE.
カチッ
FSK
GO!
ポーン
TOSS
ポトッ
THUMP

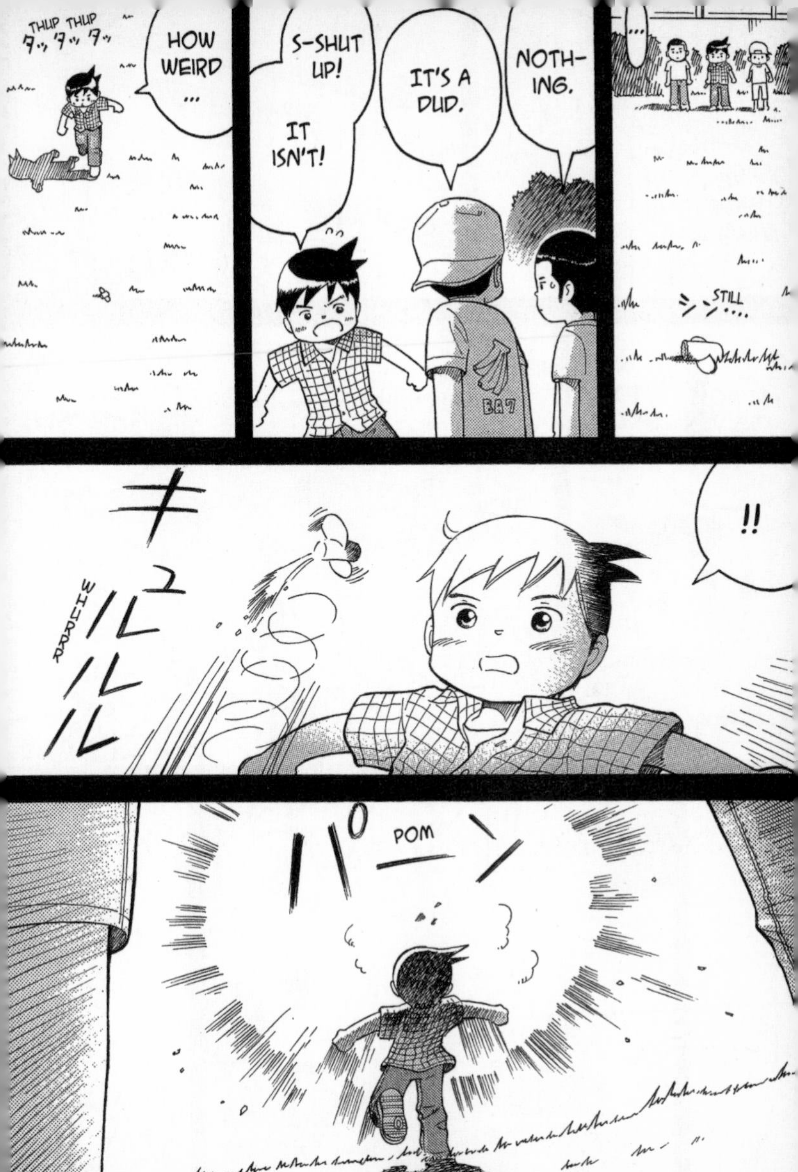
...
STILL
NOTH-ING.
IT'S A DUD.
S-SHUT UP!
IT ISN'T!
THUP THUP
タッタッタッ
HOW WEIRD ...
!!
キュルルルル
WHIRRR
パーン
POM

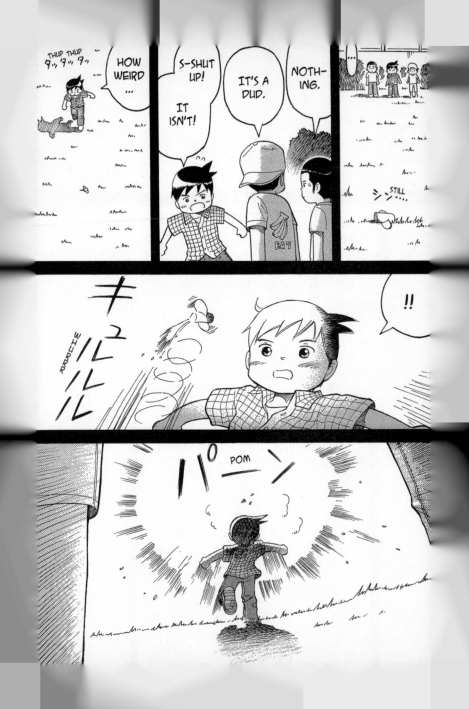

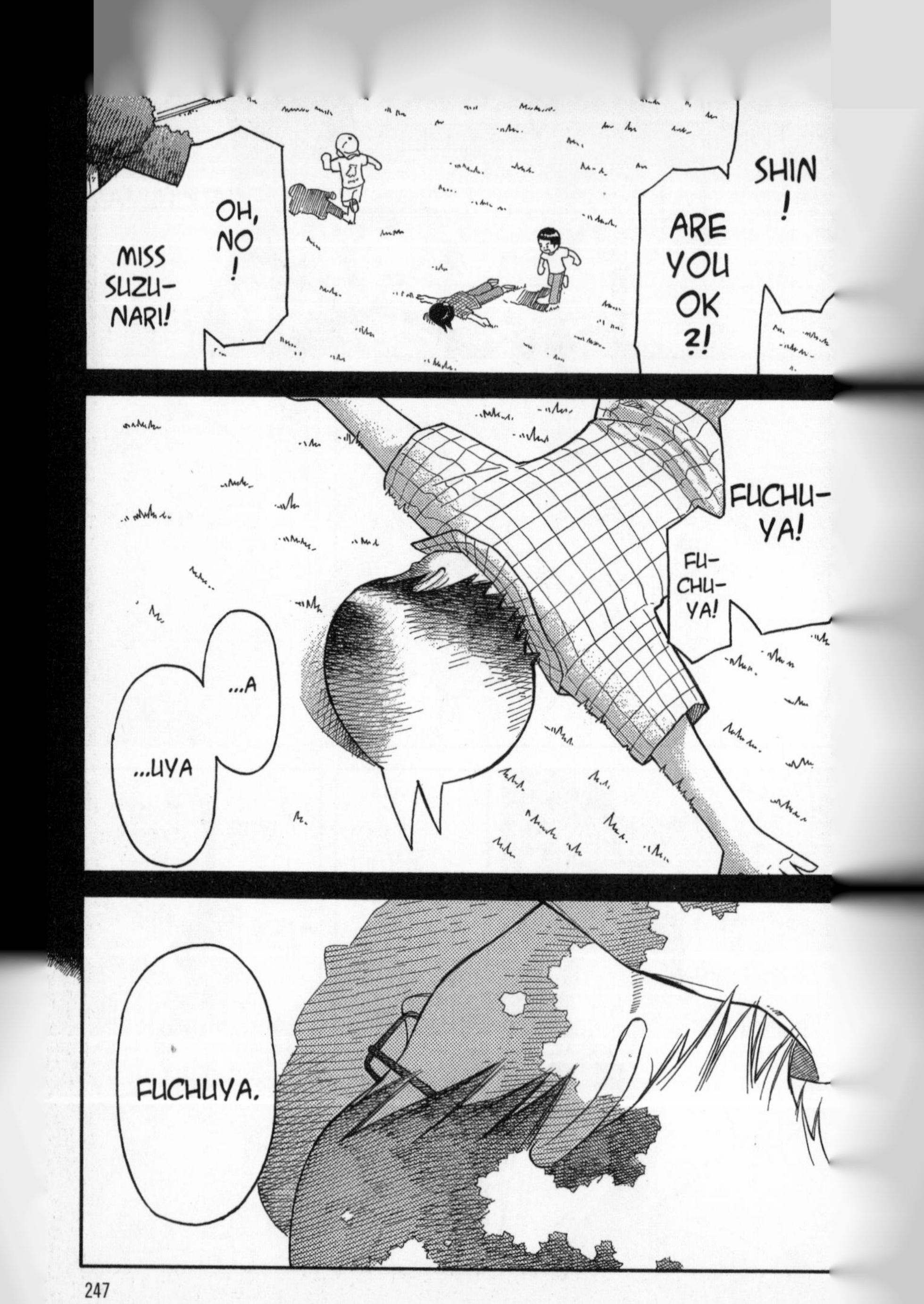
SHIN!
ARE YOU OK?!
OH, NO!
MISS SUZU-NARI!
FUCHU-YA!
FU-CHU-YA!
...A ...UYA
FUCHUYA.

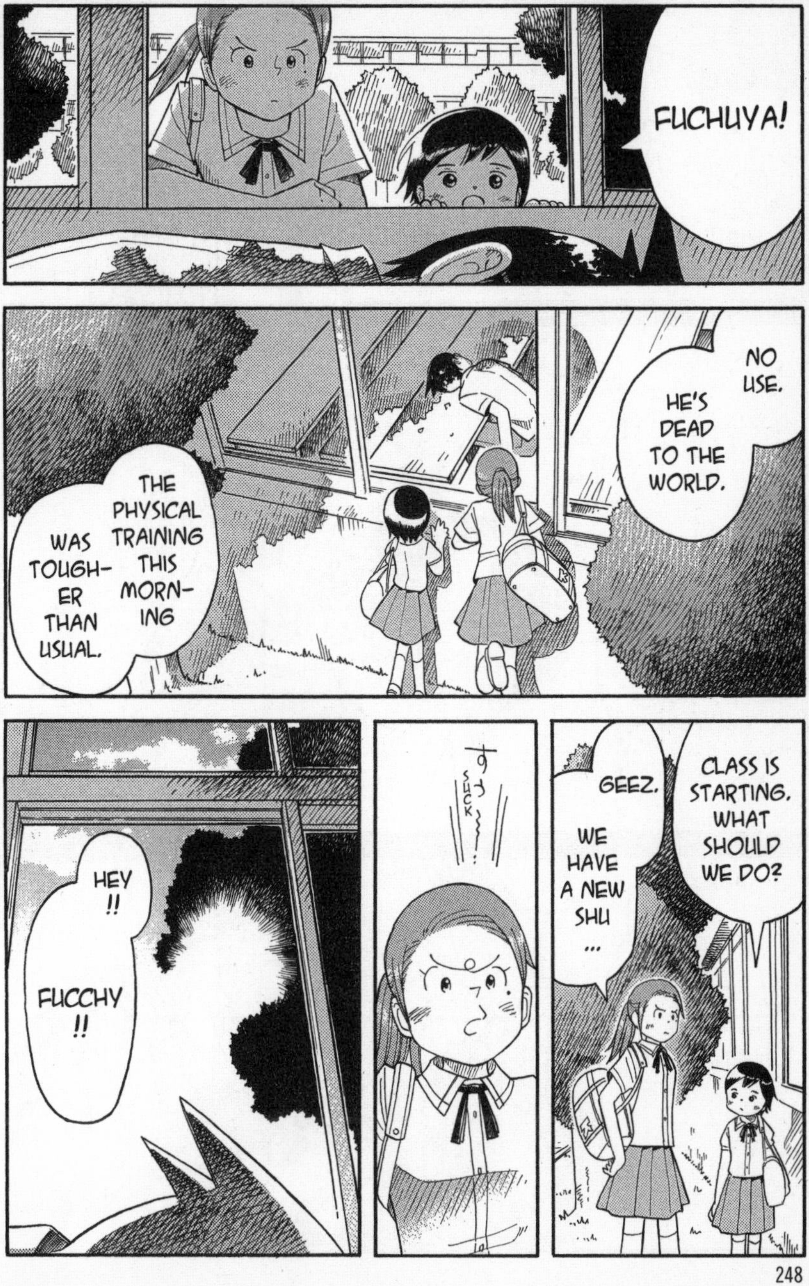
FUCHUYA!
NO USE.
HE'S DEAD TO THE WORLD.
THE PHYSICAL TRAINING THIS MORNING WAS TOUGHER THAN USUAL.
CLASS IS STARTING. WHAT SHOULD WE DO?
GEEZ.
WE HAVE A NEW SHU...
すっ〜!
SUCK
HEY!!
FUCCHY!!

MISSION:64

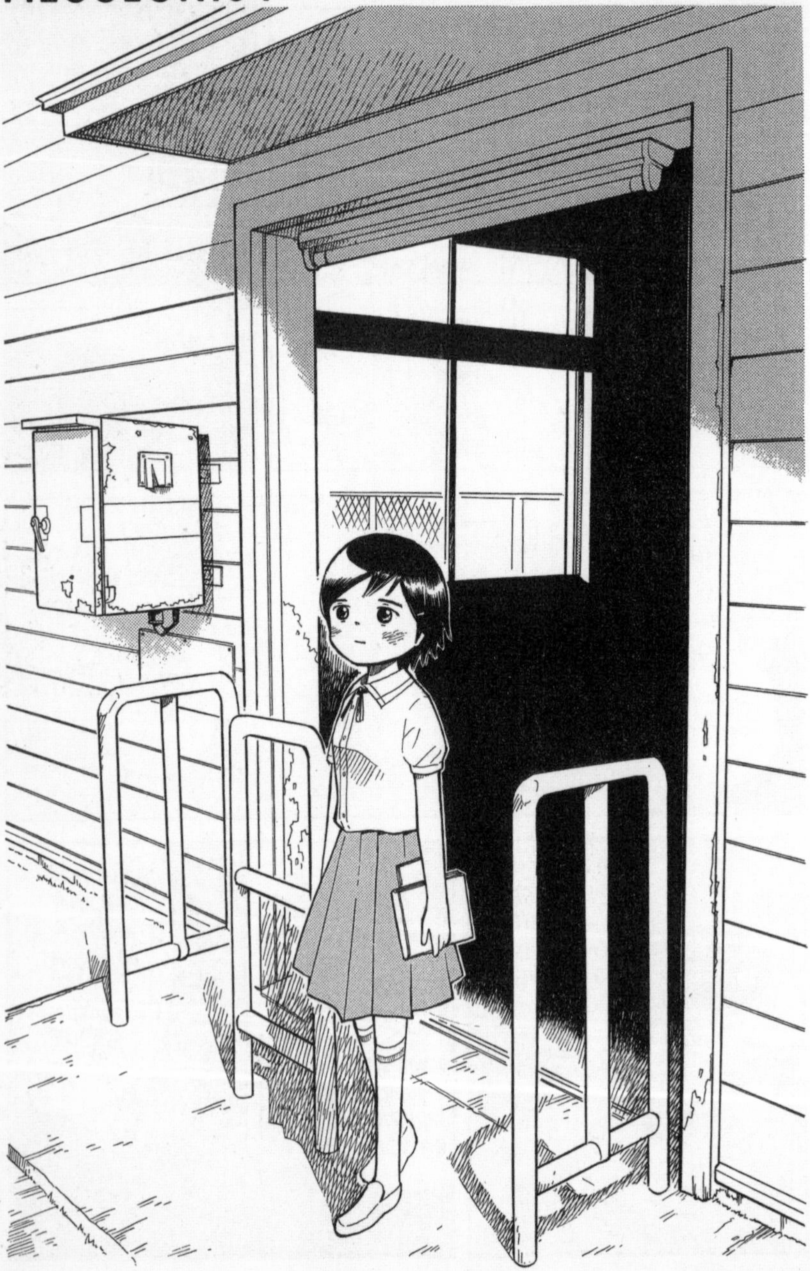

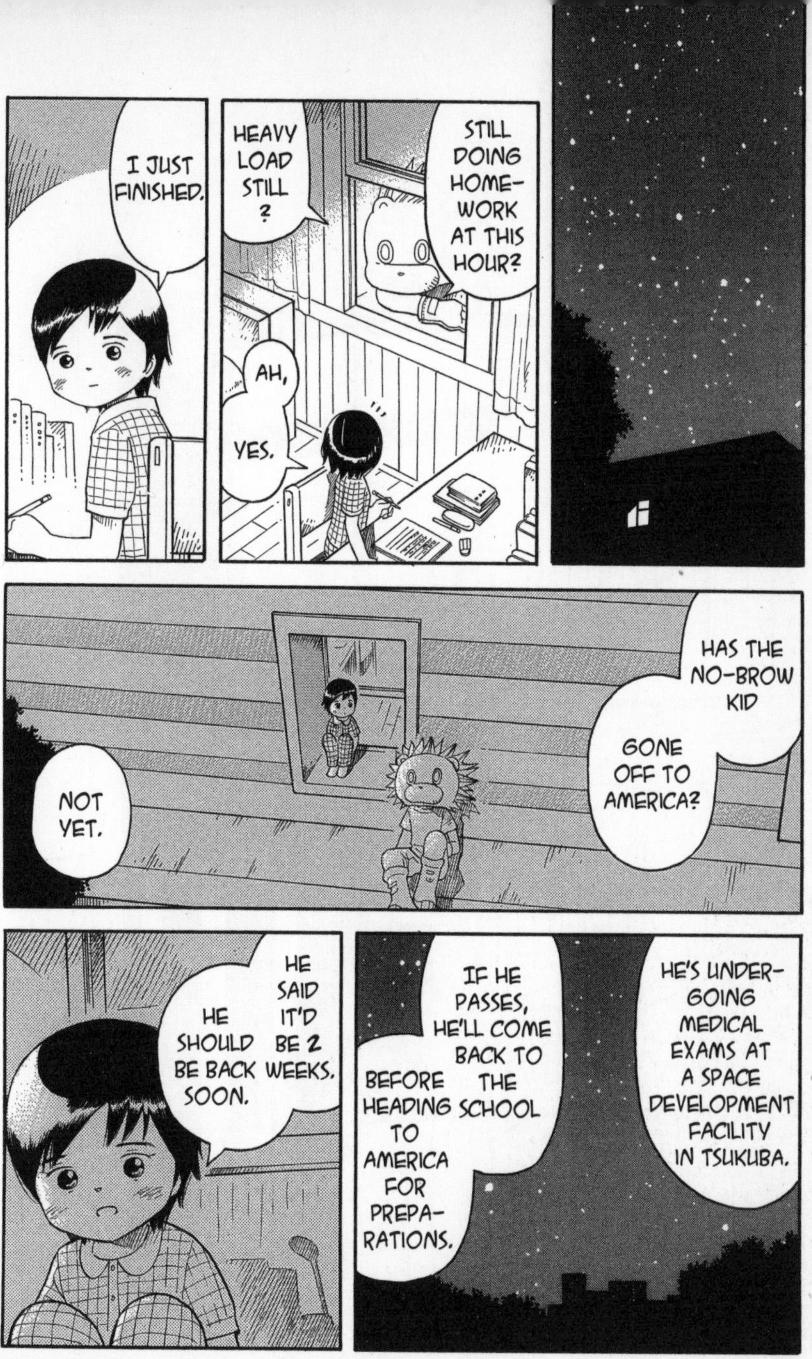
STILL DOING HOME-WORK AT THIS HOUR?
HEAVY LOAD STILL?
AH,
YES.
I JUST FINISHED.
HAS THE NO-BROW KID
GONE OFF TO AMERICA?
NOT YET.
HE'S UNDER-GOING MEDICAL EXAMS AT A SPACE DEVELOPMENT FACILITY IN TSUKUBA.
IF HE PASSES, HE'LL COME BACK TO THE SCHOOL
BEFORE HEADING TO AMERICA FOR PREPA-RATIONS.
HE SAID IT'D BE 2 WEEKS.
HE SHOULD BE BACK SOON.

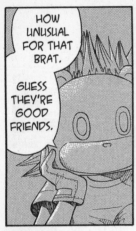

HMM.
SO HE'LL BE OVERSEAS.
YOU WON'T SEE HIM FOR A WHILE.
FUCHUYA LOOKED KINDA SAD.
THE WHOLE SCHOOL SEEMED A LITTLE LESS CHEERY.
HOW UNUSUAL FOR THAT BRAT.
GUESS THEY'RE GOOD FRIENDS.
YEAH.
THEY WERE ALWAYS TOGETHER.
THEY WERE BEST FRIENDS.
PARTINGS MAKE PEOPLE GROW UP.
ALWAYS.

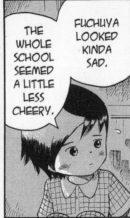

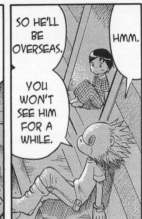

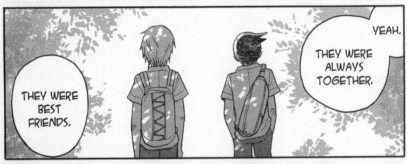

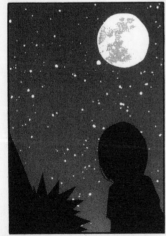

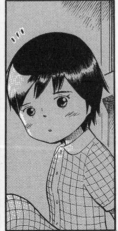

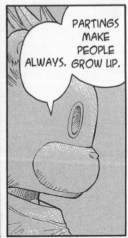

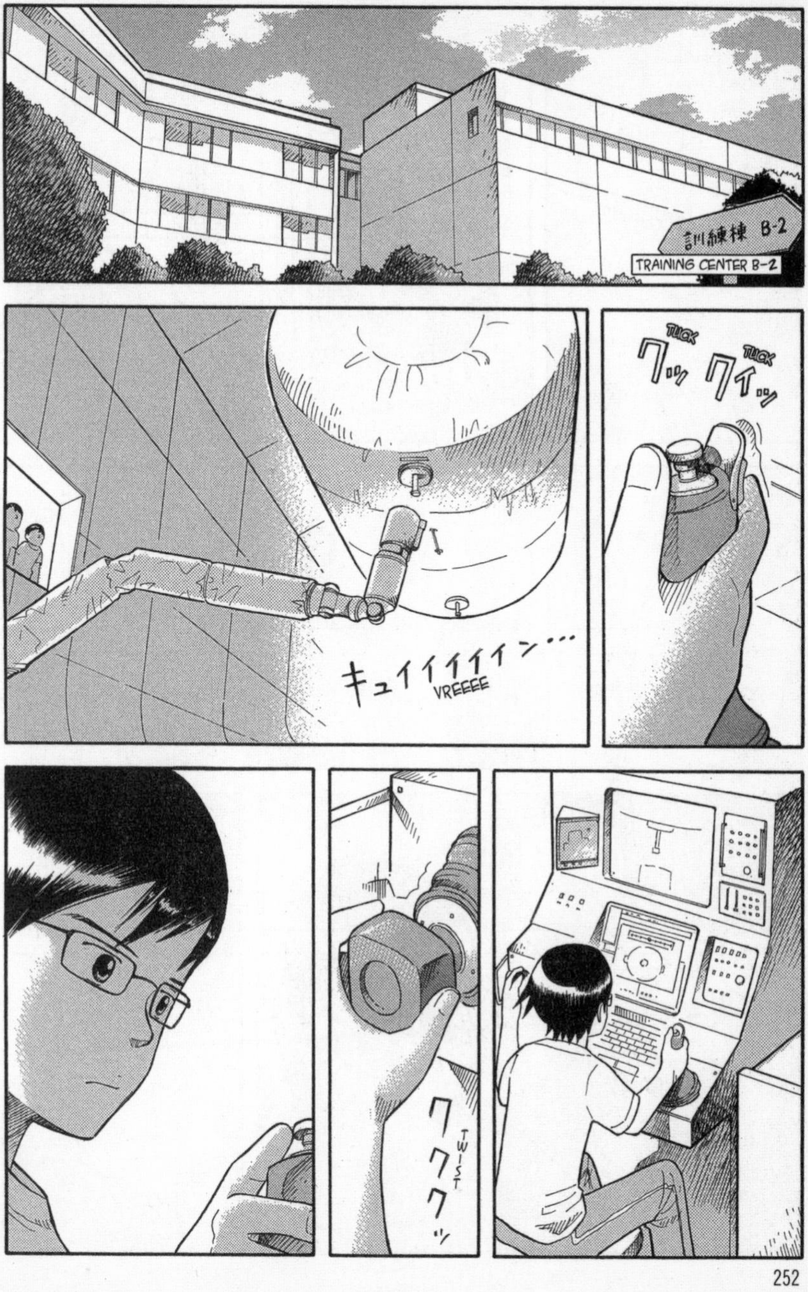
訓練棟 B-2
TRAINING CENTER B-2
クッ クイッ
TUCK TUCK
キュイイイイイン…
VREEEE
クククッ
TWIST

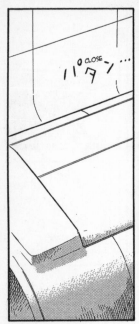

CLOSE
パタン…

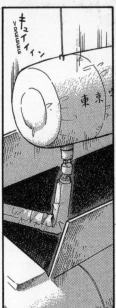

キュイィン
VOUUUUU

東京

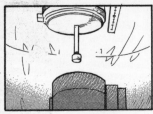

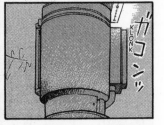

グググ
REE REE

ググ
REE

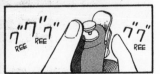

ガコンッ
KLONK

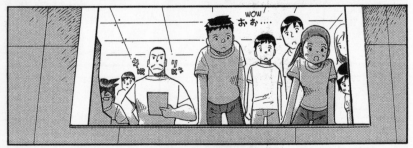

WOW
おお…

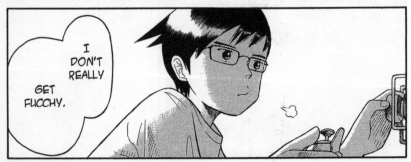

I DON'T REALLY GET FUCCHY.

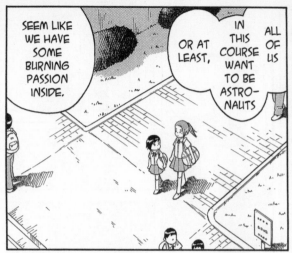

WHY?
ALL OF US IN THIS COURSE WANT TO BE ASTRONAUTS OR AT LEAST,
SEEM LIKE WE HAVE SOME BURNING PASSION INSIDE.
BUT FUCCHY SEEMS TO BE JUST DRIFTING ALONG,
JUST GOING WITH THE FLOW.
I TRIED ASKING HIM WHY HE WANTS TO BE AN ASTRONAUT, BUT IT WASN'T ANY HELP.
IF A CHILDHOOD FRIEND COULDN'T GET IT OUT OF HIM, THEN I CERTAINLY NEVER COULD.
WELL, HE'S A LITTLE ODD.

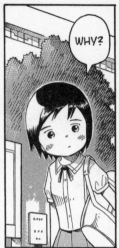

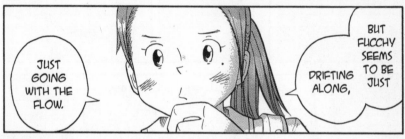

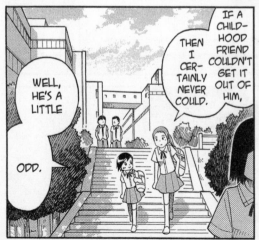

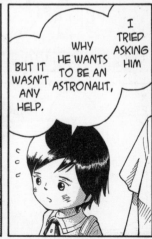

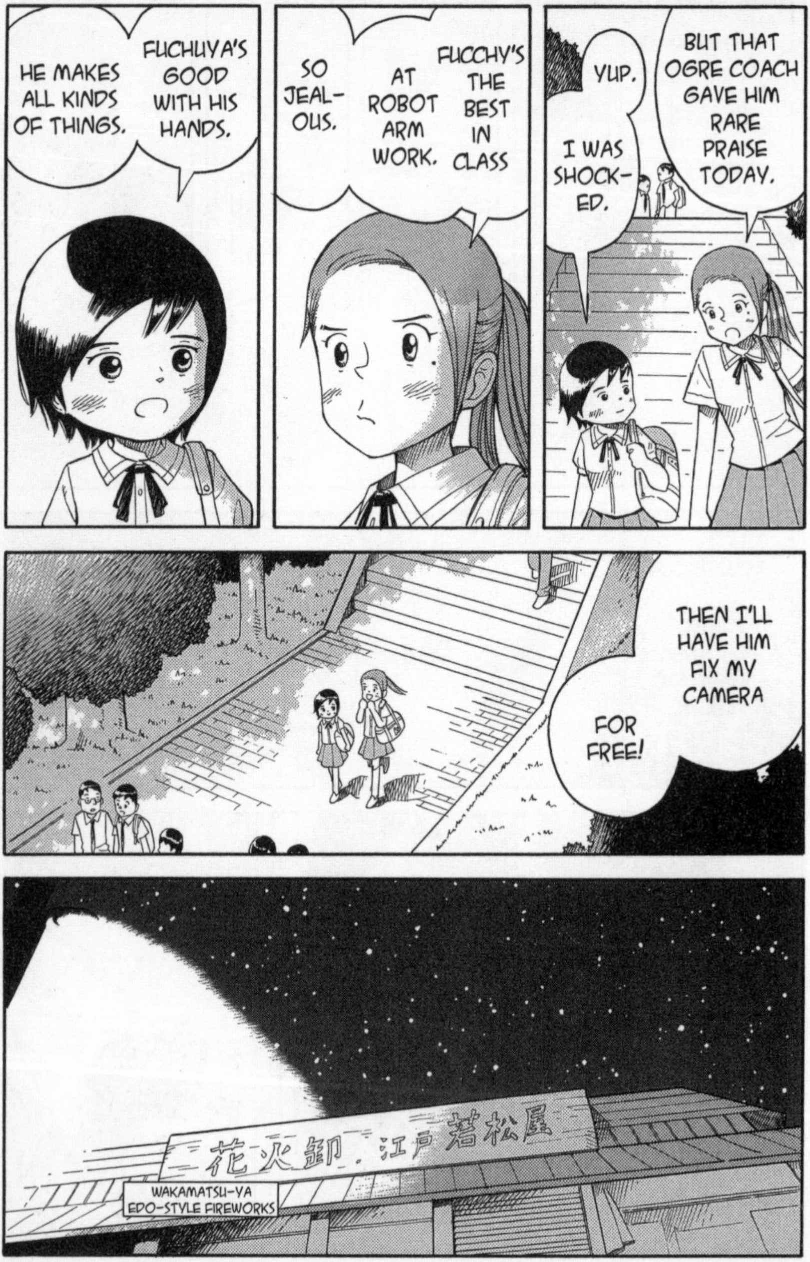
BUT THAT OGRE COACH GAVE HIM RARE PRAISE TODAY.
YUP.
I WAS SHOCKED.
FUCCHY'S THE BEST IN CLASS
AT ROBOT ARM WORK.
SO JEALOUS.
FUCHUYA'S GOOD WITH HIS HANDS.
HE MAKES ALL KINDS OF THINGS.
THEN I'LL HAVE HIM FIX MY CAMERA
FOR FREE!
花火卸・江戸 若松屋
WAKAMATSU-YA EDO-STYLE FIREWORKS

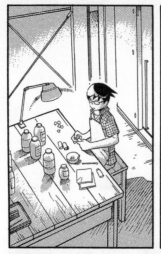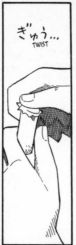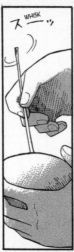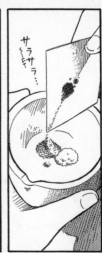

ぎゅう…
TWIST

スーッ
WHISK

サラサラ…

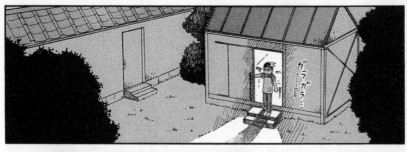

ガラガラ…
SLIDE

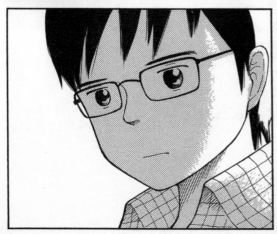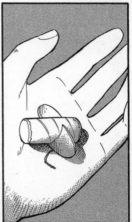

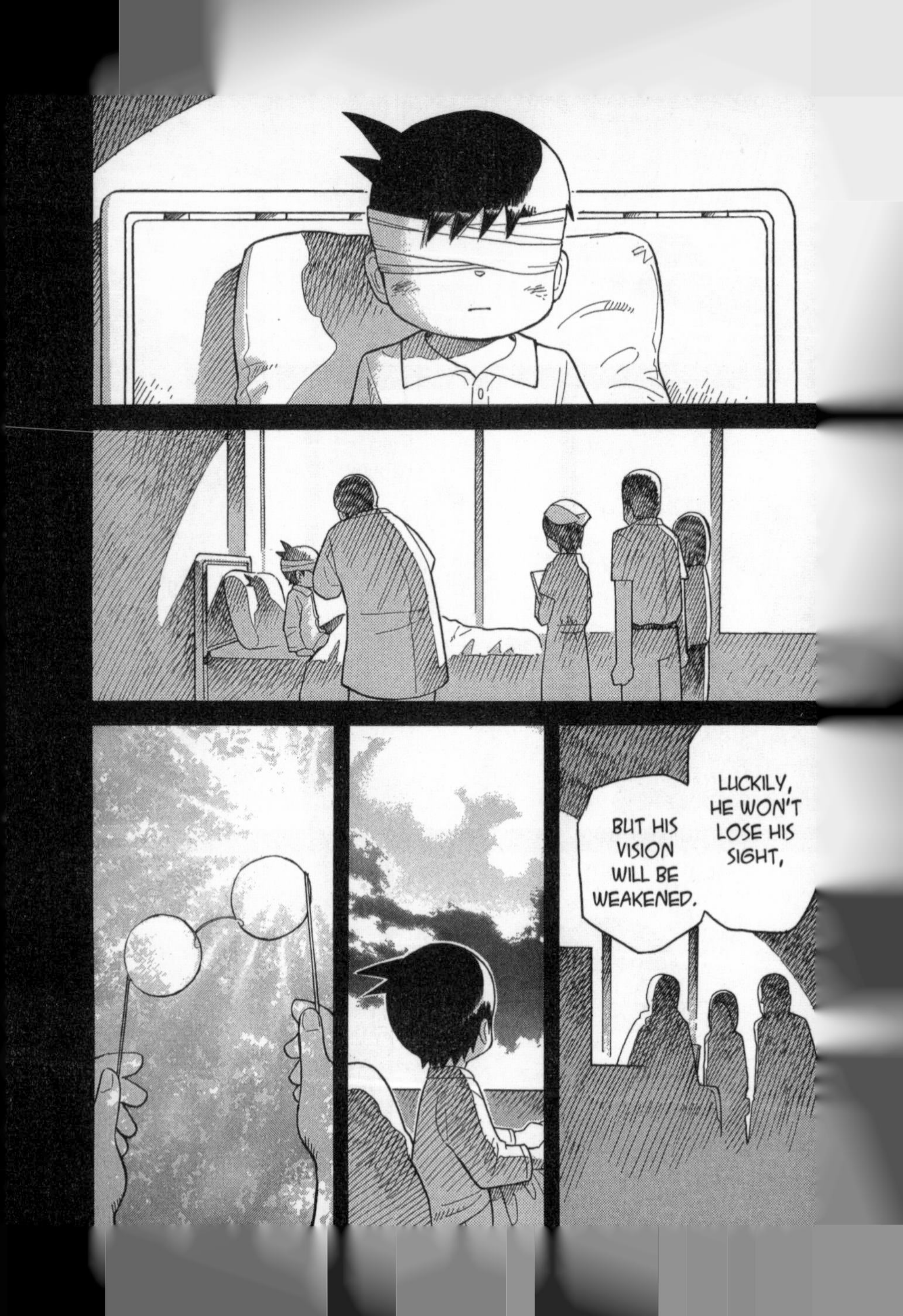
LUCKILY, HE WON'T LOSE HIS SIGHT,
BUT HIS VISION WILL BE WEAKENED.

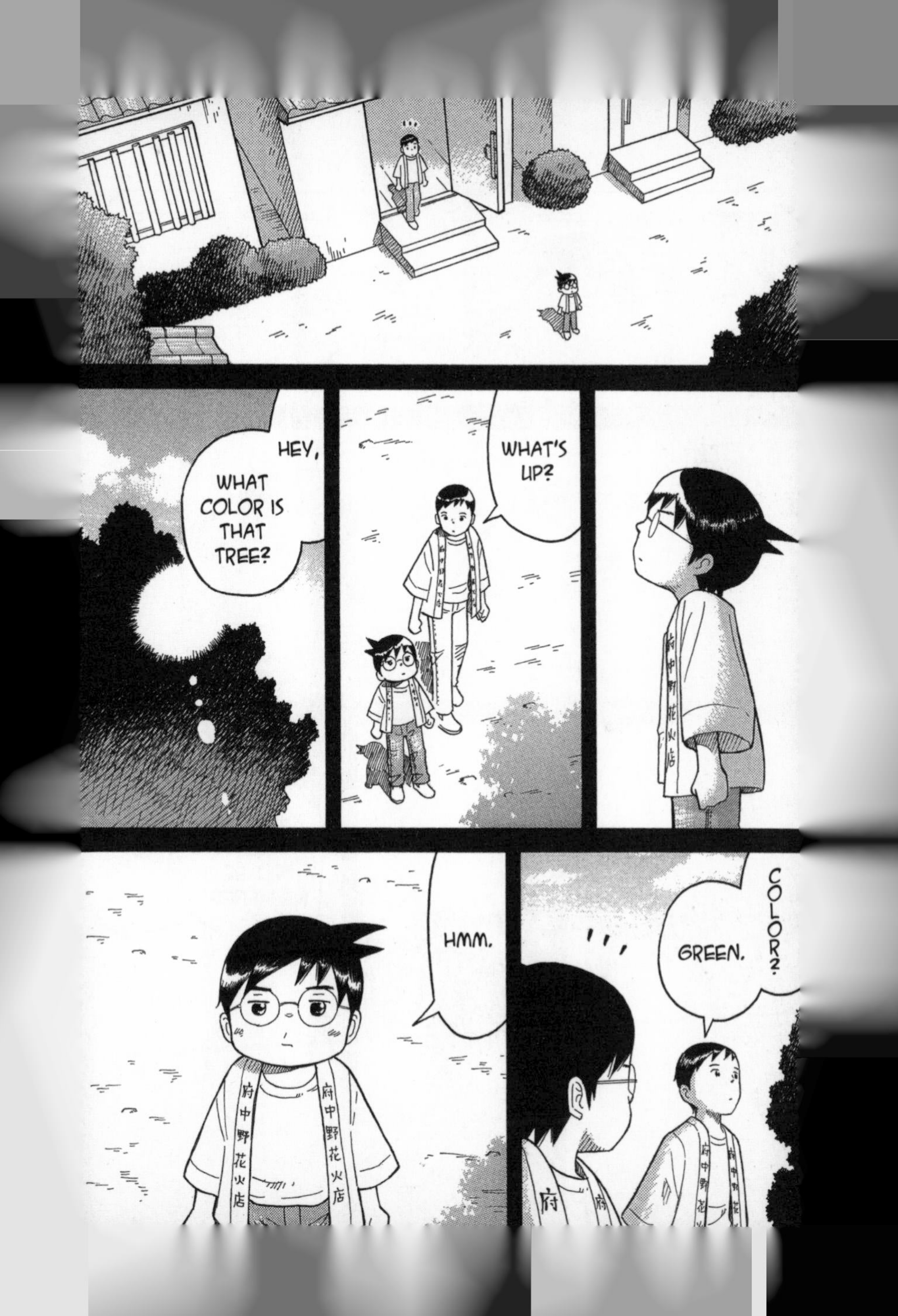
WHAT'S UP?
HEY, WHAT COLOR IS THAT TREE?
COLOR?
GREEN.
HMM.

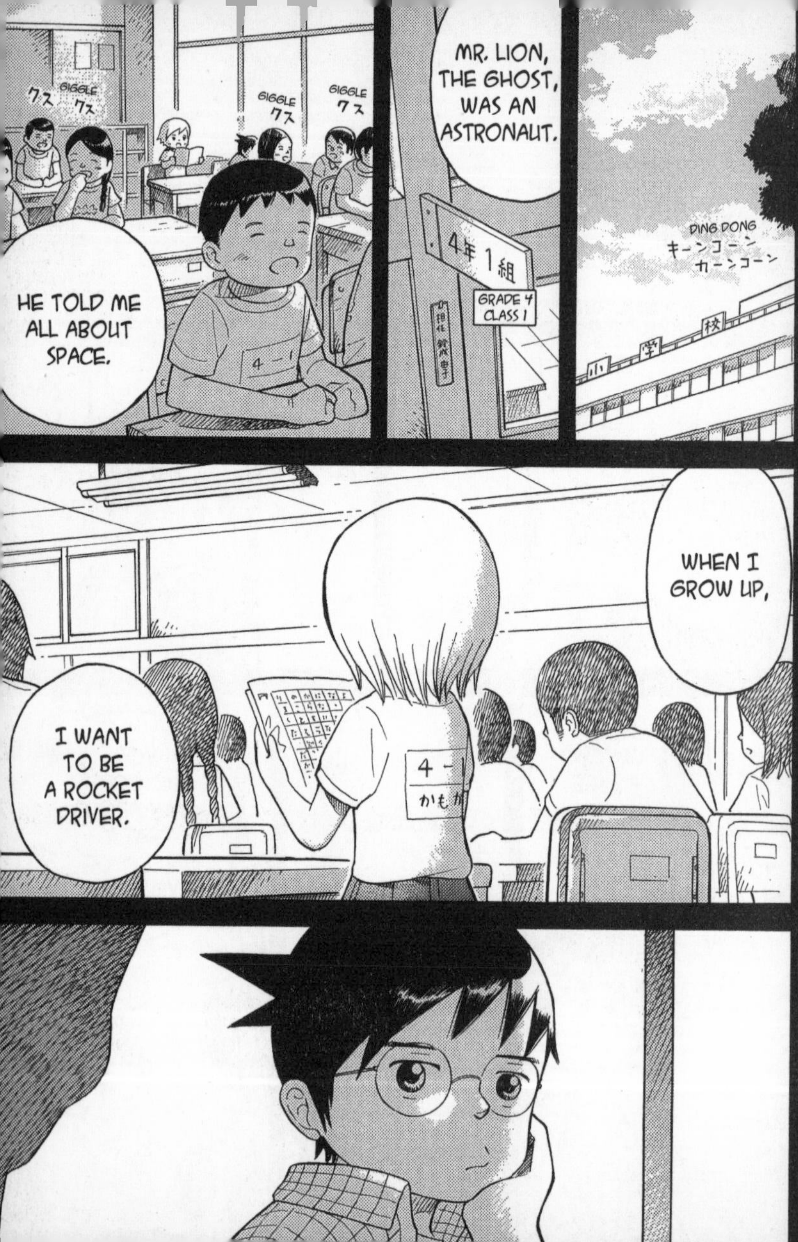
DING DONG
キーンコーン
カーンコーン
小
学
校
MR. LION, THE GHOST, WAS AN ASTRONAUT.
4年1組
GRADE 4 CLASS 1
クス
GIGGLE
クス
GIGGLE
クス
GIGGLE
クス
HE TOLD ME ALL ABOUT SPACE.
4-1
WHEN I GROW UP,
I WANT TO BE A ROCKET DRIVER.
4-1

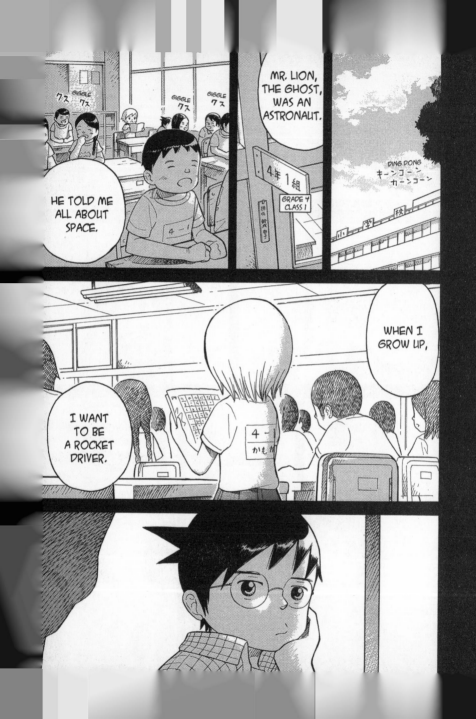

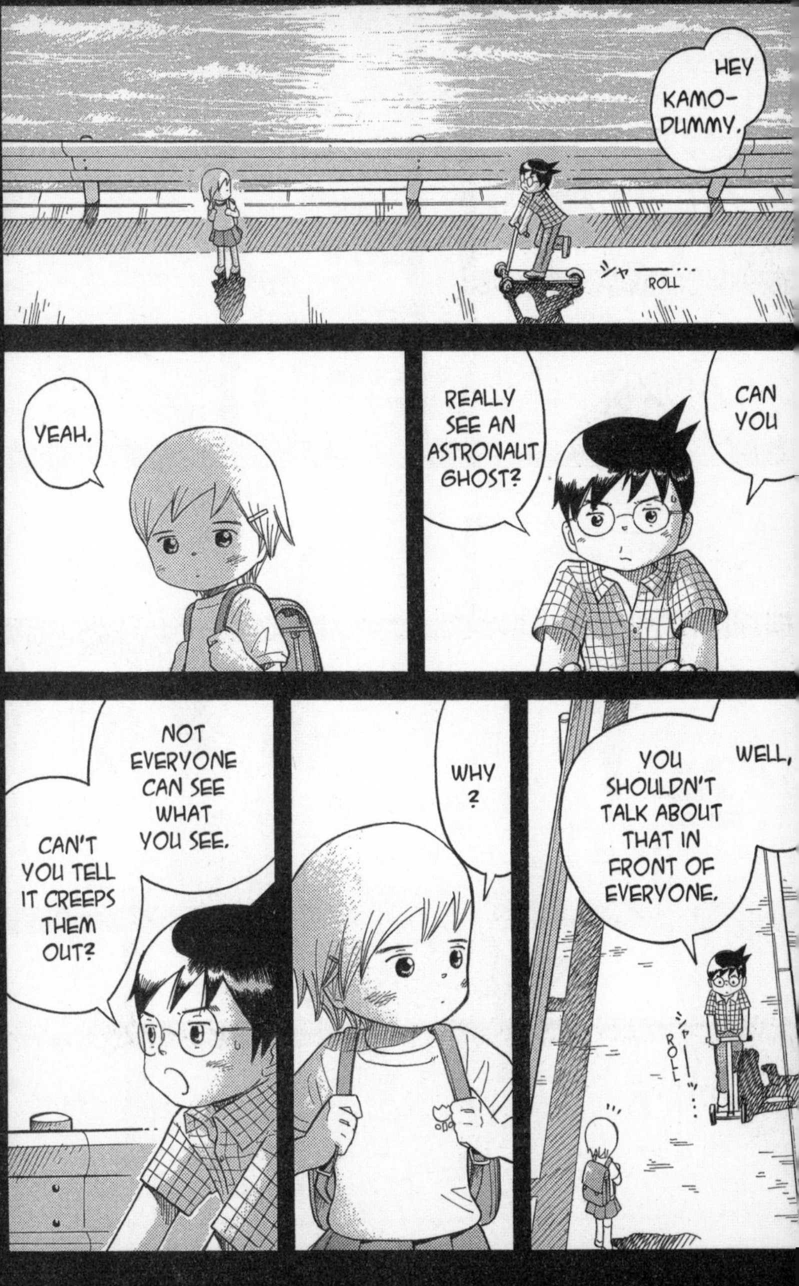
HEY KAMO-DUMMY.
シャーー…
ROLL
CAN YOU
REALLY SEE AN ASTRONAUT GHOST?
YEAH.
WELL,
YOU SHOULDN'T TALK ABOUT THAT IN FRONT OF EVERYONE.
シャーーッ…
ROLL
WHY?
NOT EVERYONE CAN SEE WHAT YOU SEE.
CAN'T YOU TELL IT CREEPS THEM OUT?

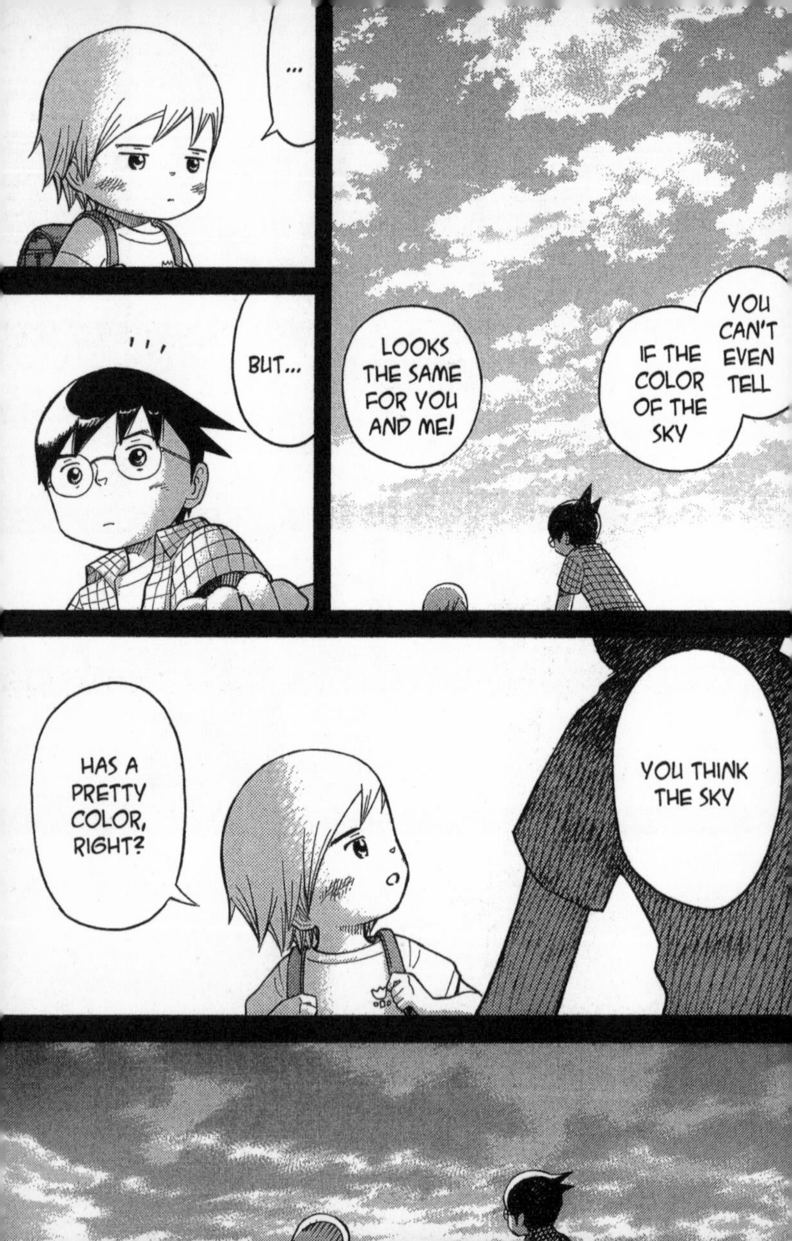
YOU CAN'T EVEN TELL IF THE COLOR OF THE SKY
LOOKS THE SAME FOR YOU AND ME!
...
BUT...
YOU THINK THE SKY
HAS A PRETTY COLOR, RIGHT?

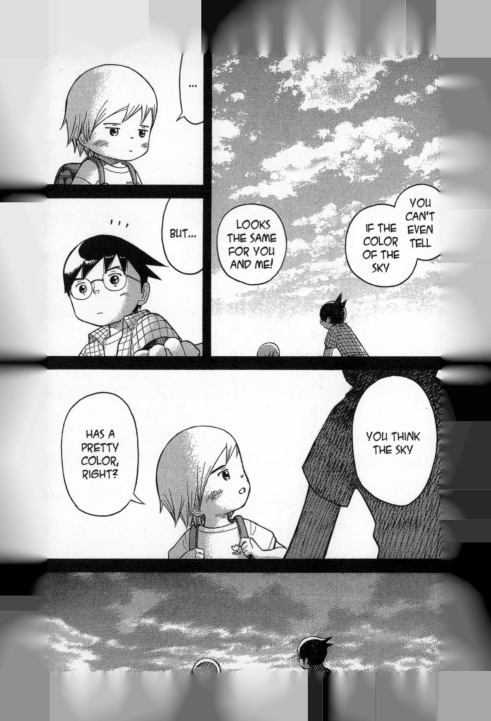

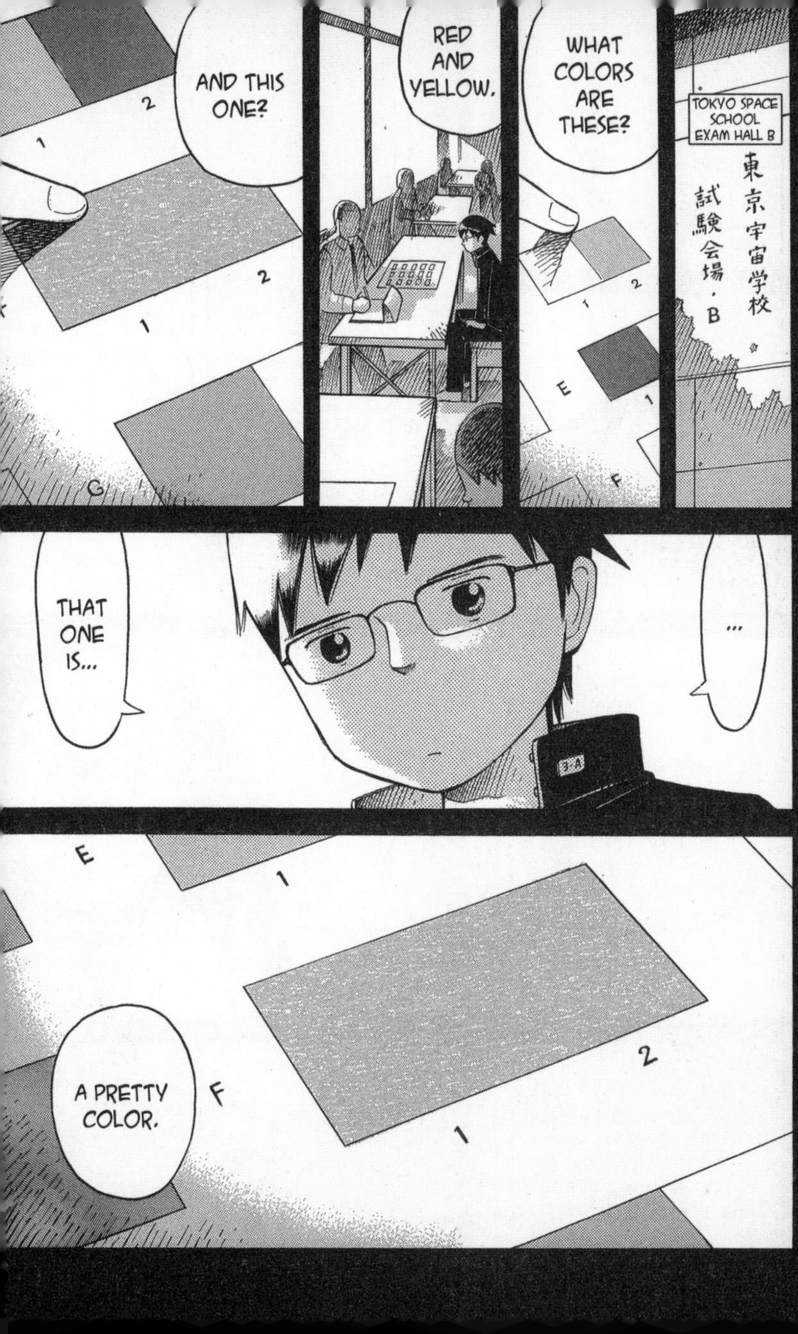
TOKYO SPACE SCHOOL EXAM HALL B
東京宇宙学校
試験会場・B
WHAT COLORS ARE THESE?
RED AND YELLOW.
AND THIS ONE?
...
THAT ONE IS...
A PRETTY COLOR.

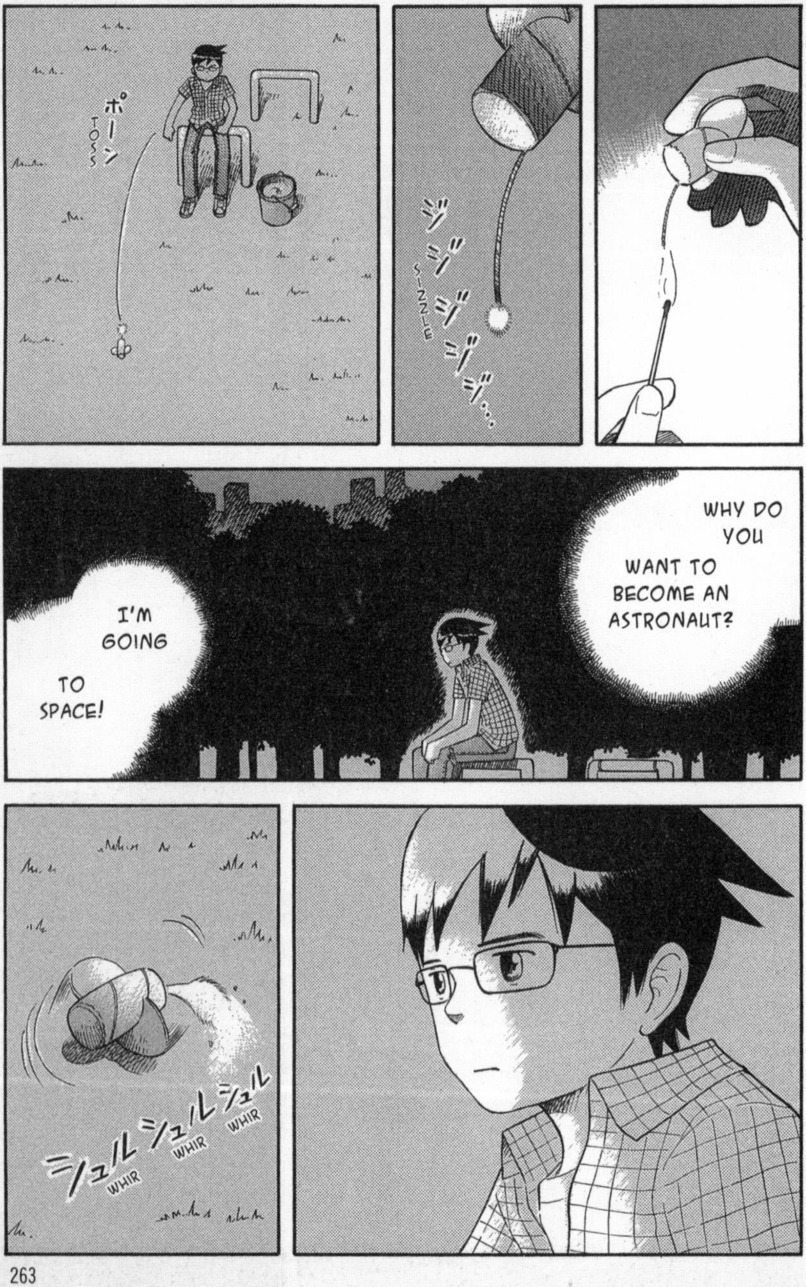
ジジジジジ...
SIZZLE
ポーン
TOSS
WHY DO YOU WANT TO BECOME AN ASTRONAUT?
I'M GOING TO SPACE!
シュルシュルシュル
WHIR WHIR WHIR

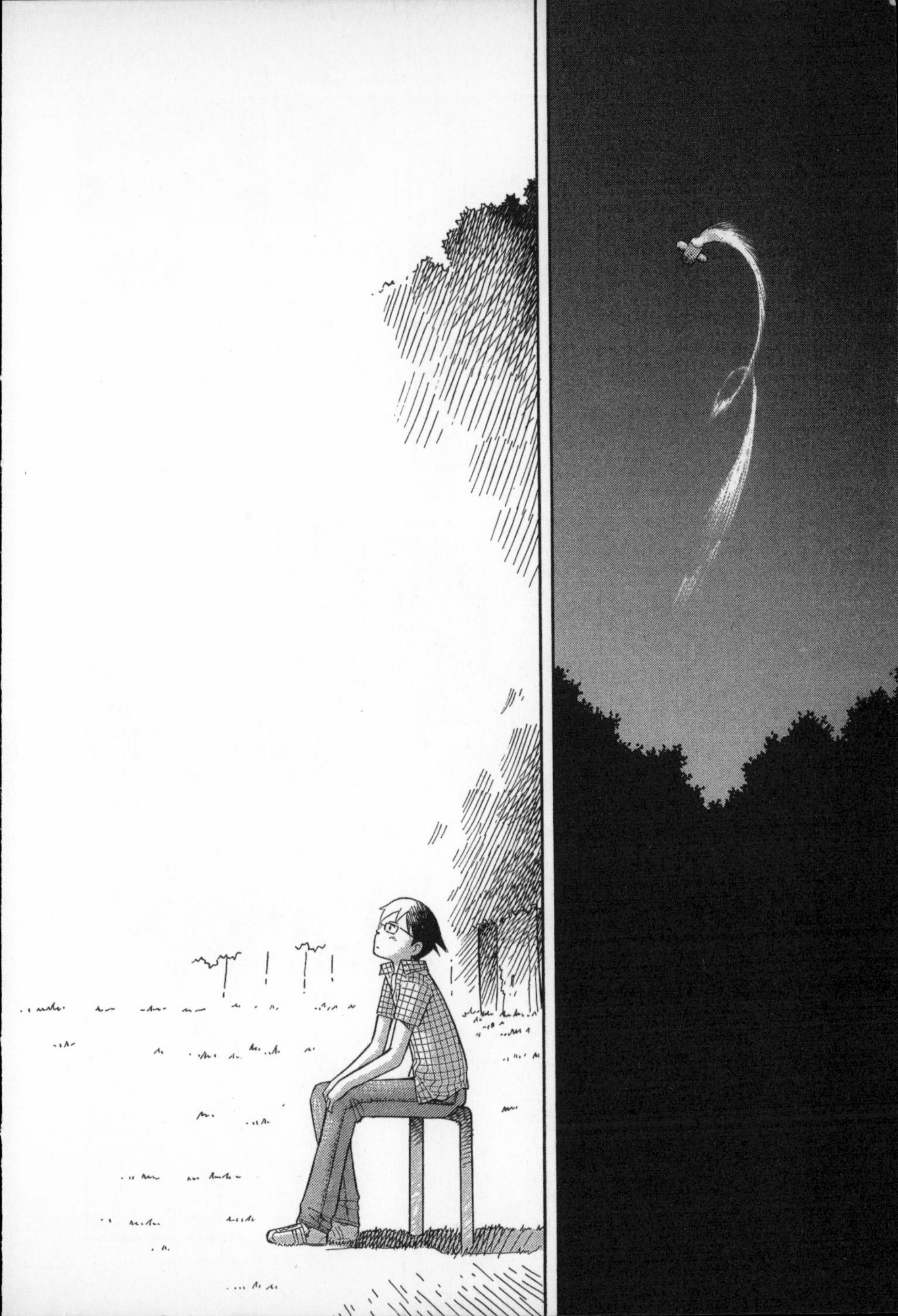

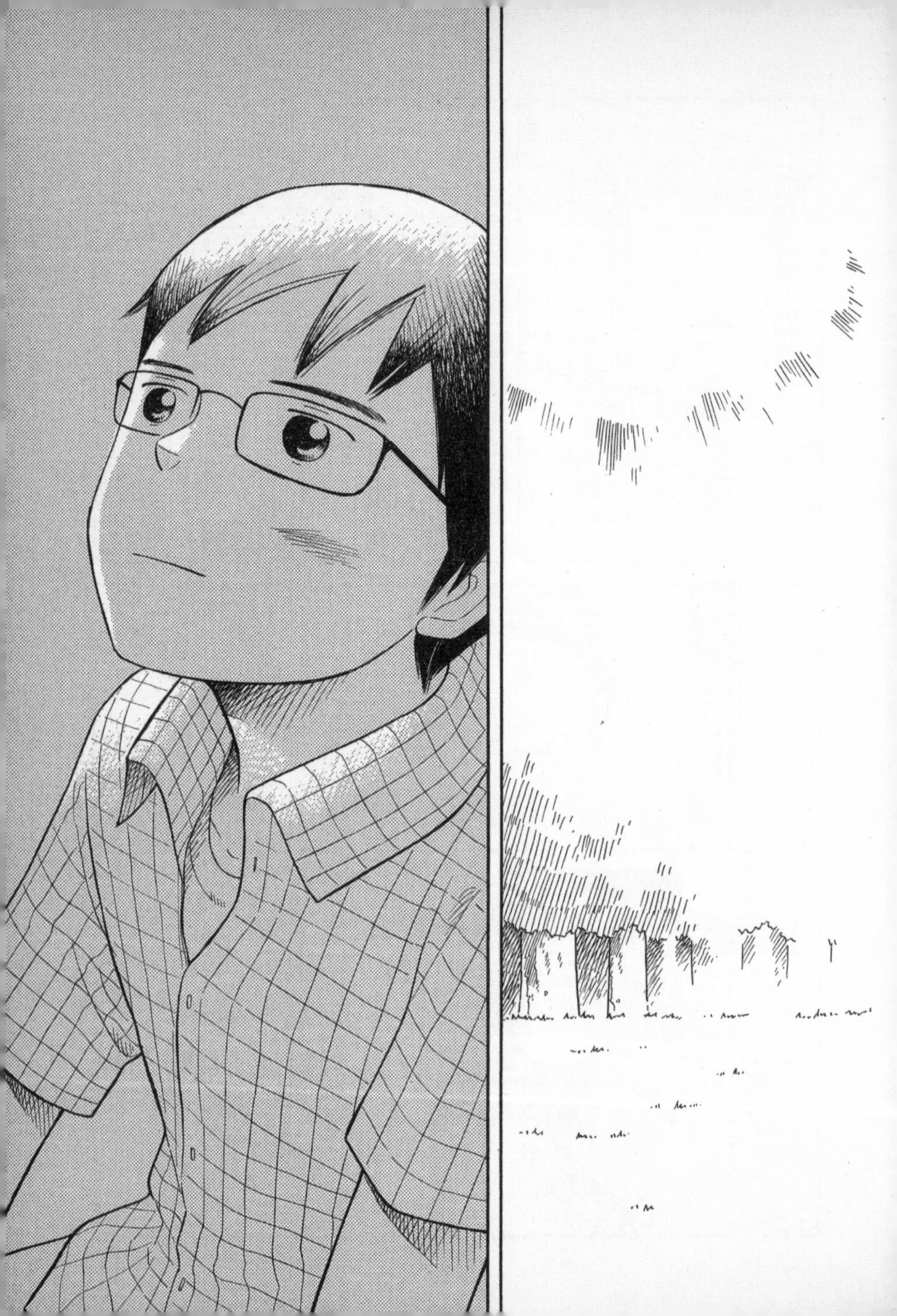

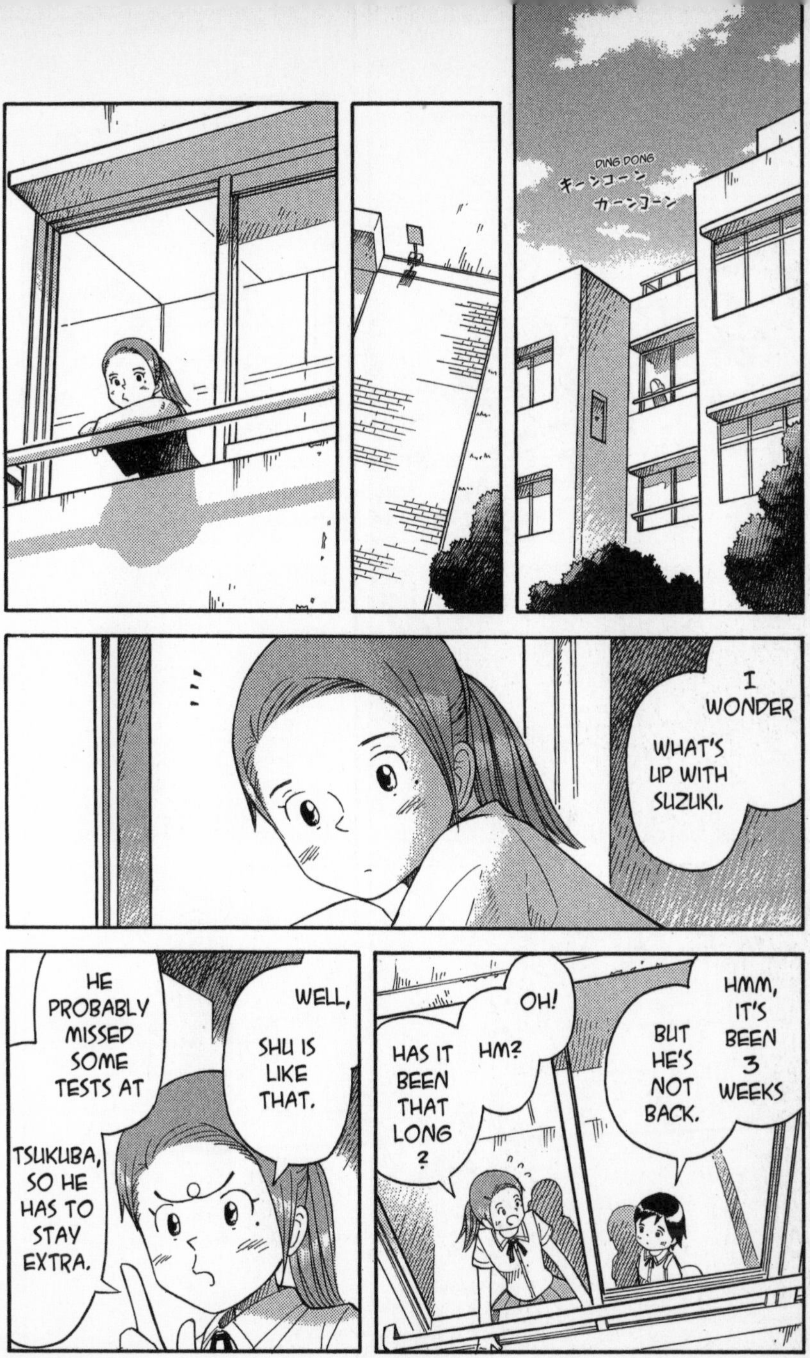
DING DONG
キーンコーン
カーンコーン
I WONDER WHAT'S UP WITH SUZUKI.
HMM, IT'S BEEN 3 WEEKS
BUT HE'S NOT BACK.
OH!
HM?
HAS IT BEEN THAT LONG?
WELL,
SHU IS LIKE THAT.
HE PROBABLY MISSED SOME TESTS AT
TSUKUBA, SO HE HAS TO STAY EXTRA.

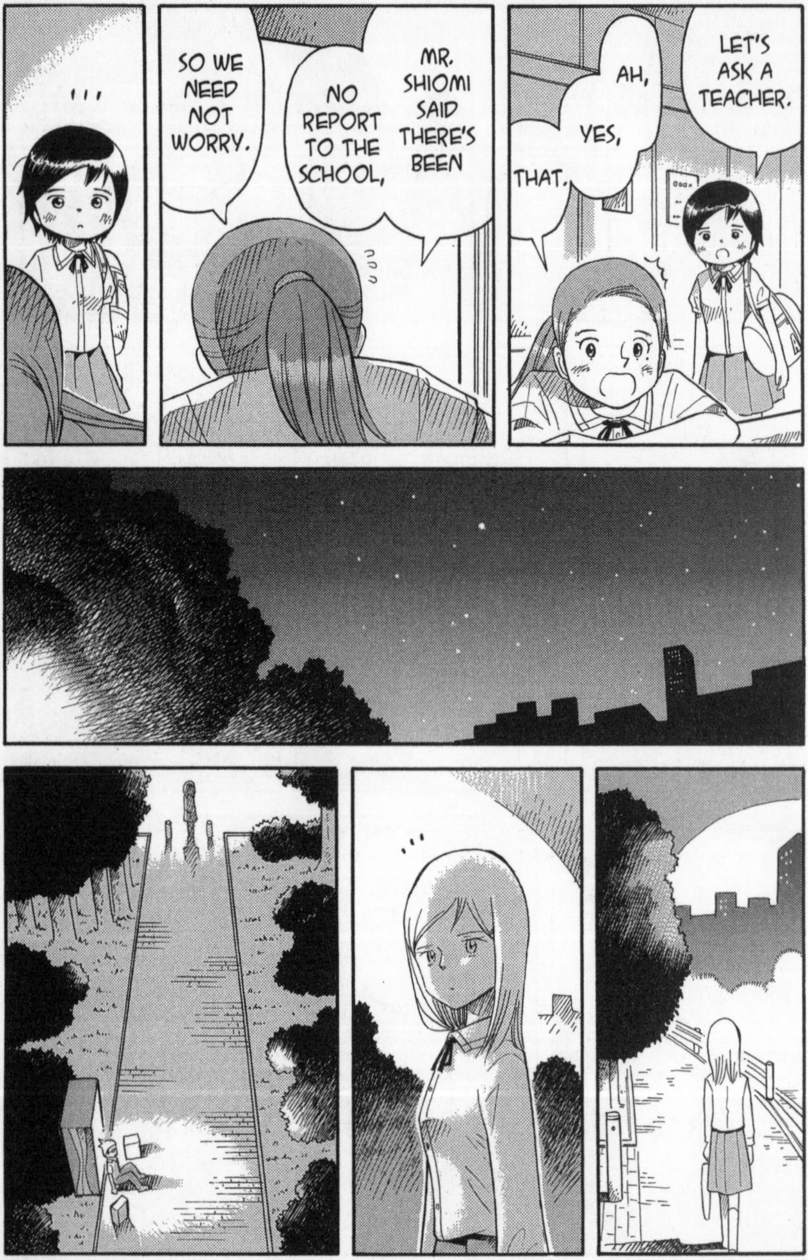
LET'S ASK A TEACHER.
AH, YES, THAT.
MR. SHIOMI SAID THERE'S BEEN
NO REPORT TO THE SCHOOL,
SO WE NEED NOT WORRY.
...
...

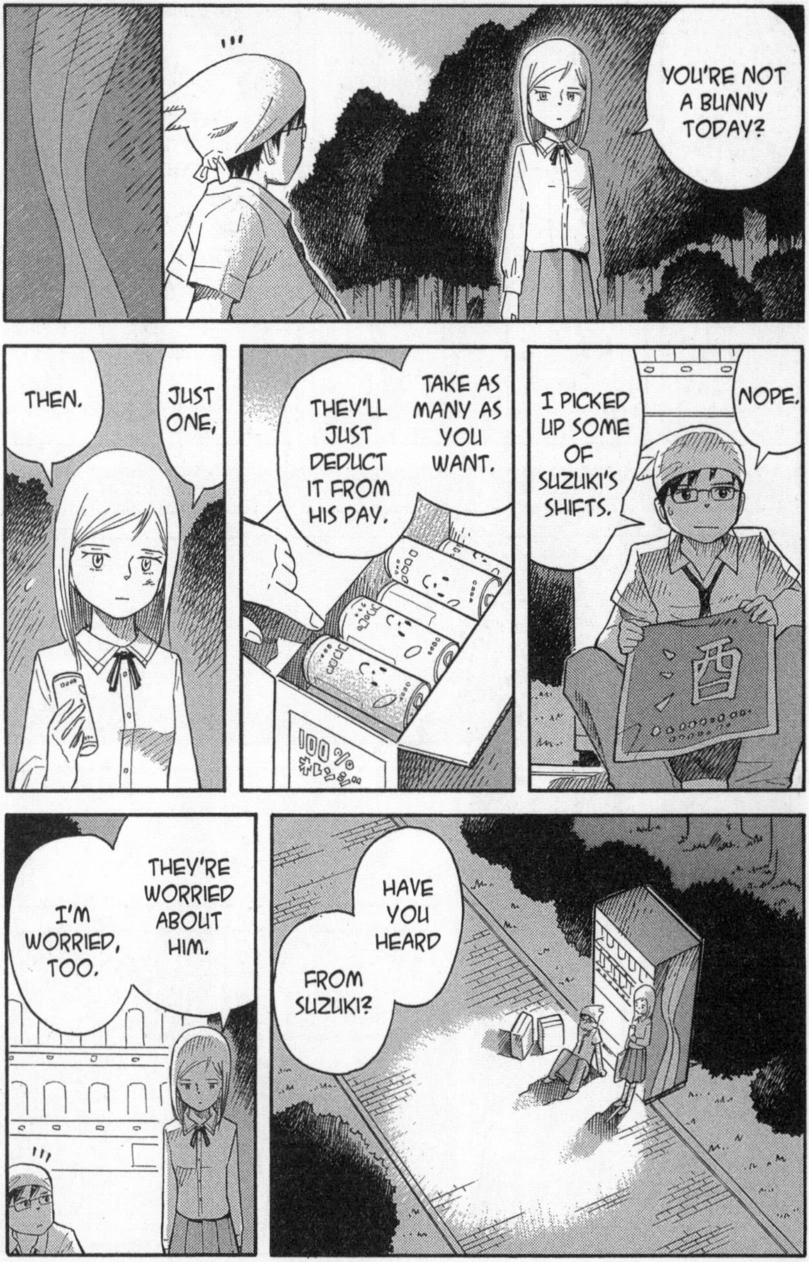
YOU'RE NOT A BUNNY TODAY?
NOPE.
I PICKED UP SOME OF SUZUKI'S SHIFTS.
TAKE AS MANY AS YOU WANT.
THEY'LL JUST DEDUCT IT FROM HIS PAY.
JUST ONE,
THEN.
HAVE YOU HEARD FROM SUZUKI?
THEY'RE WORRIED ABOUT HIM.
I'M WORRIED, TOO.

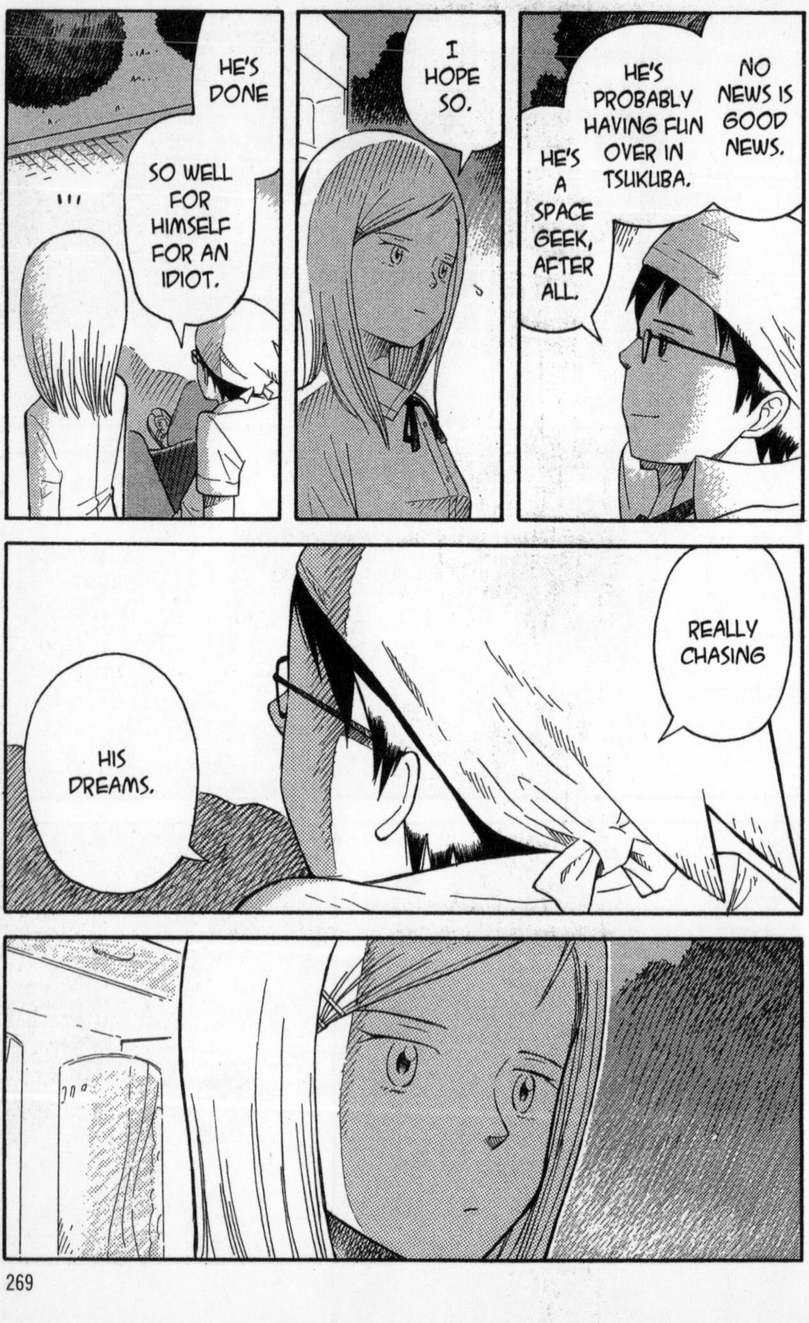
NO NEWS IS GOOD NEWS.
HE'S PROBABLY HAVING FUN OVER IN TSUKUBA.
HE'S A SPACE GEEK, AFTER ALL.
I HOPE SO.
HE'S DONE
SO WELL FOR HIMSELF FOR AN IDIOT.
REALLY CHASING
HIS DREAMS.

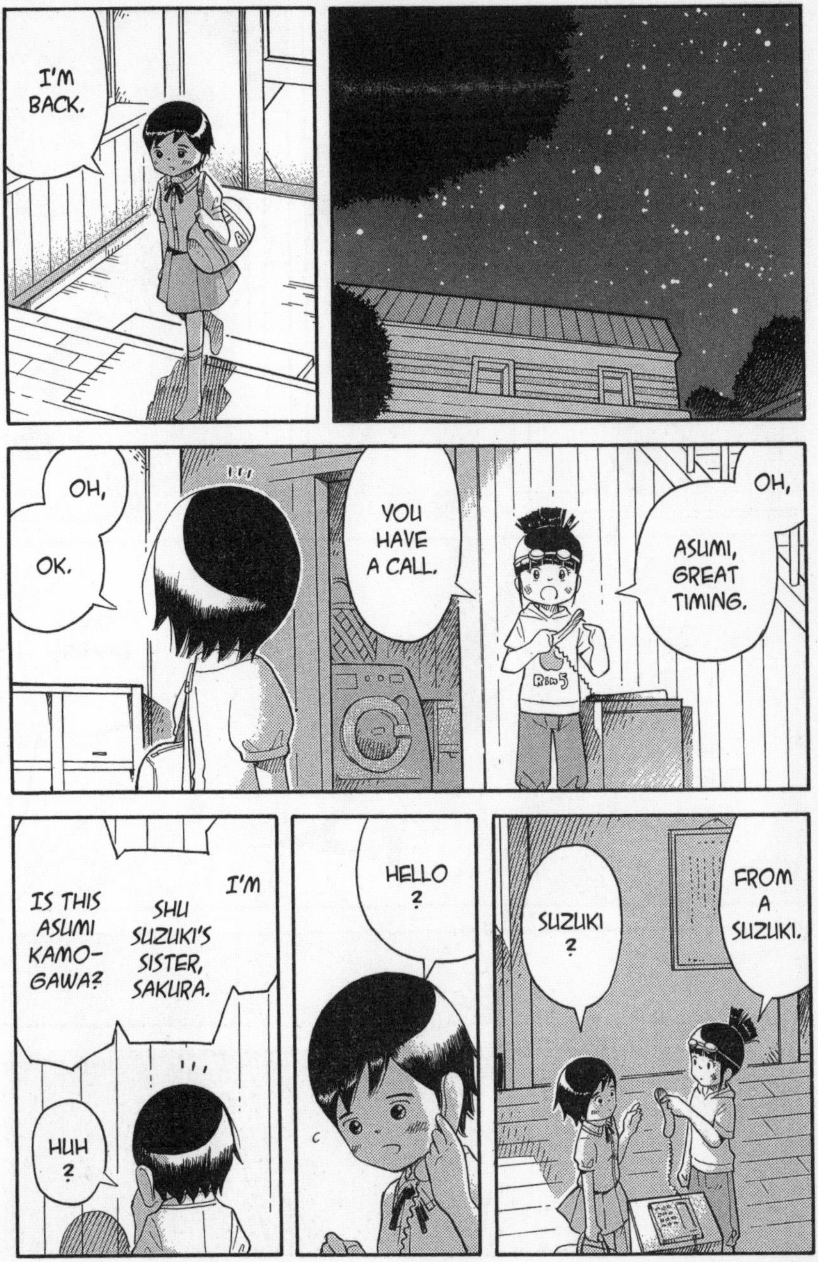
I'M BACK.
OH, ASUMI, GREAT TIMING.
YOU HAVE A CALL.
OH, OK.
FROM A SUZUKI.
SUZUKI?
HELLO?
I'M SHU SUZUKI'S SISTER, SAKURA.
IS THIS ASUMI KAMOGAWA?
HUH?

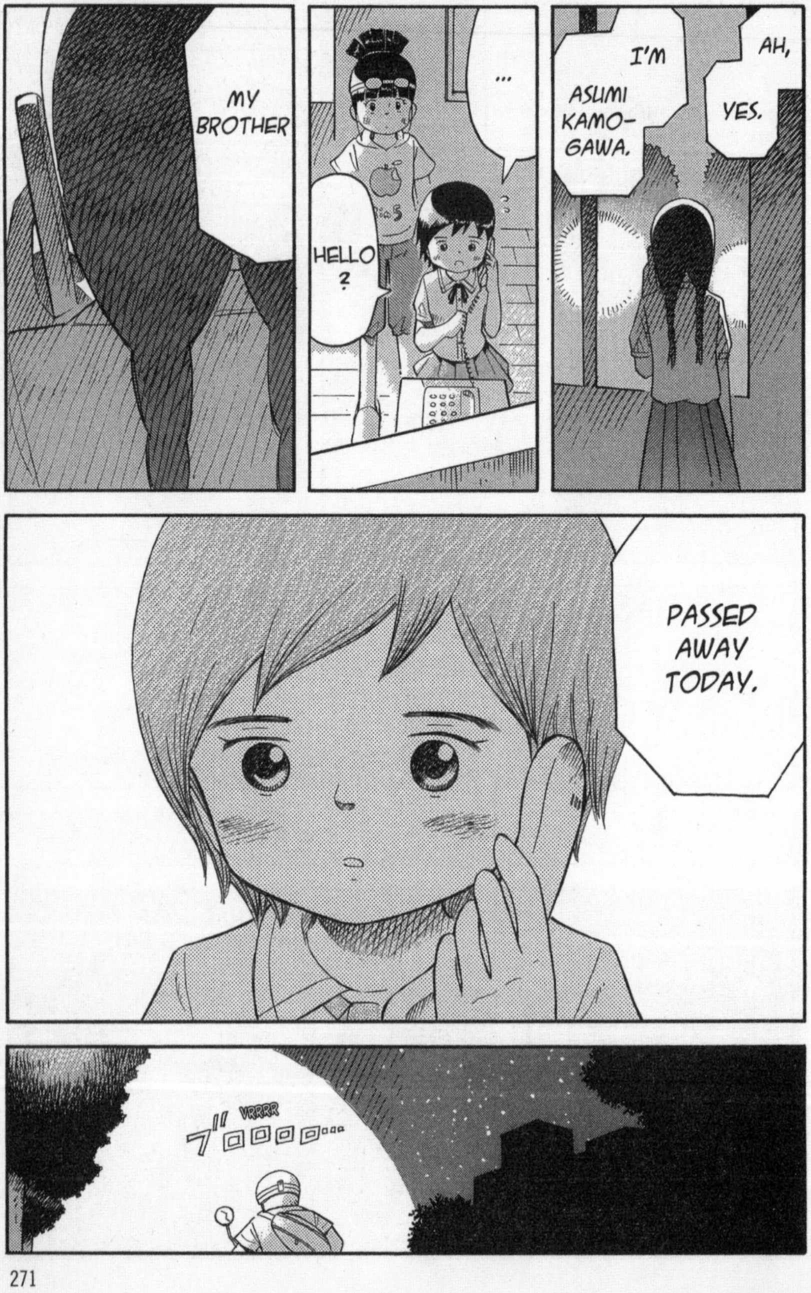
AH, YES.
I'M ASUMI KAMO-GAWA.
...
HELLO?
MY BROTHER
PASSED AWAY TODAY.
VRRRR
ブロロロロ...

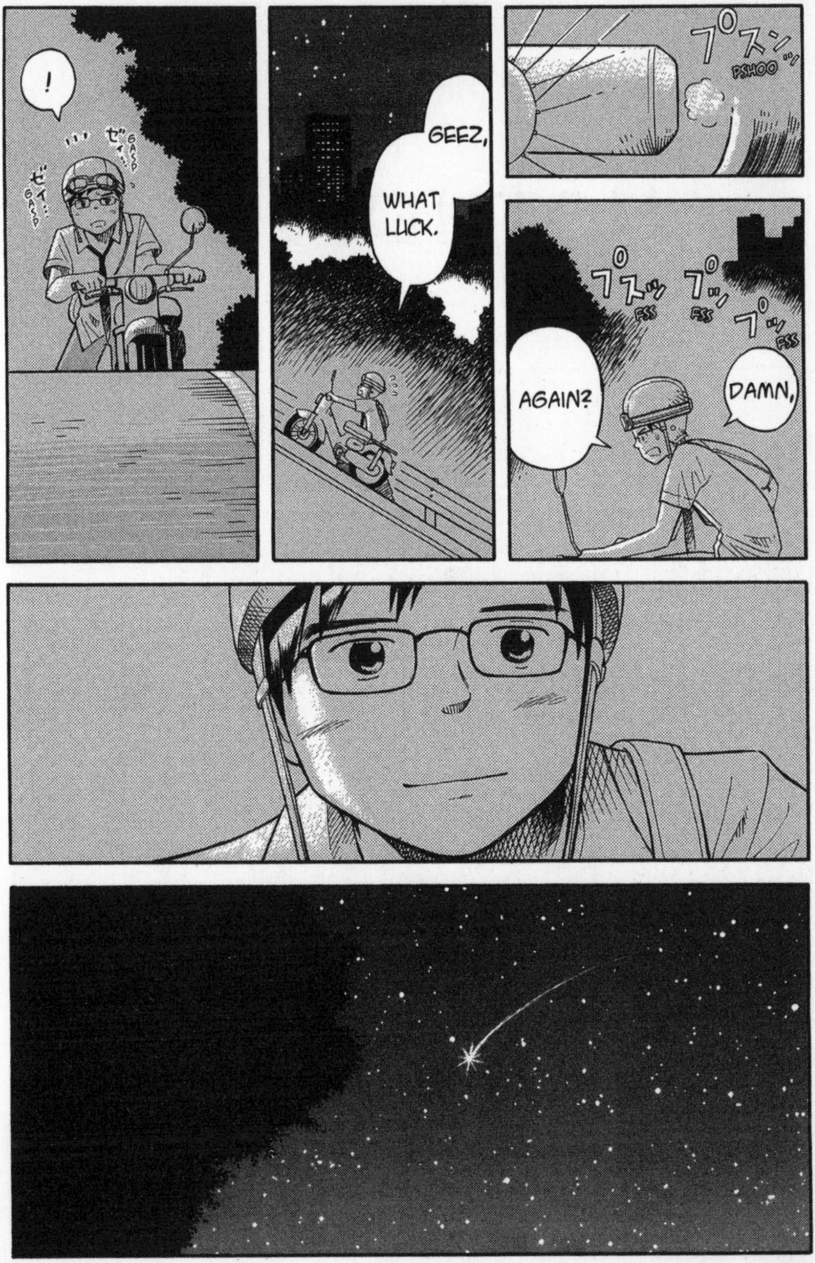
プスン
PSHOO
プスッ
FSS
プッ
FSS
プッ
FSS
DAMN,
AGAIN?
GEEZ,
WHAT LUCK.
!
ゼイ…
GASP
ゼイ…
GASP

ANOTHER SPICA

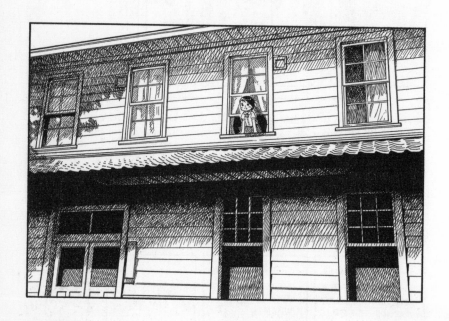

KOU YAGINUMA

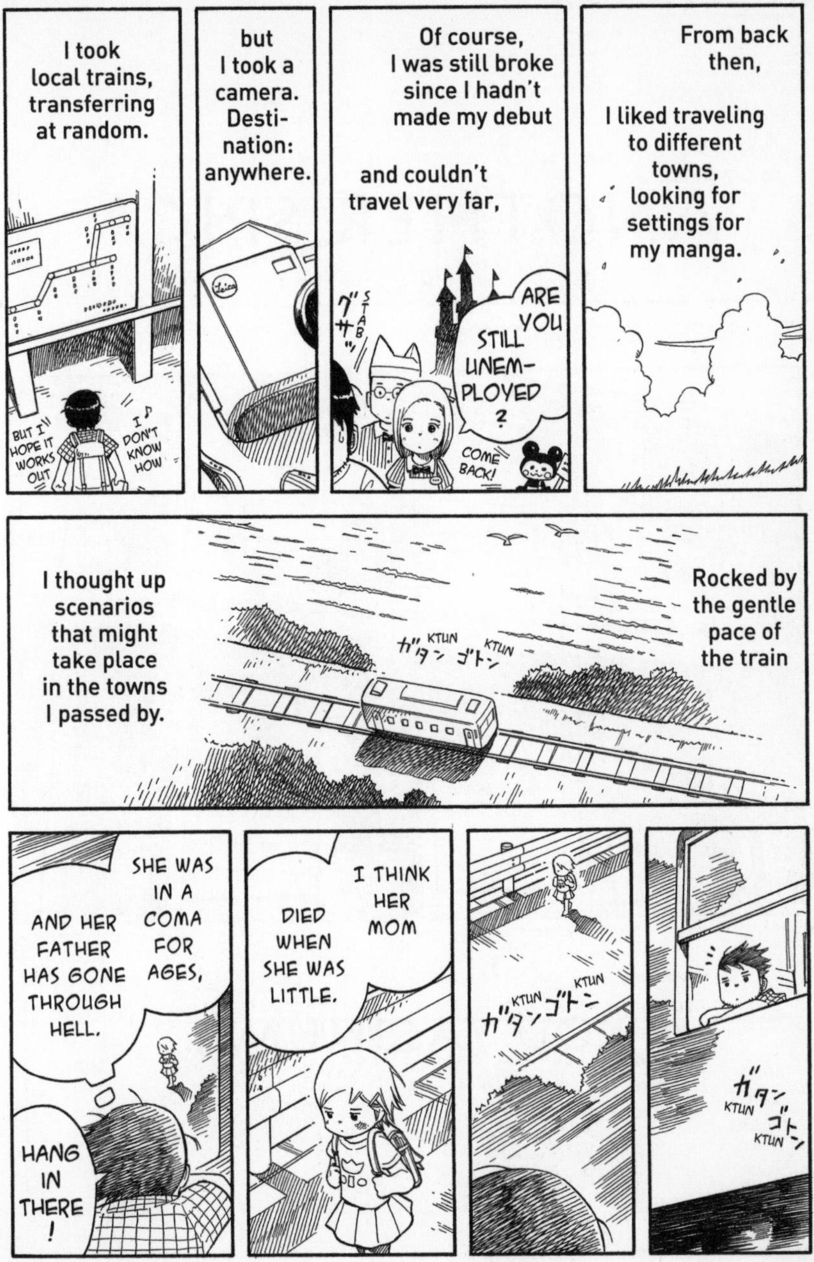

From back then,
I liked traveling to different towns, looking for settings for my manga.
Of course, I was still broke since I hadn't made my debut
and couldn't travel very far,
グサッ STAB
ARE YOU STILL UNEMPLOYED?
COME BACK!
but I took a camera. Destination: anywhere.
I took local trains, transferring at random.
I DON'T KNOW HOW
BUT I HOPE IT WORKS OUT
Rocked by the gentle pace of the train
ガタン KTUN ゴトン KTUN
I thought up scenarios that might take place in the towns I passed by.
ガタン KTUN ゴトン KTUN
ガタン KTUN ゴトン KTUN
I THINK HER MOM
DIED WHEN SHE WAS LITTLE.
SHE WAS IN A COMA FOR AGES,
AND HER FATHER HAS GONE THROUGH HELL.
HANG IN THERE!

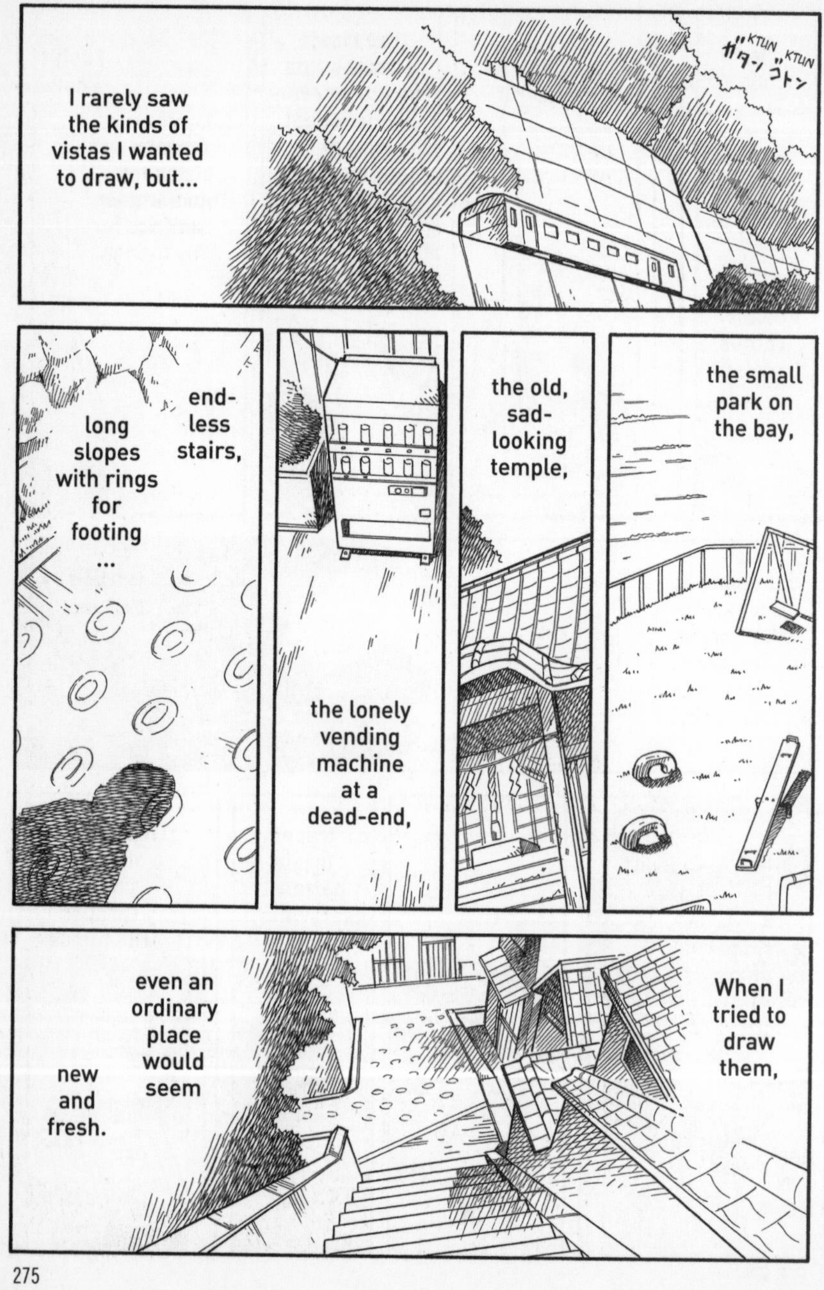
ガタン KTUN
ゴトン KTUN
I rarely saw the kinds of vistas I wanted to draw, but...
the small park on the bay,
the old, sad-looking temple,
the lonely vending machine at a dead-end,
end-less stairs,
long slopes with rings for footing ...
When I tried to draw them,
even an ordinary place would seem
new and fresh.

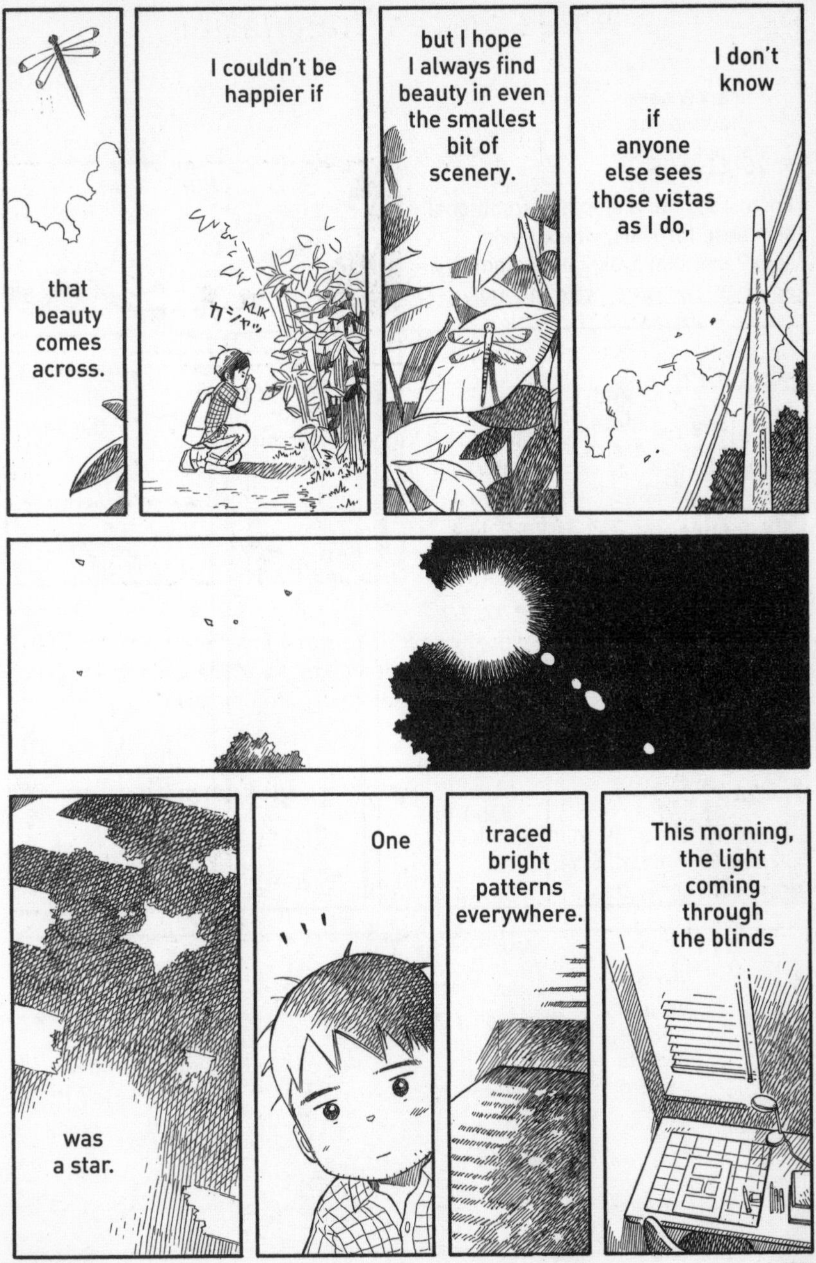
I don't know
if anyone else sees those vistas as I do,
but I hope I always find beauty in even the smallest bit of scenery.
I couldn't be happier if
KLIK
カシャッ
that beauty comes across.
This morning, the light coming through the blinds
traced bright patterns everywhere.
One
was a star.

THE END

Notes on the Translation

P. 20-21, 156

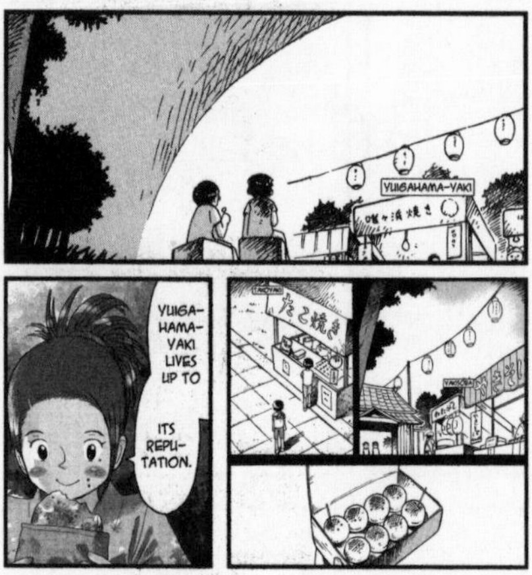
YUIGAHAMA-YAKI
YUIGA-HAMA-YAKI LIVES UP TO
ITS REPU-TATION.

Food stalls are a staple at traditional Japanese festivals, where "yaki-soba" and "takoyaki" are commonly on offer. The word "yaki" literally means *burn*, and in the context of food, *fry/cook*. Thus "yakisoba" are fried soba noodles, while "takoyaki" are balls of flour with a piece of octopus ("tako") at the center. The recipe for the enticing "Yuigahama-yaki," on the other hand, is a mystery. There does exist a Yuigahama (written with different characters) in the area of Japan where the fictional town also seems to be located, namely Kamakura. The historically important region boasts as many "specialty" foods and snacks as it does significant architecture. The real-life version of "Yuigahama-yaki," if there is any, is therefore hard to pin down.

P. 153

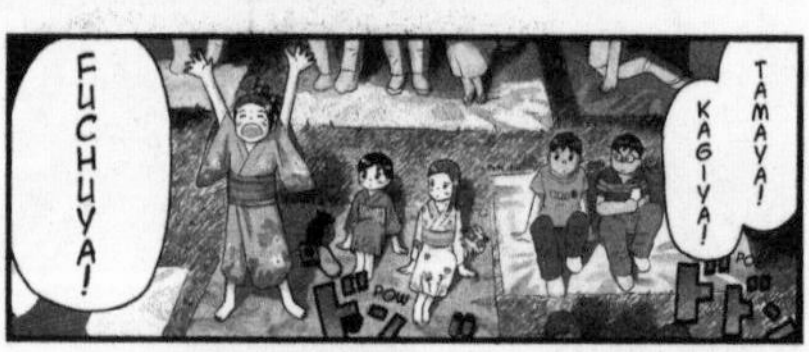
TAMAYA!
KAGIYA!
FUCHUYA!
POW

"Tamaya, Kagiya" is an interjection specific to celebrating fireworks, while adding "Fuchuya" is a pun on Kei's part.

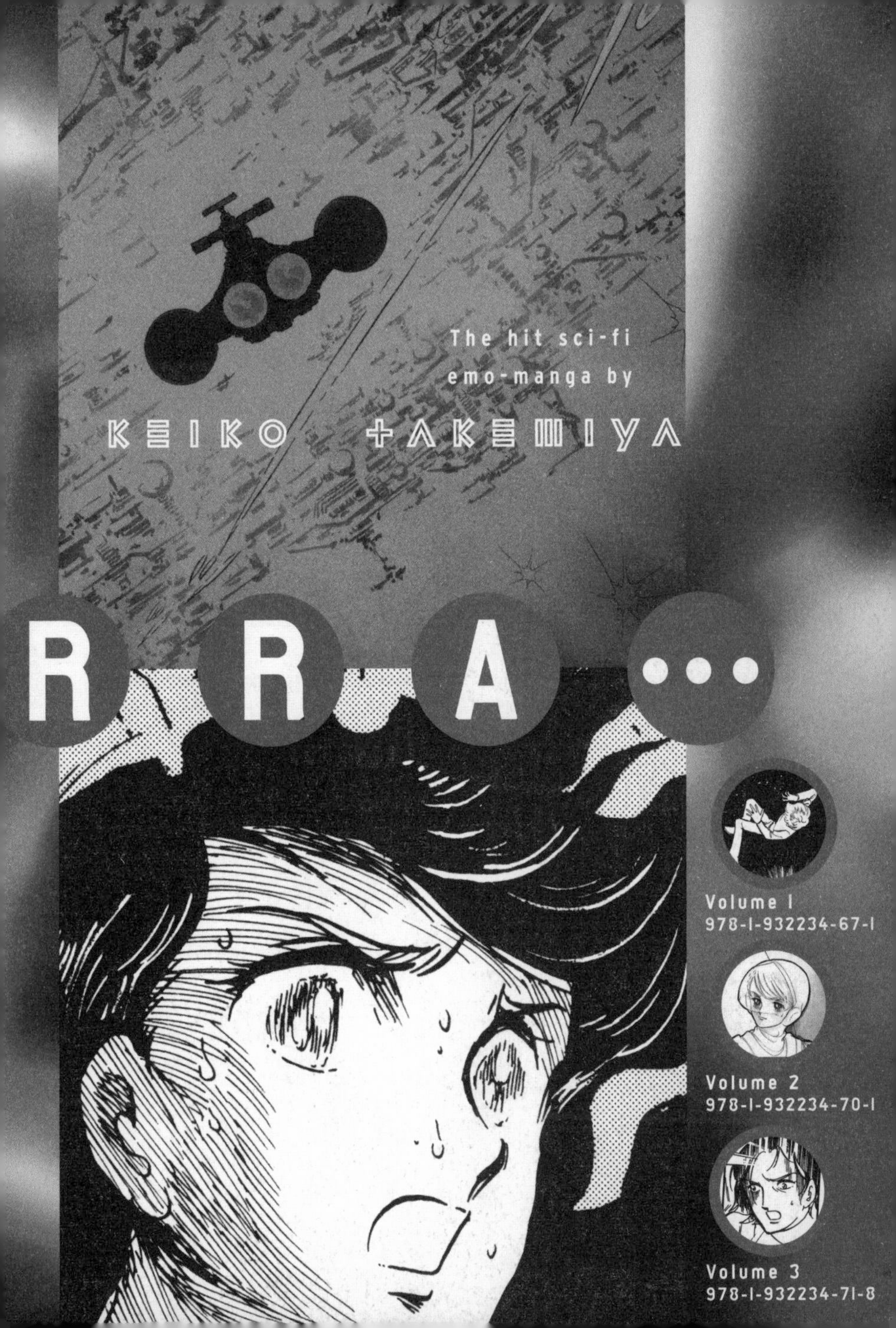
The hit sci-fi
emo-manga by
KEIKO TAKEMIYA
R R A ...
Volume 1
978-1-932234-67-1
Volume 2
978-1-932234-70-1
Volume 3
978-1-932234-71-8

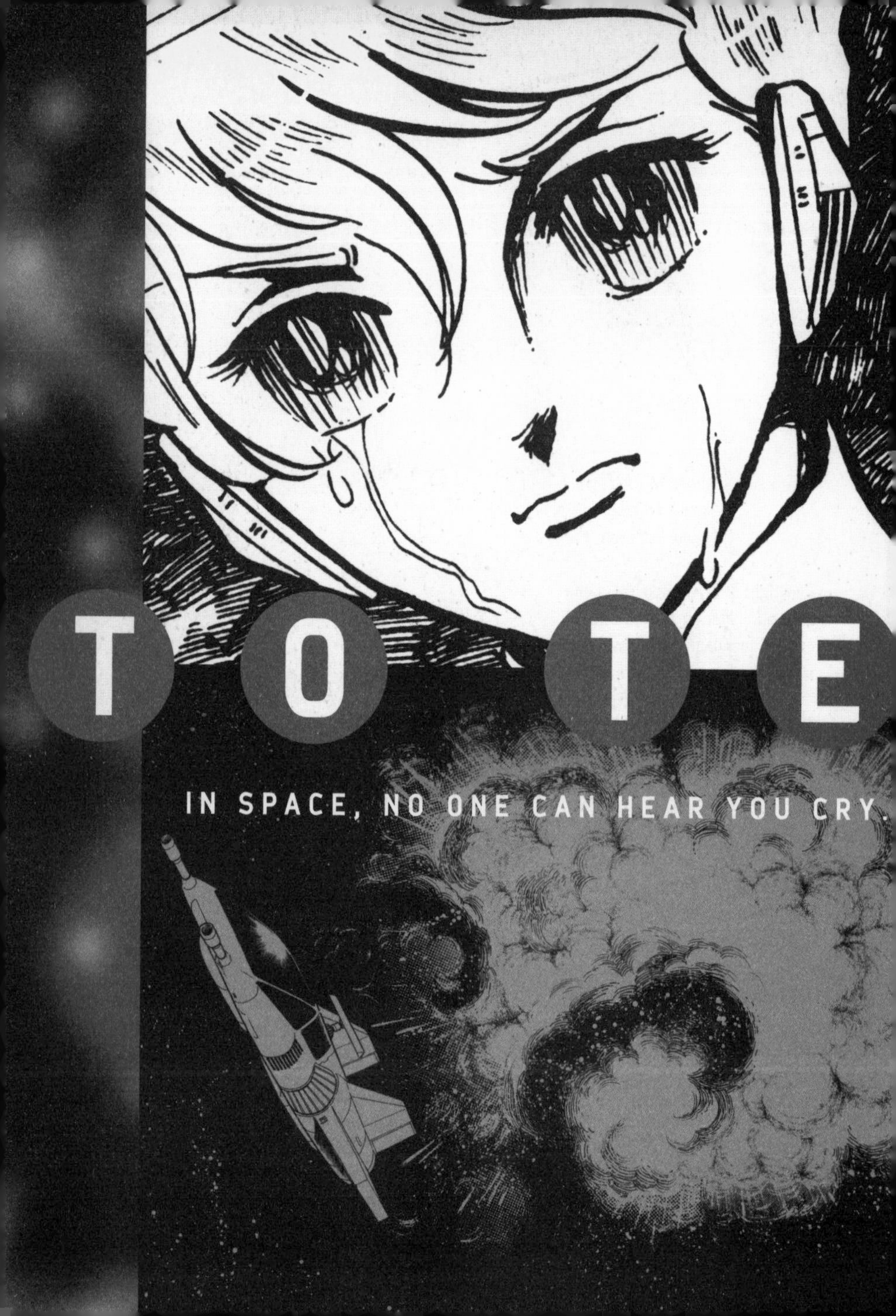
T O T E
IN SPACE, NO ONE CAN HEAR YOU CRY.

Production - Hiroko Mizuno
Tomoe Tsutsumi
Nicole Dochych

Originally published in Japanese as *Futatsu no Supika 11, 12*
by MEDIA FACTORY, Inc., Tokyo, 2006, 2007
Futatsu no Supika first serialized in Gekkan Comic Flapper,
MEDIA FACTORY, Inc., 2001-2009

This is a work of fiction.

ISBN: 978-1-935654-24-7

Manufactured in Canada

First Edition

Vertical, Inc.
451 Park Avenue South, 7th Floor
New York, NY 10016
www.vertical-inc.com